eighth edition

Classroom Assessment

What Teachers Need to Know

W. James Popham

Professor Emeritus,
University of California, Los Angeles

PEARSON

Boston   Columbus   Indianapolis   New York   San Francisco
Amsterdam   Cape Town   Dubai   London   Madrid   Milan   Munich   Paris   Montréal   Toronto
Delhi   Mexico City   São Paulo   Sydney   Hong Kong   Seoul   Singapore   Taipei   Tokyo

Vice President and Editorial Director: Jeffery W. Johnston

Vice President and Publisher: Kevin M. Davis

Editorial Assistant: Marisia Styles

Executive Field Marketing Manager: Krista Clark

Senior Product Marketing Manager: Christopher Barry

Project Manager: Pamela Bennett

Program Program Manager: Janelle Criner

Operations Specialist: Carol Melville

Text Designer: Cenveo

Cover Design Director: Diane Lorenzo

Cover Art: Getty Images, ©KidStock

Media Project Manager: Lauren Carlson

Full-Service Project Management: Cenveo

Composition: Cenveo

Printer/Binder: LSC Communications/ Crawfordsville

Cover Printer: Phoenix Color/Hagarstown

Text Font: 10.25/12 Sabon LT Std

Cataloging-in-Publication Data is available on file at the Library of Congress.

2 18

PEARSON

ISBN 10:   0-13-489463-4

ISBN 13: 978-0-13-489463-8

For Sarah:
Former Teacher, Former Principal,
Current Colleague, Current and Future Spouse

about the author

W. James Popham has spent the bulk of his educational career as a teacher. His first teaching assignment, for example, was in a small eastern Oregon high school where he taught English and social studies while serving as yearbook advisor, class sponsor, and unpaid tennis coach. The recompense meshed well with the quality of his coaching.

Most of Dr. Popham's teaching career took place at UCLA where, for nearly 30 years, he taught courses in instructional methods for prospective teachers as well as courses in evaluation and measurement for graduate students. At UCLA he won several distinguished teaching awards. In January 2000, he was recognized by *UCLA Today* as one of the university's top 20 professors of the twentieth century. (He notes that the twentieth century was a full-length century, unlike the current abbreviated one.) In 1992, he took early retirement from UCLA upon learning that emeritus professors received free parking.

Because at UCLA he was acutely aware of the perishability of professors who failed to publish, he spent his nonteaching hours affixing words to paper. The result: over 30 books, 200 journal articles, 50 research reports, and 175 papers presented before research societies. Although not noted in his official vita, while at UCLA he also authored 1,426 grocery lists.

His most recent books are *Transformative Assessment* (2008); *Instruction That Measures Up* (2009); *Transformative Assessment in Action* (2011, ASCD); *Mastering Assessment* (2011, Pearson); *Unlearned Lessons* (2009, Harvard Education Press); *Everything School Leaders Need to Know About Assessment* (2010); and *Evaluating America's Teachers: Mission Possible?* (2013, Corwin). He encourages purchase of these books because he regards their semi-annual royalties as psychologically reassuring.

In 1968, Dr. Popham established IOX Assessment Associates, an R&D group that formerly created statewide student achievement tests for a dozen states. He has personally passed all of those tests, largely because of his unlimited access to the tests' answer keys.

preface

Educational Assessment in Flux

Perhaps you have heard the ancient Chinese curse, *May you live in an interesting time!* Perhaps you haven't.

Well, I can definitely tell you where and when I first heard this curse—and how puzzled I was by its meaning. The year was 1961, and I was a rookie assistant professor at San Francisco State College. A campuswide speech was to be delivered by Robert Maynard Hutchins, an educational celebrity of that era. Hutchins was the founder of the Great Books Movement and had been the youngest-ever chancellor of the University of Chicago.

It was a simply marvelous speech—so fine, in fact, that I subsequently obtained an audiotape of the address and played it often in my classes. Hutchins opened his address with the following sentence: "Perhaps you have heard the ancient Chinese curse, '*May you live in an interesting time!*'"

As I indicated, upon hearing Hutchins's first sentence, I was immediately perplexed by the meaning of this "curse" that I'd never heard before. After all, if the time in which one lives is "interesting," this would seem to be a positive—not a negative. What's interesting is typically better than what's dull. But then, as Hutchins continued, he pointed out that an "interesting time" invariably involves *changes*. Indeed, the more profound the changes, the more "interesting" the time. And changes, at least for most of us, cause *discomfort*. We must accommodate to what's new. Routine, experience-honed approaches no longer work. New, "interesting" times simply bristle with uncertainty. Hutchins was warning his audience that education in the United States was entering an era of unprecedented change and, as a consequence, U.S. educators should clearly regard themselves as consummately cursed.

Well, if you look at what's taking place these days regarding this nation's *educational assessment*, you'll quickly conclude that we are smack in the middle of what is, most certainly, an especially "interesting time." To illustrate, as the revision of the classroom-assessment textbook you're currently reading was nearing the finish line, U.S. educators were still perplexed about how to deal with the Common Core State Standards, a set of curricular aims that, chiefly because of federal financial incentives, had been adopted by many, but not all, states. Beyond that, two different consortia of states that had set out to create "next generation" assessments to measure students' mastery of those Common Core State Standards were beginning to assess students in many parts of the nation. Because those new assessments measured students' mastery of what were widely regarded as more challenging curricular goals, students' performances on the new consortium-built tests were predictably lower than students' scores on other tests in previous years. Finally, Congressional reauthorization of the Elementary and Secondary Education Act of 1965 (ESEA) was long overdue and, although the current version of that federal statute—the No Child Left Behind Act—was clearly in need of a serious re-do, realistic estimates of when Congress might finally get around to reauthorizing this law ranged widely.

Yet, because American educators are now coping with assessment events that, in concert, constitute a truly "interesting time," I hope you will be patient with a textbook author who must come up with a sensible eighth edition of a classroom assessment textbook in such a setting. Unlike any of its previous versions, this rendition of *Classroom Assessment* was written in the midst of kaleidoscopic confusion about what sorts of assessments are around the corner and what roles those assessments are going to play in our schools. This eighth edition of *Classroom Assessment*, I fear, is apt to have been afflicted by a curse—probably of Chinese origin.

Formative Assessment in Action

This most recent revision of *Classroom Assessment*, however, is fundamentally different than its seven predecessors, and that difference stems directly from a phone call I received a couple of years ago from my editor, Kevin Davis. It was a phone call that seriously mucked up the next two years of my life.

My editor opened with an upbeat inquiry: "We'd like the next edition of *Classroom Assessment* to be digital. Do you have any problem with that?" Having always believed in electricity, I had no problem with it at all—especially after Kevin described what the possibilities were for a digitally presented textbook. The more I considered this new publication strategy, the more enthused I became—for I realized that a digitized eighth edition would make it possible for the book to be revised so it could become *an actual incarnation of the formative-assessment process*. And, even though it took much, much more work to revise the book, that's precisely what this eighth edition of *Classroom Assessment* is—an exemplification of how the formative-assessment process can support learning.

When formative assessment is present, students periodically provide assessment-elicited evidence that teachers can use to tell if adjustments are needed in their instruction or that students can use to tell if adjustments are needed how they're trying to learn. Happily, we now have an impressive collection of empirical evidence indicating the formative-assessment process is a research-ratified way of helping both teachers and students become more effective. When you read this eighth edition as a student, you should be on the receiving end of formative assessment's payoffs.

Thus, at the outset of each of this new edition's 16 chapters, a *chief chapter outcome* has been identified. This outcome is the most significant understanding you should gain from reading the chapter. Then, at the chapter's conclusion, two different self-tests are provided for you to determine how well you have mastered that chapter's chief outcome. (One of these mastery checks employs selected-response items, and one calls on you to generate a short constructed-response essay.) Having completed a chapter's two mastery checks, and decided how well you achieved the chapter's chief outcome, you then have three options available to you. If you judged that you demonstrated satisfactory mastery of the chapter's chief outcome, you could simply move ahead to the book's next chapter. If, however, you performed satisfactorily on the chapter's two mastery checks—and also found the chapter's content to be particularly fascinating—you could consult the array of digital options representing a *deeper dig* into one or more chapter-related issues. Finally, if your performance on one or both of the end-of-chapter mastery checks suggests that you need to spend more time in pursuit of the chapter's chief outcome, then you can refer to the digitally presented segments constituting *another take* regarding the chapter's content. In this book's application of the formative-assessment process, as in similar successful applications of formative assessment, it is the learner (you) who often uses assessment results to determine what should be done next.

Hopefully, reconfiguring the eighth edition of *Classroom Assessment* into a model of the formative-assessment process will have two clear-cut benefits. First, if you use each chapter's mastery checks to decide how well you have attained the chapter's chief intended outcome, you can then benefit by making your next activity an evidence-informed choice rather than a data-free conjecture. Second, because this new edition represents an attempt to adopt, insofar as a textbook-only approach to formative assessment permits—it is anticipated that this modeling may incline at least a portion of its teacher-readers to employ some variation of formative assessment in their own classes.

Classroom Assessment's embrace of digitization, as indicated earlier, required a far more laborious revision of this book than I had ever undertaken with previous editions. Yet, I am more optimistic about this new, formatively oriented revision than I have ever been. I truly hope that you not only like the eighth edition's approach, but that its digitized dazzle works as advertised.

New to This Edition

Given the uncertain nature of tomorrow's high-stakes assessments and the legal requirements regarding how they must be used, I've tried to comb through the book to make sure that heretofore unequivocal statements about state-level assessments and state-level accountability laws have been suitably softened with dollops of uncertainty. The varnish-free truth is that, as I was readying this revision, education leaders in a good many states had told me, off the record, they simply had no idea about what sorts of state-level assessment programs would be present during the next few years. What, a few years earlier, had been uniform adulation of the *Common Core State Standards* is currently a much more mixed bag of support or disdain. Similarly, early optimism had been widely registered regarding the two emerging sets of consortium-built tests that would allow American educators to gauge students' mastery of challenging "college and career-ready" content. More recently, however, doubts have been voiced by some educators regarding these "next generation" assessments.

In mid-2014, three of our nation's organizations most concerned with educational measurement released a genuinely significant document—namely, the *Standards for Educational and Psychological Testing*. The standards (guidelines) included therein describe how education tests should be constructed, evaluated, and used. Because the standards in this publication are often relied on to resolve assessment-related courtroom litigation, the tenets set forth in this volume will have a profound impact on the way U.S. educational testing takes place in the coming years. The most important of these new standards have been incorporated into all relevant sections of *Classroom Assessment*. Given today's pervasive pressure to boost students' test scores, a number of test publishers are hawking what they characterize as "diagnostic tests." To help teachers understand what's necessary for a diagnostic test to make a meaningful contribution to instruction, a new section on *instructionally diagnostic testing* has been included in Chapter 13. Readers who understand what's needed in a test that is truly diagnostic will be better able to choose among an ever-expanding array of supposedly diagnostic assessments. Many of today's allegedly useful diagnostic tests should, regrettably, be sent to a shredder. The new section on instructionally diagnostic tests will help readers evaluate the merits of commercial or locally developed "diagnostic" assessments.

The "Legacy" Elements of the Book

A number of features in this current edition, as might be expected, are inherited from previous renditions of the book. As in past editions, this new version is attentive to the *instructional* payoffs of well-designed classroom tests. Whenever I can, I've attempted to highlight the implications that testing has on teaching. In each chapter, there's even a section titled *But What Does This Have to Do with Teaching?* In those instances, I spell out the instructional implications of a chapter's content.

All chapters contain a description of fictitious classroom teachers who must make decisions related to one or more of the topics treated in the chapter. These are called *Decision Time* features, and each one concludes with a decision that needs to be made by the teacher being described. Readers are then asked to put themselves in the place of the teacher and decide how they would proceed. These vignettes are intended to set out a series of practical problems squarely on a reader's plate, and then see how readers might munch on them.

Considerable attention is also given in this eighth edition to an important audience for teachers—namely, *parents*. Teachers often need to explain to parents such assessment-related topics as why a child scored a certain way on a standardized test or how a teacher's classroom exams are related to the grades a child receives. So, in every chapter, you'll find a feature titled *Parent Talk*. In these Parent Talk segments, I've described a situation in which a teacher needs to explain something about assessment to parents. I then indicate what I would have said to the parents if I had been the teacher in that situation. What I hope readers will do, then, is decide how *they* would have responded had they been placed in this same situation. In fact, readers might even say *aloud* (in private, if they have any sense) what they'd tell parents. Teachers who can talk sensibly to parents about assessment-related concerns will find they're able to establish more effective rapport with parents. Such teachers will get along far better with parents than will teachers who convey to parents the idea that assessment is an exotic measurement mystery, well beyond the perceptive powers of mere parents.

I realize all too well that most readers are not likely to regard the content of a book on assessment as enthralling. For myself, if I had the choice between whether I would read an assessment book or a cracking good espionage novel, I'd shove the assessment book aside in a millisecond. In recognition of a reader's likely response to the book's content, I've tried to lighten the load with cartoons and an occasional dash of levity. If readers don't find the light style to be acceptable, they are encouraged to frown during the funny parts.

MyEducationLab®: Digitalization Does Its Dance

Now, to describe how the digital features of the eighth edition work, here are the basics of that operation. In the MyEdLab for this book, at the end of each chapter you will find three links:

- MyEdLab: Selected-Response Check of Outcome Mastery
- MyEdLab: Constructed-Response Check of Outcome Mastery
- MyEdLab: Learning Outcome Mastery Determination

The first two links take you to interactive mastery checks (one selected-response and the other constructed-response). Both these mastery checks contain feedback that enable you to reach a judgment regarding whether you have mastered the chapter's chief intended outcome. The following provide examples of the two types of Outcome Mastery checks.

Determining Your Outcome Mastery

The importance of validity to educational assessment really cannot be over-emphasized. It is, unarguably, the most influential concept in all of education-al testing. Teachers need to know what valid sort of evidence is needed to support test-ba purposes. Let's look, then, at the major outc after you completed this chapter:

A sufficiently deep understanding of as essential nature can be explained, its es and the most appropriate kinds of validity evidence can be selected for specific uses of educational tests

With the completion of the chapter, you should now describe what validity is, (2) explain how validity c (3) choose suitable validity evidence for diverse uses essence, you should have the ability to display a fun ment validity by being able to carry out three related tasks regarding validity. Using nonfancy language, it understand what's going on when people talk about well that you can comfortably do all three things ide chief intended learning outcome.

Complete both the Selected-Response and the Const and think about the feedback you receive for each q

MyEdLab *Selected-Response Check of Outcome Mastery*
MyEdLab *Constructed-Response Check of Outcome Mastery*

After completing both quizzes, go to the Learning Outcome Mastery Determination, where you will decide whether you've mastered the chapter's learning outcome or whether you need further study.

MyEdLab *Learning Outcome Mastery Determination*

After completing both mastery checks, you will be instructed to go to the third link—Learning Outcome Mastery Determination, where you will decide whether you have mastered the chapter's intended outcome or whether you need further study. If you believe that you have not mastered the chapter's chief outcomes, you are not directed to re-read the chapter. Instead, new explanations are provide in *Another Take* segments. If, based on how well you did on the mastery checks, you believe you have mastered the chapter's chief intended outcome, you will be given an opportunity to extend your knowledge of the chapter's contents by exploring material that probes further into the assessment concepts presented in the chapter. These materials are called *Deeper Digs* segments.

Here, of course, is where the heart of the formative-assessment process beats. You will be collecting your own evidence of content mastery, then deciding what the next step in your learning efforts should be. If you think you performed well on a chapter's two mastery checks, are you obliged only to consider the Deeper Dig segments—and never dip into the *Another Take* segment? Of course not. Similarly, you can surely probe any *Deeper Dig* segments even if you didn't do all that well on a given chapter's mastery checks. In general, the decisions you make about your own learning activities at the close of a chapter are apt to be more defensible if you base those decisions on your assessed mastery of the chapter's most significant learning outcome. Nonetheless, in this digital age—and with this digitized new edition—the choices are clearly yours.

Why This Book Will Help Today's Teachers

Teachers these days who don't recognize that educational assessment impinges on their work are teachers in serious need of impingement therapy. Rarely, indeed, does a day go by in the Monday-through-Friday life of today's teachers when testing does not have an impact on one or more of their classroom decisions. It was not always this way.

Eons ago, I was a high school teacher in eastern Oregon. (It was so long ago that my friends contend Oregon must have been a territory rather than a state.) Way back then, we administered standardized achievement tests in our classes. However, students' scores on those tests made no difference in how we taught. Pressure to raise our students' scores on those achievement exams was nonexistent. We taught pretty much as we saw fit. But, of course, the world of education is different today—much different.

And even before those teaching days, when I was preparing to be a teacher, little attention was given to testing. In truth, the only time my professors actually taught us about educational tests was when, during an educational psychology class, we spent an entire week on the making and massaging of multiple-choice items. My fellow prospective teachers and I were not being prepared for educational assessment because, back then, educational assessment truly did not have an impact on teachers' decision-making.

But today, educational tests certainly make a difference regarding what currently takes place in our classrooms. For openers, today's teachers find themselves directly in the cross-hairs of some heavy-duty accountability artillery aimed at evaluating schools *and teachers* according to students' scores on accountability tests. A school's staff can be "restructured" or a school can be completely shut down if its students don't perform well enough on externally administered accountability exams. Teachers can be tossed. It is a scary time.

Second, during the last two decades, growing numbers of educators have learned that the skillful use of classroom testing can make huge differences in how well students learn. Classroom assessment, if employed *formatively,* can dramatically increase the effectiveness of a teacher's *teaching.* And yet, sadly, we rarely see more than token use of classroom assessment in the way that research clearly tells us will benefit students.

For both of those reasons, then, every experienced teacher and every teacher-in-training need to master the essentials of educational assessment. And that's why this book was first written and then revised so frequently. Its title, *Classroom Assessment: What Teachers Need to Know,* captures the book's intent. Readers won't be asked to learn any nice-to-know exotics about educational measurement. No, what's contained in this book is the stuff today's teachers *need to know* if they are going to be first-rate professionals.

Acknowledgments

To my colleagues who offered recommendations about how to improve this latest edition, I offer my sincere appreciation: Deborah Bennett, Purdue University; Jean Ragin, Coppin State University; Marilyn Roseman, Mount Aloysius College; and Christy Tirrell-Corbin, University of Maryland.

I am especially grateful to Dolly Bulquerin, great friend and word-processor nonpareil, who prepared the very first edition of *Classroom Assessment.* She then helped transform that first edition into second, third, fourth, fifth, sixth, and seventh versions. Now, once more, she has helped me birth this exciting new eighth edition. I suspect those efforts clearly have established Dolly as a multi-edition midwife.

W. J. P.

brief contents

contents

4 Validity   94

5 Fairness   124

6 Selected-Response Tests   150

7 Constructed-Response Tests   174

11 Improving Teacher-Developed Assessments   257

12 Formative Assessment   274

13 Making Sense Out of Standardized Test Scores 307

14 Appropriate and Inappropriate Test-Preparation Practices 339

15 The Evaluation of Instruction 353

16   Assessment-Based Grading   385

Why Do Teachers Need to Know about Assessment?

CHIEF CHAPTER OUTCOME

An understanding of why it is that four traditional and three recent reasons for educators to assess students should dispose teachers to learn more about the fundamentals of educational assessment

Teachers teach students. That hardly constitutes a break-through insight. Just as preachers preach and flyers fly—teachers teach. That's why they're called teachers.

But what is a bit less obvious is that most teachers teach because they *like* to teach. Primary teachers like to teach little people. High school teachers like to teach bigger people. Most high school teachers also like to teach about a particular subject matter. (Have you ever seen how mathematics teachers' eyes get misty when they introduce their students to the raptures of the Pythagorean theorem?) Yes, most teachers love to teach. It is because they enjoy what they do that they waded through a medley of preservice teacher education courses, conquered the challenges of student teaching, and hopped the myriad hurdles of the certification process. Teachers overcame these obstacles in order to earn annual salaries that, particularly during the first few years, are laughably low. Yes, there's little doubt that teachers enjoy teaching.

Although teachers like to *teach,* they rarely like to *test*. Yet, here you are—beginning a book about testing. How can I, the author, ever entice you, the reader, to become interested in testing when your heart has already been given to teaching? The answer is really quite straightforward. Teachers who can test well will be better teachers. Effective testing will enhance a teacher's instructional effectiveness. Really!

If you're willing to suspend any preconceptions about testing while you're reading this book, particularly any negative ones, I'll make a pledge to you. If you tackle this text with even half the enthusiasm you might bring to a teaching assignment, I promise you'll discover how *testing will make you a much better teacher*. And, because I've been a teacher for over 50 years, it's a promise I'll keep. Teachers definitely should not break promises to teachers. Teachers' promises to administrators, on the other hand, should be regarded as eminently renegotiable.

But before I attempt to convince you, ever so subtly, that testing can be a boon to teaching, I want you to get a fix on your own *current* views about educational testing. And, because this is a book about testing, what better way to have you learn about those attitudes than to have you take a self-test I devised just for readers of this book?

So, on the adjacent page (it's on the *right* from where you're currently reading!) you'll find a brief self-test similar to the ones you've surely encountered in many widely read magazines. I saw one such self-test in a health magazine recently. It was entitled "How Long Will You Live? A Self-Test." Frankly, I was afraid to try it. As one gets older, one becomes more cautious.

But you have nothing to fear by taking the self-test I've whipped up for you. To emphasize its brevity, I have entitled it "A Terse Self-Test about Testing." It is an example of an attitudinal inventory. Later, in Chapter 10, you'll learn more about attitudinal inventories. But for now, please take a crack at page 3's teensy self-test. The way to interpret your responses is given as a footnote at the bottom of page 4.

FEDERAL LAWS RULE

Anyone who has completed even an introductory course in U.S. Government knows that while state laws can overturn the laws enacted by local communities, federal laws can overturn state laws. When it comes to the art of overturning, federal folks hold all the trump cards.

Any consideration of educational testing these days cannot be sensibly undertaken without understanding the nature of whatever assessment-related federal laws are on the books. When I began working on this eighth edition of *Classroom Assessment,* the most significant education-related federal law then in place was the No Child Left Behind Act (NCLB). Although NCLB has exercised considerable influence on the way U.S. teachers tested and taught in their classrooms, the law elicited intense criticism from many quarters. Moreover, NCLB was supposed to be revised sometime during 2009 or, at the latest, 2010. Yet, by early-to-mid-2015, genuinely serious movement to revise NCLB had not yet surfaced in the U.S. Congress. Accordingly, because this eighth edition of the book would most likely be completed before a successor-law to NCLB had been enacted, it seemed silly to speculate about what the key assessment-related features of such a yet-unwritten law might be.

Instead, very briefly, I want to describe the background of the most pivotal federal legislation that, in one form or another, will surely have an impact on the way teachers are obliged to think about educational testing. Hopefully, based on that familiarity, you will then be more easily able to learn about the particulars of any federal law bearing directly on how students' achievements are supposed to be assessed. All educators will definitely need to attend to those assessment-related particulars.

By all odds, the most significant federal statute influencing U.S. educational testing was the Elementary and Secondary Education Act (ESEA) of 1965.

A Terse Self-Test about Testing

Directions: For each of the statements below, use the following answer key to indicate how you react to the statement:

SA = *Strongly Agree*
A = *Agree*
U = *Uncertain*
D = *Disagree*
SD = *Strongly Disagree*

There are no right or wrong answers, so please answer frankly by circling the appropriate response for each statement.

1. The chief reason that teachers should give classroom tests is to determine students' grades.   SA   A   U   D   SD

2. Teachers should typically plan instruction that focuses on the skills or knowledge represented by a test.   SA   A   U   D   SD

3. In their classroom tests, teachers should only use items that can be scored objectively.   SA   A   U   D   SD

4. There are other legitimate indicators of a teacher's instructional effectiveness besides students' test scores.   SA   A   U   D   SD

5. A teacher has no business measuring students' confidence in their ability to do schoolwork.   SA   A   U   D   SD

6. Today's nationally standardized achievement tests should never be used to supply evidence about how well teachers are instructing children.   SA   A   U   D   SD

7. Teachers really don't need to determine the reliability of their own classroom tests.   SA   A   U   D   SD

8. It is impossible to judge the quality of students' written compositions with any meaningful accuracy.   SA   A   U   D   SD

9. The enormous pressure to boost students' scores on important tests permits teachers to employ almost any sort of score-improvement preparation activities.   SA   A   U   D   SD

10. Significant classroom tests should typically be built before a teacher plans instruction.   SA   A   U   D   SD

Enacted as a key component of President Lyndon B. Johnson's "great society," ESEA set out to provide a more appropriate education for historically underserved student groups such as students who were economically disadvantaged. Over the years (actually, every two to eight years), ESEA was periodically reauthorized with, sometimes, serious shifts in its assessment provisions. No Child Left Behind, for instance, the eighth reauthorization of 1965's ESEA, contained some significant alterations to that law's testing requirements. In the earliest incarnations of ESEA, educational assessments were focused on evaluating the progress made by those statutorily designated underserved groups—for example, minority students. However, in the reauthorization immediately preceding NCLB, the reauthorization enacted in 1994, the assessment of *all* students rather than statute-designated underserved groups was required. Clearly, this was a change of considerable importance.

Because the responsibility for education is not identified as a federal responsibility in the United States Constitution, U.S. education has historically been seen as a state rather than federal responsibility. Thus, prior to the 1994 incarnation of ESEA, known as the Improving America's Schools Act (IASA), states were relatively free to carry out whatever sorts of educational assessments they thought appropriate, with the chief exception being the assessment of those students being educated, at least in part, via federal dollars dispensed by the then-operative version of ESEA. But in 1994's IASA, that game changed. When a state took IASA dollars, this state agreed to assess the achievement of all its students in several IASA-designated grade ranges. And when NCLB was signed into law by President George W. Bush on January 8, 2002, the assessment of *all* students became more emphatic by far. Students in twice as many grade levels (grade *levels,* not grade ranges) were to be assessed—even though many of those students were not on the receiving end of federal dollars.

Moreover, whereas in the IASA statute, federal oversight of state-level testing of students in certain grade ranges was fairly light, NCLB's controls over the testing of more than twice as many students assessed under that law was not light but, instead, quite tight indeed. In short, the most recent two versions of ESEA (IASA and NCLB) embodied increasingly stringent requirements regarding which students were to be tested and how this testing was to be done. While the dominant function of IASA and NCLB was to be accountability—that is, the identification of which schools and districts were doing a satisfactory instructional job—certain specifics of those laws make a real difference in how teachers need to think about educational assessment.

Assuming that the next reauthorization of ESEA will not be in place at the point when this book must go into actual production, I entreat you to become knowledgeable about the assessment-related aspects of a reauthorized ESEA. Although there may be numerous features of such a law that can have an impact on the way teachers teach, it is almost certain that the assessment-related provisions of such a law will have great impact, if not the greatest impact, on how a teacher needs to think about *instruction*. In the realm of educational assessment, federal laws tend to rule. That's because federal legislators craft their statutes so that unless a state's officials comply with a federal statute's ground rules, that state must forego receipt of substantial federal dollars. The history of American public education is, as you might guess, not replete with instances wherein state authorities turned down federal dollars.

Interestingly, when the NCLB statute experienced its decade-old anniversary, the federal government's stance regarding how best to foster state and local accountability initiatives had shifted considerably. The early years of NCLB's existence had been marked by the threat of penalties for low-performing schools. However, after President Barack Obama's administration had taken office, federal officials soon set out meaningful financial incentives for states who subscribed to the U.S. Department of Education's accountability preferences. As usual, state education officials responded predictably to the lure of federal largesse. In essence, then, federal implementation of ESEA had shifted—in just a few years—from the stick to the carrot.

Arrival of the Common Core State Standards

One of the most salient of these carrot-induced shifts in state education policies was associated with the adoption, by all but a few states, of a set of identical curricular aims: the *Common Core State Standards (CCSS)* in English language arts (ELA) and mathematics. Because states that adopted these identical curricular aims became eligible for receipt of substantial federal subsidies, and because a markedly slowing national economy found most states facing serious fiscal shortfalls, educators soon saw almost all states accepting—as their state's official curricular aims—the *CCSS* in ELA and math. This event, almost unthinkable just a few years earlier, was near certain to have a substantial impact on the instructional and assessment practices of the nation's public school teachers in the coming years. Although educational authorities in the vast majority of U.S. states have adopted the *CCSS* as the official curricular aims in their state, since the early months of what seemed, in retrospect, to be an "adoption orgy" with almost all states hopping aboard the *CCSS* bandwagon, educational leaders in some states have now hopped off. The reasons for this turnaround in educational policy during a relatively brief span of years are several. Most often, we have seen officials in some states arguing that the *CCSS* represents a federal intrusion into the education of our young—historically an enterprise undertaken by states, not the federal government. Thus, backpedalling by *CCSS* states regarding adoption of the *CCSS* appears to be based more on political than educational rationales. In at least a few states, however, the educational leaders of those states (or, sometimes, the members of a state's legislature) found themselves in disagreement with certain of the curricular emphases of the *CCSS*. Although, as this edition of *Classroom Assessment* headed off happily to the publishers, the final number of U.S. states adopting the *CCSS* was uncertain, a good many states have either adopted the aims embodied in the *CCSS* or have made only slight modifications in the *CCSS* curricular goals, then adopted those substantively similar curricular aims. To be sure, in certain states we have seen truly acrimonious disputes among educational policymakers regarding their state's acceptance of the curricular aspirations embodied in the *CCSS*.

Let's look, ever so briefly, at what these curricular aims are—with a definite commitment to return in the next chapter for a deeper dip into the viscera of the *CCSS*. In Chapter 2, you will see how the two sets of curricular aims identified in the *CCSS* are organized, as well as hear what some of the developers of those state standards were hoping to accomplish.

Let's be clear about what the *Common Core State Standards* are. They represent the curricular outcomes sought for the nation's students—that is, the knowledge and cognitive skills students are supposed to acquire in school. Because NCLB had allowed each state to select its own curricular aims (that is, content standards), its own tests to assess students' mastery of those aims, and its own cut-scores (that is, achievement standards) to signify students' mastery of those curricular aims, making sense out of the NCLB-spawned accountability picture in U.S. public schools was almost impossible. In an effort to rectify this chaotic situation, the Council of Chief State School Officers (CCSSO) and the National Governors Association (NGA) Center for Best Practices set out in late 2009 to provide a more suitable set of curricular targets for the nation's schools. The CCSSO is the organization of the state officials, elected or appointed, who head each state's public schools. The NGA performs a comparable function for the nation's governors.

On June 2, 2010, the CCSSO and the NGA released the *Common Core State Standards for English Language Arts and Mathematics* (National Governors Association, 2010). As noted earlier, many states have accepted these standards—these "expectations for student knowledge and skills that high school graduates need to master to succeed in college and careers." Given the long-standing reluctance of state education officials to abandon "local control" over important educational decisions such as curricular outcomes for students, the widespread adoption of the *CCSS* was genuinely astonishing. In essentially a single year, the CCSSO and the NGA crafted sets of national mathematics and ELA curricular aims that seem sufficiently defensible so that all but a few states soon hopped aboard the *CCSS* Express.

The widespread and remarkably rapid adoption of the *CCSS* by so many states, however, did not take place merely because of the merits of a more uniform set of curricular targets for America. The recent role of philanthropic organizations in nurturing such significant changes in U.S. education is now being better understood.

In the June 7, 2014, issue of *The Washington Post*, Lyndsey Layton reports that a major player in the adoption of the *CCSS* was the Bill and Melinda Gates Foundation. In an article entitled "How Bill Gates Pulled off the Swift Common Core Revolution," Layton reveals that the Gates Foundation supplied more than $200 million not only to the actual development of the *CCSS* itself but also to building political support across the nation—often convincing state officials to make systematic and expensive changes in their curricular aspirations. Moreover, the foundation spread funds across the entire political spectrum, distributing dollars galore to the two major U.S. teachers unions and such business groups as the U.S. Chamber of Commerce—organizations that have historically clashed, but soon became outspoken proponents of the Common Core. As Layton reports, within two years of the Gates Foundation's decision to support the Common Core, 45 states and the District of Columbia had fully endorsed the *CCSS*.

But the curricular aims embodied in the *CCSS* were destined to serve as much more than lofty statements of curricular intent that, like so many previously crafted sets of curricular aims, typically languished in rarely read reports. This is because, soon after the release of the *CCSS* in mid-2010, the federal government announced its intention to fund one or more consortia of states whose mission it would be to create assessments suitable for measuring students' mastery of the skills and knowledge embodied in the *CCSS*. Two such assessment consortia were selected by federal authorities (from competing bidders) and were funded with approximately $175 million each to create assessments that, by the 2014–15 school year, could be used to determine students' mastery of the *CCSS*. The two consortia were the ***Partnership for the Assessment of Readiness for College and Careers (PARCC)*** and the ***Smarter Balanced Assessment Consortium (SBAC)***. Each of the consortia was initially composed of about 20 to 25 states, all of which agreed to promote students' mastery of the curricular goals represented by the *CCSS*.

It should be clear that the nature of the assessments devised by PARCC and SBAC would most likely have a considerable impact on America's public schools. Because the curricular aims being pursued by so many states would be identical, and the assessments used in those states would also be identical, comparisons among states' student performances would now be possible in ways that heretofore were impossible. The evaluative impact of such evidence, of course, is apt to be substantial.

As the assessments created by the two consortia became more widely understood, it has become less likely that the sorts of straightforward comparisons among states—comparisons originally foreseen by most proponents of the two assessment consortia—would be less likely to be present. Not only are the reporting categories and the cut-scores set by the two consortia dissimilar, but states are being allowed to infuse unanticipated degrees of local determination into what's taught and what's tested. In the middle of 2015, it appeared that considerable uncertainty existed regarding the degree to which identical curricular aims would be pursued by most of the 50 states, and how students' mastery of those states would be measured.

It is reasonably safe to assume that, under whatever federal revision of ESEA ultimately is enacted by Congress, there will continue to be state accountability tests. The nature and number of those tests may be modified in any ESEA reauthorization, of course, but it seems likely that in one form or another, we will continue to see federal laws calling for state-operated accountability tests. Perhaps those state tests will have been chosen from the *CCSS* tests provided by one of the two federally funded assessment consortia. Perhaps a state's accountability tests will be state-grown rather than consortium-built. But, one way or the other, state-level accountability tests are apt to be with us for a long while to come. That's the premise that will be employed in the coming pages.

An Updating of the *Standards for Educational and Psychological Testing*

The *Standards for Educational and Psychological Testing* (2014), first published in 1966, contains a set of professionally approved expectations for the way educational and psychological tests ought to be built and used. The *Standards* contain not only a series of comments regarding the way that educational and psychological tests should be evaluated, but they also lay out a specific series of detailed "standards," that is, mandates regarding what is appropriate in the nature and use of educational and psychological tests. This significant document is published by the American Educational Research Association (AERA) and is approved by that organization as well as the American Psychological Association (APA) and the National Council on Measurement in Education (NCME).

Because the *Standards* are often invoked in high-visibility courtroom contests involving educational tests, their influence on members of the educational measurement community is considerable. Thus, for example, those who write textbooks about educational testing almost always try to make sure what they are recommending in those textbooks is in accord with the latest rendition of the AERA, APA, NCME *Standards*. (I readily count myself among those writers who defer to the *Standards* when recommending how to play in the educational-testing sandbox.)

Periodically revised, for about one and a half decades the 1999 version of the *Standards* held sway, because until mid-2014 the 1999 *Standards* were essentially the only game in town. During that 1999–2014 period, a series of extraordinarily important uses of educational testing took place (for example, the role of students' test scores in educational accountability programs such as those fostered by NCLB). Not surprisingly, then, the 1999 *Standards* were regarded by many educators as being somewhat out of date. And so, when, after a 5-year revision and review process, the 2014 edition of the *Standards* was published, great interest in their contents was predictably displayed by assessment specialists. To illustrate, if pivotal concepts regarding educational assessment had been altered, or even if such concepts had been more clearly explicated, these alterations and these clarified explications would, in a very few years, be incorporated into the set of guidelines governing not only what is being professionally recommended about educational testing, but what educators ought to be learning about educational testing.

Candidly, I had been putting the bulk of this eighth edition of *Classroom Assessment* on hold until the updated version of the *Standards* hit the streets. I was reluctant to be advocating practices that might have been acceptable in 1999, but had been meaningfully modified in the new incarnation of the *Standards*. Happily, even though the final publication of the new *Standards* was many months overdue—largely due to the stringent level of scrutiny to which the revised testing standards were subjected by review groups representing AERA, APA, and NCME—the 2014 *Standards* appeared in time to have its contents completely integrated into this edition of *Classroom Assessment*. Although its publication in July 2014 caused the validity and reliability chapters in *Classroom Assessment* to be largely rewritten, at least what you will be reading in the remainder of this book will be in accord with the new *Standards*.

Although I run the risk of oversimplifying a bit, my take on the new *Standards* is that they do not introduce any dramatic reconceptualizations of the fundamental notions of educational testing that have guided educational measurement specialists since the 1999 version of the *Standards*. However, I think the new edition of this potent document both clarifies and tightens the interpretation of several key concepts in educational assessment. We will consider the most salient of those clarified "tightenings" in Chapters 3 and 4 regarding reliability and validity. The 2014 *Standards* did, however, more clearly emphasize the importance of assessment *fairness* than had been seen in earlier revisions. Thus, in the new *Standards* it is appropriate to assert that the three chief emphases are validity, reliability, and fairness.

Do teachers need to become knowledgeable regarding what's contained in the new 2014 *Standards?* I don't think so. Let the educational measurement specialists of America fuss with adhering to and interpreting content in the new edition of the *Standards*. But it is a reasonable expectation that teachers at least realize that the ground-rules of educational assessment did not arrive from outer space or from a far Eastern measurement guru. No, these nuts and bolts guidelines about educational testing undergo a rigorous review, rewriting, and approval process every decade or two by three national organizations most concerned with such testing. What teachers need to know, however, is that if they ever find themselves embroiled in any sort of test-related controversy, there exists an authoritative collection of definite dos and don'ts that can be consulted. It is called the *Standards for Educational and Psychological Testing* (2014) and it is available to all.

ASSESSMENT VERSUS TESTING

So far, I've been contrasting teaching to testing when, if you'll glance at this book's cover, you'll find that it's supposed to be a book about assessment. If you're alert, you've already started to wonder—What's this author trying to pull off? Am I going to learn about *testing* or am I going to learn about *assessment*? Is *assessment* simply a more fashionable word for *testing?* In short, what's he up to? These are reasonable questions, and I'll now try to supply you with a set of compelling, confidence-engendering answers.

Almost everyone knows about the kinds of tests typically encountered in school. Most of today's adults, indeed, were on the receiving end of a hoard of teacher-dispensed tests during their own days in school. There were final exams, midterm exams, end-of-unit tests, pop quizzes, and (in the interest of gender equity) mom quizzes. All of those tests had one thing in common. They represented the teacher's attempt to get a fix on how much the teacher's students had learned. More accurately, such tests were employed to determine a student's status with respect to the knowledge or skills the teacher was attempting to promote. This is an altogether praiseworthy endeavor for teachers—to find out how much students know. If teachers are reasonably sure about what their students currently know, then teachers can more accurately tailor any future instructional activities to promote what their students need to learn.

The sorts of tests referred to in the preceding paragraph, such as the quizzes and examinations most of us took in school, have historically been paper-and-pencil instruments. When I was a student, many years ago, the three most common forms of tests I encountered were essay tests, multiple-choice tests, and true-false tests. Until the past decade or so, those three kinds of tests were, by far, the most prevalent sorts of tests found in classrooms.

In recent years, however, educators have been urged to broaden their conception of testing so students' status is determined via a wider variety of measuring devices—a variety extending well beyond traditional paper-and-pencil tests. The reason teachers have been challenged to expand their repertoire of testing techniques is not merely for the sake of variety. Rather, thoughtful educators have recognized there are a number of important kinds of student learning not measured most appropriately by paper-and-pencil tests. If, for example, a teacher wants to determine how well students can function orally in a job-interview situation, it's pretty clear that a written true-false test doesn't cut it.

Thus, because there are many worthwhile learning outcomes not best measured by paper-and-pencil tests, and because when most people use the word *test* they automatically think of traditional paper-and-pencil tests, the term *assessment* has been increasingly adopted by many educators and measurement specialists. Assessment is a broader descriptor of the kinds of educational measuring teachers do—a descriptor that, while certainly including traditional paper-and-pencil tests, covers many more kinds of measurement procedures. Here is a working definition of *assessment* as it is used in an educational context:

> *Educational assessment is a formal attempt to determine students' status with respect to educational variables of interest.*

Lest you be put off by this fairly foreboding definition, let's briefly consider its chief elements. Note that the kind of assessment we're talking about is aimed at determining the status of students regarding "educational variables of interest." *Variables* are merely things that vary. (I suspect you could have figured this out all on your own!) In education, for example, we find that students vary in how much they know about a subject, how skilled they are in performing such operations as long division, and how positive their attitudes are toward school. Those are the sorts of variables with which a teacher is typically concerned; thus they are the "variables of interest" teachers typically measure. If the teacher's instructional focus is on the industrial revolution, then the teacher may wish to assess how much students know about the industrial revolution. In that case, the variable of interest would be the degree of students' knowledge regarding the industrial revolution. If the teacher is interested in how confident students are regarding their own written composition skills, then students' composition confidence would be a variable of interest. Educational assessment deals with such variables.

Our working definition also indicates that educational assessment constitutes a "formal" attempt to get a fix on students' status. As human beings, we make all sorts of informal determinations regarding people's status. For example, we may conclude that the woman who cut into the supermarket line ahead of us is rude, or that the man who keeps stumbling as he climbs a set of stairs is clumsy. But these are informal status determinations. Teachers, too, make informal judgments about their students. For instance, a teacher might conclude that a student, based on the student's glum demeanor during the first few moments of class, is definitely

grumpy. Such informal appraisals, although they may be useful to teachers, should not be regarded as educational assessment.

When I was a high school teacher, for example, I employed informal judgment to conclude that Raymond Gonty, one of the seniors in my U.S. Government class, was not really interested in what I was teaching. I reached this conclusion chiefly because Raymond usually slept during class. I became more firmly convinced, however, when he began arriving at class carrying a pillow!

The kind of educational assessment you'll be reading about in this book is formal—that is, it's a deliberate effort to determine a student's status regarding such variables as the student's knowledge, skills, or attitudes. The kind of educational assessment you'll be considering is more than a teacher's "impressions." Rather, you'll be learning about systematic ways to get a fix on a student's status.

Assessment, therefore, is a broad and relatively nonrestrictive label for the kinds of testing and measuring teachers must do. It is a label to help remind educators that the measurement of students' status should include far more than paper-and-pencil instruments. Assessment is a word that embraces diverse kinds of tests and measurements. In the remaining pages, you'll find that although I'll use the term *assessment*, I'll often use the words **test** and **measurement**. I'll not be trying to make any subtle distinctions at those times. Instead, I'm probably just tired of using the A-word.

WHY SHOULD TEACHERS KNOW ABOUT ASSESSMENT? YESTERYEAR'S ANSWERS

Let's play a bit of time travel. Suppose you were magically transported back to the 1950s or 1960s. And, as long as we're in a let's-pretend mode, imagine you're a new teacher taking part in a fall orientation for first-year teachers in a large school district. The thematic topic of the particular session you're attending is Why Should Teachers Know about Testing? The session's lecturer, Professor Tess Tumm, is supplying the audience with a set of traditional answers to this thematic question based on how teachers actually can use classroom tests. Because you are a docile new teacher (remember, this is imaginary), you are compliantly taking notes to help guide you during the coming school year.

What I'm suggesting, as you've probably guessed, is that there are a number of fairly traditional answers to the question of why teachers should learn about assessment. Those answers have been around for several decades. There is also a set of more current answers to the question of why teachers should know about assessment. Let's give tradition its due and, initially, consider four time-honored answers to the question of why teachers should know about testing. Although these reasons for knowing about classroom assessment may have been around for a while, they're still compelling because they are rooted in the realities of what skilled teachers can do with classroom assessment. These four reasons may well have been the major points treated by Professor Tumm during our imaginary orientation session of yesteryear.

Determining Students' Current Status

One important reason that a teacher might assess students is to determine what they presently know and can do—for instance, what a group of students' current levels of knowledge are or what their current cognitive skills happen to be. If, for example, a teacher has been instructing students about a series of mathematical operations, there are moments during an instructional sequence when it would be useful for the teacher to know which of those operations have been mastered—and which ones haven't. Based on students' test performances, then, a teacher can decide which mathematical operations seem to need more instructional attention and which ones seem to have been mastered by the students.

There is one oft-encountered instance in which teachers can benefit considerably by using tests to determine students' current status, and it comes up many times during a school year. When teachers are trying to promote their students' attainment of knowledge or skills that are relatively *new* to the students, it is remarkably helpful to get a fix on what it is that students already know and can do.

For instance, if Jaime is already truly proficient in solving simultaneous equations, it's a waste of Jaime's time to make him plow through practice piles of such equations. When I was growing up, the expression "That's like carrying coal to Newcastle" was used to disparage any scheme that reeked of redundancy. (I always assumed that coal mining was a big deal in Newcastle.) Well, teachers who relentlessly keep instructing students regarding knowledge or skills that the students have already mastered are definitely lugging coal lumps to Newcastle. Assessment can allow teachers to identify students' current capabilities and, as a consequence, can help teachers avoid superfluous and wasteful instruction.

Thus, by measuring students' status, teachers can discern (1) where to put their instructional energies to ameliorate a student's shortcomings and (2) what already mastered skills or knowledge can be instructionally avoided. Such assessment is particularly useful for a teacher's planning if the assessment is carried out at the beginning of an instructional sequence. This kind of early diagnosis is often referred to as *preassessment* because it is assessment that takes place prior to the teacher's initiation of instruction.

Monitoring Students' Progress

A second, related answer to the question, Why should teachers assess? is that such assessments help teachers determine whether their students are making satisfactory progress. Sometimes, of course, it's easy for teachers to tell whether their students are or are not progressing satisfactorily. I can still recall, with suitable embarrassment, the absolutely scintillating lesson I provided as a high school English teacher on the topic of Modifying Gerunds with Possessives. It was a lesson designed for a full-class period, and I was confident that at its conclusion my students would not only understand the topic but also be able to explain to others why one of the following sentences contains an appropriate pronoun and one does not:

Improper
Pronoun Gerund
↓ ↓

☹ **Sentence 1:** I really appreciate you sending the brownies.

Proper
Pronoun Gerund
↓ ↓

☺ **Sentence 2:** I really appreciate your sending the brownies.

At the end of a bravura 40-minute lesson, replete with all sorts of real-life examples and a host of on-target practice activities, I was certain I had effectively taught students that because a gerund was a noun-form of a verb, any modifiers of such gerunds, including pronouns, must be possessive. And yet, at the end of the lesson, when I looked into my students' baffled faces, I realized that my optimism was unwarranted. After asking several students to explain to me the essence of what I'd been talking about, I quickly discerned that my lesson about gerund modifiers was not an award-winning effort. Most of my students couldn't distinguish between a gerund and a geranium.

Although teachers can occasionally discern informally, as I did, that their students aren't making satisfactory progress, more often than not we find teachers' believing their students are progressing quite well. (Note in the previous sentence that the modifier of the gerund *believing* is the possessive form of *teachers*. Yes, I'm still trying.) It's only human nature for teachers to believe they're teaching well and their students are learning well. But unless teachers systematically monitor students' progress via some type of assessment, there's too much chance that teachers will improperly conclude progress is taking place when, in fact, such progress is not.

A useful function of classroom assessment, therefore, is to determine whether students are moving satisfactorily toward the instructional outcomes the teacher is seeking to promote. If progress for all students is satisfactory, of course, then the teacher need make no instructional adjustments. If progress for most students is satisfactory, but a few students are falling behind, then some separate doses of remedial assistance would seem to be in order. If progress for most students is inadequate, then the teacher should substantially modify whatever instructional approach is being used because, it is all too clear, this approach is not working. Progress monitoring is a time-honored and altogether sensible use of classroom assessment.

I've run into a number of teachers in recent years who refer to this use of assessment as "dip-sticking." When I think back to the days that I occasionally used a dip-stick to determine if my second-hand automobile was running low on oil (as it typically was), that label definitely rings true.

A teacher ought to monitor students' progress via classroom assessment because, more often than you'd think, the teacher can stop instructing on a certain topic well in advance of what the teacher had anticipated. Suppose, for instance, you're attempting to get your students to acquire a certain skill, and you've set aside two weeks to promote their mastery of the skill. If you monitor students' progress with an assessment after only a week, however, and discover your students have already mastered the skill, you should simply scrap your week-two plans and smilingly move on to the next topic.

Another way of thinking about the monitoring of student progress is that it positions teachers to use the results of classroom tests as part of *formative assessment*—that is, the use of assessment-elicited evidence intended to improve unsuccessful yet still modifiable instruction. *Summative assessment,* in contrast, refers to the use of tests whose purpose is to make a final success/failure decision about a relatively unmodifiable set of instructional activities. In a review of research studies focused on the instructional payoffs of formatively oriented classroom assessment, two British investigators (Black and Wiliam, 1998) concluded that the use of progress-monitoring classroom assessments can promote striking gains in student learning on both teacher-made and external exams.

Based on the Black and Wiliam conclusions regarding the major instructional dividends of formatively oriented classroom assessment, members of Britain's Assessment Reform Group introduced the idea of classroom assessment *for* learning—in contrast to assessment *of* learning. They describe this approach as follows:

> *Assessment for learning is any assessment for which the first priority in its design and practice is to serve the purpose of promoting pupils' learning. It thus differs from assessment designed primarily to serve the purpose of accountability, or of ranking, or of certifying competence. (Black et al., 2002)*

Stiggins and Chappuis (2012) have also pushed assessment for learning as the cornerstone of effective classroom measurement. Later, in Chapter 12, you will learn much more about the fundamentals of formative assessment.

Assigning Grades

If I were somehow able to carry out an instant nationwide survey of beginning teachers and asked them, "What is the most important function of classroom assessment?" I know what answer I'd get from most of the surveyed teachers. They'd immediately respond: *to give grades.*

That's certainly what I thought testing was all about when I taught in public schools. To be honest (confession, I am told, is good for the soul), the *only* reason I tested my students was to give them grades. I've talked to hundreds of teachers during the past few years, and I've been dismayed at how many of them continue to regard testing's *exclusive* function to be grade giving. A third reason, therefore, that teachers assess students is to assemble the evidence necessary to give their students grades. Most school systems are structured so the end-of-course or end-of-year grades a student earns constitute the beginnings of a record of the student's personal accomplishments—a record destined to follow the student throughout life. Thus, it is imperative teachers not assign grades capriciously. Whether we like it or not, students' grades are important.

The best way to assign grades properly is to collect evidence of a student's accomplishments so the teacher will have access to ample information before deciding whether to dish out an A, B, C, D, or F to a student. Some school systems employ less traditional student grading systems—for example, the use of descriptive verbal reports that are relayed to parents. Yet, whatever the reporting system used, it is clear the teacher's assessment activities can provide the evidence necessary to make sensible student-by-student appraisals. The more frequent and varied the evidence of student accomplishments, the more judiciously the teacher can assign to students the grades they deserve.

A corollary principle linked to "tests as grade determiners" is that some teachers also employ the prospect of upcoming tests to motivate their students. Because a student's grade is often dependent on the student's test performances, teachers will frequently employ admonitions such as, "Be sure to study this chapter carefully, because you have an important end-of-chapter exam coming up on Thursday!" Some teachers surely employ impending tests as a motivational device.

In recent years, several thoughtful educators have proffered sensible guidance regarding how teachers ought to award grades to their students (for example, Guskey, 2015). A consensus of these writers' thinking—a consensus focused on "standards-based" grading—will be presented in Chapter 16 to wrap up this edition of *Classroom Assessment*.

Determining One's Own Instructional Effectiveness

A fourth and final reason teachers have traditionally been told they should test students is that students' test performances can help teachers infer how effective their teaching has been. Suppose a teacher sets out to have students master a set of worthwhile skills and knowledge regarding Topic X during a 3-week instructional unit. Prior to instruction, a brief test indicated students knew almost nothing about Topic X but, after the unit was concluded, a more lengthy test revealed students had mastered most of the skills and knowledge addressed during the Topic X unit.

Because the comparison of students' pretest and posttest results indicated the teacher's students had acquired ample knowledge and skills regarding Topic X, the teacher has a charming chunk of evidence that the instructional approach being used appears to be working. If the teacher's instruction seems to be promoting the desired outcomes, then it probably shouldn't be altered much.

On the other hand, let's say a teacher's Topic X pretest-to-posttest results for students suggest students' progress has been piffling. After comparing results on the end-of-instruction posttest to students' performance on the preinstruction test, it appears students barely knew more than they knew before the instruction commenced. Such trivial student growth should suggest to the teacher that adjustments in the instructional activities seem warranted when teaching Topic X again next term or next year.

I'm not suggesting students' pretest-to-posttest results are the only way for teachers to tell whether they're flying or flopping, but students' end-of-instruction performances on assessment devices constitute a particularly compelling indication of whether teachers should retain, alter, or jettison their current instructional procedures.

In review, then, we've considered four fairly traditional answers to the question of why teachers should assess students. Here they are again:

Traditional Reasons That Teachers Assess Students

- To determine students' current status
- To monitor students' progress
- To assign grades to students
- To determine instructional effectiveness

You will notice that each of these four uses of educational assessment is directly related to *helping the teacher make a decision*. When a teacher assesses to determine students' current status, the teacher uses test results to *decide* what instructional objectives to pursue. When a teacher assesses students' progress, the teacher uses test results to *decide* whether certain parts of the ongoing instructional program need to be altered. When a teacher assesses students to help assign grades, the teacher uses students' performances to *decide* which students get which grades. And, finally, when a teacher uses pretest-to-posttest assessment results to indicate how effective an instructional sequence has been, the teacher is trying to *decide* whether the instructional sequence needs to be overhauled. Teachers should never assess students without a clear understanding of what the decision is that will be informed by results of the assessment. The chief function of educational assessment, you see, is to improve the quality of educational decision-making.

Taken in concert, the four traditional reasons just described should incline teachers to assess up a storm in their classrooms. But these days even more reasons can be given regarding why teachers need to know about assessment.

WHY SHOULD TEACHERS KNOW ABOUT ASSESSMENT? TODAY'S ANSWERS

In addition to the four traditional reasons teachers need to know about assessment, there are three new reasons that should incline teachers to dive joyfully into the assessment pool. These three reasons, having emerged during the past decade or so, provide compelling support for why today's teachers dare not be ignorant regarding educational assessment. Let's consider three new roles for educational assessment and see why these new functions of educational testing should incline you to feverishly pump up your assessment knowledge and skills.

Influencing Public Perceptions of Educational Effectiveness

When I was a high school teacher a long while ago, teachers were occasionally asked to give nationally standardized achievement tests. But, to be honest, no one really paid much attention to the test results. My fellow teachers glanced at the test-score reports, but were rarely influenced by them. The public was essentially oblivious of the testing process and altogether disinterested in the results unless, of course, parents received a report that their child was performing below expectations. Testing took place in the fifties and sixties, but it was definitely no big deal.

During the seventies and eighties, however, a modest journalistic wrinkle changed all that. Newspaper editors began to publish statewide educational test results on a district-by-district and even school-by-school basis. Citizens could see how their school or district stacked up in comparison to other schools or districts in the state. Districts and schools were *ranked* from top to bottom.

From a news perspective, the publishing of test results was a genuine coup. The test scores were inexpensive to obtain, and readers were really interested in the scores. Residents of low-ranked districts could complain; residents of high-ranked districts could crow. More importantly, because there are no other handy indices of educational effectiveness around, test results became the measuring-stick by which citizens reached conclusions about how well their schools were doing. There are many reports of realtors trying to peddle homes to prospective buyers on the basis that a house was located "in a school district with excellent test scores."

Let me be as clear as I can possibly be about this issue, because I think it is a terrifically important one. As matters stand, students' performances on a state's accountability tests are certain to influence the way that *all* teachers are evaluated—even if a particular teacher's own students never come within miles of an accountability test. Here's how that will happen.

Suppose you teach ninth-grade social studies, and your ninth-graders aren't required to take federally required accountability tests. Suppose you're a second-grade teacher, and your students aren't required to take any kind of accountability test. Suppose you're a high school teacher who teaches subjects and grade levels where no federal or state accountability tests are required. In all these "suppose" situations, *your* students won't be taking accountability exams. However, the public's perception of *your* personal effectiveness will most certainly be influenced by the scores of *your* school's students on any accountability tests that are required for such schools. Let's be honest—do you want to be a teacher in a "failing" school? Do you want your students' parents to regard *you* as ineffective because you happen to do your teaching in what's thought to be a sub-par school? I doubt it.

The reality is that the performance of any school's students on federally stipulated accountability tests will splash over on every teacher in that school. If you teach in a school that's regarded as successful, then you will be seen as a member of an effective educational team. The opposite is also true. Unless federal accountability requirements are substantially softened, no public school teacher will be able to remain isolated from the impact of externally imposed accountability tests.

And, as I'll try to point out later in the book, the nature of a school's success on high-stakes external assessments, such as federally required accountability tests, will (and, indeed, *should*) have an impact on the sorts of classroom assessments you personally choose to employ. We live in an era when public perceptions of schooling are more important than some educators might prefer. Yet, like it or not, that's the reality today's teachers must face.

DECISION TIME

Pressure from "Higher Ups"

Laura Lund has been teaching second-graders at Horace Mann Elementary School for the past 3 years. During that period, Laura has become increasingly convinced that "developmentally appropriate instruction" is what she wants in her classroom. Developmentally appropriate instruction takes place when the instructional activities for children are not only matched with the typical developmental level of children in that grade but also matched with the particular developmental level of each child. Because of her growing commitment to developmental appropriateness, and its clear implications for individualized instruction, Laura's students now no longer receive, in unison, the same kinds of massed practice drills in reading and mathematics Laura provided earlier in her career.

Having discovered what kinds of changes are taking place in Laura's second grade, however, the third-grade and fourth-grade teachers in her school have registered great concern over what they regard as less attention to academics, at least less attention of the traditional sort. Because state accountability tests are given to all third- and fourth-grade students each spring, Laura's colleagues are afraid their students will not perform well on those tests because they will not be skilled at the end of the second grade.

A year or so earlier, when Laura was teaching her second grade in a fairly traditional manner, it was widely recognized that most of her students went on to the third grade with a solid mastery of reading and mathematics. Now, however, the school's third- and fourth-grade teachers fear that "Horace Mann's accountability scores may plummet."

As Laura sees it, she has to decide whether to (1) revert to her former instructional practices or (2) maintain her stress on developmentally appropriate instruction. In either case, she realizes that she has to try to justify her action to her colleagues.

 If you were Laura Lund, what would your decision be?

Helping Evaluate Teachers

Teaching skill is coming under increasing scrutiny these days. With the push for more rigorous evaluation of a classroom teacher's performance, we now see many teacher appraisal systems in which students' test performances constitute one key category of evidence being used to evaluate teachers. Sometimes, teachers are directed to assemble pretest and posttest data that can be used to infer how much learning by students was promoted by the teacher. And, of course, teachers whose students are *required* to take a state's annual accountability tests understand all too well that their students' scores on those tests will play a prominent role in teacher evaluation—that is, in the evaluation of *their* teaching.

Although we will consider the topic of teacher evaluation far more thoroughly in Chapter 15, it should be noted at this point that a pair of federal initiatives have spurred much greater use of students' test scores in the appraisal of teachers. In 2009, the federal

Race to the Top Program offered some serious financial grants to states that would be willing, among other reforms, to install teacher evaluation systems in which students' test performances played a prominent role. Two years later, in 2011, once again federal officials offered the ESEA Flexibility Program that allowed states to seek a waiver from the harsh penalties linked to the final days of the No Child Left Behind Act. In that second initiative, states were once more informed that they had a better chance of snaring a waiver from Washington, DC, if they installed teacher evaluation programs in which students' test scores were regarded as a significant factor in evaluating the state's teachers.

Even though the education officials of most states sought one or both of these federal incentive programs, and promised to implement systems for evaluating teachers (and principals) using programs featuring student's assessed growth, a good many states now seem to be treading water regarding the implementation of their promised educator evaluation programs. Nonetheless, in all but a few of our states, descriptions of the current state-decreed teacher evaluation system calls for use of students' *measured* growth as one key evaluative criterion.

As a practical matter, then, because educational assessments will be employed to collect evidence of students' learning, and because this evidence will be used to evaluate teachers, a teacher would have to be a downright dunce to dodge the acquisition of information about sensible and senseless ways to measure students' status.

However, as you will learn in later chapters, only certain kinds of educational assessments can properly carry out this sort of test-rooted task. Most of the tests proposed for this purpose are altogether inappropriate for such an evaluative assignment. Nonetheless, if judgments about teachers' quality are—because of well-intentioned legislative actions—to be based in part on students' assessment performances, then it is apparent that teachers need to learn about the kinds of tests that will support or, possibly, distort this sort of evaluative endeavor.

Experienced teachers will be quick to tell you that the caliber of students' test performances is dramatically influenced by the caliber of the students being tested. It should be apparent that a teacher who is blessed with a flock of bright students will almost always get better test results than a teacher who must work with a less able group of students. And let's not forget about the quality of students' previous teachers. Wouldn't you rather be receiving a new group of students who had been effectively taught by Mrs. X than a group of students who had been ineffectively taught by Mrs. Y? Nonetheless, increasing numbers of statewide and districtwide teacher evaluation systems now call for teachers to assemble tangible evidence of student accomplishments based on external exams or teacher-made classroom assessments. It is clear, therefore, that today's teachers need to know enough about educational assessment so they can corral compelling evidence regarding their own students' growth. We will consider today's teacher evaluation tempest in more detail in Chapter 15.

Clarifying Teachers' Instructional Intentions

For many years, educational tests were regarded as instructional afterthoughts. As soon as an instructional unit was over, the teacher got busy cranking out a test. Tests were rarely created before instruction was initiated. Instead, tests were devised *after* instruction to fulfill some of the traditional functions of educational assessment described earlier in the chapter—for example, the assignment of grades.

Today, however, many educational measuring instruments have become high-stakes tests. A *high-stakes test* is an assessment for which important consequences ride on the test's results. One example of an educational high-stakes test would be a statewide basic skills test that must be mastered before a student graduates. (Note that the important consequences are for the test taker.) Another example would be the results of a districtwide achievement test that are publicized so local taxpayers' judgments about educational effectiveness are influenced by the test results. (Note that in this second case the important consequences apply to the educators who prepared the students, not the test-takers themselves.)

A federally required accountability test will fall into this second category of high-stakes tests. Because students' performances on these tests will so powerfully influence the way people regard a school staff's quality, such accountability tests will be genuinely high stakes in nature. You should know, however, there was nothing in NCLB that required diploma denial or that obliged students to be held back at grade level if they fail to perform well enough on a test. A *state's* decision can transform a federal test into one that has an adverse impact on a particular student. Many people continue to be confused by this, for they assume that any federally mandated accountability test automatically requires diploma-denial or promotion-denial testing. It's just not so.

Insofar as important consequences are directly linked to assessment results, the content of such high-stakes tests tends to be emphasized instructionally by teachers. Because teachers want their students to perform well on high-stakes tests (for the students' own good and/or for the teacher's benefit), high-stakes tests tend to serve as the kind of curricular magnet seen in Figure 1.1.

figure 1.1 ■ **The Curricular Impact of High-Stakes Tests**

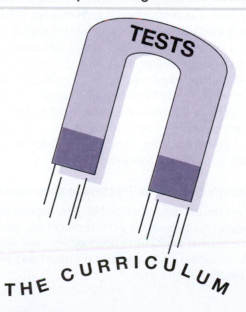

On some educational grounds, teachers might prefer that tests did not influence instruction so directly, but the reality is that high-stakes assessment will definitely have an impact on classroom instructional practices. Because this curricular influence is certain to be present, it will be in teachers' and students' best interests if the nature of the upcoming assessment is sufficiently well understood so the teacher can organize the most effective, on-target instruction possible. (Later in the book, we will consider the deficits of teaching exclusively toward assessment targets.) In a sense, however, the more that teachers understand what the innards of a test are, the more effectively they can use this understanding to clarify what's to be sought instructionally.

Earlier in the chapter, the *Common Core State Standards* were identified as a set of widely adopted curricular goals for many of our states. It was also pointed out that two assessment consortia (SBAC and PARCC) had been commissioned with substantial funds to create assessments intended to measure students' mastery of the curricular aims embodied in the *CCSS*. Well, when many of the nation's educators attempted to promote students' attainment of those curricular aims, they soon realized that although teachers could get a rough, general idea of what learner outcomes were sought by the *CCSS*, it was really necessary to await the release of the PARCC and SBAC test items before one could really know what was meant by many of the *CCSS* goals. Curricular aims are often just words—words so ambiguous in their meaning that it is sometimes necessary to use tests to operationalize those nice-sounding but often too general words. Thus, when SBAC and PARCC released many sample items in 2014 and 2015, American educators arrived at a much clearer idea of what the *CCSS* curricular aims actually mean.

Even the low-stakes classroom tests routinely employed by teachers can be used to help teachers clarify their instructional targets. Tests should obviously not, then, be instructional afterthoughts. Rather, classroom assessment instruments should always be prepared *prior* to any instructional planning in order for the teacher to better understand what is being sought of students and, therefore, what to incorporate in instructional activities for students. Assessment instruments prepared prior to instruction concretely exemplify a teacher's instructional intentions and, as a consequence, clarify those intentions. Clarified instructional intentions characteristically lead to more effective instructional decisions by the teacher. The better you understand where you're going, the more efficiently you can get there.

To reiterate, we've now looked at three reasons today's teachers, unlike their counterparts of a few decades ago, need to know about assessment. These reasons are supplemental to, not in place of, the previously considered traditional reasons teachers assess students. Here are the three new reasons for teachers' familiarization with educational assessment:

Today's Reasons for Teachers to Know about Assessment

- Test results determine public perceptions of educational effectiveness.
- Students' assessment performances are increasingly being included as part of the teacher evaluation process.
- As clarifiers of instructional intentions, assessment devices can improve instructional quality.

These reasons are also linked to decisions. For instance, when citizens use test results to reach judgments about a school district's effectiveness, those judgments can play a major role in determining what level of taxpayer support will be provided in that district. There are also decisions on the line when students' test scores are used as evidence to evaluate teachers. Such decisions as whether the teacher should be granted tenure or receive merit-pay awards are illustrative of the kinds of decisions that can ride, at least in part, on the results of educational assessments. Finally, from the teacher's perspective, when tests serve as clarifiers of the teacher's instructional intentions, the teacher can make better decisions about how to put together instructional activities likely to help students attain the instructional intentions represented by the assessment. With these three current roles of educational assessment, as was true with the four more traditional roles of educational assessment, test results should contribute to educational *decisions*.

WHAT DO CLASSROOM TEACHERS REALLY NEED TO KNOW ABOUT ASSESSMENT?

Whether you are already a teacher or are preparing to become a teacher, you really do need to know about educational assessment. But the field of educational assessment contains huge chunks of information. In fact, some educators devote their entire careers to assessment. Clearly, there's more to educational assessment than you probably care to know. The question is, What should *classroom teachers* know about assessment?

The title of this book suggests an answer—namely, *Classroom Assessment: What Teachers Need to Know*. The key word in the title, at least for purposes of this discussion, is *need*. There are oodles of fascinating things about assessment you might learn. You'd even find a few of them interesting (not all that many, I suspect). But to help your students learn, you really don't *need* to know a host of assessment esoterica. This book about educational assessment is deliberately focused on only those things that you really *must know* in order to promote your students' learning most effectively. I am altogether reluctant to clutter your skull with a galaxy of nice-to-know but nonessential knowledge about educational assessment. Such nice-to-know content often crowds out the need-to-know content. There is, after all, only so much skull space available.

As a preview, I want to describe briefly what you will have learned by the time you reach the book's index. (I have never had much confidence in any book's index as a teaching tool, so if you haven't learned what's needed by that time—it's likely to be too late.) It may be easier for you to get a handle on what you'll be reading if you realize you'll be covering topics dealing chiefly with:

1. Constructing your own assessment instruments
2. Using assessment instruments constructed by others
3. Planning instruction based on instructionally illuminating assessments

Creating Classroom Assessment Devices

Let's start with the kinds of classroom assessment devices you will personally need to create. The chief thing you will learn in this book is how to construct a wide variety of assessment instruments you can use as part of your day-to-day classroom instruction. You really do need to know how to determine what your students have learned—for example, whether they comprehend what they have read. You also really do need to know how to get a fix on your students' educationally relevant attitudes—such as how positively disposed your students are toward the subject(s) you're teaching. Thus, you are going to be learning about how to create classroom assessment approaches to measure students' *achievement* (that is, the knowledge and/or skills students acquire) as well as students' *affect* (that is, the educationally pertinent attitudes, interests, and values influenced by school).

As suggested earlier, the kinds of classroom assessment procedures you'll be learning about will extend well beyond traditional paper-and-pencil testing instruments. You may even learn about several assessment approaches with which you are currently unfamiliar.

In a related vein, you will also learn how to judge the quality of the assessment devices *you* create. And, at the same time, you will learn how to judge the quality of assessment devices created by others. Those "others" might be your own colleagues or, perhaps, the folks who devise large-scale assessment instruments such as districtwide or statewide tests. It may seem presumptuous for me to suggest that you, a classroom teacher (in practice or in preparation), could be judging the efforts of folks who create large-scale standardized educational tests. But you'll discover from this book that you will, indeed, possess the knowledge and skills necessary to distinguish between tawdry and terrific practices by those who create such large-scale educational tests. In particular, you can use your new knowledge to judge the quality of any accountability tests that may be used in your state. Those tests are going to be so important that, if you are teaching in a state whose accountability tests are educationally unsound, you definitely need to know it. What can you do if you discover that your state's high-stakes tests are inappropriate? Well, two action-options come quickly to mind. For openers, you can learn enough about the shortcomings of the state's tests so that you are able to explain coherently to your students' parents why the high-stakes tests your state has chosen are unsound. Second, and this may require a nontrivial expenditure of effort on your part, you can take part in educator organizations that are willing to bring about the installation of more suitable educational assessments. You can do neither of these things, of course, if you have only a skimpy knowledge of what makes your state's tests tick—and how they really ought to be ticking.

It is also important for you to know enough about educational assessment so that you can assist your colleagues in evaluating an ever-increasing array of commercially developed educational tests. Educators have seen a spate of such tests developed in the years following emergence of the *Common Core State Standards*. Some of these vendor-produced tests may be quite useful to teachers. Some of those tests, however, are seriously flawed—apparently cranked out merely to bring in a few bucks from desperate educators. There is no guarantee that a published

Assessment Literacy: Only for Grown-ups?

Students' performances on tests can have an enormous impact not only on the students who actually take educational tests but also on the test-taker's family. Teachers, too, are often affected by their students' test scores. To illustrate, today's teachers seem to be frequently buffeted by educational accountability tests on which students' test scores can have an impact on teachers' tenure, assignment, and salaries. Clearly, educators at all levels, whether teachers or administrators, need to learn enough about educational tests to carry out their responsibilities successfully.

What those educators need, then, is a reasonable dose of *assessment literacy*. And here's a definition of it:

> *Assessment literacy consists of an individual's understandings of the fundamental assessment concepts and procedures deemed likely to influence educational decisions.*

Notice that this definition is focused on someone's understandings of educational measurement's *basic* concepts and procedures of educational assessment. The stuff an assessment-literate person needs to understand is not esoteric and incomprehensible. Rather, most of what an assessment-literate person should know is just common sense applied to educational measurement. Describing assessment literacy a bit differently, it represents the main-line measurement procedures and concepts thought to make a difference in the decisions made about the students who take educational tests.

Well, if that's what assessment literacy is, who needs to have it? There's considerable pressure these days on teachers to become more assessment literate. You are currently reading a book that, unless the book's author has really mucked up, ought to help you personally become more assessment literate. But what about educational policymakers? And what about parents of school-age children? And, finally, *what about students themselves?* Don't all three of these groups need to beef up their understandings about the key assessment-related principles and processes that can influence students' lives?

I certainly think so. I hope, as you read this book, you'll occasionally pause to think how you might relay to policymakers (such as school board members), parents (such as (such as your own students' parents) and students (such as the ones you're teaching) the most essential things about the assessment-related concepts and procedures you're encountering in these pages. Remember, because test results these days can increasingly enhance or impair the decisions made about students, don't those students *at least* have the right to know what's going on behind the assessment curtain? A reasonable lump of assessment literacy is good for almost everyone!

test ought ever to have been published. Only an educator who possesses at least a small sack-full of assessment sophistication will be able to tell whether a commercially created educational test is yummy or gummy.

Fundamentally, educational assessment rests on a foundation of common sense. Once you learn the technical vocabulary of assessment, you'll be able to identify departures from commonsensical assessment practices, whether those departures are seen in your own tests, in the tests of a teacher down the hall, or in the tests created by district, state, or national assessment specialists. In short, after you finish this book, you really need not be deferent to any "measurement experts." You'll know enough to spot serious shortcomings in their work.

In Chapter 3, for example, you will learn about three criteria you can use to evaluate all educational tests. Those criteria apply with equal force to tests you might develop as well as to tests that are commercially developed. Once you get the hang of how to evaluate tests, you can apply this evaluative skill in many settings.

Interpreting Standardized Test Results

Because your students will often be assessed with nationally standardized or state-developed tests, you will need to know how to interpret the results of such tests. In general, commercially developed educational tests focus either on students' *achievement*, which, as noted earlier, deals with the knowledge and skills that students have acquired, or commercial tests focus on *aptitude*, which is a term used to describe a student's learning *potential*. You should know, however, that the term *aptitude* is definitely falling from grace these days. In the old days, when I was a tyke, people talked about intelligence. As a prospective teacher, I learned all about the intelligence quotient (IQ), which was a numerical way of indicating the degree to which a particular individual's intellectual abilities exceeded or fell short of conventional expectations for such individuals.

To calculate someone's IQ, you simply divided a student's *mental age* (based on how well a student's test score stacked up against a norm group's scores) by a student's *chronological age* (based on a calendar). The result of this was

$$\frac{MA}{CA} = IQ$$

But "intelligence" has fallen decisively out of favor with educators during the past few decades. The term *intelligence* conveys the notion that students possess an inborn potential about which schools can do little to influence. Yet, the so-called intelligence tests, widely used until recently, often measured what students had learned at school or, more importantly, what students had learned at home. Thus, the term *aptitude* has been increasingly used rather than *intelligence* in order to convey a notion of a student's academic potential. But even the term *aptitude* tends to create the perception there is some sort of innate cap on one's potential. Because of this perception, we now find that the commercial test makers who formerly created so-called intelligence tests, and then renamed them aptitude tests, are looking for a less negatively loaded descriptor. Interestingly, the tests themselves, although they've been relabeled, haven't really changed all that much.

At any rate, you'll learn how to make sense out of the kinds of reports regarding student performance released by those who conduct large-scale assessments. You will

But What Does This Have to Do with Teaching?

This chapter contains over a half-dozen reasons teachers need to learn about assessment. Actually, there are seven reasons in the chapter, and that's one more reason than a half-dozen. (Notice how low-level the arithmetic in this book is going to be!)

But let me single out the *two* reasons I think, *from an instructional perspective,* all teachers need to know about testing. The first of these reasons is the last of the seven reasons cited in the chapter—namely, the *instructional-planning payoffs* teachers can get from a more clear understanding of what they're trying to have their students accomplish. Because a properly constructed classroom test can truly exemplify what a teacher is trying to achieve, the resulting *clarity of intention* helps teachers make more astute decisions when they plan their instruction.

When I recall my own early years as a high school teacher, I remember how often I simply whipped together lesson plans that *seemed* somewhat instructional. Yet, my planning was almost never guided by a truly clearheaded notion of what knowledge, skills, or attitudes I wanted my students to possess when the instruction was over. If I had relied on my classroom tests to clarify what I wanted my students to become, I'm certain my lessons would have been far better focused on my intended instructional outcomes.

The second reason I think all teachers should become more astute regarding assessment is also instructionally rooted. It's the second of the four traditional reasons considered in the chapter—namely, so teachers can *monitor students' progress.* If teachers use students' assessed levels of achievement to determine whether the current instructional plan is stellar or sickly, then teachers' adjustments in lessons can, if warranted, be made. Without the evidence yielded by the classroom formative-assessment process, a teacher will often fail to spot instructional inadequacies. As Black and Wiliam, the British investigators, made quite clear, the instructional dividends from monitoring students' progress can be striking. And their views were based on solid research investigations, not wishful yearnings. My grandparents came to the United States from Great Britain, so I typically groove on anything that's asserted with a British accent. But, then, doesn't everyone?

need this knowledge not only to inform your own decisions about classroom instruction but also to interpret students' test performances to parents who may demand answers to questions such as, "What does my son's standardized test performance at 40th percentile really mean?" or "If my fifth-grade daughter earned a grade-equivalent score at the eighth-grade level on this year's standardized achievement test, why shouldn't she be promoted?" In short, you'll learn how to interpret students' performances on both **achievement tests** and **aptitude tests**. Moreover, given the relatively recent arrival of computer-administered and computer-adaptive educational tests, you'll find that parents are apt to be raising questions about such technologically abetted tests. Teachers need to be able to answer such questions—preferably with the correct answers.

Instructionally Illuminating Assessment

Earlier, it was suggested that because assessment devices exemplify a teacher's instructional intentions, those assessment instruments can clarify the teacher's instructional decision-making. You'll learn more about how the link between testing and teaching can prove beneficial to your students because you can provide more on-target and effective instruction.

On the other hand, you'll also learn how some teachers inappropriately prepare their students for tests, particularly for high-stakes tests. You will learn about ways of judging whether a given test-preparation practice is (1) in students' best interests from an educational perspective and (2) in educators' best interests from an ethical perspective. In short, you'll learn about the increasingly important relationship between instruction and assessment.

Later, you'll learn about a way to build classroom assessments so that they'll have a decisively positive impact on how well you teach. *Tests*, if deliberately created with instruction in mind, *can boost your personal success as a teacher*. We'll dig into that topic in Chapter 12.

There's one other issue that I'd like to bring to your attention—namely, the possibility (after you've finished the book) of your helping *parents* learn more about educational assessment. And why, you might ask, should a teacher be messing around trying to promote parental measurement moxie? It's a good question. And the answer is this: Parents who are *assessment literate* will be better able to *help you help their children learn* more successfully.

You see, most parents know little more about testing than what they can recall, often vaguely, from their own classroom days as students. But the nature of classroom testing has changed dramatically since that time. Not only are there new approaches to assessment being used in classrooms (all of which you'll learn about in this book), but students' test scores are also being used to judge the success of teachers' instructional efforts. You'll learn in Chapter 15 that, depending on the tests being used, this may be a dumb idea. If you and your students' parents truly understand the fundamentals of educational assessment, you can work together in many ways that will benefit your students. Assessment-literate parents can be a potent force to counter the serious misuses of educational tests we see so often today. And, if you are teaching in a state whose officials have opted to use instructionally inappropriate accountability tests, you'll find that assessment-literate parents can be a potent political force who might, if you're lucky, help get more appropriate accountability tests installed in your state.

There's another audience for assessment literacy that you'll hopefully give some thought to as you wend your way through this book. Please recognize that the lives of today's students are increasingly influenced by their performances on various kinds of educational tests. Why not, therefore, provide at least a dose of assessment literacy to students themselves? As you will see, most of the assessment concepts treated in the book are not particularly complicated. Indeed, the truly essential assessment understandings needed by students are well within the grasp of those students. Why not splash a bit of assessment literacy on those students? They really need it!

PARENT TALK

Mr. and Mrs. Smothers are attending a back-to-school night at a middle school where their daughter, Cathy, is a fifth-grader. After briefly leafing through Cathy's math portfolio and language arts portfolio, they get around to the real reason they've come to school. Mrs. Smothers, looking more than a little belligerent, says, "Cathy tells us she gets several teacher-made tests in class every week. All that testing can't be necessary. It obviously takes away the time you spend teaching her! Why is there so darn much testing in your class?"

 If I were you, here's how I'd respond to Mrs. Smothers:

"I suppose that it might seem to you there's too much testing going on in my class, and I can understand your concern about testing-time taking away from teaching-time. But let me explain how the time my students spend doing classroom assessments really leads to much *better* use of instructional time.

"You see, the way I use classroom assessment is to make sure my instruction is on target and, most importantly, that I don't waste the children's time. Last month, for instance, we started a new unit in social studies and I gave students a short pretest to find out what they already knew. To my delight, I discovered that almost all of the students—including Cathy—knew well over half of what I had been planning to teach.

"Based on the pretest's results, I was able to shorten the social studies unit substantially, and spend the extra time giving students more practice on their map-interpretation skills. You probably saw some of the maps Cathy was interpreting as part of her homework assignments.

"Mr. and Mrs. Smothers, I want Cathy's time in class to be as well spent as possible. And to make sure of that, I use formal and informal classroom tests to be certain that I'm teaching her and her classmates what they really need to learn."

 Now, how would you respond to Mrs. Smothers?

CHAPTER SUMMARY

In this chapter, the emphasis was on why teachers really need to know about assessment. Early in the chapter, the assessment-related features of various reauthorizations of the Elementary and Secondary Education Act of 1965 were briefly described because this oft-revised federal law's impact on most teachers' instructional and assessment decisions is becoming profound. *Educational assessment* was defined as a formal attempt to determine students' status with respect to educational variables of interest. Much of the chapter was devoted to a consideration of why teachers must become knowledgeable regarding educational assessment. Based on teachers' classroom activities, four traditional reasons were given for why teachers assess—namely, to (1) determine students' current status, (2) monitor students' progress, (3) assign grades, and (4) determine a teacher's own instructional effectiveness. Based on recent uses of educational assessment results, three more current reasons teachers need to know about instruction were identified. Those more recent functions of educational tests are to (1) influence public perceptions of educational effectiveness, (2) help evaluate teachers, and (3) clarify teachers' instructional intentions. Regardless of the specific application of test results, however, it was emphasized that teachers should use the results of assessments *to make better decisions.* That's really the only excuse for taking up students' time with assessment.

The chapter identified three major outcomes to be attained by those reading the book—namely, becoming more knowledgeable about how to (1) construct and evaluate their own classroom tests, (2) interpret results of standardized tests, and (3) teach students to master what's assessed in classroom and high-stakes tests. It was also suggested that an assessment-literate teacher should attempt to promote parents' and students' assessment literacy.

Determining Your Outcome Mastery

This is your first opportunity to decide how well you have achieved the chief chapter outcome for one of the chapters in *Classroom Assessment.* You will have 15 additional opportunities to do the very same thing as you spin through each of the book's 16 chapters.

Remember, although other topics were addressed in Chapter 1, the most important intended learning outcome was that you would become conversant with what underlies the reasons teachers test their students. As a reminder, here is the chapter's chief outcome:

> *An understanding of why it is that four traditional and three recent reasons for educators to assess students should dispose teachers to learn more about the fundamentals of educational assessment*

To engage fully in the formative-assessment process, complete both Mastery Checks, reach a mastery-determination judgment and, thereafter, make an adjustment decision. This simple assessment-governed process exemplifies how students employ formative assessment. For teachers, the process is similar, but when teachers review their students' performances on carefully selected tests, those teachers will use students' performances to decide whether to make any instructional adjustments.

Complete both the Selected-Response and the Constructed-Response quizzes and think about the feedback you receive for each quiz.

> **MyEdLab** *Selected-Response Check for Outcome Mastery*
> **MyEdLab** *Constructed-Response Check for Outcome Mastery*
>
> After completing both quizzes, go to the Learning Outcome Mastery Determination, where you will decide whether you've mastered the chapter's learning outcome or whether you need further study.
>
> **MyEdLab** *Learning Outcome Mastery Determination*

References

Andrade, H. (Ed.). (Winter 2009). "A special issue on classroom assessment," *Theory into Practice, 48,* no. 1.

Black, P., and Wiliam, D. (1998). "Inside the black box: Raising standards through classroom assessment," *Phi Delta Kappan, 80,* no. 2 (October): 139–148.

Curwin, R. L. (2014). "Can assessments motivate?" *Educational Leadership, 72,* no. 1 (September): 38–41.

Goodwin, B. (2014). "Better tests don't guarantee better instruction," *Educational Leadership, 71,* no. 6 (March): 78–81.

Gotch, C. M., and French, B. F. (2014). "A systematic review of assessment literacy measures," *Educational Measurement: Issues and Practice, 33,* no. 2 (Summer): 14–18.

Hess, F. M. (2008/2009). "The new stupid," *Educational Leadership, 66,* no. 4 (December/January): 12–17.

Layton, L. (June 7, 2014, Issue). "How Bill Gates pulled off the swift Common Core revolution," *The Washington Post.*

National Governors Association Center for Best Practices and Council of Chief State School Officers. (2010). *Common Core State Standards for English Language Arts and Mathematics.* Washington, DC: Author.

Nichols, S. L., and Berliner, D. C. (2008). "Testing the joy out of learning," *Educational Leadership, 65,* no. 6 (March): 14–18.

Popham, W. J. (2009). *Unlearned lessons: Six stumbling blocks to our schools' success.* Cambridge, MA: Harvard Education Press.

Stiggins, R. J., and Chappuis, J. (2012). *An introduction to student-involved assessment FOR learning* (6th ed.). Boston: Pearson.

Wiliam, D. (2013). "Assessment: The bridge between teaching and learning," *Voices from the Middle, 21,* no. 2 (December): 15–20.

2

Deciding What to Assess

CHIEF CHAPTER OUTCOME

An ability to identify, and understand the impact of, key factors that can help teachers determine the measurement targets for their classroom assessments

If classroom assessment does not help teachers do a better job of educating their students, then classroom assessment has no reason to exist. Consistent with that premise, this book about classroom assessment is really a book about teaching, not testing. That's because well-conceived classroom assessment will almost always lead to better educated students. So, before getting into some of the measurement concepts typically linked to educational testing, this second chapter addresses an overridingly important *educational* question that each teacher must answer about classroom assessment. This whopper question, suitably highlighted in uppercase type, is presented here:

WHAT SHOULD A CLASSROOM TEACHER TRY TO ASSESS?

In this chapter you'll encounter a collection of factors that teachers should consider before deciding what sorts of things their classroom assessments should measure.

WHAT TO ASSESS

Far too many teachers simply stumble into an assessment pattern without giving serious consideration to why they're assessing what they're assessing. Many teachers, for example, test students in order to dispense grades in a manner that somehow resembles the levels of academic performances students have displayed. Students who score well on the teacher's tests are given good grades; low-scoring students get the other kind. Traditionally, the need to dole out grades to students has been a key factor spurring teachers to assess their students. Other teachers, of course, also employ classroom tests as motivational tools—that is, to encourage students to "study harder."

Yet, as suggested in Chapter 1, there are a number of other significant reasons these days that teachers construct and use assessment instruments. For instance, results of classroom assessments may be employed to identify certain students' areas of deficiency so the teacher can more effectively target additional instruction at those content or skill areas where there's the greatest need. Another important function of classroom assessment is to help teachers, *prior* to the design of an instructional sequence, understand more clearly what their end-of-instruction targets really are. This clarification occurs because properly constructed assessment procedures can exemplify and, thereby, illuminate the nature of instructional targets for teachers.

Decision-Driven Assessment

Teachers use tests to get information about their students. Teachers typically make score-based interpretations about their students' status with respect to whatever curricular aims are being represented by the tests. Based on these interpretations, teachers then make decisions. Sometimes the decisions are as straightforward as whether to give Steve Smith an A or a B. Sometimes the decisions are more difficult, such as how to adjust an ongoing instructional unit based on students' performances on a mid-unit exam. But, whatever the decisions are, classroom assessment should be unequivocally focused on the *action options* teachers have at their disposal. The information garnered from assessing students is then used to help a teacher make the specific decision that's at issue. Because the nature of the decision to be illuminated by the test results will usually influence the kind of assessment approach the teacher selects, it is important to clarify, *prior to the creation of a test*, just what decision or decisions will be influenced by students' test performances.

I realize it may seem silly to you, or at least somewhat unnecessary, to identify *in advance* what decisions are linked to your classroom assessments, but it really does make a difference in determining what you should assess. For instance, suppose the key decision riding on a set of test results is how to structure a series of remedial instructional activities for those students who performed poorly during a teaching unit promoting a higher-order thinking skill. In this sort of situation, the teacher would definitely need some fine-grained diagnostic information about the "building block" subskills or enabling knowledge each student did or didn't possess. Thus, instead of designing a test so it merely assessed students' mastery of the overall skill being taught, there would also need to be a sufficient number of items assessing students' mastery of each building-block subskill or enabling knowledge. Based on the diagnostic data derived from the test, a sensible set of remedial instructional activities could then be designed for the low performers.

If, on the other hand, the key decision linked to test results is a simple determination of whether the teacher's instruction was sufficiently effective, a pretest–posttest assessment of more global (and less diagnostic) outcomes would suffice. It's also appropriate, by the way, when judging the effectiveness of a teacher's instruction, that separate assessments can be used containing items intended to assess students' *attitudes* regarding what was being taught, not merely the knowledge and/or skills being addressed. We'll look into how you can measure your students' attitudes in Chapter 10.

In short, the decisions to be informed by assessment results should always influence the nature of the assessments themselves. Teachers should, therefore, routinely consider the decision(s) at issue prior to creating a classroom assessment device.

A fairly easy way to decide if a test's results will really influence a classroom teacher's decision is to imagine that the test results turn out in two opposite ways—for example, a set of excellent student test performances versus a set of inferior student test performances. If the teacher would be likely to make a *different* decision based on those disparate sets of performances, then the teacher truly has a test that can help inform decisions. If the teacher's decision would be pretty much the same no matter what the test results were, there's a strong likelihood the assessment procedure is more ritual than genuine help for the teacher.

The Role of Curricular Aims

Much classroom assessment takes place after an instructional sequence has been completed. There are exceptions, of course, such as the during-instruction monitoring of students' progress as part of the formative-assessment process (about which you'll learn lots more in Chapter 12). There's also the pretesting a teacher might use as part of a pretest–posttest evaluation of the teacher's instructional effectiveness. Yet, many classroom tests are used at the close of instruction. And, because much classroom instruction is intended to help students achieve specified outcomes, it is quite reasonable to think that if teachers consider the outcomes they want their students to achieve, those teachers can more readily answer the what-to-assess question. What teachers should assess will, in most instances, stem directly from the intended consequences of instruction because it will be those hoped-for consequences that influence what the teacher will be teaching and, in all probability, what the students will be learning.

Let's pause for just a moment to consider how best to label a teacher's instructional intentions. This might seem unnecessary to you because, after all, why should the way teachers label their instructional aspirations make any real difference? Aren't a teacher's instructional aspirations simply what a teacher hopes, as a consequence of the teacher's instruction, will happen to kids?

Regrettably, there is considerable confusion among educators regarding how to describe the outcomes we hope students will achieve. If you become aware of this potential confusion, you can adroitly dodge it and move on to more important concerns. If you don't understand the nature of curriculum-label confusion, however, it is likely you will end up either being confused or, worse, adding to the confusion.

Getting down to basics, *curriculum* refers to the sought-for *ends* of instruction—for example, changes in students' knowledge or skills that a teacher hopes students will experience as a result of what was taught. In contrast, *instruction* describes the *means* teachers employ in an attempt to promote students' achievement of the curricular ends being sought. Instruction, therefore, refers to the set of activities a teacher has students carry out in an attempt to accomplish one or more intended curricular outcomes. Simply put, *curriculum equals ends* and *instruction equals means*. Where confusion careens onto the scene is when educators try to plaster diverse sorts of labels on the curricular ends they hope their students will accomplish.

No widespread consensus among educators exists regarding what to call the intended outcomes of instruction. During my own 50-plus years in the classroom, I've been in settings where curricular outcomes are referred to as goals, objectives, outcomes, expectations, benchmarks, and standards. In most of those locales, certain labels were supposed to apply to broader, more general curricular outcomes while other labels were given to more specific, less general outcomes. What's important when carving out what you want your classroom assessments to measure is that you understand precisely the meaning of whatever curricular labels are being used by colleagues in your school, district, or state. In most instances, whatever the curricular labels are, they are presented (often with examples) in some sort of official curricular document. Be sure you have a handle on what sorts of curricular descriptors are being used in your own part of the world. You'll dodge much curricular chaos if you do.

More often than not, throughout this book I will be employing the label *curricular aim* to characterize the desired outcomes of instruction. That phrase, *curricular aim*, has not been around for all that long and, therefore, has not had all of its meaning leeched from it. I'll sometimes use such phrases as "educational objectives" or "instructional objectives" to describe curricular aims—just for a descriptive change-of-pace. But, as I've indicated, you need to find out what sorts of curricular labels are being used where you teach. Odds are that those labels will be different from the descriptors I'm using here. That's okay, so long as you know what's going on.

Consideration of your own curricular aims, then, is one action you can take to help get a fix on what you should assess. The more clearly you state those aims, the more useful they will be to you in answering the what-to-assess question. In the 1960s and 1970s, there was widespread advocacy of *behavioral objectives*—that is, educational objectives stated in terms of the postinstruction behavior of learners. The push for behavioral objectives was fueled, at least in part, by dissatisfaction with the traditional form of general and ambiguous instructional objectives historically used by educators. An example of such general objectives would be the following: "At the end of the course, students will understand the true function of our federal government." My favorite gunky instructional objective of that era was one I ran across in a state-level language arts syllabus: "The student will learn to relish literature." After that time, I kept on the lookout for an objective such as "The student will mayonnaise mathematics." I haven't encountered one—yet.

DECISION TIME

On-Demand Assessment

Dolly Davis is a fourth-grade teacher who has set up her social studies activities on a mastery learning basis. Students are allowed to work through most of their social studies assignments at their own speed. Much of the social studies program in Dolly's class is based on reading assignments, so students can move at their own pace. When students believe they are ready to demonstrate mastery of the social studies skills and knowledge Dolly has described in written documents she distributes early in the school year, students set up an oral assessment. Dolly then spends 10 to 15 minutes presenting a series of short-answer items students must answer orally. So students do not discover from previously assessed students what the items on the assessment are, Dolly selects items at random from a pool of nearly 50 items for each of the four major social studies assessments during the year.

Although most students seem to appreciate Dolly's willingness to let them be assessed when they're ready, several students have complained that they "got a harder test" than some of their classmates. The dissatisfied students have encouraged Dolly to retain her mastery learning model, but to assess all students at the same time.

Dolly is deciding whether to maintain her on-call oral assessments or to revert to her former practice of written examinations administered to the entire class at the same time.

 If you were Dolly, what would your decision be?

Still, in their attempt to move from unclear general objectives toward super-clear behavioral objectives, the proponents of behavioral objectives (and I was right in there proponing up a storm) made a serious mistake. We failed to realize if we encouraged teachers to use instructional objectives that were *too* specific, the result would be an abundance of small-scope behavioral objectives. The resulting piles of hyperspecific instructional objectives would so overwhelm teachers that those overwhelmed teachers would end up paying attention to no objectives at all.

If you are currently a classroom teacher, you know you can't realistically keep track of whether your students are achieving hundreds of curricular aims. If you are preparing to be a classroom teacher, you'll soon discover that dozens and dozens of curricular aims will overwhelm you. The trick in conceptualizing curricular aims that help rather than hinder is to frame those aims broadly enough so you can sensibly organize instruction around them while making sure that the aims are still measurable. The degree of *measurability* is clearly a key in the way you should state your curricular aims. The broader the objective is, while still measurable, the more useful the objective will be because you can be guided by an intellectually manageable set of curricular intentions. If you can conceptualize your curricular aims so that one broad, measurable aim subsumes a bevy of lesser, smaller-scope objectives, you'll have a curricular aim that will guide your instruction more effectively and, at the same time, will be a big help in deciding what to assess.

In language arts instruction, for example, when teachers set out to have their students become good writers, a curricular aim is focused on the students' ability to generate an original composition. That aim, although still measurable (by simply having students churn out an original essay), encompasses a number of smaller-scope aims such as the students' ability to employ appropriate syntax, word choice, and proper spelling.

The concept of *measurability* is trickier than it first appears to be. Let's see why. A mere two paragraphs ago you were urged to frame your curricular aims broadly—so they subsumed more specific curricular intentions. However, you must also be sure your students' mastery of a curricular aim can be measured by a single, conceptually *unitary* assessment approach—not a fragmented flock of separate assessment tactics.

To illustrate, when teachers measure a student's ability to compose an original persuasive essay by asking the student to whip up such an essay (a writing sample) from scratch, those teachers can use the writing sample to get a fix on the student's punctuation skills, content mastery, spelling, and word usage—all at one time. A unitary assessment strategy has been employed that, in one fell swoop, captures students' mastery of lesser, contributory subskills and bodies of knowledge. The way to use students' writing samples to arrive at an inference about a student's composition prowess—and the separate subcomponents of that prowess—represents an example of *unitary* measurability.

On the other hand, if the only way to measure a student's mastery of a curricular aim is by relying on a collection of substantively *different* assessment tactics, then unitary measurability is not present. To illustrate, suppose a teacher had formulated a curricular aim labeled "Geometry" that embraced (1) congruence, (2) similarity, (3) circles, (4) equations, and (5) geometric measurement. However, in order to determine students' mastery of the "Geometry" goal, five separate sets of items were constructed, each focused on one of the five separate subcomponents of the "Geometry" curricular aim. This conceptualization, as you can see, does not constitute unitary measurement of students' curricular-aim mastery. The five distinct subcomponents of the curricular aim have not been truly coalesced in such a way that a single assessment strategy can accurately reflect students' attainment of an amalgam of the five subcomponents. What we would have here is what might be characterized as "counterfeit coalescence." What teachers should try to identify is a modest number of high-import curricular aims that can be measured via a unitary assessment approach. A flock of different, noncoalesced subtests clearly does not constitute unitary measurability.

Many educators these days use the concept of **grain-size** to represent the breadth of a curricular aim. More specific curricular aims are considered "small grain-size" instructional objectives, whereas more general curricular aims are regarded as "large grain-size" instructional objectives. One useful way of distinguishing among curricular aims according to their grain-sizes is to estimate the amount of instructional time it will take for students to accomplish what's embodied in a particular curricular aim. If the curricular aim can be achieved by students in a short while, perhaps in a few days or even in one class session, then the aim is usually thought of as a small grain-size outcome. If, on the other hand, a curricular aim seems likely to take days, weeks, or months to accomplish, such an aim is regarded as a large grain-size outcome.

Here's an example of two small-scope (small grain-size) curricular aims in language arts:

- When presented with reading passages containing unfamiliar words, students can employ context clues to infer the unfamiliar words' meanings.
- The student will be able to write sentences in which verbs agree in number with relevant nouns and pronouns.

Now let's look at a broad-scope (large grain-size) language arts curricular aim that subsumes these small-scope objectives plus a load of similar small-scope objectives:

- After reading an age-appropriate nonfiction essay, the student will be able to compose two paragraphs, the first of which summarizes the essay's central message and the second of which provides the student's personal reaction to the essay's message.

Strive to come up with a half dozen or so truly salient, broad, yet measurable, curricular aims for your own classroom. Too many small-scope, hyperspecific objectives will be of scant value to you because, if you're at all normal, you'll soon disregard an overwhelming array of super-specific curricular targets. On the other hand, a small number of intellectually manageable, broad, yet measurable, curricular aims will not only prove helpful to you instructionally but will also help you answer the what-to-assess question. Simply put, you need to create assessments to help you determine whether your students have, as you hoped, achieved your chief curricular aims. What this will often mean is that when deciding what to measure in your classroom tests, you will frequently need *curricular courage*—that is, the courage to measure well what's most important.

Cognitive, Affective, and Psychomotor Assessment

In thinking about what to assess, classroom teachers can often be helped by considering potential assessment targets according to whether they are chiefly focused on cognitive, affective, or psychomotor targets. *Cognitive assessment* targets are those that deal with a student's intellectual operations—for instance, when the student displays acquired knowledge or demonstrates a thinking skill such as decision-making or problem-solving. ***Affective assessment*** targets are those that deal with a student's attitudes, interests, and values, such as the student's self-esteem, risk-taking tendencies, or attitudes toward learning. ***Psychomotor assessment*** targets are those focused on a student's large-muscle or small-muscle skills. Examples of psychomotor assessments that take place in schools would include tests of the student's keyboarding skills in a computer class or the student's prowess in shooting a basketball in gym class.

The distinction among cognitive, affective, and psychomotor educational outcomes was first introduced in 1956 when Benjamin Bloom and his colleagues (Bloom et al., 1956) proposed a classification system for educational objectives organized around those three categories. While recognizing there are usually ad-mixtures of all three domains of behavior in most things that teachers ask students to do on tests, the 1956 *Taxonomy of Educational Objectives* made it clear there is typically a dominant kind of student behavior sought when teachers devise educational objectives for their students. For example, if a student is completing an essay examination in a social studies class, the student may be using a pencil to write *(psychomotor)* the essay and may be feeling remarkably confident *(affective)* about the emerging quality of the essay. But the chief domain of performance involved is *cognitive* because it is the student's intellectual analysis of the test's items and the student's intellectual organization of a response that mostly account for what the student's essay contains. Bloom's cognitive taxonomy included six levels of students' intellectual activity—ranging from the lowest level, *knowledge*, all the way up to the highest level, *evaluation*.

Standards-Based Classroom Assessment

Whether you are an elementary teacher who has instructional responsibility for a number of subject areas, or a secondary teacher who has instructional responsibility for one or two subject areas, you should be concerned that your instruction and your assessments address appropriate content. Fortunately, in the last decade or so, various national organizations have attempted to isolate the most important content to teach in their respective subject areas. These content-delineation efforts can prove quite helpful to teachers who are trying to "teach the right things." These national content-delineation efforts were a pivotal part of the 1990s *educational standards movement*.

First off, let's define what an educational *standard* actually is. Unfortunately, you'll find that different educators use the term all too loosely and often incorrectly. Actually, there are two types of educational standards you need to know about:

- A ***content standard*** describes the knowledge or skills that educators want students to learn. Such curricular aims are also referred to as "academic content standards."
- A ***performance standard*** identifies the desired level of proficiency at which educators want a content standard mastered. Such sought-for performance levels are also referred to as "academic achievement standards."

It should be apparent that although we might refer to both of the above as "standards," they are very different creatures. Just as cowboys in a western movie might loosely refer to "cattle," those cowpokes know that boy-cattle and girl-cattle perform decisively different functions. It's the same story today when educators utter the many-meaning word *standards*. An academic content standard (a curricular aim) is patently different from an academic achievement standard (a performance level). To refer to them both as "standards" can cause a cattle-car full of confusion!

From a classroom teacher's perspective, the most useful kinds of standards, without question, will be *content* standards because those standards set forth the things that whoever chose the standards regarded as the most important content for children to learn. Years ago, when I was a high school teacher, we had a district "curriculum guide" and a state "scope and sequence" manual, both of which attempted to identify the most important knowledge and skills that students should learn in each subject area. To be honest, those documents weren't all that wonderful. My fellow teachers and I found those curriculum materials to be vague, ambiguous, and altogether unhelpful.

During the 1990s, however, standards were recommended by many organizations, led by the National Council of Teachers of Mathematics (NCTM) 1989 publication of *Curriculum and Evaluation Standards for School Mathematics*. In that publication, NCTM made a major effort to reconceptualize how mathematics should be taught by identifying a set of important new content standards. Those content standards defined the chief curricular aim of mathematics education as the promotion of students' mathematical power—that is, students' ability to use mathematical thinking and understanding to solve problems and communicate the results of those solutions mathematically.

Soon thereafter, other national subject-matter associations began to bring forth their own sets of content standards and, in some instances, performance standards as well. I have had a chance to review many of these standards documents. Most of them are very impressive. All of the standards documents represent the efforts of top-flight subject-area specialists who devoted enormous time to circumscribing the knowledge and skills that students should learn.

I think it would be great if *you* spent some time reviewing these standards documents to identify what you might be teaching (and, therefore, testing). But I do *not* believe you should meekly succumb to the curricular preferences expressed in those standards collections. The reason for such a warning is straightforward. These standards documents were produced by subject-matter *specialists*. And subject-matter specialists really adore their subject matters. Subject-matter specialists would like to see students master almost *everything* in their field.

Subject specialists often approach their standards-identification tasks not from the perspective of a busy classroom teacher, but from the perch of a content devoteé. Content devoteés and classroom teachers, just like steers and cows, are different members of the cattle crowd. If teachers tried to teach students to do *all* the things set forth in most standards documents, there'd be no time left for food, sleep, or movies! So, what I recommend you do is *consult* the most recent national standards document(s) relevant to your own teaching responsibilities, and then see which of the content standards you have time to address. Without question, you'll get some wonderful ideas from the standards documents. But select your own content standards judiciously; don't try to stuff the whole wad of standards into your students' skulls. That wad won't fit.

Norm-Referenced versus Criterion-Referenced Assessment

There are two rather distinctive, yet widely used, assessment strategies available to educators these days: *norm-referenced measurement* and *criterion-referenced measurement*. The most fundamental difference between these two approaches to educational assessment is the nature of the interpretation that's used to make sense out of students' test performances.

With ***norm-referenced measurement***, educators interpret a student's performance in relation to the performances of students who have previously taken the same examination. This previous group of test takers is referred to as the *norm group*. Thus, when educators try to make sense out of a student's test score by "referencing" the score back to the norm group's performances, it is apparent why these sorts of interpretations are characterized as norm referenced.

To illustrate, when a teacher asserts a student "scored at the 90th percentile on a scholastic aptitude test," the teacher means the student's test performance has exceeded the performance of 90 percent of students in the test's norm group. In education, norm-referenced interpretations are most frequently encountered when reporting students' results on academic aptitude tests, such as the SAT, or on widely used standardized achievement tests, such as the Iowa Tests of Basic Skills or the California Achievement Tests. In short, norm-referenced interpretations are *relative* interpretations of students' performances because such interpretations focus on how a given student's performance stacks up in relation to the previous performances of other students.

In contrast, a ***criterion-referenced measurement*** is an *absolute* interpretation because it hinges on the extent to which the criterion (that is, curricular aim) represented by the test is actually mastered by the student. Once the nature of an assessed curricular aim is properly described, the student's test performance can be interpreted according to the degree to which the curricular aim has been mastered. For instance, instead of a norm-referenced interpretation such as the student "scored better than 85 percent of the students in the norm group," a criterion-referenced interpretation might be that the student "mastered 85 percent of the test's content and can be inferred, therefore, to have mastered 85 percent of the curricular aim's skills and/or knowledge represented by the test." Note that a criterion-referenced interpretation doesn't depend at all on how other students performed on the test. The focus is on the curricular aim represented by the test.

As you can see, the meaningfulness of criterion-referenced interpretations is directly linked to the clarity with which the assessed curricular aim is delineated.

Accurately described curricular aims can yield crisp, understandable criterion-referenced interpretations. Ambiguously defined curricular aims are certain to yield fuzzy criterion-referenced interpretations of little utility.

Although loads of educators refer to "criterion-referenced tests" and "norm-referenced tests," there are, technically, no such creatures. Rather, there are criterion and norm-referenced *interpretations* of students' test performances. For example, educators in a school district might have built a test to yield criterion-referenced interpretations, used the test for several years and, in the process, gathered substantial data regarding the performances of district students. As a consequence, the district's educators could build normative tables permitting norm-referenced interpretations of the test which, although born to provide criterion-referenced inferences, can still provide meaningful norm-referenced interpretations.

Because most of the assessment-influenced decisions faced by classroom teachers are benefited by those teachers' understanding of what it is students can and cannot do, not merely their relative standing in relationship to one another, classroom teachers will generally want to arrive at criterion-referenced rather than norm-referenced interpretations. A teacher's instructional choices, for example, are better serviced by evidence about particular students' skills and knowledge than by evidence about how those students compare with one another.

About the only instance in which classroom teachers will need to employ norm-referenced interpretations occurs when there are fixed-quota settings—that is, when there are insufficient slots for all of a teacher's students to be assigned to a given educational experience. For example, suppose there were five students to be chosen for a special outside-of-class enrichment program in mathematics, and the teacher had been directed by the school principal to choose the "best" mathematics students for the program. In such a situation, because *best* is, by definition, a relative descriptor, norm-referenced interpretations would be warranted. A teacher might build a test to spread students out according to their mathematics skills so the top students could be identified. Barring those rare situations, however, most classroom teachers would be better off using tests yielding criterion-referenced interpretations. Criterion-referenced interpretations provide a far more lucid idea of what it is students can and can't do. Teachers need such clarity if they're going to make solid instructional decisions.

Later, in Chapter 13, you'll be considering standardized achievement tests, assessment devices usually built to provide norm-referenced interpretations. At that time, the appropriate and inappropriate uses of test results from such commercially distributed assessment instruments will be identified. For most classroom assessment, however, the measurement strategy should almost always be criterion referenced rather than norm referenced.

Before saying farewell to the distinction between criterion-referenced and norm-referenced assessment strategies, I need to highlight a confusion that I first encountered about 50 years ago, but am running into again in recent years.

When Robert Glaser first introduced the notion of criterion-referenced measurement more than five decades ago (Glaser, 1963), there were actually two different meanings he provided for the term *criterion*. On the one hand, Glaser used it in a fairly traditional manner to represent a *level of performance*, such as one might employ when saying, "Let's get the quality of all trainees' performance up to a suitable criterion." In the sixties, most people I knew tended to use the word *criterion* in precisely that way—as a desired level of performance. On the other hand, in Glaser's article he also used "criterion" to represent a clearly defined criterion behavior such as a well-explicated cognitive skill or a tightly delineated body of knowledge. Well, in those early days, many educators who were beginning to learn about criterion-referenced testing were not sure which of those two very different notions to employ.

Yet it soon became apparent that only the "criterion as defined behavior" notion really made much sense because, if the "criterion as level of performance" interpretation were adopted, then all of the existing education tests could become instantly criterion-referenced simply by designating a desired performance level for those tests. Such an approach to assessment would be fundamentally no different from the traditional approaches to educational testing so widely used at the time. Glaser was looking for a new way of thinking about educational testing, not more of the same. Thus, in the 1970s and 1980s, criterion-referenced testing was seen as a way of ascertaining a test taker's status with regard to one or more well-defined criterion behaviors. This interpretation was sensible.

Just during the last few years, however, I have encountered measurement specialists who are once more touting the "criterion as level of performance" notion. This is a clear instance of regression toward dumbness. It is not a suitable way to think about criterion-referenced assessment. I just want you to be on guard so you can spot such flawed thinking when it crosses your path. Criterion-referenced measurement is built on an assessment strategy intended to determine a test taker's status with respect to a clearly defined set of criterion behaviors, typically well-defined skills or knowledge. I treat these issues elsewhere (Popham, 2014).

Selected Responses and Constructed Responses

Assuming a classroom teacher has come up with a reasonable answer to the what-to-assess question, an important point in determining how to assess it arises when the teacher must choose between assessment strategies that elicit ***selected responses*** or ***constructed responses*** from students. If you think for a moment about the way educators assess students' educational status, you'll realize there are really only two kinds of responses students can make. Students *select* their responses from alternatives we present to them—for example, when we give students multiple-choice tests and students' responses must be selected from each item's available options. Other examples of selected-response assessment procedures are binary-choice items, such as those found in true–false tests where, for each item, students must select either a true or a false answer.

In contrast to selected-response sorts of tests, students *construct* all kinds of responses. In an English class, for instance, students construct original essays. In a woodshop class, students construct end tables. In a speech class, students construct 5-minute oral speeches. In a drama class, students construct their responses while they present a one-act play. In a homemaking class, students construct soufflés and upside-down cakes. Constructed-response tests lead either to student *products*, such as the end tables and soufflés, or to *behaviors*, such as the speeches and the one-act plays. When the students' constructed responses take the form of a tangible product, classroom teachers have the luxury of judging the quality of the product at their leisure. For instance, after students create an original essay, the teacher can take this product home on the weekend and, while relaxing in the jacuzzi, either grade or immerse each essay.

When students' constructed responses are in the form of behaviors, however, such as when students are asked in a physical education class to run a mile in less than 12 minutes, the teacher must somehow make a record of the behavior or else it disappears. The record might be created by the teacher's use of written records or be captured electronically via an audio or video recording. For example, when students in a speech class give a series of impromptu speeches, the teacher typically fills out some sort of evaluation form for each speech. Similarly, physical education teachers use their stopwatches to note how much time it takes for students to run a mile, and then note the elapsed time in a record book.

It was formerly thought that although selected-response tests were difficult to create, they were easy to score. Similarly, it was once believed constructed-response tests were just the opposite—simple to create but tough to score. These days, however, educators have become more sophisticated about constructed-response tests and are employing many more types of constructed-response assessment procedures than only essay tests or short-answer tests. It is generally conceded that both selected-response and constructed-response tests require considerable care when being created. It is still true, however, that the scoring of selected-response tests is substantially easier than the scoring of constructed-response tests.

If, as a classroom teacher, you're really choosing between these two assessment schemes, you need to focus on the nature of the score-based inference you wish to make. Some score-based inferences simply shriek out for selected-response assessment schemes. For instance, if you want to make inferences about how many historical facts your students know, a selected-response procedure will not only fill the bill but will also be simple to score. Other score-based inferences you might wish to make really require students to display complex behavior, not merely choose among options. If, for example, you want to make inferences about how well students can compose sonnets, then selected-response assessment schemes just won't cut it. To see if students can churn out a sonnet, you need to have them construct sonnets. Reliance on a selected-response test in such a situation would be psychometrically silly. It is, as usual, the *test-based inference* the teacher needs to make that should guide the choice between selected-response and constructed-response assessment strategies. Nonetheless, if teachers plan to incorporate constructed-response items in their tests, they *must be sure to have sufficient time available to score students' responses accurately*.

PARENT TALK

Suppose that Ms. Collins, a parent of one of your students, has cornered you after school and asked for a few minutes of your time. She wants to know what all the talk about "new, challenging standards" really means. She's read an article about educational standards in the local newspaper, and she wonders whether the "new" standards are really new. Her question to you is, "Why is there all this fuss about educational standards these days when it seems that teachers in this school are still teaching pretty much what they've always taught and testing what they've always tested?"

 If I were you, here's how I'd respond to Ms. Collins:

"I really understand your concern about educational standards, Ms. Collins. They've certainly been receiving plenty of attention from educators during recent years. But, regrettably, there's still a fair amount of confusion about standards, even among educators.

"Actually, there are two kinds of educational standards that you and I need to consider. A *content standard* simply identifies the skills and knowledge we want students to acquire in school. For example, your daughter has recently been improving her composition skills quite dramatically. She can now write narrative and persuasive essays that are quite wonderful. An example of a content standard would be *'Students' mastery of written communication skills.'*

"A *performance standard*, on the other hand, indicates *how well* a content standard should be mastered. We score our students' essays on a four-point scale, and the school's teachers have agreed that a student should achieve at least a three in written communication to be considered satisfactory.

"What we now call *content standards,* we formerly described as goals, objectives, or outcomes. What we now call *performance standards,* we formerly described as passing levels or cut scores. So some of the descriptive labels may be new, but the central idea of trying to teach children important skills and knowledge—this hasn't really changed very much.

"What is new, at least to me, is a much greater concern about the *defensibility* of our content and performance standards. All across the nation, educators are being urged to adopt more challenging standards—standards that demand more of our children. This has also been taking place in our own school. So if you look more closely at what we're teaching and testing here, I think you'll see important differences in the kinds of skills and knowledge we're pursuing—and the levels of excellence we expect of our students."

 Now, how would you respond to Ms. Collins?

It is always possible, of course, for teachers to rely on both of these two assessment strategies in their classrooms. A given assessment, for instance, might represent a blend of both selected- and constructed-response approaches. As always, the assessment procedure should be employed to help the teacher get a fix on the students' status with respect to an otherwise unobservable variable in which the teacher is interested.

A State's Official Curricular Aims

A state's designated educational policymakers typically decide on the curriculum aims—that is, the content standards—to be promoted for the state's public-school students. This is because education, not having been identified in the U.S. Constitution as a federal responsibility, has historically been regarded as a state obligation. Until recently, the usual way for a state to identify the curricular targets for its schools was to assemble groups of content-capable educators who, after substantial deliberation, identified the content standards to be promoted in the state's public schools. As might be expected, considerable agreement was seen between the official curricular aims of different states, but meaningful differences in curricular preferences were also seen among states. With the arrival of the *Common Core State Standards (CCSS)* in 2010, however, all this changed—dramatically. Many states have now accepted the mathematics and English language arts (ELA) curricular aims represented by the *CCSS*. As was true in earlier years when state-specific curricular aims were identified by each state, the adoption of the *CCSS* was usually accomplished by a state board of education or, in some instances, a state legislature.

Briefly introduced in Chapter 1 of this book, the *CCSS* seem certain to play a prominent role not only in the nature of U.S. classroom instruction and assessment but also in the sorts of assessment instruments that will be available so educators can measure students' achievement of the *CCSS*. If only from an assessment perspective, then, we need to take a look at the *CCSS*.

The *Common Core State Standards*

As noted earlier, on June 2, 2010, the *CCSS* were released by the Council of Chief State School Officers (CCSSO) and the National Governors Association (NGA) Center for Best Practices. In the next section of this chapter an attempt will be made to provide a brief introductory picture of the *CCSS* in English language arts and mathematics. Yet, because these curricular aims have now been accepted (sometimes after renaming them) by many of the 50 states, it should be apparent that any teacher in a state where the *CCSS* curricular aims have been adopted should possess much more than a nodding acquaintance with these curricular targets. Accordingly, educators are encouraged to consult either the CCSSO (http://www.ccsso.org) or the NGA (http://www.nga.org/cms/home.html) for a far more detailed depiction of what makes up the *CCSS*. Moreover, if you are a teacher in a state where the *CCSS* have been adopted, it is likely that your state or district will have information available regarding the nature of these curricular aims.

Before presenting what I hope will be an accurate but terse introduction to the *CCSS*, however, I feel compelled to offer one or two stage-setting remarks regarding these important curricular aims. First off, remembering that the *CCSS*, at least their official publication, did not take place until June 2010—at least in the early months thereafter—it was clear that many U.S. educators were not familiar with the nature of the *CCSS*. As many educators began to dig into the substance of the *CCSS*, they anticipated that these newly spawned curricular targets would be similar to the sets of state-specific content standards seen throughout the country during recent decades. Those state-identified curricular aims had typically consisted of a list of content standards (that is, sets of the knowledge and skills students were supposed to master)—typically grouped under subject-area headings such as reading, writing, mathematics, and so on. Beneath those subject headings, the content standards themselves usually were grouped under a set of general labels (sometimes called "strands") such as geometry, numeration, algebra, and so on. Beneath those content standards, we usually found further particularization such as the specific bodies of knowledge or skills a student should achieve in order to attain mastery of any content standard. Although these collections of state curricular aims were often too numerous, as least in the view of the educators who had to promote students' mastery of those aims, these state-specific aims—as typically formulated—were relatively easy to understand.

I regret to report that such is not the case with the *CCSS*. Several categorization strata have been employed to describe the curricular targets in the *CCSS* and, unfortunately, the labeling scheme employed for the ELA curricular targets is not the same as the labeling approach employed in mathematics. Thus, elementary teachers who are instructionally responsible for both English language arts and math will be obliged to engage in gobs of mental gear-shifting when seeking guidance from *CCSS* documents regarding appropriate curricular targets for those two content fields.

In the next few paragraphs, then, a particularly brief introduction to the organizational structure of the *CCSS* ELA and mathematics content standards will be provided. This "handshake" with the *CCSS* should, hopefully, be followed up with a much more meaningful "hug" that can only be obtained by your spending time—more than might be initially thought—with the actual content of the *CCSS* (NGA and CCSSO, 2010). Let's begin with English language arts.

English Language Arts *Common Core Standards*

In an effort to identify K–12 standards to help ensure that all U.S. students would be college and career ready in *literacy* no later than the close of high school, those crafting the *CCSS* identified a set of curricular targets in both English Language Arts as well as Literacy in History/Social Studies, Science, and Technical Subjects. When reviewing the complete array of these standards, your comprehension of them will usually be enhanced if you are aware of the several ways the ELA and literacy standards have been categorized in the *CCSS*. Let's consider those categorizations.

For openers, there's a fairly straightforward distinction between grades K–8 and grades 9–12. For grades K–8, the standards are set out on a grade-by-grade basis. At the secondary level, however, we find grade bands being used to describe the standards for grades 9–10 and 11–12.

Then, at each K–8 grade level you will find sets of standards for *reading, writing, speaking and listening*, and *language*. For the reading outcomes, there's an important distinction drawn between standards based on students' reading of *literature* versus *informational text*. Architects of the *CCSS* reading standards definitely wanted U.S. students to have greater exposure to informational text than has often been the case in years past. In grades K–5, in fact, the standards are broken out separately for literature and for informational texts. Ten "College and Career Readiness Anchor Standards" are presented under the following four general categories: (1) Key Ideas and Details, (2) Craft and Structure, (3) Integration of Knowledge and Ideas, and (4) Range of Reading and Level of Text Complexity. In addition to a more equitable split between students' exposure to informational texts and literature, framers of the *CCSS* reading standards want students to be able to read increasingly complex texts through the grades. After grades K–5, the reading standards are identified separately for literature and informational text at grades, 6, 7, and 8 as well as for grade ranges 9–10 and 11–12.

Here, then, is an example of a *CCSS* grade 5 standard in *reading*—in this instance for students' reading of informational text (rather than literature):

> *Explain how an author uses reasons and evidence to support particular points in a text, identifying which reasons and evidence support which point(s).*
> © Copyright 2010. National Governors Association Center for Best Practices and Council of Chief State School Officers. All rights reserved.

In addition to the ELA reading standards, the *CCSS* also spell out anchor standards for writing, for speaking and listening skills, and for language. As was the case with reading, these curricular aims are broken out by separate grades in K–8, and then use two grade ranges in grades 9–10 and 11–12. Here's an example of a *CCSS writing* standard for grade 3 students:

> *Write informative/explanatory texts to examine a topic and convey ideas and information clearly. (This standard is accompanied by four attributes sought of these early writers—for example, "Provide a concluding statement or section.")*
> © Copyright 2010. National Governors Association Center for Best Practices and Council of Chief State School Officers. All rights reserved.

Beyond the identification of ELA standards as described here, separate standards are also provided in the *CCSS* for literacy in grades 6–12 dealing with history/ social studies, science, and technical subjects. Both reading and writing standards are given for students in three grade ranges, that is, 6–8, 9–10, and 11–12. Authors of these grade 6–12 literacy standards in reading intend for instructional attention to those standards to be integrated along with instruction focused on the K–5 reading standards described earlier. It was hoped by the creators of the *CCSS* that attention to the K–5 reading standards would provide broad curricular targets, while the literacy standards in 6–12 reading would supply additional specificity (NGA and CCSSO ELA Standards, 2010, p. 61).

The original June 2, 2010, publication by CCSSO and NGA (2010) not only contains substantial introductory material related to the *CCSS* but, in the case of the ELA standards, also presents a number of components intended to assist in the implementation of the standards. To illustrate, the *CCSS* authors strongly advocate that students become ever more able to engage in "close analysis" of increasingly complex textual materials. Accordingly, helpful illustrations of increasingly complex materials—both literary and informational text—are supplied (NGA and CCSSO ELA Standards, 2010, p. 32). Suggestions are also proffered regarding how to stay on topic within a grade and across grades (NGA and CCSSO ELA Standards, 2010, p. 33).

Given the several ways in which the designers of the *CCSS* attempt to organize the curricular aims embodied in their conceptualization of what students should learn, educators who wish to take full advantage of the *CCSS*—not only in ELA but also in mathematics, should become flat-out familiar with any *CCSS* segments in which they are interested. Thus, rather than being overwhelmed and/or confused by a set of seemingly off-putting curricular aims, educators can become truly knowledgeable about these significant collections of curriculum goals.

Mathematics *Common Core Standards*

Let's look now at the *CCSS* for *mathematics*. The working group that identified the math standards divided those standards into two groups, the mathematical *practice* standards and the mathematical *content* standards. The content standards are identified for each grade level, kindergarten through grade 8, and also at high school. These mathematics curricular aims are categorized in three ways as seen here:

> *Standards* define what students should understand and be able to do. An example of a standard would be: "Use place value understanding to round whole numbers to the nearest 10 or 100."
>
> *Clusters* represent groups of related standards. An example of a cluster that includes the illustrated (preceding) standard would be: "Use place value understanding and properties of operations to perform multi-digit arithmetic."
>
> *Domains* are larger groups of related standards, for example, "Number and Operations in Base Ten."

To illustrate how this sort of categorization system works, let's take a look at one grade level and the numbers of domains, clusters, and standards identified for that particular grade. In the fourth grade, for instance, we find five domains, each of which contains one, two, or three clusters of standards. And each of these grade 4 clusters contains one to three standards. (Several of the standards have been broken down further into subdivisions reflecting two, three, or four different aspects of a student's understanding of a given standard.) In all, then, there are 28 grade 4 *CCSS* standards with, if one also considers the three "subdivided" standards, a grand total of 37 curricular targets in the *CCSS* mathematics standards.

A given grade's domains, then, constitute the broadest descriptors of the curricular aims designated at that grade level. In some instances, we encounter slight differences between the mathematical domains at two different grade levels, but frequently these domains are identical at different grades. To illustrate, the *CCSS* grade 6 overview in mathematics presents the following five domains: (1) Ratios and Proportional Relationships, (2) The Number System, (3) Expressions and Equations, (4) Geometry, and (5) Statistics and Probability. In the seventh grade, precisely the same five domains are seen. However, beneath these domain labels, there are often differences in the set of standards that a given cluster represents.

Clearly, then, although there is surely substantial coherence and consistency in mathematical emphases as one moves through the grades, there are also meaningful differences in the math skills and knowledge sought of students. Teachers whose state authorities have adopted the *CCSS* should certainly become conversant with relevant grade-level variations in the knowledge and skills sought of students not only for the particular grade at which a teacher teaches but also at nearby grade levels. The creators of the *CCSS* mathematics curricular targets have attempted to fashion a series of multigrade curricular emphases that, from an instructional perspective, build sensibly on one another.

Turning from the math *content* standards, let's look at the mathematical *practice* standards. The practice standards remain the same across the grades because they describe varieties of expertise that mathematics educators at all levels should seek to foster in their students. These practice standards are drawn from processes and proficiencies that have traditionally occupied important places in mathematics education. They are presented in Figure 2.1.

As the designers of the *CCSS* see it, the Mathematical Practice standards describe ways in which those who engage in the discipline of mathematics should increasingly engage with the subject matter as they grow in mathematical expertise and maturity. It is the hope of those who crafted the *CCSS* mathematical standards that educators will make a serious effort to connect the Standards for Mathematical Practice to the Standards for Mathematical Content. Candidly, given the few years that the *CCSS* math standards have been with us, there is much work to be done in discerning the most sensible ways to interrelate these two meaningfully different sets of standards.

Turning to high school, the *CCSS* mathematics standards are listed as conceptual categories: (1) Number and Quantity, (2) Algebra, (3), Functions, (4) Modeling, (5) Geometry, and (6) Statistics and Probability. These six categories are believed to represent a coherent view of high school mathematics. To illustrate, a student's work with functions can cross a number of traditional course boundaries up through and including calculus.

Each of these conceptual categories is broken out at the high school level by the *CCSS* architects. For example, the geometry category is subdivided into

figure 2.1 ■ *Common Core Standards* for Mathematical Practice

1. Make sense of problems and persevere in solving them.
2. Reason abstractly and quantitatively.
3. Construct viable arguments and critique the reasoning of others.
4. Model with mathematics.
5. Use appropriate tools strategically.
6. Attend to precision.
7. Look for and make use of structure.
8. Look for and express regularity in repeated reasoning.

Source: © Copyright 2010. National Governors Association Center for Best Practices and Council of Chief State School Officers. All rights reserved.

(1) Congruence, (2) Similarity, Right Triangles, and Trigonometry, (3) Circles, (4) Expressing Geometric Properties with Equations, (5) Geometric Measurement and Dimension, and (6) Modeling with Geometry. And each of these subdivisions typically represents several further subdivisions. Slight differences also exist for high school in the mathematical *practices* for the conceptual categories that, in elementary grades, had remained the same.

It should be apparent that the manner in which the *CCSS* mathematics standards are organized and presented to the nation's educators could easily become confusing. There are so many curricular targets—in different categories and at different levels—embraced by the math standards, that educators really do need to arrive at a "mentally manageable" way of representing the diverse mathematical outcomes being sought of students.

When one spends much time with the *CCSS* mathematics standards, it is apparent that those who built these mathematical curricular aims desperately wish the nation's educators to stress "greater focus and coherence." Indeed, in the initial paragraphs of the materials describing the math standards, we are given frequent reminders that not only should mathematical *focus* be achieved, but *coherence* among those standards should also be attained. "The mathematics curriculum in the United States must become substantially more focused and coherent in order to improve mathematics achievement in this country" (NGA and CCSSO Mathematics Standards, 2010, p. 3).

In their quest for "focus," the architects of the *CCSS* in mathematics are not merely advocating a smaller number of curricular targets—as might be achieved merely by stuffing numerous narrow but clearly stated standards into a smaller collection of broader curricular statements that mask much, if not all, of the original standards' clarity. Jason Zimba, one of three *CCSS* mathematics team coordinators, provides a powerful argument supporting the need for focus in the *CCSS* mathematics standards. As he suggests, "Not everything in the Standards *should* have equal priority" (Zimba, 2011, p. 2). He continues:

> *Moreover, at every level in mathematics, there are intricate, challenging, and necessary things that serve as prerequisites for the next level's intricate, challenging, and necessary things. In order to keep as many students as possible on the path to readiness for college and careers, we need to give students enough time to succeed in these areas. (Zimba, 2011, pp. 2–3)*

To illustrate, the *CCSS* mathematics team coordinators believe there should be a definite focus on numbers and operations in the elementary school, but that this focus should be diminished in later grades. In short, the developers of the *CCSS* mathematics standards clearly recommend that more time be spent on fewer things at each grade level. Because both focus *and* coherence are emphasized throughout the *CCSS* mathematics standards, the designers of these standards want teachers to recognize how the curricular aims focus on progress from one grade to the next. According to *Webster's*, when something *coheres*, it "sticks together, that is, holds together as parts of the same mass." Well, such *coherence* among the *focused CCSS* mathematics curricular aims is what the originators of these mathematics standards apparently had in mind.

Mathematics curricular aspirations that are both coherent *and* focused will surely constitute a collection of curricular targets capable of influencing what takes place in our nation's classrooms. Teachers who set out to have their students master the *CCSS* goals in math (or ELA) need to become sufficiently familiar with what (to some educators) is the initially off-putting *CCSS* structure to arrive at their own judgments regarding the coherence and focus of the *CCSS* curricular aims.

"Many a Slip ..."

The older I get, there are fewer and fewer folks who know the maxims that I've relied on most of my life. One of those sayings is: "There's many a slip twixt the cup and the lip!" Besides giving me an opportunity to use the word "twixt" (an option that doesn't come along all that often), the maxim reminds us that, as we raise our cups of hot cocoa toward our mouths, numerous things can go wrong. Through the years, loads of laps have definitely been doused by errant, about-to-be-consumed drinks of one sort or another. Yet, this little-used adage still alerts us to the possibility, perhaps the *probability*, that well-conceived hopes often take a tumble en route to the finish line. And so it is with curricular aims such as those embodied in the *CCSS*.

I have concluded that the *CCSS* English language arts and mathematics curricular targets are really quite commendable. For the most part, I believe the *CCSS* curricular aims are equal to or better than the state curricular goals they are replacing—that is, the ones we have seen adopted by individual states during the last several decades. Some months after I had reached this conclusion, a report was issued in late 2011 by the respected nonpartisan Center on Education Policy in Washington, DC, which seemed to confirm such an estimate of *CCSS* quality. After surveying school districts in the 44 states where the *CCSS* had been officially adopted, this report concluded that almost 60 percent of officials in those districts agreed "that the new standards in math and English language arts are more rigorous than the ones they are replacing" (Center on Educational Policy Press Release, September 14, 2011, p. 1).

So it appears that the curricular aims embodied in the *CCSS* may, indeed, be worthwhile. Moreover, many district-level officials recognize the merits of those curricular aims. Where, then, does "slip twixting" slither into this happy picture? Here's my answer to that question: *Curricular aims—whether local, state, or national—until decisions have been made about how students' mastery of those aims will be assessed, are just words—sometimes fairly meaningless words.* That's right, no matter how laudable the curricular aspirations embodied in the *CCSS* are, if they are poorly assessed, then the positive impact of the *CCSS* will most certainly be minimal.

You see, curricular aims set an outer limit of how a sensible assessment might take place. For instance, if a curricular aim calls for students to be able to comprehend the main idea of a written passage, then we know that measuring such an aim by asking students to perform long division is obviously off target. Long division is *outside* the limits set by a main-idea curricular aim. However, *within* that main-idea curricular aim, there are various ways to get at a student's main-idea mastery. And it is the way students perform on the tests chosen to measure attainment of a curricular aim that really lets us know the degree to which we've been successful in promoting students' curricular-aim mastery.

To determine how well a teacher, school, or district has succeeded in getting students to master any of the *CCSS* curricular aims, we must consider students' postinstruction performances. Those postinstruction performances will most often be displayed as *scores on tests*. And that's where the two assessment consortia—Partnership for the Assessment of Readiness for College and Careers (PARCC) and Smarter Balanced Assessment Consortium (SBAC)—will come rumbling onto our education's center-stage.

What's to Be Assessed on Your State's Accountability Test

Teachers working with students who are on the receiving end of a state's annual accountability tests should, without question, take into consideration what's to be assessed each year on state accountability tests. Results from such tests, typically administered in the spring near the close of a school year, can have a substantial impact on the kind of evaluations awarded to schools, school districts, and teachers. Accordingly, when deciding what to measure in a teacher's own classroom tests, it would be foolish not to consider what's being assessed by such unarguably significant tests.

Because the education officials of each state must determine what sorts of accountability tests will be employed in their state, a teacher needs to find out for certain what's to be measured by state assessments in that teacher's state.

Having done so, then the teacher needs to determine whether the teacher's students, because of grade-levels-taught or subject-matter-taught, will be assessed each year regarding what the teacher was supposed to be teaching. Obviously, what's eligible for assessment on such high-stakes tests should have a major impact on what the teacher tries to teach and what the teacher tries to assess.

Even teachers whose students will be assessed only in later years should become conversant with what's to be measured in those later-year assessments. For example, teachers of first-graders or second-graders—whose students will not be tested each year—should surely consider what's to be tested in the third grade when state-level accountability testing commences. Similarly, a ninth-grade English teacher whose students won't be taking an accountability test until the tenth or eleventh grade should still look into what to be assessed in English language arts when accountability testing resumes.

Because many U.S. states have adopted the *Common Core State Standards* as the curricular aims for their own states, then what's measured by the two previously described assessment consortia, that is, PARCC and SBAC—should be seriously considered by any teacher whose students must take those tests or any teacher whose instructional efforts should contribute to students' subsequent mastery of CCSS-based accountability tests. Fortunately, both assessment consortia have provided ample descriptions of what their tests assess, and even provide sample items and tests intended to help educators understand what the consortium-built tests measure.

As this eighth edition of *Classroom Assessment* was about to be sent to the publisher for its periodic pummeling by editors, an intriguing set of developments was taking place in America. A group of states that had originally been members of one of the assessment consortia were pulling out of those consortia (for example, Kansas, Florida, and South Dakota). Moreover, some states that had been committed to rely on consortium-built tests as their annual accountability assessments were looking elsewhere for such tests. Alaska, for example, had requested the state of Kansas and its test-development group at the University of Kansas to develop Alaska's annual accountability test.

Indeed, for a variety of reasons, such as (1) cost considerations, (2) a public backlash against too much testing, and (3) the perception that the *Common Core State Standards* had been a federal rather than a state initiative, some states were withdrawing their acceptance of the *CCSS* altogether, only to adopt a set of "locally" developed curricular aims that, unsurprisingly, often resembled the CCSS themselves. Putting it simply, substantial uncertainty was prevalent regarding what curricular aims would be endorsed by many states and, beyond that, what assessments would be used to assess students' achievement of those curricular aims.

Accordingly, because what's to be assessed by important external tests can and should have an impact on a teacher's decisions about the content of classroom assessments—especially if the teacher's own students will be taking those assessments immediately or in later years. This doesn't mean that whatever's tested on a later, important test needs to be completely mirrored by a teacher. Instead, what's needed is some serious scrutiny of what's to be measured by any subsequent significant assessment.

If one or both consortia do a nifty job in generating instructionally useful assessments—assessments that can provide accurate evidence regarding students' attainment of the *CCSS* targets—then all will be well. But, as has been pointed out, "twixt-slips" often happen between aspiration and culmination. Accordingly, it becomes particularly important for U.S. educators to carefully scrutinize the caliber of the assessments that will emerge from the SBAC and PARCC consortia. Wonderful curricular hopes can be hobbled by less than wonderful assessments. Wonderful curricula can be made even more marvelous by truly wonderful assessments.

It is invariably expected that a state's accountability tests should be *aligned* with the state's official curricular aims. Let's look briefly at the term *alignment*. In the field of education, *alignment* is the only 9-letter word that seems to function as a 4-letter word. This is because many people play fairly fast and loose with a term that, by its nature, seems to evoke fast-and-loose play. **Alignment** refers to the degree to which there is a meaningful agreement between two or more of the following: curriculum, instruction, and assessment. What is generally called for, of course, is the agreement of a state's accountability tests with a state's content standards. To the extent that such a *curriculum-assessment* alignment has been achieved, a teacher would have to be a ninny not to recognize that it is sensible to also align the teacher's classroom curricula and assessments with whatever state content standards are to be assessed by the accountability tests in that teacher's state.

A major difficulty with the concept of alignment, unfortunately, is that it is decidedly *squishy*. What constitutes alignment in one educator's eyes may be seen as nonalignment by another educator. And there is often much self-interested "seeing alignment where none exists." So, whenever you hear someone touting the alignment between instruction and curriculum and assessment, try to dig a bit deeper so you can see whether the alignment being described is based on rigorous or relaxed ways of determining agreement levels.

But what do teachers do to align their classroom tests with important exams such as a state's annual accountability tests? This constitutes a nontrivial quandary for most teachers, and it turns out to depend—almost totally—on the quality of the accountability exams. If your state's accountability exams are capable of accurately detecting instructional quality, then you should make sure your classroom assessments mesh with what's assessed on those accountability tests. If your state's accountability tests, on the other hand, are *not* capable of accurately detecting instructional quality, then you need to pay less heed to what's assessed by those statewide tests. If you continue reading until you arrive at this book's final chapter, you'll learn how to distinguish between state-level accountability tests that are grubby versus those that glisten.

Of Standards and Emperors

Then a small voice called out from the crowd, "But the emperor's not wearing new standards at all; he's wearing old objectives!" According to a classic but uncorroborated fairy tale, a ruler can be persuaded to parade around in the buff if he's made to believe he's wearing wonderful but invisible garments. The moral of "The Emperor's New Clothes" fable, of course, is that a ruler is not apt to redress his state of undress unless someone informs him that he's naked as a jaybird.

Standards, of course, is a warmth-inducing word. Although perhaps not in the same league with *motherhood, democracy*, and *babies*, I suspect that *standards* ranks right up there with *oatmeal, honor,* and *excellence*. It's really tough not to groove on *standards*, especially if those standards are *high*. Everyone wants students to reach high standards. And, because high standards are so intrinsically praiseworthy, if teachers pursue such standards, then teachers can sleep tranquilly at night. Teachers are clearly questing after that which, like the Holy Grail, warrants such questing.

If by the expression *content standards* we refer to the knowledge and skills we want our students to achieve as a consequence of education, how is a content standard different from an instructional objective? The answer (all emperors and emperors-in-training take heed) is that there really is *no* difference between instructional objectives and content standards. Both phrases describe the educational intentions—that is, the curricular aims—we have for our students.

One reason that content standards are much more appealing to almost everyone than instructional objectives, as noted earlier, is that *content standards* is a warmth-inducing phrase; *instructional objectives* is not. What right-minded politician or educational policymaker would not leap with enthusiasm to be "in solid support of high content standards"? It's far less exciting for someone to applaud even meritorious instructional objectives.

So, for both of these reasons, I foresee continued widespread support for the identification and promotion of defensible content standards. As I listen, however, to today's enthusiastic endorsements of "challenging" or "world-class" content standards and their pivotal role in educational improvement, I find myself doing a bit of mental transformation, so I'm covertly thinking about curricular aims or instructional objectives. (I don't tell anyone, of course. One needs to be regarded as up-to-date.)

NAEP Assessment Frameworks

The National Assessment of Educational Progress (NAEP) is a congressionally mandated project of the U.S. Department of Education. It assesses U.S. students' knowledge and skills in geography, reading, writing, mathematics, science, U.S. history, the arts, civics, and other academic subjects. Since 1969, NAEP has periodically surveyed the achievement of students at *ages* 9, 13, as well as 17 and, since the 1980s, in *grades* 4, 8, and 12. As originally conceptualized, NAEP was intended to measure U.S. students' levels of academic achievement over time.

The National Assessment Governing Board (NAGB) was created by Congress in 1988 to formulate policy for NAEP. Among its responsibilities is the development of assessment objectives for NAEP through a national consensus approach. Although NAGB strives to avoid the perception that its objectives for various academic subjects at grades 4, 8, and 12 constitute a national curriculum, the assessment frameworks produced under NAGB's aegis are typically first-rate curricular documents, hence represent another source teachers might wish to consult as they attempt to decide what to assess.

The NAEP frameworks can be downloaded from the NAGB (https://www.NAGB.org) website. Although never intended to serve as a one-size-fits-all set of assessable objectives for an entire nation, the NAEP assessment/curricular frameworks typically reflect thoughtful analyses regarding what ought to be assessed (taught) at three key grade levels. Beyond the curricular insights obtainable from the NAEP assessment frameworks, the NAGB website supplies a wide range of illustrative items from previously administered NAEP tests. These illustrative items can give teachers useful ideas about how to measure students' mastery of important outcomes.

The No Child Left Behind Act required all states to participate in the biennial administration of NAEP reading and mathematics tests to representative samples of students in grades 4 and 8. The NAEP results are reported as the numbers of students who score in each of the following three categories: *advanced, proficient*, and *basic*. Scores that fail to be classified in one of these three categories are regarded as *below basic*. Many states currently report the percentages of students who score in those categories *on the state's own accountability tests*. Accordingly, how do you think it will look to the public if on the state's accountability test, 60 percent of the students score at proficient-or-above but, on NAEP, only 20 percent of the state's students earned proficient-or-above scores? That's right, it will look fiercely fishy!

Assessment Blueprints

A number of teachers find it helpful, especially when constructing major examinations, to develop what's called an *assessment blueprint* or a *test blueprint*. These blueprints are essentially two-way tables in which one dimension represents the curricular aims the teacher wants to assess, while the other dimension represents the levels of cognitive functioning being sought. For instance, the following example from a teacher's assessment blueprint will illustrate how these sorts of organizational schemes work by dividing each curricular aim's items into (1) knowledge (low-level recall of information) and (2) cognitive levels higher than mere recall.

	Number of Items	
	Cognitive Level	
Curricular Aim	*Knowledge*	*Above Knowledge*
1	3	1
2	1	4
3	2	2
etc.	etc.	

Assessment blueprints can help teachers identify curricular aims not being measured with sufficient items or with sufficient items at an appropriate level of *cognitive demand*.

As noted earlier in the chapter, the Bloom *Taxonomy of Educational Objectives* (Bloom et al., 1956) has been around for well over a half century and, frankly, for about 50 years was the *only* system used to contrast different levels of cognitive demand. As you can see in the previous illustration, sometimes Bloom's six levels of cognitive demand were scrunched into a smaller number, for instance, into a simple dichotomy between Bloom's lowest cognitive level (that is, memorized *knowledge*) and any cognitive demand above knowledge.

However, in 2002, Norman Webb of the University of Wisconsin provided educators with a procedure for gauging the alignment between a test's items and the curricular aims supposedly being measured by that test (Webb, 2002). A key component of Webb's alignment process was his proposed four *Depth of Knowledge* categories which functioned as a cognitive-demand classification system similar to Bloom's. Because Webb's depth of knowledge (DOK) system is often used by today's educators not only in connection with assessment blueprints, but also when choosing among contending curricular aims, you should be familiar with its composition as shown here:

DOK Level	Title of Level
1	Recall and Reproduction
2	Skills and Concepts
3	Short-Term Strategic Thinking
4	Extended Thinking

As you can see, the DOK levels range from a lowest level of Recall and Reproduction, which is similar to Bloom's lowest levels of *Knowledge* and *Comprehension*, up to a highest level of Extended Thinking, which is akin to Bloom's highest levels of *Synthesis* and *Evaluation*.

Clearly, if you are ever involved in making any sort of curricular choices among competing curricular aims or are attempting to create an assessment blueprint for your own tests or for those of your colleagues, you should become more knowledgeable about both the Bloom and Webb frameworks for categorizing the cognitive demands reflected in different curricular goals. It is much tougher to get an accurate fix on the levels of cognitive challenge associated with diverse curricular aims than it first might appear.

Collar a Colleague

Too many classroom teachers carry out their professional chores in isolation. If you're trying to figure out what to assess in your own classroom, one straightforward scheme for tackling the task is to seek the counsel of a colleague, particularly one who teaches the same sort of class and/or grade level you teach.

Always keeping in mind that what you assess should be governed by the decisions to be influenced by your students' assessment results, simply solicit the advice of a respected colleague regarding what sorts of things you should be assessing in your class. If you're uncomfortable about making such a request, simply read (with feeling) the following scripted question: "If you were I, what would you assess?" I admit the phrasing of the question isn't all that exotic, but it will get the job done. What you're looking for is some sensible advice from a nonpartisan co-worker. If you do choose to solicit the advice of one or more colleagues regarding what you plan to test, remember you are getting their *advice*. The final decision is yours.

If you've already devoted a significant chunk of thought to the what-to-assess question, you might simply ask your colleague to review your ideas so you can discern whether your planned assessment targets seem reasonable to another teacher. A second pair of eyes can frequently prove useful in deciding whether you've really staked out a defensible set of emphases for your planned classroom assessments.

A COLLECTION OF WHAT-TO-ASSESS CONSIDERATIONS

So far, nine factors have been identified for potential consideration by teachers who are trying to decide what to measure with their classroom tests. Teachers who consider all or most of these factors will generally come up with more defensible assessment targets for their classroom assessments than will teachers who do not take these factors into consideration. Accordingly, this chapter's chief intended outcome was that you will not only remember what these nine factors are but will understand the nature of the likely impact of each of those factors on a teacher's choice regarding what to measure with the teacher's classroom tests.

Presented next, then, are nine potential factors a teacher should consider when determining what to assess via classroom tests. You'll note that each consideration is now framed as a question to be answered, and brief labels have also been added to each factor in a transparent attempt to make the factors more readily memorable if you ever choose to employ them in your own test-construction efforts.

1. **Decision Focus:** Are clearly explicated decision options directly linked to a test's results?
2. **Number of Assessment Targets:** Is the number of proposed assessment targets for a test sufficiently small so that those targets represent an instructionally manageable number?
3. **Assessment Domain Emphasized:** Will the assessments to be built focus on the cognitive domain, the affective domain, or the psychomotor domain?

4. **Norm-Referencing and/or Criterion-Referencing:** Will the score-based inferences to be based on students' test performances be norm-referenced, criterion-referenced, or both?

5. **Selected versus Constructed Response Mode:** Can students' responses be selected-responses, constructed-responses, or both?

6. **Relevant Curricular Configurations:** Will students' performances on this classroom assessment contribute to students' mastery of your state's officially approved set of curricular aims such as, for example, the *Common Core State Standards*?

7. **National Subject-Matter Organizations' Recommendations:** Are the knowledge, skills, and/or affect assessed by this classroom assessment consonant with the curricular recommendations of national subject-matter associations?

8. **NAEP Assessment Frameworks:** If the proposed classroom assessment deals with a subject matter routinely measured by the National Assessment of Educational Progress, is what it measures similar to the NAEP assessment frameworks?

9. **Collegial Input:** If a knowledgeable colleague is available, has this educator reacted to the proposed assessment targets in a to-be-built classroom test?

Tests as Instructional Influencers

Historically, teachers have used classroom tests at or near the close of an instructional sequence. And, of course, teachers would like their students to perform well on any end-of-instruction tests. If students are successful on end-of-instruction classroom tests, it usually means that they have learned well and, accordingly, teachers have taught well. More often than not, teachers' classroom tests have been constructed only *after* instruction is over or when instruction is nearing its conclusion (for instance, near the end of a semester, a school year, or a short-duration teaching unit). Obviously, classroom assessments devised *after* instruction is over will have little impact on what the teacher teaches. The teacher's instruction, or at least the majority of it, is a "done deal" by the time the test is constructed.

Classroom assessments, therefore, have typically had little impact on instructional planning. At least this was true until the era of *educational accountability* arrived in the 1970s and 1980s. During that period, legislators in most states enacted a string of laws requiring students to pass basic skills tests in order to receive high school diplomas or, in some cases, to be advanced to higher grade levels. Thus was born what educators have come to call "high-stakes" tests because there were important consequences for the students who were required to take those tests.

There was another sense in which statewide tests became high stakes. In schools where all, or almost all, students passed the tests, a school's teachers and administrators were applauded. But in schools where many students failed the tests, a school's teachers and administrators were blamed. The stakes associated with statewide testing were elevated even more when newspapers began, in the 1980s, to publish annual statewide test scores of all districts and all schools in the state. Each school and district was *ranked* in relation to the state's other schools and districts. There were, of course, numerous winners as well as an equal number of losers.

As noted in Chapter 1, what was being measured by the tests began to influence the nature of what was taught in classrooms. The phrase *measurement-driven instruction* became widely used during the eighties to depict an educational reform strategy in which it was hoped the content of high-stakes tests would have a substantial and positive influence on the content of classroom instruction.

Because of this heightened attention to student performance on important statewide and districtwide tests, we also saw increased attention being given to the evidence of student success on teacher-made *classroom* tests. Many educational administrators and policymakers concluded that if students' performances on statewide tests reflected a school's educational effectiveness, then even at the classroom level, test results could indicate whether good teaching was taking place. Greater and greater emphasis was given to "evidence of effectiveness" in the form of improved student performance on whatever types of classroom tests were being employed. Increasingly, *evidence* of student learning—evidence in the form of student performance on classroom tests—is being used in personnel appraisals of teachers. In many settings, a teacher's competence is currently being determined, and often significantly, by how well a teacher's students perform on the teacher's classroom tests. During the past several years, considerable pressure has been brought on educational leaders to make students' test scores a prominent factor when evaluating individual teachers. We will look into recent developments regarding teacher evaluation in Chapter 15.

Given this ever-increasing administrative reliance on student test results as one indicator of a teacher's instructional effectiveness, it was only natural that many teachers tried to address instructionally whatever was to be tested. Tests had clearly begun to influence teaching. And it was increasingly recognized by teachers not only that the content of their tests *could* influence their teaching but also that, perhaps, the content of those tests *should* influence their teaching.

If testing should influence teaching, why not construct classroom assessments *prior* to instructional planning? In this way, any planned instructional sequence could mesh more effectively with the content of the test involved. Moreover, why not build classroom assessments with the instructional implications of those assessments deliberately in mind? In other words, why not build a classroom assessment not only before any instructional planning, but in such a way that the assessment would beneficially inform the teacher's instructional planning? A contrast between a more traditional educational approach in which instruction influences assessment and the kind of assessment-influenced instruction being described here can be seen in Figure 2.2.

In a traditional approach to instructional design, an approach in which instruction influences assessment, the teacher (1) is guided by the curriculum that's been adopted by the state and/or district, (2) plans instructional activities to promote the educational objectives set forth in that curriculum, and (3) assesses students. In an assessment-influenced approach to instructional design, also indicated

figure 2.2 ■ **Traditional Instruction-Influenced Assessment versus Assessment-Influenced Instruction, Both of Which Are Governed by Curricular Aims**

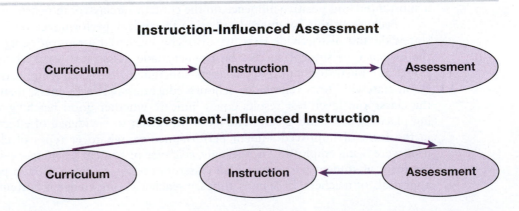

in Figure 2.2, the teacher still (1) starts with curricular aims, (2) then moves to create assessments based on those goals, and (3) only thereafter plans instructional activities intended to promote students' mastery of the knowledge, skills, and/or attitudes to be assessed. In both approaches, curriculum is the starting point. Curricular aims still govern the entire process. But in the two contrasting approaches, the sequence of instructional planning and assessment development is reversed.

Dividends of Assessment Illumination

Assessment-illuminated instruction rests on the assumption that, in many instances, what is to be assessed *will* influence the teacher's instructional decisions. Consequently, if the assessment can be created prior to the teacher's instructional planning, the resultant clarity provided to the teacher will help the teacher make more appropriate instructional choices.

When teachers develop their classroom assessments *before* instructional plans are made, teachers are meaningfully *clarifying* the curricular aims being pursued. In other words, the assessment serves as the operational definition of whether a curricular aim has been achieved. Such clarity provides far more insight for teachers when, subsequently, they make their instructional plans.

It is important to remember that classroom assessments *represent* the knowledge and/or skills being promoted. Teachers should *never* teach toward the classroom test itself. Instead, teachers should teach toward the knowledge, skills, and/or attitudes sampled by the classroom test. But, when teachers construct classroom assessments prior to instructional decision-making, those teachers will have a markedly better understanding of what the instructional objectives really are. And, of course, the more clearheaded teachers are about curricular *ends*, the more skillfully such teachers can select suitable instructional *means* to accomplish those ends.

With increased clarity regarding the nature of the curricular aims being promoted, there are all sorts of derivative instructional-planning benefits. Here are a few of the most salient dividends you, as a teacher or a teacher-in-preparation, will receive:

- *More accurate learning progressions.* Because you'll know more clearly what the terminal results of an instructional sequence are supposed to be, you can better pinpoint the enabling knowledge or the subskills your students must acquire before mastering what's being taught. You'll learn more about "learning progressions" in Chapter 12.
- *More on-target practice activities.* Because you'll know better what kinds of end-of-instruction outcomes are being sought for your students, you can make sure to select guided-practice and independent-practice activities more accurately aligned with the target outcomes.
- *More lucid expositions.* Because you'll understand more clearly what's to be assessed at instruction's conclusion, during instruction you can provide clearer explanations to your students about the content involved and where the instructional activities are heading.

Instructional planning will benefit from early development of classroom assessments most fundamentally because you will, as a consequence of prior assessment development, better understand what it is hoped that your students will be able to do when instruction has been concluded.

A Profusion of Item Types

Beyond the basic constructed-response versus selected-response distinction considered earlier, there are numerous types of items available for inclusion in classroom assessment procedures. Certain of these item types have been employed for many, many years. The essay test, for example, has probably been around since Socrates was strutting his instructional stuff. Multiple-choice tests have been with us for more than a century. True–false tests were probably used, at least in oral form, by prehistoric teachers who might have put such true–false toughies to their students as "True or False: Today's dinosaur was a leaf-munching brontosaurus rather than a people-munching tyrannosaurus rex."

During recent years, however, there have been some significant advances in educational measurement procedures so that, for example, some educational measurement specialists now advocate wider use of *portfolio assessment* and *performance assessment*. These significant item types must now be added to the menu of assessment alternatives open to today's classroom teacher. In coming chapters you'll be learning how to create classroom assessments using all of the major item types now available in the classroom teacher's assessment arsenal. And, of course, as each hour goes by, we find advances being made in technology—advances that allow teachers to rely on a number of sophisticated computer programs to provide online or other forms of computer-controlled assessments. Fortunately, states and districts are substantially expanding the range of electronic options available to today's (and tomorrow's) teachers.

We're going to start off with the more traditional sorts of selected- and constructed-response types of items because, quite frankly, you're more likely to be familiar with those item types, and you'll have less difficulty in learning about how to crank out, for instance, a simply splendid short-answer test item. Thereafter, in separate chapters, we'll be considering portfolios and how they can be used for classroom assessment, as well as performance tests and how they can be employed. After that, we'll deal with the special kinds of item types to be used when you're trying to get a fix on students' affective status.

As a preview, then, in subsequent chapters you'll be encountering the following types of items that can be employed in classroom assessments:

- Binary-choice items (Chapter 6)
- Multiple binary-choice items (Chapter 6)
- Multiple-choice items (Chapter 6)
- Matching items (Chapter 6)
- Short-answer items (Chapter 7)
- Essay items (Chapter 7)

- Observational approaches (Chapter 8)
- Performance tests (Chapter 8)
- Portfolios (Chapter 9)
- Affective assessment procedures (Chapter 10)

But What Does This Have to Do with Teaching?

As a first-year teacher, I had only a foggy idea of what stuff I should be teaching. Oh, of course, there was a state curriculum syllabus setting forth a seemingly endless array of knowledge and skills that students such as mine might possess. But, as was true with most of my colleagues, I found the syllabus altogether overwhelming.

So, when a new teacher is curricularly overwhelmed, the teacher gravitates toward whatever content is addressed in textbooks. And that's just what I did. Along with courses in high school English, speech, and U.S. government, I also had to teach a course in geography. Having never taken a college course in geography, and knowing barely more than the four major directions on a compass, I thanked heaven each night for the bright red geography text that allowed me to appear geographically suave. Had it not been for that comforting red textbook, I surely would have perished pedagogically before I learned the difference between the equator and a Mercator map projection.

In short, my first year's curricular choices were often made almost unthinkingly. I simply scrambled to fill my lesson plans with something resembling relevant content. But, during my *second* year of teaching, I had a solid basis for my curricular choices—namely, I had taught about those things the previous year!

It should be apparent to you that if teachers carry out a consummately classy instructional act, but focus on the wrong curricular content, this would be a genuine waste. Yet, many beginning teachers (like me) don't devote sufficient thought to what they need to teach and, therefore, what they need to assess. And even seasoned teachers often can't provide a solid rationale for what they're teaching.

The impact of the federal accountability legislation on most teachers' instruction—and classroom assessment—has been considerable. That's why you really need to find out how *your* state carries out its accountability program. If your state's leaders have installed suitable accountability tests, you'll be in a good position to key off those tests and supply your students with equally sensible classroom tests and on-target instruction. If your state's accountability tests are inappropriate, however, you'll find yourself in the midst of an insoluble testing-teaching puzzle.

This chapter's focus on what to test and how to test it should help you recognize that you should be *assessing* the most important skills, knowledge, and affect you want your students to acquire. And this recognition, of course, should help you realize you should make sure that you're *teaching* your students such stuff.

Unless, of course, you're using a red textbook. If so, forget everything I've just said.

As you can see, there are plenty of options open to classroom teachers when it comes to item types. When you're choosing among item types, select the one that best allows you to make the test-based inference in which you're interested and whatever decision is linked to it. Sometimes it won't make much difference which types of items you choose. I suspect in many instances it really isn't the case that a batch of multiple-choice items is vastly superior to a set of matching items. In other cases, however, there will be substantial differences in the suitability of differing item types. To make your own choice, simply ask yourself the question, Will my students' responses to this type of item allow me to reach a defensible inference contributing to the educational decision facing me?

As we consider various types of items in later chapters, you'll become more conversant with the particulars of each item type, and thus more skilled in identifying their utility to you in your own classroom assessments.

WHAT DO CLASSROOM TEACHERS REALLY NEED TO KNOW ABOUT WHAT TO ASSESS?

What is the main message of this chapter for classroom teachers who must decide what to assess? The answer is rather straightforward. All you need to do is to think seriously about this issue. Any experienced teacher will, if pressed, confess that *instructional inertia* plays a key role in what usually goes on in the teacher's classroom. Classroom teachers find it far easier to engage in activities this year that they engaged in last year simply because it takes less effort to employ "same-old, same-old" instructional procedures than to install new instructional procedures. There's also *assessment inertia* inclining teachers to rely on whatever assessment schemes they've previously utilized. It's so much simpler to re-use or slightly massage last year's true–false exams than to whip out a brand-new performance test.

In recognition of these all-too-human tendencies to adopt the path of least resis-tance, it becomes more important to try to "get it right the first time" or, putting it in more pedantic parlance, to "eschew egregiously inferior initial assessment conceptualizations." In other words, the more up-front thought teachers give to answering the what-to-assess question, the more likely they'll be able to avoid the kind of serious assessment errors that, because of practical pressures, may plague them for years.

Because of the impact of federal accountability laws on you and your fellow teachers, you need to understand the nature of the tests your state's leaders have chosen to satisfy the state's accountability needs. For instance, you may end up teaching in a state in which the state's officials have chosen to employ the assessments constructed during recent years to measure students' mastery of the *Common Core State Standards* described earlier in the chapter. Do not assume, without careful consideration, those tests are going to help you do a better teaching job. Nor should you assume your state's accountability tests will have an adverse impact on what goes on in the state's classrooms. You definitely need to find out whether the state's accountability tests are winners or losers. Those tests will have an enormous impact on what you try to teach, what you try to test, and how you try to teach it.

A THREE-CHAPTER PREVIEW

Because the next three chapters in the book are highly related, I'm going to do a little previewing of what you'll be encountering in those chapters. Later in the book, you'll learn all sorts of nifty ways to assess your students. Not only will you learn how to create a variety of traditional paper-and-pencil tests, such as the true-false and multiple-choice instruments, but you'll also discover how to generate many of the alternative forms of educational assessment receiving so much attention these days. To illustrate, you will learn how to create really demanding performance tests, student portfolios, and assessment devices that can gauge your students' attitudes and interests. But when you read about these assessment approaches in later chapters, it will make it easier for you to determine their worth *to you* if you know how to evaluate the quality of educational assessment approaches. The next three chapters give you the concepts you will need to do such evaluating.

If you're evaluating a test—whether it's your own test, a test developed by another teacher, or a test distributed by a commercial test publisher—you will need some criteria to help you decide whether the test should be wildly applauded or, instead, sent swiftly to a paper shredder.

Judging educational tests, in fact, is fundamentally no different from evaluating brownies. If, for example, you are ever called on to serve as a judge in a brownie bake-off, you'll need some evaluative criteria to use when you appraise the merits of the contending brownies. I realize your preferences may differ from mine, but if I were chief justice in a brownie-judging extravaganza, I would employ the three evaluative criteria presented in Table 2.1. If you are a brownie aficionado

table 2.1 ▪ Potential Criteria for Brownie Judging

Criterion	Optimal Status
Fudginess	Should reek of chocolate flavor—so much, indeed, as to be considered fundamentally fudgelike.
Chewiness	Must be so chewy as to approximate munching on a lump of fudge-flavored Silly Putty.
Acceptable Additives	Although sliced walnuts and extra chocolate chips are praiseworthy, raw shredded brussels sprouts are not.

and prefer other evaluative criteria, I can overlook such preferences. You may, for example, adore nut-free and high-rise brownies. However, I have no personal interest in establishing a meaningful brownie-bond with you.

When we evaluate just about anything, we employ explicit or implicit evaluative criteria to determine quality. And although there may be substantial disagreements among brownie devoteés regarding the criteria to employ when appraising their favorite baked goods, there are far fewer disputes when it comes to judging the quality of educational assessment devices. In the next three chapters, we're going to look at the three widely accepted criteria that are used to evaluate educational assessment procedures. Two of the criteria have been around for a long while. The third is a relative newcomer, having figured in the evaluation of educational tests only during the last few decades.

In Table 2.2 are the three criteria we'll be considering in the next three chapters. The capsule description of each criterion presented in the table will let you know what's coming. After considering each of these three criteria in its very own chapter, I'll level with you regarding what classroom teachers *really* need to know about the three criteria. In other words, I'll toss my personal opinion at you regarding whether you should establish an intimate relationship or merely a nodding acquaintance with each criterion.

Of all the things you will learn from reading this book, and there will be lots of them, the topics treated in the next three chapters are regarded by psychometricians as the most important. (*Psychometrician*, by the way, is simply a ritzy descriptor for a measurement specialist.) Chapters 3, 4, and 5 will familiarize you with the pivotal criteria by which assessment specialists tell whether educational assessment procedures are fabulous or feeble. But because this book is focused on classroom assessment, we'll be looking at the content of the next three chapters in relation to *educational decisions* that must be made by classroom teachers.

table 2.2 ■ **A Preview of the Three Test-Evaluation Criteria to Be Considered in Chapters 3, 4, and 5**

Criterion	Brief Description
Reliability	Reliability represents the *consistency* with which an assessment procedure measures whatever it's measuring.
Validity	Validity reflects the degree to which evidence and theory support the accuracy of interpretations of test scores for proposed uses of tests.
Fairness	Fairness signifies the degree to which assessments are free of elements that would *offend* or *unfairly penalize* particular groups of students on the basis of students' gender, ethnicity, and so on.

CHAPTER SUMMARY

One major question guided the content of this chapter—namely, what should a classroom teacher assess? It was contended that decisions must be primarily influenced by the decisions the teacher hopes to illuminate on the basis of assessment data gathered from students.

In determining what to assess, it was suggested that a teacher's curricular aims play a prominent role in the teacher's choice of assessment emphases. In particular, large grain-size measurable objectives were recommended as helpful vehicles for identifying potential assessment targets. The three domains of student outcomes contained in Bloom's *Taxonomies of Educational Objectives* were also suggested as a helpful framework to decide whether there are instructional or assessment overemphases on certain kinds of outcomes. Because many of the nation's educators will soon be, if not already doing so, promoting their students' mastery of the *Common Core State Standards* now adopted by many, many states, the background and nature of those standards in mathematics and English language arts were described in the chapter. It was emphasized that those curricular aims, as is true with almost all intended curricular outcomes, will be clearly understood only when assessments to measure students' mastery of the aims have been created. Accordingly, teachers were urged to be particularly attentive to the nature of the tests being developed by two large, federally funded assessment consortia of states whose tests are scheduled to be available by the time this edition of *Classroom Assessment* is published.

In all, then, when addressing the what-to-assess question, this chapter identified nine isolatable considerations for teachers. Treated during the chapter were (1) decision focus, (2) number of assessment targets, (3) assessment domain emphasized, (4) norm-referencing and/or criterion-referencing, (5) selected versus constructed response mode, (6) relevant curricular configurations, (7) national subject-matter organizations' recommendations, (8) NAEP assessment frameworks, and (9) collegial input. Teachers who attend to all or most of these nine considerations will be more likely to arrive at defensible decisions regarding what to measure in their classroom assessments.

Determining Your Outcome Mastery

This chapter focused on enhancing a teacher's ability to arrive at defensible decisions about what to measure in the teacher's classroom assessments. As a reminder, here is the chapter's chief outcome:

An ability to identify, and understand the impact of, key factors that can help teachers determine the measurement targets for their classroom assessments

Complete both the Selected-Response and the Constructed-Response quizzes and think about the feedback you receive for each quiz. Note that the Selected-Response Mastery check is composed of binary-choice items, which can prove quite useful for measuring students' mastery of certain sorts of outcomes. Later, after you've mastered Chapter 6, you'll see that I've violated one of my item-writing guidelines for binary-choice items: "Include only one concept in each statement." However, "guidelines" are just what they say they are—namely, guidelines. My blatant disregard for an item-writing guideline stems from my belief that in this instance most Measurement Gods would smile indulgently at my guideline-shunning, concluding that I had a good reason for doing so.

MyEdLab *Selected-Response Check for Outcome Mastery*
MyEdLab *Constructed-Response Check for Outcome Mastery*

After completing both quizzes, go to the Learning Outcome Mastery Determination, where you will decide whether you've mastered the chapter's learning outcome or whether you need further study.

MyEdLab *Learning Outcome Mastery Determination*

References

Arffman, I. (2013). "Problems and issues in translating international educational achievement tests," *Educational Measurement: Issues and Practice, 32,* no. 2 (Summer): 2–14.

Bloom, B. S., et al. (1956). *Taxonomy of educational objectives: Handbook I: Cognitive domain.* New York: David McKay.

Center on Education Policy. (2011). *District officials view common state standards as more rigorous, expect new standards to improve learning.* Press Release, September 14. Washington, DC: Author.

Davis-Becker, S. L., and Buckendahl, C. W. (2013). "A proposed framework for evaluating alignment studies," *Educational Measurement: Issues and Practice, 32,* no. 1 (Spring): 23–33.

Glaser, R. (1963). "Institutional technology and the measurement of learning outcomes: Some questions," *American Psychology, 18,* 519–521.

McMillan, J. H. (2013). *Classroom assessment: Principles and practice for effective standards-based instruction* (6th ed.) Boston: Pearson.

National Council of Teachers of Mathematics. (1989). *Curriculum and evaluation standards for school mathematics.* Reston, VA: The Council.

National Governors Association and the Counsel of Chief State School Officers. (2010). *The Common Core State Standards initiative.* Washington, DC: Author.

Pellegrino, J. W., Chudowsky, N., and Glaser, R. (Eds.). (2001). *Knowing what students know: The science and design of educational assessment.* National Research Council, Division of Behavioral and Social Sciences and Education, Center for Education, Board on Testing and Assessment, Washington, DC: National Academy Press.

Popham, W. J. (2014). "Criterion-referenced measurement: Half a century wasted?" *Educational Leadership, 71,* no. 6 (March): 62–67.

Popham, W. J. (2014). "The right test for the wrong reason," *Phi Delta Kappan, 96,* no. 1 (September): 46–52.

Rutkowski, D, Rutkowski, L., and Plucker, J. A. (2014). "Should individual schools participate in PISA?" *Phi Delta Kappan, 96,* no. 4 (December): 68–73.

Webb, N. L. (2002) *Alignment Study in Language Arts, Mathematics, Science, and Social Studies of State Standards and Assessment for Four States,* Washington, DC: Council of Chief State School Officers.

Zimba, J. (2011). *Priorities in the* Common Core State Standards' *standards for mathematical content,* Discussion Draft, March 31, 2011.

3

Reliability of Assessment

CHIEF CHAPTER
OUTCOME

An understanding of commonly
employed indicators of a test's
reliability/precision that is
sufficient to identify the types
of reliability evidence already
collected for a test and, if
necessary, to select the kinds
of reliability evidence needed
for particular uses of
educational assessments

Reliability is such a cherished commodity. We all want our automobiles, washing machines, and spouses to be reliable. The term *reliability* simply reeks of solid goodness. It conjures up visions of meat loaf, mashed potatoes, and a mother's love. Clearly, reliability is an attribute to be sought.

In the realm of educational assessment, reliability is also a desired attribute. We definitely want our educational assessments to be reliable. In matters related to measurement, however, reliability has a very restricted meaning. When you encounter the term *reliability* in any assessment context, you should draw a mental equal sign between *reliability* and *consistency*, because reliability refers to the consistency with which a test measures whatever it's measuring:

Reliability = Consistency

From a classroom teacher's perspective, there are two important ways the concept of reliability can rub up against your day-to-day activities. First, there's the possibility your own classroom assessments might lack sufficient reliability to be doing a good job for you and your students. Second, if your students are obliged to complete any sort of commercially published standardized tests, you're apt to find a parent or two who might want to discuss the adequacy of those tests. And reliability, as noted in the previous chapter's preview, such as for your state's accountability tests, is an evaluative criterion by which external standardized tests are judged. You may need to know enough about reliability's wrinkles so you'll be able to talk sensibly with parents about the way reliability is employed to judge the quality of standardized tests.

As explained in Chapter 2, a particularly influential document in the field of educational assessment is the *Standards for Educational and Psychological Testing* (2014).[1] Commonly referred to simply as "the *Standards*," this important compilation of dos and don'ts regarding educational and psychological measurement was developed and distributed by the American Educational Research Association

(AERA), the American Psychological Association (APA), and the National Council on Measurement in Education (NCME). What's prescribed about educational testing in the *Standards* are the nuts and bolts of how educational tests should be created, evaluated, and used. Because the 2014 *Standards* constituted the first revision of this significant AERA-APA-NCME publication since 1999, assessment specialists everywhere will be particularly attentive to its contents and, we can safely predict, most of those specialists will adhere to its mandates. Let's consider, then, what the new *Standards* say about reliability.

Well, for openers, the architects of the *Standards* use a different label to describe what has historically been referred to as the "reliability" of tests. The authors of the new *Standards* point out that the term *reliability* has been used not only to represent (1) the *traditional reliability coefficients* so often employed through the years when describing a test's quality, but the term *reliability* refers more generally to (2) the consistency of students' scores across replications of a testing procedure *regardless of the way such consistency is estimated or reported.*

In case you are unfamiliar with the meaning of the technical term *coefficient* as used in this context, that term typically refers to a *correlation coefficient*—that is, a numerical indicator of the relationship between the same persons' status on two variables such as students' scores on two different tests. The symbol representing such a coefficient is r. If students score pretty much the same on the two tests, the resulting correlation coefficient will be strong and positive. If the individuals score high on one test and low on the other test, the resulting r will be negative. If there's a high reliability coefficient, this doesn't necessarily signify that students' scores on the two testing occasions are *identical*. Rather, a high r indicates students' *relative* performances on the two testing occasions are quite similar. Correlation coefficients can range from a high of +1.00 to a low of −1.00. Thus, what a *reliability coefficient* really means is that a correlation coefficient has typically been computed for test takers' performances on two sets of variables—as you will soon see.

To illustrate, if the developers of a new achievement test report that when their test was administered to the same students on two occasions—for example, a month apart—and that the resulting test-retest correlation coefficient was .86, this would be an instance involving the sort of traditional reliability coefficient that measurement experts have relied on for roughly a full century. If, however, a test-development company creates a brand new high school graduation test, and supplies evidence about what percentage of students' scores can consistently classify those test takers into "diploma awardees" and "diploma denials," this constitutes a useful way of representing a test's consistency—but in a way that's clearly not the same as reliance on a traditional reliability coefficient. A variety of different indices of classification consistency are often employed these days to supply test users with indications about the reliability with which a test classifies test takers. Don't be surprised, then, if you encounter an indicator of a test's reliability that's expressed in a manner quite different from oft-encountered reliability coefficients.

Architects of the 2014 *Standards* wanted to provide a link to traditional conceptions of measurement consistency (in which a single reliability coefficient typically indicated a test's consistency), yet avoid the ambiguity of using the single label *reliability* to refer to a wide range of reliability indicators such as measures of classification consistency. Accordingly, the 2014 *Standards* architects employ the term ***reliability/precision*** to denote the more general notion of score consistency across instances of the testing procedure. The label ***reliability coefficient*** is used to describe more conventionally used coefficients representing different forms of test-takers' consistency.

The descriptor *reliability/precision,* then, describes not only traditional reliability coefficients but also various indicators of classification consistency and a number of less readily understandable statistical indices of assessment consistency. As the writers of the *Standards* make clear, the need for precision of measurement increases as the consequences on test-based inferences and resultant decisions become more important.

Whether the label *reliability/precision* becomes widely employed by those who work with educational tests remains to be seen. In this chapter, you will encounter descriptions of reliability in several contexts. Hopefully, it will be clear to you whether the term applies to a quantitative indicator representing a traditional relationship between two sets of test scores—that is, a *reliability coefficient*—or, instead, refers to another way of representing a test's consistency of measurement—that is, a *reliability/precision* procedure.

What does a teacher really need to know about reliability or about reliability/precision? Well, hold off for a bit on that question, and I suspect my answer may surprise you. But one thing you do need to recognize is that the fundamental notion of reliability is downright important for those whose professional lives bump up against educational tests in any meaningful manner. This overriding truth about the significance of assessment consistency is well represented in the very first, most basic expectation set forth in the 2014 *Standards*:

> *Appropriate evidence of reliability/precision should be provided for the interpretation of each intended score use. (Standards, 2014, p. 42)*

Based on this call for appropriate evidence supporting the reliability/precision of an educational test, fully 20 subordinate standards are presented in the new *Standards* dealing with various aspects of reliability. Taken together, they spell out how the authors of the 2014 *Standards* believe the consistency of educational tests ought to be determined.

So, recognizing that we can estimate a test's consistency in a number of ways, and that the expression *reliability coefficient* refers to particular sorts of evidence that's traditionally served up when educational tests are scrutinized, let's look at the three traditional reliability coefficients presented in Table 3.1: *test-retest coefficients, alternate-form coefficients,* and *internal consistency coefficients.* Along the way, while describing how these three sorts of reliability coefficients are obtained,

table 3.1 ■ Three Types of Reliability Evidence

Type of Reliability Coefficient	Brief Description
Test-Retest	Consistency of results among different testing occasions
Alternate Form	Consistency of results among two or more different forms of a test
Internal Consistency	Consistency in the way an assessment instrument's items function

we will consider other approaches to be employed when describing a test's reliability/precision.

If you have only recently been tussling with different conceptions of assessments' consistency (such as in the last few paragraphs), an altogether reasonable question for you to ask about reliability coefficients is: How big must a reliability coefficient be? For instance, looking at the three sorts of reliability coefficients tersely described in Table 3.1, how high do those correlation coefficients need to be for us to regard a test as sufficiently reliable? Regrettably, the answer to this altogether straightforward question is apt to be more murky than you might like.

For openers, if a correlation coefficient is involved, it needs to be positive rather than negative. If test developers from an educational measurement company are trying to measure how consistently their newly created history test does its measurement job regardless of when it is administered, they would typically ask a group of students to take the same test on two separate occasions. Thereupon a test-retest correlation could be computed for the test-takers' two sets of scores. Clearly, the hope would be that students' scores on the two administrations would be decisively positive—that is, the scores would reveal substantial similarity in the way students performed on both of the two test administrations. Okay, the test's developers want a positive *test-retest reliability* coefficient to signify their test's stability in doing its measurement job. But how large does that coefficient need to be before the test's developers start clinking glasses during a champagne toast?

Well, get ready for an answer that's often to be encountered when judging the quality of educational tests. That's right: *It depends.* The size that a correlation coefficient needs to be before we regard a test as sufficiently reliable depends on the context in which a test is being used and, in particular, on the nature of the test-based decision that will be influenced by test-takers' scores.

In general, the higher the stakes involved, the higher should be our expectations for our tests' reliability coefficients. For instance, let's suppose that a teacher is working in a state where the awarding of a high school diploma requires a student to perform above a specific cut-score on both a mathematics test and an English language arts test. Given the considerable importance of the decision that's riding on students' test performances, we should be demanding a much greater indication of test consistency than we would with, say, a teacher's exam covering a one-month unit on the topic of punctuation.

But because the contexts in which educational tests are used will vary so considerably, it is simply impossible to set forth a definitive table presenting minimally acceptable levels for certain kinds of reliability coefficients. Experience shows us that when teachers attempt to collect evidence for their own teacher-constructed tests, it is not uncommon to encounter a test-retest r of .60 plus or minus .10 and an alternate-form r reflecting about the same range. Accordingly, when deciding whether a test's reliability coefficients are sufficiently strong for the test's intended use, this decision boils down to *professional judgment* based on the correlation coefficients seen over the years in similar settings. Yes, we use historical precedent to help us arrive at realistic expectations for what's possible regarding reliability coefficients. For instance, with significant high-stakes examinations such as nationally standardized achievement tests that have been developed and revised many times at great cost, it is not uncommon to see the test developers report internal-consistency coefficients hovering slightly above or slightly below .90. However, for a district-made test requiring far fewer developmental dollars, the identical sorts of internal consistency coefficients might be closer to .80 or .70.

In general, reliability coefficients representing test-retest or alternate-form consistency tend to be lower than internal consistency coefficients. However, in certain contexts—when a test has been developed in an effort to provide distinguishable subscores—we should expect internal consistency coefficients to be much lower because the overall test is not attempting to measure a single, all-encompassing trait but, rather, a set of related subscales scores. As indicated earlier, *it depends*. To judge whether a test's reliability coefficients are sufficiently strong, that judgment should hinge on what is a realistic expectation for such coefficients in such situations.

Similarly, when looking at reliability/precision more generally—for instance, when considering the consistency with which a set of test scores allow us to classify test takers' levels of proficiency accurately, once more we need to be guided by historical precedent. That is, based on the experience of others, what expectations about reliability/precision are realistic—irrespective of the quantitative indicator employed? For example, if we look back at recent percentages of identical classifications of students on district-developed end-of-course exams, and find that these decision-consistency percentages almost always reach at least 80 percent (that is, 80 percent of the test takers given the same classifications irrespective of the test form they completed), then educators ought to be wary if a new test yielded only a 60 percent estimate of decision consistency.

TEST-RETEST RELIABILITY EVIDENCE

The first kind of reliability evidence we'll be looking at is called *test-retest*. This conception of reliability often comes to people's minds when someone asserts that reliability equals consistency. Formerly referred to in earlier versions of the *Standards* as "stability reliability," *test-retest evidence* refers to consistency of test results over time. We want our educational assessments of students to yield similar results even if the tests were administered on different occasions. For example, suppose you gave your students a midterm exam on Tuesday, but later in the afternoon a masked thief (1) snatched your briefcase containing the students' test papers, (2) jumped into a waiting armored personnel-carrier, and (3) escaped to an adjacent state or nation. The next day, after describing to your students how their examinations had been purloined by a masked personnel-carrier person, you ask them to retake the midterm exam. Because there have been no intervening events of significance, such as more instruction from you on the topics covered by the examination, you would expect your students' Wednesday examination scores to be fairly similar to their Tuesday examination scores. And that's what the *test-retest coefficient* conception of test reliability refers to—consistency over time. If the Wednesday scores aren't rather similar to the Tuesday scores, then your midterm exam would be judged to have little test-retest reliability.

To get a fix on how stable an assessment's results are over time, we usually test students on one occasion, wait a week or two, and then retest them with the same instrument. Because measurement specialists typically use the descriptors *stability reliability* and *test-retest reliability* interchangeably, you are hereby allowed to do the same thing. Simply choose which of the two labels you prefer. It is important, however, for no significant events that might alter students' performances on the second assessment occasion to have taken place between the two testing occasions. For instance, suppose the test you are administering assessed students' knowledge regarding World War II. If a widely viewed television mini-series about World War II is presented during the interval between the initial test and the retest, it is likely the performances of the students who watched the mini-series will be higher on the second test because of their exposure to test-relevant information in the mini-series. Thus, for test-retest coefficients to be interpreted accurately, it is imperative that no significant performance-influencing events occur during the between-assessments interval.

A reliability/precision procedure for calculating the stability of students' performances on the same test administered on two assessment occasions is to determine the percentage of student classifications that were consistent over time. Such a **classification-consistency** approach to the determination of a test's reliability might be used, for instance, when a teacher is deciding which students would be exempted from further study about Topic X. To illustrate, let's say that the teacher establishes an 80 percent correct level as the degree of proficiency required in order to exempt students from further Topic X study. Then, on a test-retest basis, the teacher would simply determine the percentage of students who were classified the same way on the two assessment occasions. The focus in such an approach would not be on the specific scores a student earned, but only on whether the *same classification* was made about the student. Thus, if Jill Jones earned an 84 percent correct score on the first testing occasion and a 99 percent correct score on the second testing occasion, Jill would be exempted from further Topic X study in both cases because she had surpassed the 80 percent correct standard both

DECISION TIME

Quibbling over Quizzes

Wayne Wong's first-year teaching assignment is a group of 28 fifth-grade students in an inner-city elementary school. Because Wayne believes in the importance of frequent assessments as motivational devices for his students, he typically administers one or more surprise quizzes per week to his students. Admittedly, after the first month or so, very few of Wayne's fifth-graders are really "surprised" when Wayne whips out one of his unannounced quizzes. Students' scores on the quizzes are used by Wayne to compute each student's 6-weeks' grades.

Mrs. Halverson, the principal of Wayne's school, has visited his class on numerous occasions. Mrs. Halverson believes that it is her "special responsibility" to see that first-year teachers receive adequate instructional support.

Recently, Mrs. Halverson completed a master's degree from the local branch of the state university. As part of her coursework, she was required to take a class in "educational measurement." She earned an A. Because the professor for that course stressed the importance of "reliability as a crucial ingredient of solid educational tests," Mrs. Halverson has been pressing Wayne to compute some form of reliability evidence for his surprise quizzes. Wayne has been resisting her suggestion because, in his view, he administers so many quizzes that the computation of reliability indices for the quizzes would surely be a time-consuming pain. He believes that if he's forced to fuss with reliability estimates for each quiz, he'll reduce the number of quizzes he uses. And, because he thinks students' perceptions that they *may* be quizzed really stimulates them to be prepared, he is reluctant to lessen the number of quizzes he gives. Even after hearing Wayne's position, however, Mrs. Halverson seems unwilling to bend.

 If you were Wayne Wong and were faced with this problem, what would your decision be?

times. The classifications for Jill would be consistent, so the teacher's decisions about Jill would also be consistent. However, if Harry Harvey received a score of 65 percent correct on the first testing occasion and a score of 82 percent correct on the second testing occasion, different classifications on the two occasions would lead to different decisions being made about Harry's need to keep plugging away at Topic X. To determine the percentage of a test's classification consistency, you would simply make the kinds of calculations seen in Table 3.2.

Whether you use a correlational approach or a classification-consistency approach to the determination of a test's consistency over time, it is apparent you'll need to test students twice in order to determine the test's stability. If a test is yielding rather unstable results between two occasions, it's really difficult to put much confidence in that test's results. Just think about it—if you can't tell whether your students have really performed wonderfully or woefully on a test because their

table 3.2 ■ **An Illustration of How Classification Consistency Is Determined in a Test-Retest Context**

A. Percent of students identified as exempt from further study on both assessment occasions	=	42%
B. Percent of students identified as requiring further study on both assessment occasions	=	46%
C. Percent of students classified differently on the two occasions	=	12%
D. Percentage of the test's classification consistency (A + B)	=	88%

scores might vary depending on the day you test them, how can you proceed to make defensible test-based instructional decisions about those students?

Realistically, of course, why would a sane, nonsadistic classroom teacher administer the identical test to the same students on two different testing occasions? It's pretty tough to come up with a decent answer to that question. What's most important for teachers to realize is that there is always a meaningful level of *instability* between students' performances on two different testing occasions, *even if the very same test is used.* And this realization, of course, should discline teachers to treat a student's test score as though it is a super-scientific, impeccably precise representation of the student's achievement level.

ALTERNATE-FORM RELIABILITY EVIDENCE

The second of our three kinds of reliability evidence for educational assessment instruments focuses on the consistency between two forms of a test—forms that are supposedly equivalent. *Alternate-form reliability evidence* deals with the question of whether two or more allegedly equivalent test forms are, in fact, equivalent.

In the classroom, teachers rarely have reason to generate two forms of a particular assessment instrument. Multiple forms of educational tests are more commonly encountered in high-stakes assessment situations, such as when high school students must pass graduation tests before receiving diplomas. In such settings, students who fail an examination when it is initially administered are usually given other opportunities to pass the examination. Clearly, to make the assessment process fair, the challenge of the assessment hurdle faced by individuals when they take the initial test must be the same as the challenge of the assessment hurdle faced by individuals when they take the make-up examination. Alternate-form reliability evidence bears on the comparability of two (or more) test forms.

Multiple test forms are apt to be found whenever educators fear that if the same test were simply re-used, students who had access to subsequent administrations of the test would be advantaged because those later test takers would have learned about the test's contents, and thus have an edge over the first-time test takers. Typically, then, in a variety of high-stakes settings such as (1) those involving high school diploma tests or (2) the certification examinations governing entry to a profession, multiple test forms are employed.

To collect alternate-form consistency evidence, procedural approaches are employed that are in many ways similar to those used for the determination of test-retest reliability evidence. First, the two test forms are administered to the same individuals. Ideally, there would be little or no delay between the administration of the two test forms. For example, suppose you were interested in determining the comparability of two forms of a district-developed language arts examination. Let's say you could round up 100 suitable students. Because the examination requires only 20 to 25 minutes to complete, you could administer both forms of the language arts test (Form A and Form B) to each of the 100 students during a single period. To eliminate the impact of the order in which the two forms were completed by students, you could ask 50 of the students to complete Form A and then Form B. The remaining students would be directed to take Form B first and then Form A.

When you obtain each student's scores on the two forms, you could compute a correlation coefficient reflecting the relationship between students' performances on the two forms. As with test-retest reliability, the closer the alternate-form correlation coefficient is to a positive 1.0, the more agreement there is between students' relative scores on the two forms. Alternatively, you could use the kind of classification-consistency approach for the determination of alternate-form reliability/precision that was described earlier for stability. To illustrate, you could decide on a level of performance that would lead to different classifications for students, and then simply calculate the percentage of identically classified students on the basis of the two test forms. For instance, if a pass/fail cutoff score of 65 percent correct had been chosen, then you would simply add (1) the percent of students who passed both times (scored 65 percent or better) and (2) the percent of students who failed both times (scored 64 percent or lower). The addition of those two percentages yields a classification-consistency estimate of alternate-form reliability for the two test forms under consideration.

As you can see, although both species of reliability evidence we've considered thus far are related—in the sense that both deal with consistency—they represent very different conceptions of consistency evidence. Test-retest reliability evidence deals with consistency over time for a single examination. Alternate-form reliability evidence deals with the consistency inherent in two or more supposedly equivalent forms of the same examination.

Alternate-form reliability is not established by proclamation. Rather, evidence must be gathered regarding the between-form consistency of the test forms under scrutiny. Accordingly, if you're ever reviewing a commercially published or state-developed test that claims to have equivalent forms available, be sure you inspect the evidence supporting those claims of equivalence. Determine how the evidence of alternate-form comparability was gathered—that is, under what circumstances. Make sure that what's described makes sense to you.

Later in the book (Chapter 13), we'll consider a procedure known as *item response theory* that, whenever large numbers of students are tested, can be employed to adjust students' scores on different forms of tests that are not equivalent in difficulty. For purposes of our current discussion, however, simply remember that evidence of alternate-form reliability is a special form of consistency evidence dealing with the comparability of two or more test forms.

INTERNAL CONSISTENCY RELIABILITY EVIDENCE

The final entrant in our reliability evidence sweepstakes is called *internal consistency reliability evidence*. It really is quite a different creature than stability and alternate-evidence form of reliability. Internal consistency evidence does not focus on the consistency of students' scores on a test. Rather, internal consistency evidence deals with the extent to which the *items* in an educational assessment instrument are functioning in a consistent fashion.

Whereas evidence of stability and alternate-form reliability require two administrations of a test, internal consistency reliability can be computed on the basis of only a single test administration. It is for this reason, one suspects, we tend to encounter internal consistency estimates of reliability far more frequently than we encounter its two reliability brethren. Yet, as you will see, internal consistency reliability evidence is quite a different commodity than stability and alternate-form reliability evidence.

Internal consistency reliability reflects the degree to which the items on a test are doing their measurement job in a consistent manner—that is, the degree to which the test's items are functioning *homogeneously*. Many educational tests are designed to measure a single variable, such as students' "reading achievement" or their "attitude toward school." If a test's items are all truly measuring a single variable, then each of the test's items ought to be doing fundamentally the same assessment job. To the extent the test's items are tapping the same variable, of course, the responses to those items by students will tend to be quite similar. For example, if all the items in a 20-item test on problem solving do, in fact, measure a student's problem-solving ability, then students who are skilled problem solvers should get most of the test's items right, whereas unskilled problem solvers should miss most of the test's 20 items. The more homogeneous the responses yielded by a test's items, the higher will be the test's internal consistency evidence.

There are several different formulae around for computing a test's internal consistency.[2] Each formula is intended to yield a numerical estimate reflective of the extent to which the assessment procedure's items are functioning homogeneously. By the way, because internal consistency estimates of a test's reliability are focused on the homogeneity of the items on a test, not on any classifications of test takers (as you saw with stability and alternate-form reliability), decision-consistency approaches to reliability are not used in this instance.

PARENT TALK

One of your strongest students, Raphael Hobbs, has recently received his scores on a nationally standardized achievement test used in your school district. Raphael's subtest percentile scores (in comparison to the test's norm group) were the following:

Subject	Percentile
Language Arts	85th
Mathematics	92nd
Science	91st
Social Studies	51st

Raphael's father, a retired U.S. Air Force colonel, has called for an after-school conference with you about the test results. He has used his home computer and the Internet to discover that the internal consistency reliabilities on all four subtests, as published in the test's technical manual, are higher than .93. When he telephoned you to set up the conference, he said he couldn't see how the four subtests could all be reliable when Raphael's score on the social studies subtest was so "out of whack" with the other three subtests. He wants you to explain how this could happen.

 If I were you, here's how I'd respond to Colonel Hobbs:

"First off, Colonel Hobbs, I'm delighted that you've taken the time to look into the standardized test we're using in the district. Not many parents are willing to expend the energy to do so.

"I'd like to deal immediately with the issue you raised on the phone regarding the reliability of the four subtests and then discuss Raphael's social studies result. You may already know some of what I'll be talking about because of your access to the Internet, but here goes.

"Assessment reliability refers to the *consistency* of measurement. But there are very different ways that test developers look at measurement consistency. The reliability estimates that are supplied for Raphael's standardized test, as you pointed out, are called internal consistency correlation coefficients. Those correlations tell us whether the items on a particular subtest are performing in the same way—that is, whether they seem to be measuring the same thing.

"The internal consistency reliability for all four subtests is quite good. But this kind of reliability evidence doesn't tell us anything about how Raphael would score if he took the test again or if he took a different form of the same test. We don't know, in other words, whether his performance would be stable across time or would be consistent across different test forms.

"What we do see in Raphael's case is a social studies performance that is decisively different from his performance on the other three subtests. I've checked his grades for the past few years and I've seen that his grades in social studies are routinely just as high as his other grades. So those grades do cast some doubt on the meaningfulness of his lower test performance in social studies.

"Whatever's measured on the social studies subtest seems to be measured by a set of homogeneous items. That doesn't mean, however, the content of the social studies subtest meshes with the social studies Raphael's been taught here in our district. To me, Colonel, I think it's less likely to be a case of measurement unreliability than it is to be a problem of content mismatch between what the standardized examination is testing and what we try to teach Raphael.

"I recommend that you, Mrs. Hobbs, and I carefully monitor Raphael's performance in social studies during the school year so that we can really see if we're dealing with a learning problem or with an assessment not aligned to what we're teaching."

 Now, how would you respond to Colonel Hobbs?

For tests containing items on which a student can be right or wrong, such as a multiple-choice item, the most commonly used internal consistency approaches are the *Kuder-Richardson* procedures (usually referred to as the K-R formulae). For tests containing items on which students can be given different numbers of points, such as essay items, the most common internal consistency coefficient is called Cronbach's *coefficient alpha* after its originator Lee J. Cronbach. Incidentally, if you want to impress your colleagues with your newfound and altogether exotic assessment vocabulary, you might want to know that test items scored right or wrong (such as true–false items) are called *dichotomous* items, and those that yield multiple scores (such as essay items) are called *polytomous* items. Try to work *polytomous* into a casual conversation around the watercooler. Its intimidation power is awesome.

Incidentally, other things being equal, the more items there are in an educational assessment device, the more reliability/precision it will tend to possess. To illustrate, if you set out to measure a student's mathematics achievement with a 100-item test dealing with various aspects of mathematics, you're apt to get a more precise fix on a student's mathematical prowess than if you asked students to solve only a single, lengthy mathematical word problem. The more times you ladle out a taste from a pot of soup, the more accurate will be your estimate of what the soup's ingredients are. One ladleful might fool you. Twenty ladlesful will give you a much better idea of what's in the pot. In general, then, more items on educational assessment devices will yield higher reliability/precision estimates than will fewer items.

THREE COINS IN THE RELIABILITY/PRECISION FOUNTAIN

You've now seen that there are three different ways of conceptualizing the manner in which the consistency of a test's results are described. Consistency of measurement is a requisite for making much sense out of a test's results. If the test yields inconsistent results, of course, how can teachers make sensible decisions based on what appears to be a capricious assessment procedure? Yet, as we have seen, reliability evidence comes in three flavors. It is up to you to make sure the reliability evidence supplied with a test is consonant with the use to which the test's results will be put—that is, the decision linked to the test's results. Although there is surely a relationship among the three kinds of reliability evidence we've been discussing, the following is unarguably true:

Test-Retest Reliability Evidence	$\neq$	Alternate-Form Reliability Evidence	$\neq$	Internal Consistency Reliability Evidence

To illustrate, suppose you were a teacher in a school district where a high school diploma test had been developed by an assistant superintendent in collaboration with a committee of district teachers. The assistant superintendent has claimed the test's three different forms are essentially interchangeable because each form, when field-tested, yielded a Kuder-Richardson reliability coefficient of

.88 or higher. "The three test forms," claimed the assistant superintendent at a recent school board meeting, "are reliable and, therefore, equivalent." You now know better.

If the assistant superintendent really wanted to know about between-form comparability, then the kind of reliability evidence needed would be alternate-form reliability, not internal consistency. (Incidentally, I do not recommend that you rise to your feet at the school board meeting to publicly repudiate an assistant superintendent's motley mastery of measurement reliability. Simply send the assistant superintendent a copy of this book, designating the pages to be read. And send it anonymously.)

Yet, even those educators who know something about reliability and its importance will sometimes unthinkingly mush the three brands of reliability evidence together. They'll see a K-R reliability coefficient of .90 and assume the test is not only internally consistent but that it will also produce stable results. That's not necessarily so.

THE STANDARD ERROR OF MEASUREMENT

Before bidding adieu to reliability and all its raptures, there's one other thing you need to know about consistency of measurement. So far, the kinds of reliability/ precision evidence and reliability coefficient evidence we've been considering deal with the reliability of a *group* of students' scores. For a few paragraphs, please turn your attention to the consistency with which we measure an *individual's* performance. The index used in educational assessment to describe the consistency of a particular person's performance(s) is referred to as the **standard error of measurement (SEM)**. Often a test's standard error of measurement is identified as the test's SEM. A standard error of measurement would be another indicator that writers of the 2014 *Standards* would classify as a reliability/precision procedure.

You should think of the standard error of measurement as a reflection of the consistency of an individual's scores if a given assessment procedure were administered to that individual again, and again, and again. However, as a practical matter, it is impossible to re-administer the same test innumerable times to the same students because such students would revolt or, if exceedingly acquiescent, soon swoon from exhaustion. (Swooning, these days, is rarely encountered.) Accordingly, we need to *estimate* how much variability there would be if we were able to re-administer a given assessment procedure many times to the same individual. The standard error of measurement is much like the plus or minus "sampling errors" or "confidence intervals" so frequently given in the media these days for various sorts of opinion polls. We are told that "89 percent of telephone interviewees indicated they would consider brussels sprouts in brownies to be repugnant" (±3 percent margin of error).

Other things being equal, the higher the reliability of a test, the smaller the standard error of measurement will be. For all commercially published tests, a technical manual is available that supplies the standard error of measurement for the test. Sometimes, if you ever have an occasion to check out a test's standard error, you'll find it's much larger than you might have suspected. As is true of sampling errors for opinion polls, what you'd prefer to have is small, not large, standard errors of measurement.

In many realms of life, big is better. Most folks like big bank accounts, houses with ample square footage, and basketball players who tower over other folks. But with standard errors of measurement, the reverse is true. Smaller standard errors of measurements signify more accurate assessment.

I don't want you to think that a test's standard error of measurement is computed by employing some type of measurement mysticism. Accordingly, presented here is the formula assessment folks use in order to obtain a standard error of measurement. If, however, you don't really care if the standard error of measurement was spawned on Mysticism Mountain, just skip the formula as well as the explanatory paragraph that follows it.

$$S_e = S_x \sqrt{1 - r_{xx}}$$

where s_e = standard error of measurement

s_x = standard deviation of the test scores

r_{xx} = the reliability of the test

Take a look at the formula for just a moment (especially if you get a kick out of formula looking), and you'll see that the size of a particular test's standard error of measurement (s_e) depends on two factors. First, there's the standard deviation (s_x) of the test's scores—that is, how spread out those scores are. The greater the spread in scores, the higher the scores' standard deviation will be. Second, there's the coefficient representing the test's reliability (r_{xx}). Now, if you consider what's going on in this formula, you'll see that the *larger* the standard deviation (score spread), the larger the standard error of measurement. Similarly, the *smaller* the reliability coefficient, the larger the standard error of measurement. So, in general, you see a test will have a smaller standard error of measurement if the test's scores are not too widely spread out and if the test is more reliable. A smaller standard error of measurement signifies that a student's score is more accurately reflective of the student's "true" performance level.[3]

The standard error of measurement is an important concept because it reminds teachers about the *imprecision* of the test scores an individual student receives. Novice teachers often ascribe unwarranted precision to a student's test results. I can remember all too vividly making this mistake myself when I began teaching. While getting ready for my first group of students, I saw as I inspected my students' files that one of my students, Sally Palmer, had taken a group intelligence test. (Such tests were popular in those days.) Sally had earned a score of 126. For the next year, I was absolutely convinced that Sally was not merely above average in her intellectual abilities. Rather, I was certain that her IQ was *exactly* 126.

I was too ignorant about assessment to realize there may have been a sizeable standard error of measurement associated with the intelligence test Sally had taken. Her "true" IQ score might have been substantially lower or higher. I doubt, if Sally had retaken the same intelligence test 10 different times, she'd ever get another score of precisely 126. But, in my naivete, I blissfully assumed Sally's intellectual ability was dead-center 126. The standard error of measurement helps remind teachers that the scores earned by students on commercial *or* classroom tests are not so darned exact.

There's one place a typical teacher is apt to find standard errors of measurement useful, and it is directly linked to the way students' performances on a state's accountability tests are reported. Most states classify a student's performance in at least one of three levels: *basic*, *proficient*, or *advanced*. A student is given one of these three (or more) labels depending on the student's test scores. So, for instance, on a 60-item accountability test in mathematics, the following classification scheme might have been adopted:

Student's Mathematics Classification	Student's Mathematics Accountability Test Score
Advanced	54–60
Proficient	44–53
Basic	37–43
Below Basic	36 and below

Now, let's suppose one of your students has a score *near the cutoff* for one of this fictitious state's math classifications. To illustrate, suppose your student had answered 53 of the 60 items correctly, and was therefore classified as a *proficient* student. Well, if the accountability test has a rather large standard error of measurement, you recognize it's quite likely your *proficient* student really might have been an *advanced* student who, because of the test's inaccuracy, didn't earn the necessary extra point. This is the kind of information you can relay to both the student and to the student's parents. But to do so, of course, you need to possess at least a rudimentary idea about where a standard error of measurement comes from and how it works.

The more students' scores you find at or near a particular cut-score, the more frequently there will be misclassifications. For example, using the previous table, the cut-score for an "Advanced" classification is 54—that is, a student must get a score of 54 or more to be designated "Advanced." Well, if there are relatively few students who earned that many points, there will be fewer who might be misclassified. However, for the cut-score between "Basic" and "Proficient," 44 points, there might be many more students earning scores of approximately 44 points, so the likelihood of misclassifications rises accordingly.

Although teachers who understand that a standard error of measurement can reveal how much confidence we can place in a student's test performance, and that this is a useful cautionary mechanism for users of test results. Particularly for important tests employed to classify test takers, SEMs can be tailored so that they allow test users to make more precise interpretations at or near classification cut-scores.

Here's how this process works: As you probably know already, in a given distribution of students' scores on a particular test, we will ordinarily find substantial differences in the number of students who earn certain sorts of scores. Usually, for example, there are more students who score toward the middle of what often turns out to be a "bell-shaped curve" than there are students who earn either very high or very low scores. Well, assume for the moment that five classification categories have been established for a state-administered achievement test, and that there are four cut-scores separating students' performances into the five groups.

Because it will be important to assign test takers to one of the five groups, it is possible to calculate not only an overall standard error for the entire array of students' test scores, but we can also compute SEMs around each of the four cut-scores established for the test. Yes, these are called "conditional standard errors of measurement," and conditional SEMs can vary considerably in their sizes when calculated for cut-scores representing different areas of an overall distribution of test scores.

It seems unlikely that classroom teachers will ever want to compute standard errors for their own tests, and almost certain that they'll never wish to compute conditional SEMs for those tests. However, for particularly high-stakes tests such as students' admissions to universities or students' attainment of scholarship support, reliability/precision is even more important than usual. Teachers should recognize that it is possible to obtain both overall and conditional SEMs at the cut-score segments of a score distribution, and that access to this information can prove particularly helpful in estimating how near—or far—a given student's performance is from the closest cut-score.

WHAT DO CLASSROOM TEACHERS REALLY NEED TO KNOW ABOUT RELIABILITY/PRECISION?

What do you, as a teacher or teacher in preparation, truly need to know about reliability/precision? Do you, for example, need to gather data from your own classroom assessment procedures so you can actually calculate reliability coefficients? If so, do you need to collect all three varieties of reliability evidence? My answers may surprise you. I think you need to know what reliability is, but I don't think you'll have much call to use it with your own tests—you won't, that is, unless certain of your tests are extraordinarily significant. And I haven't run into classroom tests, even rocko-socko final examinations, that I would consider sufficiently significant to warrant your engaging in a reliability-evidence orgy. In general, if you construct your own classroom tests with care, those tests will be sufficiently reliable for the decisions you will base on the tests' results.

You need to know what reliability is because you may be called on to explain to parents the meaning of a student's important test scores, and you'll want to know how reliable such tests are. You need to know what a commercial test-manual's authors are talking about and to be wary of those who secure one type of reliability evidence—for instance, a form of internal consistency evidence (because it's the easiest to obtain)—and then try to proclaim that this form of reliability evidence indicates the test's stability or the comparability of its multiple forms. In short, you need to be at least knowledgeable about the fundamental meaning of reliability, but I do not suggest you make your own classroom tests pass any sort of reliability muster.

Reliability is a central concept in measurement. As you'll see in the next chapter, if an assessment procedure fails to yield consistent results, it is almost impossible to make any accurate inferences about what a student's score signifies. Inconsistent measurement is, at least much of the time, almost certain to be inaccurate measurement. Thus, you should realize that as the stakes associated with an assessment procedure become higher, there will typically be more attention given to establishing that the assessment procedure is, indeed, reliable. If you're evaluating an important test developed by others and you see that only skimpy attention has been given to establishing reliability for the test, you should be critical of the test because evidence regarding an essential attribute of an educational test is missing.

I also think you ought to possess at least an intuitive understanding of what a standard error of measurement is. Such an understanding will come in handy when you're explaining to students, or their parents, how to make sense of a student's scores on such high-stakes external exams as your state's accountability tests. It's also useful to know that for very important tests, conditional SEMs can be determined.

The other thing you should know about reliability evidence is that it comes in three brands—three kinds of *not interchangeable* evidence about a test's consistency. Don't let someone foist a set of internal consistency results on you and suggest that these results tell you anything of importance about test-retest evidence. Don't let anyone tell you that a stability reliability coefficient indicates anything about the equivalence of a test's multiple forms. Although the three types of reliability evidence are related, they really are fairly distinctive kinds of creatures, something along the lines of second or third cousins.

What I'm trying to suggest is that classroom teachers, as professionals in the field of education, need to understand that an important attribute of educational assessment procedures is reliability. The higher the stakes associated with a test's use, the more that educators should attend to the assessment procedure's reliability/precision. Reliability is such a key criterion by which psychometricians evaluate tests that you really ought to know what it is, even if you don't use it on a daily basis.

But What Does This Have to Do with Teaching?

Students' questions can sometimes get under a teacher's skin. For example, a student once asked me a question that, in time, forced me to completely rethink what I believed about reliability—at least insofar as it made a difference in a classroom teacher's behavior. "Why," the student asked, "is reliability *really* important for classroom teachers to know?"

The incident occurred during the early seventies. I can still recall where the student was sitting (the back-right corner of an open-square desk arrangement). I had only recently begun teaching measurement courses at UCLA, and I was "going by the book"; in other words, I was following the course's textbook almost unthinkingly.

You see, as a graduate student myself, I had never taken any coursework dealing with testing. My doctoral studies dealt with curriculum and instruction, not measurement. I wanted to learn ways of instructing prospective teachers about how to whip up winning instructional plans and deliver them with panache. But, after graduate school, I soon began to recognize that what was *tested* on important tests invariably influenced what was *taught* by most teachers. I began to read all about educational measurement so I could teach the introductory measurement course in the UCLA Graduate School of Education. Frankly, I was somewhat intimidated by the psychometric shroud that testing experts sometimes employ to surround their playpen. Thus, as a beginner in the field of measurement, I rarely strayed from the "truths" contained in traditional measurement textbooks.

I can't recall my answer to that 1970s student, but I'm sure it must have been somewhat insipid. You see, I was merely mouthing a traditional view of reliability as a key attribute of good tests. In my own mind, at that moment, I really didn't have an answer to her *Why* question. But her question kept bothering me—actually for several years. Then I finally rethought the realistic value of reliability as a concept for classroom teachers. As you'll see in this chapter's wrap-up, I now downplay reliability's importance for busy teachers. But I suspect I still might be dishing out the same old psychometric party line about reliability—if it hadn't been for this one student's perceptive question. One of those psychometrically sanctioned truths was "reliability is a good thing." Accordingly, I was in the midst of a lecture extolling the extreme goodness of reliability when this memorable student, a woman who was at the time teaching sixth-graders while also working on her master's degree, said, "I can't see any practical reason for teachers to know about reliability or to go to the trouble of computing all these reliability coefficients you've just described. Why should we?"

Teachers *do* need to make sure they evaluate their students' test performances with consistency, especially if students are supplying essay responses or other sorts of performances that can't be scored objectively. But, as a general rule, classroom teachers need *not* devote their valuable time to reliability exotica. In reality, reliability has precious little to do with a classroom teacher's *teaching*. But this doesn't make key notions about reliability totally irrelevant to the concerns of classroom teachers. It's just that reliability is way, way less germane than how to whomp up a winning lesson plan for tomorrow's class!

The situation regarding your knowledge about reliability is somewhat analogous to a health professional's knowledge about blood pressure and how blood pressure influences one's health. Even though only a small proportion of health professionals work directly with patients' blood pressure on a day-by-day basis, there are few health professionals who don't know at least the fundamentals of how one's blood pressure can influence a person's health.

I don't think you should devote any time to calculating the reliability of your own classroom tests, but I think you should have a general knowledge about what it is and why it's important. Besides, computing too many reliability coefficients for your own classroom tests might give you high blood pressure.

CHAPTER SUMMARY

This chapter focused on the reliability/precision of educational assessment procedures. *Reliability* refers to the consistency with which a test measures whatever it's measuring—that is, the absence of measurement errors that would distort a student's score.

There are three distinct types of reliability evidence. *Test-retest reliability* refers to the consistency of students' scores over time. Such reliability is usually represented by a coefficient of correlation between students' scores on two occasions, but can be indicated by the degree of classification consistency displayed for students on two measurement occasions. *Alternate-form reliability evidence* refers to the consistency of results between two or more forms of the same test. Alternate-form reliability evidence is usually represented by the correlation of students' scores on two different test forms, but can also be reflected by classification consistency percentages. *Internal consistency* evidence represents the degree of homogeneity in an assessment procedure's items. Common indices of internal consistency are the Kuder-Richardson formulae as well as Cronbach's coefficient *alpha*. The three forms of reliability evidence should *not* be used interchangeably, but should be sought if relevant to the educational purpose to which an assessment procedure is being put—that is, the kind of educational decision linked to the assessment's results.

The standard error of measurement supplies an indication of the consistency of an individual's score by estimating person-score consistency from evidence of group-score consistency. The standard error of measurement is interpreted in a manner similar to the plus or minus sampling-error estimates often provided with national opinion polls. Conditional SEMs can be computed for particular segments of a test's score scale—such as near any key cut-scores. Classroom teachers are advised to become generally familiar with the key notions of reliability, but not to subject their own classroom tests to reliability analyses unless the tests are extraordinarily important.

Determining Your Outcome Mastery

In this chapter, you encountered one of the three cornerstones of today's educational assessment—namely, *reliability*. Along with *validity* and *fairness*, reliability represents what the writers of the *Standards for Educational and Psychological Testing* (2014) regard as the three "foundations" of educational and psychological testing. Clearly, reliability is a concept with which all teachers should be reasonably familiar.

Review the chapter's chief outcome:

> *An understanding of commonly employed indicators of a test's reliability/ precision that is sufficient to identify the types of reliability evidence already collected for a test and, if necessary, to select the kinds of reliability evidence needed for particular uses of educational assessments.*

Put in other words, the outcome is for readers to understand what's meant by assessment reliability—understand it well enough to correctly label different sorts of validity evidence and, even more importantly, to know in what sorts of situations a particular type of reliability evidence is needed. The Mastery Checks, then, require identifying what sort of reliability evidence is being described in a test item, choosing what sort of reliability evidence ought to be used in the specific context depicted in a test item, and describing a key reliability indicator that's useful when making decisions about individual students.

Complete both the Selected-Response and the Constructed-Response quizzes and think about the feedback you receive for each quiz.

MyEdLab *Selected-Response Check for Outcome Mastery*
MyEdLab *Constructed-Response Check for Outcome Mastery*

After completing both quizzes, go to the Learning Outcome Mastery Determination, where you will decide whether you've mastered the chapter's learning outcome or whether you need further study.

MyEdLab *Learning Outcome Mastery Determination*

References

American Educational Research Association. (2014). *Standards for educational and psychological testing.* Washington, DC: Author.

McMillan, J. H. (2013). *Classroom assessment: Principles and practice for effective standards-based instruction* (6th ed.). Boston: Pearson.

Miller, M. D., and Linn, R. (2012). *Measurement and assessment in teaching* (11th ed.). Columbus, OH: Pearson.

Endnotes

1. A special issue of *Educational Measurement: Issues and Practice* (Volume 33, No. 4, Winter 2014) is devoted to the new *Standards*. The special issue contains a marvelous collection of articles related to the nature of the *Standards* and their likely impact on educational practice. Those who are interested in the 2014 *Standards* are encouraged to consult this informative special issue.

2. Please note the use of the Latin plural for *formula*. Because I once completed two years of Latin in high school and three years in college, I have vowed to use Latin at least once per month to make those five years seem less wasted. Any fool could have said *formulas*.

3. You should recognize that because there are different kinds of reliability coefficients used to reflect a test's consistency, the size of a test's standard error of measurement will depend on the *particular* reliability coefficient that's used when calculating a standard error of measurement.

Validity

We'll be looking at *validity* in this chapter. Validity is, hands down, the most significant concept in assessment. In order to appreciate the reasons validity is so all-fired important, however, one first needs to understand why educators carry out assessments in the first place. Thus, let's set the stage a bit for your consideration of validity by explaining why educators frequently find themselves obliged to mess around with measurement.

Before you eagerly plunge into this important chapter, I need to issue a heads-up warning. This chapter on validity contains some fairly unusual concepts—that is, ideas you're not apt to see on Saturday night television or even encounter in the "Letters to the Editor" section of your local newspaper (if you still have one).

Don't become put off by these new concepts. When you've finished the chapter, having smilingly succeeded on its end-of-chapter Mastery Checks, you'll be better able to focus on the really necessary ideas about validity. The really necessary ideas, when all the hotsy-totsy terminology has been stripped away, are simply gussied-up applications of common sense. Thus, be patient and plug away at Chapter 4. When it's over, you'll be a better person for having done so. And you'll know tons more about validity.

A QUEST FOR DEFENSIBLE INTERPRETATIONS

As noted in Chapter 1, we assess students because we want to determine a student's status with respect to an educationally relevant variable. One kind of variable of relevance to teachers is a variable that can be altered as a consequence of instruction. Such a variable, for example, would be how much students have learned about world history. Another educationally relevant variable is one that can influence the way a teacher decides to instruct students. This sort of variable might be students' attitudes toward the study of whatever content the teacher is teaching.

The more teachers know about their students' status with respect to certain educationally relevant variables, the better will be the educational decisions teachers make regarding those students. To illustrate, if a middle school teacher knows that Lee Lacey is a weak reader and has truly negative attitudes toward reading, the teacher will probably decide *not* to send Lee trotting off to the school library to tackle an independent research project based on self-directed reading. Similarly, if a mathematics teacher discovers early in the school year that her students know much more about mathematics than she had previously suspected, the teacher is apt to decide that the class will tackle more advanced topics than originally planned. Teachers use the results of assessments to make decisions about students. But appropriate educational decisions depend on the *accuracy of educational assessment*. That's because, quite obviously, accurate assessments will improve the quality of decisions, whereas inaccurate assessments will do the opposite. And this is where validity comes in.

Teachers often need to know how well their students have mastered a *curricular aim*—for example, a skill or body of knowledge that students are supposed to learn. A curricular aim is also referred to these days as a *content standard*. To illustrate, if we set out to determine how well students can comprehend what they have read, it is obviously impractical to find out how well students can read *everything*. There's too much out there to read. Nonetheless, teachers would like to get an accurate fix on how well a particular student can handle the full collection of relevant reading tasks implied by a particular curricular aim. Because it is impossible to see how well students can perform with respect to the entire array of skills or knowledge embodied in a curricular aim, we have to fall back on a *sampling* strategy. Thus, when we measure students, we try to sample their mastery of a curricular aim in a representative manner so that, based on students' performance on the sample, we can infer what their status is with respect to their mastery of the entire curricular aim. Figure 4.1 portrays this relationship graphically. Note that we start with a curricular aim. In Figure 4.1, that's the oval at the left. The left-hand oval represents, for illustration purposes, a curricular aim in reading consisting of a student's ability to

figure 4.1 ■ An Illustration of How We Infer a Student's Status with Respect to a Curricular Aim from the Student's Performance on an Educational Test That Samples the Aim

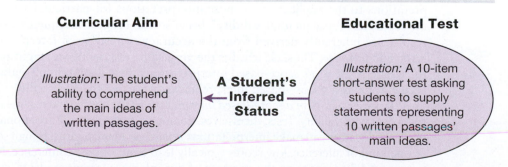

Curricular Aim

Illustration: The student's ability to comprehend the main ideas of written passages.

A Student's Inferred Status

Educational Test

Illustration: A 10-item short-answer test asking students to supply statements representing 10 written passages' main ideas.

comprehend the main ideas of written passages. The oval at the right in Figure 4.1 represents an educational assessment approach—in this instance a 10-item test—that we use to make an *inference* about a student. If you prefer, you can think of a test-based inference simply as an *interpretation* of what the test results signify. The interpretation concerns the student's status with respect to the entire curricular aim (the oval at the left). If this interpretation (inference) is accurate, then the resultant educational decisions are likely to be more defensible because those decisions will be based on a correct estimate regarding the student's actual status.

The 2014 *Standards for Educational and Psychological Testing* (2014) don't beat around the bush when dealing with the topic of assessment validity. Early on in their consideration of validity, for example, the authors of the *Standards* indicate that "validity is, therefore, the most fundamental consideration in developing and evaluating tests" (*Standards*, 2014, p. 11). Although in the intervening years between publication of the 1999 *Standards* and the 2014 *Standards,* we have seen some disagreements among members of the educational measurement community about whether assessment validity should emphasize (1) the accuracy of *the test-based interpretation* regarding what a test taker knows or can do *or* (2) the *consequences of usage*—that is, appropriateness of the uses of test-based interpretations. Indeed, some of those who stressed the importance of test-score usage introduced the concept of "consequential validity" to highlight the salience of looking at what action was taken because of test-based inference about test takers' status.

Happily, the 2014 *Standards* resolve this issue decisively by proclaiming that assessment validity involves accumulating relevant evidence to provide a sound scientific basis for "proposed uses of tests." In other words, those who set out to collect validity evidence should do so in relationship to specific intended uses of the test under consideration. If an educational test is proposed to be employed by providing an interpretation (that is, an inference) about a test taker's status to be used in a particular way (such as, for instance, a student's grade-to-grade promotion), the accuracy of that interpretation must be supported *not in general,* but, rather, for the specific, clearly identified use. If another use of the test's results is proposed, such as to help evaluate a teacher's instructional effectiveness, then this different usage requires usage-specific evidence to support any interpretation of the test's results related to teachers' instructional skills.

The 2014 *Standards,* then, definitely link the accuracy of score-based interpretations to the application of those interpretations for particular uses. There is no separate "consequential validity" because the usage consequences of a test's results are inherently derived from the accuracy of test-based interpretations *for a specific purpose.* Thus, clearly, for the very same test, evidence might reveal that for Usage X the test's score-based interpretations were resoundingly valid but, for Usage Y, the test's score-based interpretations were insufficiently valid.

It is the *validity of a score-based interpretation* that's at issue when measurement folks deal with validity. Tests, themselves, do not possess validity. Educational tests are used so educators can make interpretations about a student's status. If high scores lead to one kind of inference, low scores typically lead to an opposite inference. Moreover, because validity hinges on the accuracy of our inferences about students' status with respect to a curricular aim, it is flat-out inaccurate to talk about "the validity of a test." A well-constructed test, if used with the wrong group of students or if administered under unsuitable circumstances, can lead to a set of unsound and thoroughly invalid interpretations. Test-based interpretations may or may not be valid. It is the accuracy of the test-based interpretation with which teachers ought to be concerned.

In real life, however, you'll find a fair number of educators talking about the "validity of a test." Perhaps they really understand it's the validity of score-based inferences that is at issue, and they're simply using a shortcut descriptor. Based on my experience, it's more likely they really don't know that the focus of validity should be on test-based interpretations, not on tests themselves. *There is no such thing as "a valid test."*

Now that you know what's really at issue in the case of validity, if you ever hear a colleague talking about "a test's validity," you'll have to decide whether you should preserve that colleague's dignity by letting such psychometric shortcomings go unchallenged. I suggest that, unless there are really critical decisions on the line—decisions that would have an important educational impact on students— you keep your insights regarding validation to yourself. (When I first truly comprehended what was going on with the validity of test-based interpretations, I shared this knowledge rather aggressively with several fellow teachers and, thereby, meaningfully miffed them. No one, after all, likes a psychometric smart ass.)

Decisions about how to marshal a persuasive validity argument, either for an under-development test or for a test that's already in use, can often be abetted by developing a set of claims or propositions that support a proposed interpretation for a specified purpose of testing. Evidence is then collected to evaluate the soundness of those propositions. It is often useful when generating the propositions for a validity argument to consider rival hypotheses that may challenge the proposed interpretation. Two variations of such hypotheses hinge on whether a test measures less or more of the construct it is attempting to measure. Let's look at both of these rival hypotheses that can often, if undetected, meaningfully muck up a validity argument.

Content underrepresentation describes a shortcoming of a test that fails to capture important aspects of the construct being measured. For example, a test of students' reading comprehension that systematically failed to include certain kinds of reading passages, yet claimed it was supplying an accurate overall estimate of a child's reading comprehension, would have made a content-underrepresentation mistake.

Construct-irrelevant variance refers to a test weakness in which test takers' scores are influenced by factors that are extraneous to the construct being assessed with a specific purpose in mind. Using a reading example again, if a test included a flock of reading passages that were outlandishly too complicated or too simple, our interpretation of a student's score on such a reading test would surely be less valid than if the test's passages had meshed with the test takers' capabilities. In some cases we have seen test developers creating mathematics tests for which the required reading load clearly contaminated a test taker's mathematics prowess. Construct-irrelevant variance can cripple the validity (that is, accuracy) of the score-based interpretations we make for a test's avowed purpose.

There are some pretty fancy phrases used in the preceding paragraphs, and the idea of having to generate a compelling validity argument might seem altogether

DECISION TIME

Group-Influenced Grading

A junior high school English teacher, Cecilia Celina, has recently installed cooperative learning groups in all five of her classes. The groups are organized so that, although there are individual grades earned by students based on each student's specific accomplishments, there is also a group-based grade that is dependent on the average performance of a student's group. Cecilia decides 60 percent of a student's grade will be based on the student's individual effort and 40 percent of the student's grade will be based on the collective efforts of the student's group. This 60–40 split is used when she grades students' written examinations as well as when she grades a group's oral presentation to the rest of the class.

Several of Cecilia's fellow teachers have been interested in her use of cooperative learning because they are considering the possibility of employing it in their own classes. One of those teachers, Fred Florie, is uncomfortable about Cecilia's 60–40 split of grading weights. Fred believes that Cecilia cannot arrive at a valid estimate of an individual student's accomplishment when 40 percent of the student's grade is based on the efforts of other students. Cecilia responds that this aggregated grading practice is one of the key features of cooperative learning because it is the contribution of the group grade that motivates the students in a group to help one another learn. In most of her groups, for example, she finds students willingly help other group members prepare for important examinations.

As she considers Fred's concerns, Cecilia concludes he is most troubled about the validity of the inferences she makes about her students' achievements. In her mind, however, she separates an estimate of a student's accomplishments from the grade she gives a student.

Cecilia believes she has three decision options facing her. As she sees it, she can (1) leave matters as they are, (2) delete all group-based contributions to an individual student's grade, or (3) modify the 60–40 split.

 If you were Cecilia, what would your decision be?

off-putting to you. But let's strip away the glossy labels and here's what's really involved when test developers (for their own tests) or test users (usually for someone else's tests) set out to whomp up a winning validity argument. In turn, we need to (1) spell out clearly the nature of our intended interpretation of test scores in relation to the particular use (that is, decision) those scores will be put; (2) come up with propositions that must be supported if those intended interpretations are going to be accurate; (3) collect as much relevant evidence as is practical bearing on those propositions; and (4) synthesize the whole works in a convincing validity argument showing that score-based interpretations are likely to be accurate. Sure, it is easier said than done. But now you can see that when the exotic nomenclature of psychometrics is expunged, the basics of what needs to be done really is not that intimidating.

VALIDITY EVIDENCE

Teachers make scads of decisions, sometimes on a minute-by-minute basis. They decide whether to ask questions of their students and, if questions are to be asked, which student gets which question. Most of a teacher's *instructional* decisions are based to a large extent on the teacher's judgment about students' achievement levels. For instance, if a third-grade teacher concludes most of her students are able to read independently, then the teacher may decide to use independent reading as a key element in a social studies lesson. The teacher's judgment about students' reading abilities is, almost always, based on evidence of some sort—gathered either formally or informally.

The major contribution of classroom assessment to a teacher's decision-making is it provides reasonably accurate evidence about students' status. Although teachers are often forced to make inferences about students' knowledge, skills, or attitudes on the basis of informal observations, such unsystematic observations sometimes lead teachers to make invalid estimates about a particular student's status. I'm not knocking teachers' informal observational skills, mind you, for I certainly relied on my own informal observations when I was in the classroom. Frequently, however, I was off the mark! More than once, I saw what I wanted to see by inferring that my students possessed knowledge and skills they really didn't have. Later, when students tackled a midterm or final exam, I discovered that the conclusions I had drawn from my observation-based judgments were far too generous.

Classroom assessments, if they're truly going to help teachers make solid instructional decisions, should allow a teacher to arrive at valid interpretations about their students' status. But, more often than not, because a classroom assessment can be carefully structured, an assessment-based interpretation is going to be more valid than an on-the-fly interpretation made while the teacher is focused on other concerns.

The only reason teachers should assess their students is to make better educational decisions about those students. Thus, when you think about validity, remember it is not some abstruse measurement mystery, knowable only to those who've labored in the validity vineyards for eons. Rather, validity centers on the accuracy of the interpretations teachers make about what their students know and are able to do.

Even though there are different ways of determining whether test-based interpretations are apt to be valid, the overriding focus is on the *accuracy of an assessment-based interpretation*. It usually helps to think about validity as an overall evaluation of the degree to which a specific interpretation of a test's results is supported. People who develop important tests often try to build a ***validity argument*** in which they assemble evidence and analyses to show their tests permit the interpretations being claimed.

As a teacher or a teacher in preparation, you may wonder why you have to devote any time at all to different kinds of validity evidence. I appreciate this concern, but it's really important that you understand at least the chief kinds of evidence bearing on the validity of a score-based inference. I promise to give most attention in this chapter to the sort of validity evidence with which classroom teachers should be chiefly concerned.

In the last chapter, we saw that there are several kinds of reliability evidence that can be used to help us decide how consistently a test is measuring what it's measuring. Well, and this should come as no surprise, there are also several kinds of evidence that can be used to help educators determine whether their score-based interpretations are valid for particular uses. Rarely will one set of evidence be so compelling that, all by itself, the evidence assures us our score-based interpretation is truly accurate for a specific purpose. More commonly, several different sets of validity evidence are needed for educators to be really comfortable about the test-based inferences they make. Putting it another way, in order to develop a powerful validity argument, it is often necessary to collect *varied* kinds of validity evidence.

When I was preparing to be a high school teacher, many years ago, my teacher education classmates and I were told that "validity refers to the degree to which a test measures what it purports to measure." (I really grooved on that definition because it gave me an opportunity to use the word *purport*. Prior to that time, I didn't have too many occasions to do so.) Although, by modern standards, the traditional definition of validity is pretty antiquated, it still contains a solid seed of truth. If a test *truly* measures what it sets out to measure, then it's likely the inferences we make about students based on their test performances will be valid for the purpose at hand. Valid test-based interpretations will be made because we will typically interpret students' performances according to what the test's developers set out to measure—with a specific use in mind.

In some instances we find educators making meaningful modifications in the sorts of assessments they use with children who have physical or cognitive disabilities. We'll look into that issue in the next chapter, particularly as it has been reshaped by federal assessment-related legislation. However, I want you to think about an assessment procedure in which a reading achievement test is to be read aloud to a blind child. Let's say that the child, having heard the test's reading passages and each multiple-choice option having been read aloud, scores very well. Does this permit us to make a valid inference that the blind child can *read*? No, even though it is a reading test that's involved, a more valid interpretation is that the child can derive substantial meaning from read-aloud material. It's an important skill for visually impaired children, and it's a skill that ought to be nurtured. But it isn't *reading*. Validity resides in a test-based interpretation, not in the test itself. And the interpretation must always be made in light of a specified use that's intended.

Let's take a look, now, at the three most common kinds of evidence you are apt to encounter in determining whether the interpretation one makes from an educational assessment procedure is valid for a specific purpose. Having looked at the three varieties of validity evidence, I'll then give you my opinion about what classroom teachers *really* need to know about validity and what kinds of validity

table 4.1 ▪ Four Sources of Validity Evidence

Basis of Validity Evidence	Brief Description
Test Content	The extent to which an assessment procedure adequately represents the content of the curricular aim(s) being measured
Response Processes	The degree to which the cognitive processes test takers employ during a test support an interpretation for a specific test use
Internal Structure	The extent to which the internal organization of a test confirms an accurate assessment of the construct supposedly being measured
Relations to Other Variables	The degree to which an inferred construct appears to exist and has been accurately measured for the intended use

evidence, if any, teachers need to gather regarding their own tests. Table 4.1 previews the four sources of validity evidence we'll be considering in the remainder of the chapter.

Through the years, measurement specialists have carved up the validity pumpkin in sometimes meaningfully different ways. Going way back to earlier than the 1999 *Standards,* it was sometimes recommended that we were dealing not with types of validity *evidence* but, rather, with different types of *validity itself.* Both the 1999 and the 2014 *Standards,* however, make it clear that when we refer to validity evidence, we are describing different types of evidence—and not different types of validity.

The 2014 *Standards* make the point nicely when its authors say, "Validity is a unitary concept. *It is the degree to which all the accumulated evidence supports the intended interpretation of test scores for the proposed use*" (p. 14). I have taken the liberty of adding a dash of emphasis to the foregoing, truly important sentence by italicizing it. The italicizing was added because, if you grasp the meaning of this single sentence, you will have understood what's really meant by assessment validity.

In Table 4.1 you will find the four types of validity evidence identified in the new *Standards.* Two of those four kinds of evidence are used more frequently and, not surprisingly, we will deal with those two categories of evidence more deeply in the remainder of this chapter. Please consider, then, the four sources of validity evidence identified in the new *Standards* and barely described in Table 4.1.

As you consider the four sources of validity evidence set forth in Table 4.1, each accompanied by its tiny description, you will discover that in most settings, the most significant sources of validity evidence that teachers need to be concerned about are the first and the fourth entries: validity evidence based on *test content* and validity evidence based on *relations to other variables.* Although, on rare occasions, a teacher might bump into the remaining two sources of validity evidence—namely, the kind based on *response processes* and on a test's *internal structure*—such sorts of validity evidence aren't often encountered by most classroom teachers. Accordingly, in the remainder of the chapter we will take a serious look at two of the sources of validity evidence set forth in Table 4.1, and give only a covert sideways glance to the other two, less frequently encountered sources of validity evidence.

VALIDITY EVIDENCE BASED ON TEST CONTENT

Remembering that the more evidence of validity we have, the better we'll know how much confidence to place in score-based inferences for specific uses, let's look at the first source of validity evidence: *evidence based on test content*.

Formerly described as *content-related evidence of validity* (and described even earlier as *content validity*), **evidence of validity based on test content** refers to the adequacy with which the content of a test represents the content of the curricular aim(s) about which interpretations are to be made for specific uses. When the idea of content representatives was first dealt with by educational measurement folks many years ago, the focus was dominantly on achievement examinations, such as a test of students' knowledge of history. If educators thought that eighth-grade students ought to know 124 specific facts about history, then the more of those 124 facts that were represented in a test, the more evidence there was of content validity.

These days, however, the notion of *content* refers to much more than factual knowledge. The content of curricular aims in which teachers are interested can embrace knowledge (such as historical facts), skills (such as higher-order thinking competencies), or attitudes (such as students' dispositions toward the study of science). Content, therefore, should be conceived of broadly. When we determine the content representativeness of a test, the content in the curricular aims being sampled can consist of whatever is contained in those curricular aims. Remember, the curricular aims for most classroom tests consist of the skills and knowledge included in a teacher's intended outcomes for a certain instructional period.

During the past decade or so, the term *content standard* has become a common way to describe the skills and knowledge educators want their students to learn. Almost all states currently have an officially approved set of content standards for each of the major subject areas taught in that state's public schools. Teachers, too, sometimes pursue additional content standards (or curricular aims) associated with the particular grade level or subjects they teach.

But what is adequate representativeness of a set of content standards and what isn't? Although this is clearly a situation in which more representativeness is better than less representativeness, let's illustrate varying levels with which a curricular aim can be represented by a test. Take a look at Figure 4.2 where you see an illustrative curricular aim (represented by the shaded rectangle) and the items from

figure 4.2 ■ **Varying Degree to Which a Test's Items Represent the Curricular Aim about Which Score-Based Inferences Are to Be Made**

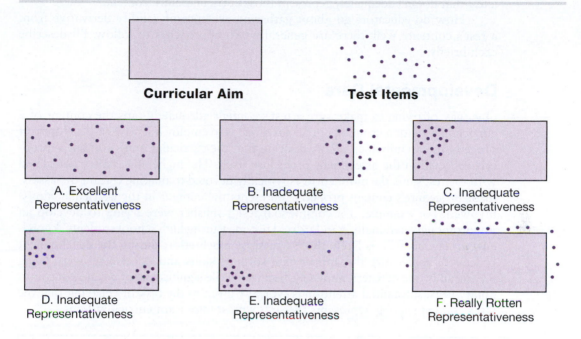

Curricular Aim   **Test Items**

A. Excellent
Representativeness

B. Inadequate
Representativeness

C. Inadequate
Representativeness

D. Inadequate
Representativeness

E. Inadequate
Representativeness

F. Really Rotten
Representativeness

different tests (represented by the dots). As the test items coincide less adequately with the curricular aim, the weaker is the evidence of validity based on test content.

For example, in Illustration A of Figure 4.2, we see that the test's items effectively sample the full range of the curricular aim's content represented by the shaded rectangle. In Illustration B, however, note that some of the test's items don't even coincide with the curricular aim's content, and that those items falling in the curricular aim don't cover it well. Even in Illustration C, where all the test's items measure content included in the curricular aim, the breadth of coverage for the curricular aim is insufficient.

Trying to put a bit of reality into those rectangles and dots, think about an Algebra I teacher who is trying to measure his students' mastery of a semester's worth of content by creating a truly comprehensive final examination. Based chiefly on students' performances on the final examination, he will assign grades that will influence whether his students can advance to Algebra II. Let's assume the content the teacher addressed instructionally in Algebra I—that is, the algebraic skills and knowledge taught during the Algebra I course—is truly prerequisite to Algebra II. Then, if the curricular aims representing the Algebra I content are *not* satisfactorily represented by the teacher's final examination, the teacher's score-based interpretations about students' end-of-course algebraic capabilities and his resultant decisions about students' readiness for Algebra II are apt to be in error. If teachers' educational decisions hinge on students' status regarding curricular aims' content, then those decisions are likely to be flawed if inferences about students' mastery of the curricular aims are based on a test that doesn't adequately represent those curricular aims' content.

How do educators go about gathering evidence of validity derivative from a test's content? Well, there are generally two approaches to follow. I'll describe each briefly.

Developmental Care

One way of trying to make sure a test's content adequately taps the content of a curricular aim (or a group of curricular aims) is to employ a set of test-development procedures carefully focused on assuring that the curricular aim's content is properly reflected in the assessment procedure itself. The higher the stakes associated with the test's use, the more effort is typically devoted to making certain the assessment procedure's content properly represents the content in the curricular aim(s) involved. For example, if a commercial test publisher were trying to develop an important new nationally standardized test measuring high school students' knowledge of chemistry, it is likely there would be much effort during the development process to make sure the appropriate sorts of skills and knowledge were being measured by the new test. Similarly, because of the significance of a state's accountability tests, substantial attention is typically given to the task of verifying that the test's content suitably represents the state's most important curricular aims.

Listed here, for example, are the kinds of activities that might be carried out during the test-development process for an important chemistry test to ensure the content covered by the new test properly represents "the content high school students ought to know about chemistry."

Possible Developmental Activities to Enhance a High-Stakes Chemistry Test's Content Representativeness

- A panel of national content experts, individually by mail or during extended face-to-face sessions, recommends the knowledge and skills that should be measured by the new test.
- The proposed content of the new test is systematically contrasted with a list of topics derived from a careful analysis of the content included in the five leading textbooks used in the nation's high school chemistry classes.
- A group of high school chemistry teachers, each judged to be a "teacher of the year" in his or her own state, provides suggestions regarding the key topics (that is, knowledge and skills) to be measured by the new test.
- Several college professors, conceded to be international authorities regarding the teaching of chemistry, having independently reviewed the content suggestions of others for the new test, offer recommendations for additions, deletions, and modifications.
- State and national associations of secondary school chemistry teachers provide reviews of the proposed content to be measured by the new test.

With lower-stakes tests, such as the kind of quiz that a high school chemistry teacher might give after a one-week instructional unit, less elaborate content reviews are obviously warranted. Even classroom teachers, however, can be attentive to the content representativeness of their tests. For openers, teachers can do so by *giving deliberate consideration* to whether the content of their classroom tests reflects the instructional outcomes supposedly being measured by those tests. For instance, whatever the test is, a teacher can deliberately try to identify the nature of the curricular aim the test is supposed to represent. Remember, the test itself should not be the focus of the teacher's concern. Rather, the test should be regarded as simply a "stand in" for a curricular aim—that is, the set of skills and/or knowledge embraced by the teacher's instructional aspirations.

To illustrate, if a teacher of tenth-grade English wants to create a final examination for a one-semester course, the teacher should first try to identify all the important skills and knowledge to be taught during the semester. An outline of such content, or even a simple listing of topics, will usually suffice. Then, after identifying the content of the curricular aims covering the English course's key content, the teacher can create an assessment instrument that attempts to represent the identified content properly.

As you can see, the important consideration here is that the teacher makes a careful effort to conceptualize the nature of a curricular aim and then tries to see if the test being constructed actually contains content that is appropriately representative of the content in the curricular aim. Unfortunately, many teachers generate tests without any regard whatsoever for curricular aims. Rather than trying to figure out what knowledge, skills, or attitudes should be promoted instructionally, some teachers simply start churning out test items. Before long, a test is born—a test that, more often than not, does a pretty poor job of sampling the skills and knowledge about which the teacher should make inferences.

We have seen, then, that one way of supplying evidence of validity based on test content is to deliberately incorporate test-development activities that increase the likelihood of representative content coverage. Having done so, these procedures should be documented. It is this documentation, in fact, that constitutes an important form of evidence of validity for specific uses. The more important the test—that is, the more important its uses—the more it is that test-development activities should be documented. For most teachers' classroom assessments, I don't believe any documentation at all is requisite.

External Reviews

A second form of evidence of validity based on test content involves the assembly of judges who rate the content appropriateness of a given test in relationship to the curricular aim(s) the test allegedly represents. For high-stakes tests, such as a state's accountability tests or a state-developed examination that must be passed before a student receives a high school diploma, these content reviews are typically quite systematic. For run-of-the-mill classroom tests, such external reviews are usually far more informal. For instance, when one teacher asks a colleague to scrutinize the content coverage of a midterm exam, that's a version of this second approach to reviewing a test's content. Clearly, the care with which external reviews of an assessment procedure's content are conducted depends on the consequences associated with students' performances. The more significant the consequences, the more elaborate the external content-review process. Let's look at a couple of examples to illustrate this point.

Suppose state department of education officials decide to construct a statewide assessment program in which all sixth-grade students who don't achieve a specified level of competence in language arts or mathematics must take part in state-designed, but locally delivered, after-school remediation programs. Once the items for the new assessment program are developed (and those items might be fairly traditional or quite innovative), a panel of 20 content reviewers for language arts and a panel of 20 content reviewers for mathematics then consider the test's items. Such reviewers, typically, are subject-matter experts who have substantial familiarity with the content involved.

Using the mathematics portion of the test for illustrative purposes, the 20 members of the Mathematics Content Review Panel might be asked to render a yes/no judgment for *each* of the test's items in response to a question such as you see on the next page. Please recognize that this sort of review task must definitely describe the test's intended use.

An Illustrative Item-Judgment Question
for Content-Review Panelists

Does this item appropriately measure mathematics knowledge and/or skill(s) that, because of the content's significance to the student's further study, should, if unmastered, result in after-school remedial instruction for the student?

Note that the illustrative question is a two-component question. Not only should the mathematical knowledge and/or skill involved, if unmastered, require after-school remedial instruction for the student, but also the item being judged must "appropriately measure" this knowledge and/or skill. In other words, the knowledge and/or skill must be sufficiently important to warrant remedial instruction on the part of the students, *and* the knowledge and/or skill must be properly measured by the item. If the content of an item is important, *and* if the content of the item is also properly measured, the content-review panelists should supply a *yes* judgment for the item. If either an item's content is not significant, or if the content is badly measured by the item, then the content-review panelists should supply a *no* judgment for the item.

By calculating the percentage of panelists who rate each item positively, an index of content-related evidence of validity can be obtained for each item. To illustrate the process, suppose we had a five-item subtest whose five items received the following positive per-item ratings from a content-review panel: Item One, 72 percent; Item Two, 92 percent; Item Three, 88 percent; Item Four, 98 percent; and Item Five, 100 percent. The average positive content per-item ratings for the entire test, then, would be 90 percent. The higher the average per-item ratings provided by a test's content reviewers, the stronger the content-related evidence of validity. This first kind of item-by-item judgment for reviewers represents an attempt to isolate (and eliminate) items whose content is insufficiently related to the curricular aim being measured.

In addition to the content-review panelists' ratings of the individual items, the panel can also be asked to judge how well the test's items represent the domain of content that *should* be assessed in order to determine whether a student is assigned to the after-school remediation extravaganza. Presented here is an example of how such a question for content-review panelists might be phrased.

An Illustrative Content-Coverage Question
for Content-Review Panelists

First, try to identify mentally the full range of mathematics knowledge and/or skills you believe to be so important that, if not mastered, should result in a student's being assigned to after-school remediation classes. Second, having mentally identified that domain of mathematics knowledge and/or skills, please estimate the percent of the domain represented by the set of test items you just reviewed. What percent is it? _____ percent

If a content panel's review of a test's content coverage yields an average response to such a question of, say, 85 percent, that's not bad. If, however, the content-review panel's average response to the content coverage question is only 45 percent, this indicates there is a solid chunk of important content not being measured by the test's items. For high-stakes tests, external reviewers' average responses to an item-by-item content question for all items and their average responses to a content coverage question for the whole test constitute solid indicators of judgmentally derived evidence of validity. The more positive the evidence, the greater confidence one can have in making score-based inferences about a student's status with respect to the curricular aims being measured.

Although it would be possible for classroom teachers to go through the same content-review machinations just described for their own classroom assessments, I know of no sane teacher who would want to expend this much energy to review the content of a typical classroom test. Instead, a teacher might ask another teacher to look over a test's items and to render judgments akin to those asked of a content-review panel. Because it takes time to provide such judgments, however, a pair of teachers might trade the task of reviewing the content of each other's classroom assessments. ("You scratch my back/review my test, and I'll scratch/review yours.")

One of the significant dividends resulting from having a fellow teacher review the content of your classroom tests is that the prospect of having such a review will usually lead to a proactive inclusion of more representative content coverage in your tests. The more carefully you consider your test's content coverage early on, the more likely the test's content coverage will be appropriate.

In review, we have considered one kind of validity evidence—namely, content-related evidence of validity—that can be used to support the defensibility of score-based inferences about a student's status with respect to curricular aims. We've discussed this form of validity evidence in some detail because, as you will see, it is the most important form of validity evidence classroom teachers need to be concerned with when they judge their own classroom assessment procedures.

Alignment

During the last decade or two, those who construct high-stakes accountability tests have been urged to make sure those assessments are in alignment with whatever curricular aims are supposed to be measured by the under-construction tests. It is not a silly notion. But it is an imprecise one.

What most people mean when they want tests to be aligned with curricular targets is that the tests will properly measure students' status with respect to those curricular targets. But "properly measure" is a fairly fuzzy concept. As one looks at the four sources of validity evidence we are dealing with in this chapter, it seems clear that the most appropriate form of alignment evidence is evidence of validity based on a test's content.

Thus, because federal assessment personnel have been calling for state accountability tests to be aligned with a state's content standards, a growth industry has emerged in recent years, especially since the enactment of No Child Left Behind. We have seen groups of assessment/curricular specialists spring up to independently determine whether a state's accountability tests are in alignment with that state's curricular aims. One of the most popular of the alignment approaches being used these days is the judgmental procedure devised by Norman Webb of the University of Wisconsin. Briefly introduced in Chapter 2, Webb's (2002) method of determining alignment is centered on judgments being made about the following four questions:

- *Categorical concurrence.* Are identical or essentially equivalent categories employed for both curricular aims and assessments?
- *Depth-of-knowledge (DOK) consistency.* To what degree are the cognitive demands of curricular aims and assessments identical?
- *Range-of-knowledge correspondence.* Is the breadth of knowledge reflected in curricular aims and assessments the same?
- *Balance of representation.* To what degree are different curricular targets given equal emphasis on the assessments?

As you can see from Webb's four evaluative criteria, the emphasis of this approach parallels other, more traditional methods of ascertaining whether the content that's supposed to be assessed by a test has, indeed, been appropriately assessed. A number of modifications of Webb's general approach have been used during the past few years, and it seems likely that we will see other approaches to the determination of a test's alignment with the curricular aims it assesses. At bottom, however, it is apparent that these alignment approaches are judgmentally rooted strategies for assembling evidence of validity based on test content.

VALIDITY EVIDENCE BASED ON RESPONSE PROCESSES

An infrequently employed source of validity evidence for educational tests is **_evidence based on response processes_**. In attempting to measure students' status with respect to certain constructs, it is assumed that test takers engage in particular cognitive processes. For example, it a test is intended to measure students' logical reasoning abilities, it becomes important to know if students are, in fact, relying on logical reasoning processes as they interact with the test.

Evidence based on response processes typically comes from analyses of individual test takers' responses during a test. For example, questions can be posed to test takers at the conclusion of a test asking for descriptions of the procedures a test taker employed during the test. More often than not, validation evidence from test takers' responses during the testing process will be used in connection with psychological assessments than the somewhat more straightforward assessment of students' knowledge and skills.

A potentially useful setting in which validity evidence would be based on students' response processes can be seen when educators monitor the evolving nature of a sought-for skill such as students' prowess in written composition. By keeping track of the development of students' writing skills in the form of en route assessments of their written or electronic drafts, validity evidence can be assembled regarding how well students can write.

The 2014 *Standards* suggests that studies of response processes are not limited to test takers, but can also focus on observers or judges who have been charged with evaluating test takers' performances or products. Careful consideration of the 2014 *Standards* will reveal that the standards consist chiefly of sound recommendations, and rarely set forth any "it must be done this way or else" proclamations.

As noted, even though this source of validity evidence has been identified as a legitimate contributor of evidence to a validity argument, and teachers should probably know that studies of response processes of students or, indeed, the judges of students' work, this source of validity evidence is rarely of interest to educators.

VALIDITY EVIDENCE BASED ON A TEST'S INTERNAL STRUCTURE

For educators, another infrequently used source of validity evidence is the internal structure of a test. For example, let's say some test developers create an achievement test they attempted to make unidimensional. The test is intended to measure only one construct (such as a student's overall mathematical prowess). That test, then, ought to behave differently than a test that had been constructed specifically to measure several supposedly different dimensions, such as students' mastery of geometry, algebra, and basic computation.

This third source of validity evidence, of course, requires us to think more carefully about the "construct" supposedly being measured by a test. For many educational tests, the construct to be assessed is abundantly obvious. To illustrate, before the arrival of nifty computer programs that automatically identify one's misspelled words and, in most instances, instantly re-spell those words, most of the students in our school actually had to *be able to spell*. The students were actually expected to be able to spell *on their own*, unabetted by electrical, digital, or extraterrestrial support. A teacher would typically choose a sample of words, for instance, 20 words randomly chosen from a district-identified set of 400 "slippery spelling" words, then read the words aloud—one by one—so students could write on their test papers how each word was spelled. The construct being assessed by such spelling tests was, quite clearly, a student's spelling ability. To tie that to-be-assessed construct down more tightly, what was being measured was a student's ability to accurately spell the words on the 400 "slippery spelling" list. A student's spelling performance on the 20-word sample was regarded as indicative of the student's ability to spell the whole 400-word list. The construct being assessed so that educators could estimate students' mastery of the construct was gratifyingly straightforward.

Not all constructs that serve as the focus of educational assessments are as easy to isolate. For example, because of several recent federal initiatives, considerable attention has been given to ascertaining students' "college and career readiness"—that is, students' readiness to be able successfully tackle higher education or to successfully undertake a career. But when assessments are created to measure students' college and career readiness, what is the actual construct to be measured? Must that construct be an amalgam of both college readiness and career readiness, or should those two constructs be measured separately? The nature of the constructs to be measured by educational tests is always in the hands of the test developers.

Moreover, depending on the way the test developers decide to carve out their to-be-assessed construct, it may be obvious that if the construct-carving has been done properly, we would expect certain sorts of statistical interactions among items representing the overall construct or certain of its subconstructs. This third source of validity evidence, then, can confirm or disconfirm that the test being considered does its measurement job that, based on our understanding of the constructs involved as well as relevant previous research dealing with this topic, the test should be doing.

One of the more important validity issues addressable by evidence regarding how a test's items are functioning deals with the unidimensionality of the construct involved. This is a pivotal feature of most significant educational tests, and if you will think back to Chapter 3's treatment of internal-consistency reliability, you will see that we can pick up some useful insights about a test's internal structure simply by calculating one or more of the available internal-consistency reliability coefficients—for instance, Cronbach's coefficient *alpha*. Such internal-consistency coefficients, if positive and high, indicate that a test is measuring test takers' status with regard to a single construct. If the construct to be measured by the test is, in fact, unidimensional in nature, then this form of reliability evidence also can make a contribution to our understanding of whether we can arrive at valid interpretations from a test—that is, valid interpretations of a test-taker's score for a specific purpose of the test being considered.

As has been noted, however, this source of internal-structure validity evidence is not often relied on by those who develop or use educational tests. Such validity evidence is more apt to be used by those who create and use psychologically focused tests where the nature of the constructs being measured is often more complex and multidimensional.

VALIDITY EVIDENCE BASED ON RELATIONS TO OTHER VARIABLES

The final source of validity evidence identified in the 2014 *Standards* stems from the nature of relationships between students' scores on the test for which we are assembling validity-relevant evidence and those students' scores on other variables. This kind of validity evidence is often seen when educational tests are being evaluated—particularly for high-stakes tests such as we increasingly encounter in education. Consequently, teachers should become familiar with the ways that this kind of validation evidence is typically employed. We will now consider the two most common ways in which validation evidence is obtainable by seeing how the scores of test-takers on a particular test relates to those individuals' status on other variables.

Test-Criterion Relationships

Whenever students' performances on a certain test are believed to be predictive of those students' status on some other relevant variable, this is an instance of a ***test-criterion relationship***. In previous years, such a relationship supplied what was referred to as *criterion-related evidence of validity*. This source of validity evidence is collected only in situations where educators are using an assessment procedure to *predict* how well students will perform on some subsequent ***criterion variable***.

The easiest way to understand what this kind of validity evidence looks like is to consider the most common educational setting in which it is collected—namely, the relationship between students' scores on (1) an aptitude test and (2) the grades those students subsequently earn. An *aptitude test,* as noted in Chapter 1, is an assessment device used in order to predict how well a student will perform academically at some later point. For example, many high school students complete a scholastic predictor test (such as the SAT or the ACT) when they're still in high school. The test is supposed to be predictive of how well those students are apt to perform in college. More specifically, students' scores on the predictor test are employed to forecast students' grade-point averages (GPAs) in college. It is assumed that those students who score well on the predictor test will earn higher GPAs in college than will those students who score poorly on the aptitude test.

In Figure 4.3, we see the classic kind of relationship between a predictor test and the criterion it is supposed to predict. As you can see, a test is used to predict students' subsequent performance on a criterion. The criterion could be GPAs, on-the-job proficiency ratings, annual income, or some other performance variable in which we are interested. Most of the time in the field of education, we are concerned with a criterion that deals directly with educational matters. Thus, grades earned in later years are often employed as a criterion. Teachers

figure 4.3 ■ The Typical Setting in Which Criterion-Related Evidence of Validity Is Sought

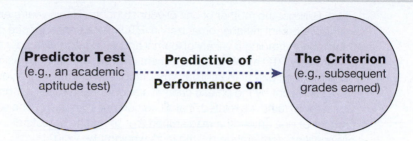

could also be interested in such "citizenship" criteria as the number of times students vote after completing high school (a positive criterion) or the number of misdemeanors or felonies that are subsequently committed by students (a negative criterion).

If we know a predictor test is working pretty well, we can use its results to help us make educational decisions about students. For example, if you discovered that Cliff Carver scored very poorly on a scholastic aptitude test while in high school, but Cliff's heart is set on attending college, you could devise a set of supplemental instructional activities so that he could try to acquire the needed academic skills and knowledge before he leaves high school. Test results, on predictor tests as well as on any educational assessment procedures, should always be used to make better educational decisions.

In some cases, however, psychometricians can't afford to wait the length of time that's needed between the administration of the predictor test and the gathering of the data regarding the criterion. For example, if the staff of a commercial testing company is developing a new academic aptitude test to predict high school students' GPAs at the end of college, the company's staff members might administer the new *high school* aptitude test to (much older) *college seniors* only a month or so before those seniors earn their baccalaureate degrees. The correlation between the aptitude test scores and the students' final college GPAs has been historically referred to as *concurrent* evidence of validity. Clearly, such evidence is far less compelling than properly gathered *predictive* evidence of validity—that is, when a meaningful length of time has elapsed between the predictor test and the collection of the criterion data. So, for instance, if we were to ask high school students to complete an academic aptitude test as eleventh-graders, then wait for three years to collect evidence of their college grades, this would represent an instance of predictive criterion-relevant validity evidence.

What teachers need to realize about the accuracy of scholastic predictor tests such as the ones we've been discussing is that those tests are far from perfect. Sometimes the criterion that's being predicted isn't all that reliable itself. (How

Mrs. Billings, the mother of one of your students, is this year's president of your school's parent-teacher organization (PTO). As a consequence of her office, she's been reading a variety of journal articles dealing with educational issues. After every PTO meeting, or so it seems to you, Mrs. Billings asks you to comment on one of the articles she's read. Tonight, she asks you to explain what is meant by the phrase *content standards* and to tell her how your classroom tests are related, if at all, to content standards. She says that the author of one article she read argued that "if teachers' tests didn't measure national content standards, the tests wouldn't be valid."

 If I were you, here's how I'd respond to Mrs. Billings:

"You've really identified an important topic for tonight, Mrs. Billings. Content standards are regarded by many of the country's educators as a key factor in how we organize our national education effort. Put simply, a *content standard* describes the knowledge or skill we want our students to master. You might think of a content standard as today's label for what used to be called an instructional objective. What's most imperative, of course, is that teachers focus their instructional efforts on *appropriate* content standards.

"As you may know, our state has already established a series of content standards at all grade levels in language arts, mathematics, social studies, and science. Each of these state-approved sets of content standards is based, more or less, on a set of content standards originally developed by the national subject-matter association involved—for example, the National Council of Teachers of Mathematics. So, in a sense, teachers in our school can consider both the state-sanctioned standards as well as those devised by the national content associations. Most of our school's teachers have looked at both sets of content standards.

"Teachers look over these content standards when they engage in an activity we call *test sharing*. Each teacher has at least one other colleague look over all the teacher's major classroom assessments to make sure that most of the truly significant content standards have been addressed.

"Those teachers whose tests do not seem to address the content standards satisfactorily are encouraged to revise their tests so the content standards are more suitably covered. It really seems to work well for us. We've used the system for a couple of years now, and the teachers uniformly think our assessment coverage of key skills and knowledge is far better."

 Now, how would you respond to Mrs. Billings?

accurate were *your* college grades?) For instance, the correlations between students' scores on academic aptitude tests and their subsequent grades rarely exceed .50. A correlation coefficient of .50 indicates that, although the test is surely predictive to some degree regarding how students will subsequently perform, there are many other factors (such as motivation, study habits, and interpersonal skills) that play a major role in the grades a student earns. In fact, the best predictor of students' future grades is not their scores on aptitude tests; it is students' earlier grades. Previous grades more accurately reflect the full range of important grade-influencing factors, such as students' perseverance, that are not directly assessable via aptitude assessment devices.

Statistically, if you want to determine what proportion of students' performances on a criterion variable (such as college grades) is meaningfully related to students' scores on a predictor test (such as the ACT or the SAT), you must *square* the correlation coefficient between the predictor and criterion variables. Thus, if the coefficient is .50, simply square it—that is, multiply it times itself—and you end up with $.50 \times .50 = .25$. This signifies that about 25 percent of students' college grades can be explained by their scores on the aptitude test. Factors such as motivation and study habits account for the other 75 percent. Your students need to understand that when it comes to the predictive accuracy of students' scores on academic aptitude tests, *effort trumps test scores.*

Convergent and Discriminant Evidence

Another kind of empirical investigation providing evidence of validity is often referred to as a *related-measures study*. In such a study, we hypothesize that a given kind of relationship will be present between students' scores on the assessment device we're scrutinizing and their scores on a related (or unrelated) assessment device. To illustrate, if we churned out a brand-new test of students' ability to comprehend what they read, we could hypothesize that students' scores on the new reading test would be positively correlated with their scores on an already established and widely used reading achievement test. To the extent that our hypothesis is confirmed, we have assembled evidence of validity supporting the validity of our score-based interpretation (using the new test's results) about a student's reading skill.

When it is hypothesized that two sets of test scores *should* be related, and evidence is collected to show that positive relationship, this is referred to as ***convergent evidence of validity***. For example, suppose you were a U.S. history teacher and you used a final exam to cover the period from the Civil War to the present. If another teacher of U.S. history in your school also had a final exam covering the same period, you'd predict that the students who scored well on your final exam would also do well on your colleague's final exam. (Your dazzling students should dazzle on his exam and your clunky students should clunk on his exam.) If you went to the trouble of actually doing this (and, of course, why would you?), this would be a form of convergent validity evidence.

Peeves Make Poor Pets

Most people have at least one or two pet peeves. When it comes to educational assessment, my Top-of-the-Charts Pet Peeve occurs when people use test results—without warrant—for a purpose other than what a test was originally created to accomplish. The "without warrant" is an important qualifier. That's because, if a test was initially built for Purpose 1 and has the validity evidence showing it can carry out that purpose well, then if evidence indicates the test can also be used for Purpose 2, I have no problem with the test's accomplishing this second purpose. (It's like a 2-for-1 sale!) What ticks me off, however, is when measurement folks build a test for one well-supported purpose, then cavalierly try to employ that test for a second, unsupported use.

That's what has been going on in the United States in recent years when we have seen hoards of policymakers call for the nation's teachers to be evaluated, as least in part, on the basis of their students' scores on achievement tests. Most of the achievement tests being trotted out for this teacher-evaluation mission were originally constructed to provide inferences about the degree of students' mastery regarding a collection of curricular aims, such as has been seen in the annual accountability tests employed throughout the land.

But when students' test scores are to be used to evaluate a teacher's *instructional quality,* then there should be ample validity evidence on hand to show that students' test scores do, indeed, distinguish between effectively taught students and ineffectively taught students. Merely because a test yields a valid interpretation about a student's mastery of curricular aims does not indicate that the test automatically yields accurate interpretations about whether particular teachers are instructionally dazzling or instructionally dismal.

Nonetheless, the proponents of test-score–based teacher evaluation blithely assume that any old test will supply the evidence we can use to differentiate among teachers' instructional skills. This is truly a dumb assumption.

When you're thinking about which test to use for which function, remember that *usage governs validity.* That is, we need to assemble validity evidence to support *any* use of a test's results. When we employ students' test scores to evaluate teachers, and the tests we use have not been *demonstrated* to be capable of doing that evaluative job, then you can safely bet that poor inferences will be made regarding which teachers are winners and which teachers are losers. And when those mistakes about teachers' competence are made, so that weak teachers get tenure while strong teachers get bounced, guess who gets harmed most? That's right; it's the students.

We'll dig more deeply into test-based teacher evaluation in Chapter 15.

In contrast, suppose as a test-crazed U.S. history teacher you also tried to compare your students' final exam scores to their scores on a final exam in an algebra class. You'd predict a weaker relationship between your students' final exam scores in your history class and their final exam scores in the algebra class. This lower relationship is referred to as *discriminant evidence* of validity. It simply means that if your test is assessing what you think it is, then scores on your test ought to relate weakly to results of tests designed to measure other constructs. (This sort of test comparison, too, would be an unsound use of your time.)

SANCTIONED AND UNSANCTIONED LABELS FOR VALIDITY EVIDENCE

Validity, as implied in the outset of the chapter, is the linchpin of educational measurement. If teachers can't arrive at valid score-based interpretations about students, there's simply no reason to measure students in the first place. However, because validity is such a central notion in educational assessment, some folks have attached specialized meanings to it that, although helpful at some level, also may introduce confusion.

One of these is *face validity,* a notion that has been around for a number of decades. All that's meant by face validity is that the *appearance* of a test seems to coincide with the use to which the test is being put. To illustrate, if an assessment procedure is supposed to measure a student's actual ability to function collaboratively with a group of other students, then a true–false test that focused exclusively on abstract principles of group dynamics would not appear to be face valid. But, appearance can be deceiving, as has been noted in a variety of ways, such as "not being able to judge a book by its cover." Thus, even though an assessment procedure may *appear* to be consonant with the assessment procedure's mission, we must still assemble evidence that inclines us to put confidence in the score-based interpretation we arrive at by using the test for a particular purpose. If an assessment procedure has no face validity, we're less inclined to assume the assessment procedure is doing its job. Yet, even in those circumstances, we still need to assemble one or more of the *Standards*-approved varieties of validity evidence to help us know how much confidence, if any, we can put in a score-based interpretation derived from using the assessment procedure.

Another more recently introduced variant of validity is something known as consequential validity. *Consequential validity* refers to whether the *uses* of test results are valid. If, for example, a test's results are inappropriately employed to deny students a reasonable expectation, such as progressing to the next grade level, the test may be said to be consequentially invalid because its results had been used improperly. Yet, because educators should obviously be attentive to the consequences of test use, the notion of consequential validity has been made superfluous because of the new *Standards'* stress on the validity of interpretations *for specific uses*. In other words, validity evidence is no longer to be collected to support just "any old interpretation," but now that interpretation must be focused on a particular, announced use of the test-based interpretation. In essence, framers of the new *Standards* have skillfully subsumed consequences into a more focused definition of assessment validity. Consequences must be heeded, of course, but they should be heeded in relation to a specified use of a test's results.

A final point is in order regarding the labels for validity evidence. No one expects classroom teachers to be psychometric whiz-bangs. Teachers should know enough about assessment so that they can do a solid instructional job. When it comes to validity evidence and how it ought to be employed by teachers, this means that when it comes to assessment validity, you do not need to keep constantly *au courant*. (This is either a French phrase for up-to-date or a scone with especially small raisins.) However, while you need not become a validity expert, you probably should know that because the 1999 *Standards* were the only game in town for about 15 years, some of the labels used in that document might linger even after the 2014 *Standards* rumbled into view.

To illustrate, some of your colleagues or even some assessment specialist might still employ the following phrases to describe validity evidence: "content-related evidence of validity" and "criterion-related evidence of validity." We've already considered both of these under slightly different labels. The one type of validity evidence that, though widely used in years past, we have not considered is "construct-related evidence of validity." Also called, at times, simply "construct validity," those labels refer to a more comprehensive approach to collecting relevant evidence and building a validity argument that supports test-based interpretations regarding the construct that test developers are attempting to measure. Because of the more usage-emphasized manner in which the new *Standards* have attempted to lay out the validity landscape, there now seems to be no need for this traditional way of characterizing the accuracy with which we make score-based interpretations about test takers—interpretations *focused on particular uses*.

THE RELATIONSHIP BETWEEN RELIABILITY AND VALIDITY

If convincing evidence is gathered that a test is permitting valid score-based interpretations for specific uses, we can be assured the test is also yielding reasonably reliable scores. In other words, valid score-based inferences almost certainly guarantee that consistent test results are present. The reverse, however, is not true. If a test yields reliable results, it may or may not yield valid score-based interpretations. A test, for example, could be measuring with remarkable consistency a construct the test developer never even contemplated measuring. For instance, although the test developer thought an assessment procedure was measuring students' punctuation skills, what was actually measured was students' general intellectual ability, which, not surprisingly, splashes over into how well students can punctuate. Inconsistent results will invariably preclude the validity of score-based interpretations. Evidence of valid score-based interpretations almost certainly requires that consistency of measurement is present.

WHAT DO CLASSROOM TEACHERS REALLY NEED TO KNOW ABOUT VALIDITY?

Well, we've spent a fair number of words worrying about the validity of score-based inferences. How much, if anything, do classroom teachers really need to know about validity? Do classroom teachers need to collect validity evidence for their own tests? If so, what kind(s)?

As with reliability, I think a classroom teacher needs to understand what the essential nature of the most common kinds of validity evidence is, but I don't think classroom teachers need to go into a frenzy of evidence-gathering regarding validity. Clearly, if you're a teacher or a teacher in preparation, you'll be far too busy in your classroom trying to keep ahead of the students to spend much time in assembling validity evidence. I do recommend, however, that for your more important tests, you devote at least some *attention* to validity evidence based on test content. As suggested in the chapter, giving serious thought to the content of an assessment domain being represented by a test is a good first step. Having a colleague review your tests' content is also an effective way to help make sure that your classroom tests represent satisfactorily the content you're trying to promote, and that your score-based interpretations about your students' content-related status are not miles off the mark.

Regarding the other types of validity evidence, however, I urge little more than a reasonable understanding of what those kinds of evidence are. If you're ever asked to help scrutinize a high-stakes educational test, you'll want to know enough about such versions of validity evidence so you're not intimidated when measurement specialists start reciting their "odes to validity."

Perhaps the most important thing classroom teachers need to understand about validity is it does *not* reside in a test itself. Rather, it is a score-based interpretation that is either accurate or inaccurate. And because score-based interpretations reflect judgments made by people, some of those judgments will be in error.

But What Does This Have to Do with Teaching?

Most teachers I talk to believe, mistakenly, that their classroom tests are pretty spiffy assessment instruments. Recently I asked five teachers whom I know, "Do you think your classroom tests are pretty spiffy assessment instruments?" Three of the five teachers said, "Yes." One said, "No." And one asked, "What does 'spiffy' mean?" (I counted this as a negative response.) Thus, based on my extensive opinion poll, I can support my contention that *most* teachers think their classroom tests are pretty good—that is, spiffy.

And that's where the concept of *validity* impinges on teaching. Many teachers, you see, believe their classroom assessments produce results that are really rather accurate. Many teachers, in fact, actually think "their tests are valid." The idea that validity resides in tests themselves is a prevalent misconception among the nation's educators. And, unfortunately, when teachers think that their *tests* are valid, then teachers begin to place unwarranted confidence in the scores their students attain on those "valid" tests.

What this chapter has been stressing, restressing, and re-restressing is the idea that validity applies to test-based interpretations, not the tests themselves. Moreover, for teachers to be confident their score-based inferences are valid, it's usually necessary to assemble some compelling evidence (three kinds of evidence are treated in the chapter) to support the accuracy of a teacher's score-based inferences. And because teaching decisions are often based on a teacher's estimate of students' current achievement levels, then it is apparent that unwarranted confidence in those test-based estimates can sometimes lead to faulty interpretations and, as a result, to unsound instructional decisions.

Ideally, teachers will accept the chapter's central contention that validity of test-based inferences requires teachers to make a *judgment* about the accuracy of their own test-based inferences. Moreover, truly compelling data are needed in order for a teacher to be super-sure that test-based *judgments* about students' achievement levels are actually on target. Yet, because compelling data are rarely at hand, then teachers will more likely recognize that their instructional decisions must often be based on a fairly fragile assessment foundation.

In today's high-stakes environment, it is even more important that teachers regard validity as a judgment-derived commodity. For example, suppose your state's officially approved curriculum contains scads of content standards. Because *scads* represents a large number (and is rarely encountered in its singular form), your state clearly has a great many content standards to be taught—and tested. Now let's suppose your state's annual accountability tests are intended to assess students' mastery of those scads of content standards—in a few hours of testing. Well, if that's the situation, do you really think there is apt to be great accuracy in the following statement by an elected state official? "Mastery of all our state's content standards can be determined on the basis of students' scores on our state's valid accountability tests." Even elected state officials, you see, can make mistakes in their judgment. For one thing, there are too many content standards for students' "mastery" to be determined. Second (and you know this by now), tests aren't valid.

Validity is a far more elusive critter than is usually thought. Indeed, valid score-based interpretations in the field of education might properly be placed on our nation's endangered species list.

CHAPTER SUMMARY

This chapter attempted to promote not only an understanding of the nature of assessment validity, but also an appreciation on the part of the reader regarding the enormously important role that validity plays in educational assessment. The chapter's content was meaningfully shaped by the publication in 2014 of the *Standards for Educational and Psychological Testing*. Because the periodically published *Standards* is developed under the aegis of the three national organizations most responsible for educational assessment, and because fully 15 years have elapsed since the previous publication of the *Standards,* it is almost certain that the new guidelines will have a substantial impact on the way that educational tests are developed, evaluated, and used.

The new *Standards,* far more explicitly than in any earlier version of that significant document, stress that validity refers to the "degree to which evidence and theory support the interpretations of test scores for proposed uses of tests" (*Standards,* 2014, p. 11). The new emphasis is on the need to collect validity evidence for any use of the tests—that is, for any usage-based interpretation of test-takers' performances. Thus, if a test had been originally created to satisfy one use (such as supplying comparative score-interpretations of students' content mastery), and the test were to be used for another purpose, validity evidence should be collected and fashioned into separate arguments supporting the validity of score-based interpretations for both the original and the new usage.

Four sources of validity evidence were described in the chapter. Two of those sources are encountered more frequently by educators and, therefore, were dealt with in greater detail. These two validity sources were evidence based on test content and evidence based on relations with other variables. The kind of validity evidence most likely to be encountered by teachers involves test-based predictions of students' performances on a criterion variable (such as high-school students' college grades). A second kind of relationship between students' test scores and other variables arises when evidence is collected so that those test scores can be correlated with both similar and dissimilar variables. As always, the quest on the part of test developers and test users it to devise a compelling argument attesting to the accuracy of score-based interpretations for particular test uses.

The relationship between validity evidence and reliability evidence was considered, as were certain unsanctioned labels for validity. It was suggested that, in general, more validity evidence is better than less, but that classroom teachers need to be realistic in how much evidence of validity to secure for their own tests. A recommendation was given to have teachers become familiar with all forms of validity evidence, but to focus only on content-based evidence of validity for their own classroom assessment procedures. Most importantly, it was stressed that teachers recognize validity as a judgmental inference about the interpretation of students' test performances—not an attribute of tests themselves.

Determining Your Outcome Mastery

The importance of validity to educational assessment really cannot be over-emphasized. It is, unarguably, the most influential concept in all of educational testing. Teachers need to know what validity is, how to corral it, and what sort of evidence is needed to support test-based interpretations for particular purposes. Let's look, then, at the major outcome it is hoped you attained after you completed this chapter:

> *A sufficiently deep understanding of assessment validity so that its essential nature can be explained, its establishment can be described, and the most appropriate kinds of validity evidence can be selected for specific uses of educational tests*

With the completion of the chapter, you should now be able to (1) accurately describe what validity is, (2) explain how validity comes into existence, and (3) choose suitable validity evidence for diverse uses of educational tests. In essence, you should have the ability to display a fundamental grasp of assessment validity by being able to carry out three related, but distinguishable, tasks regarding validity. Using nonfancy language, it is now hoped that you understand what's going on when people talk about assessment validity so well that you can comfortably do all three things identified in the chapter's chief intended learning outcome.

Complete both the Selected-Response and the Constructed-Response quizzes and think about the feedback you receive for each quiz.

MyEdLab *Selected-Response Check of Outcome Mastery*
MyEdLab *Constructed-Response Check of Outcome Mastery*

After completing both quizzes, go to the Learning Outcome Mastery Determination, where you will decide whether you've mastered the chapter's learning outcome or whether you need further study.

MyEdLab *Learning Outcome Mastery Determination*

References

American Educational Research Association. (2014). *Standards for educational and psychological testing*. Washington, DC: Author.

Haertel, E. (2013). "Getting the help we need," *Journal of Educational Measurement, 50,* no. 1 (Spring): 84–90.

Kane, M. (2013). "Validating the interpretations and uses of test scores," *Journal of Educational Measurement, 50,* no. 1 (Spring): 1–73.

Nichols, P. D., and Williams, N. (2009). "Consequences of test score use as validity evidence: Roles and responsibilities," *Educational Measurement: Issues and Practice, 28,* no. 1 (Spring): 3–9.

Popham, W. J. (1997). "Consequential validity: Right concern—wrong concept," *Educational Measurement: Issues and Practice, 16,* no. 2 (Summer): 9–13.

Webb, N. L. (2002). *Alignment study in language arts, mathematics, science, and social studies of state standards and assessment for four states*. Washington, DC: Council of Chief State School Officers.

5

Fairness

CHIEF CHAPTER OUTCOME

An understanding of the nature of assessment bias and the procedures by which it can be reduced in both large-scale tests and classroom assessments

The last of the "big three" criteria for evaluating educational assessment devices is, in contrast to reliability and validity, a relatively new kid on the block. During the past couple of decades, educators have increasingly recognized that the tests they use are often biased against particular groups of students. As a consequence, students in those groups do not perform as well on a test, not because the students are less able but because there are features in the test that distort the nature of the students' performances. Even if you had never read a single word about educational measurement, you would quickly realize that such a test would definitely be unfair. The third major factor to be used in judging the caliber of educational assessments is *fairness* and, as just pointed out, its arrival on the test-quality scene is far more recent than its time-honored evaluative cousins, reliability and validity.

Fairness in educational testing, however, has no single, technically sanctioned meaning. This is because the term *fairness* is used by educators—and noneducators alike—in many different ways. For example, educators might regard fairness in testing as a desirable aspiration in general, and yet regard a particular testing program as flagrantly unfair. Authors of the 2014 *Standards for Educational and Psychological Testing* (2014) limit their focus to fairness regarding the aspects of testing that are the responsibility of those who develop, use, and interpret the results of educational tests. Moreover, the *Standards* restrict its attention to those assessment considerations about which there is general professional and technical agreement. Accordingly, in the remainder of this chapter of *Classroom Assessment,* we'll be considering fairness in testing against a framework of what's recommended in the 2014 *Standards.*

More specifically, we'll first be looking at a potential source of unfairness that can arise when *assessment bias* is present in a test. Later, we'll consider the kinds of unfairness that can slither onto the scene when we try to assess students with disabilities or we attempt to measure the status of students whose first language is not English. Less than high-quality educational assessments of such students almost always leads to test-based interpretations—and subsequent interpretation-based educational decisions—that are far from fair.

At its most basic level, fairness in educational testing is a validity issue. As you saw in the previous chapter, validity refers to the accuracy of score-based interpretations about test takers (for specific uses). What happens to validity, however, if those interpretations are messed up because our tests contain serious assessment bias, or if we failed to accurately assess English-language learners or students with disabilities because of those students' atypicalities? Well, it is almost certain that the usage-focused interpretations we make based on students' test scores are going to be inaccurate—that is, invalid. Thus, in almost all situations, fairness in testing should be routinely regarded as a requisite precursor to assessment validity—in other words, as a necessary but not sufficient condition for assessment validity.

THE NATURE OF ASSESSMENT BIAS

Assessment bias refers to qualities of an assessment instrument that offend or unfairly penalize a group of students because of students' gender, race, ethnicity, socioeconomic status, religion, or other such group-defining characteristics. Most teachers are sufficiently familiar with the idea of test bias these days that, at least in a general way, they recognize what's being talked about when someone says, "That test was biased." In this chapter, however, we'll take a deeper look at what test bias is—and what it isn't. Moreover, we'll consider some procedures that can help classroom teachers recognize whether bias is present in assessment procedures and, as a consequence, can help reduce or eradicate bias in teachers' own classroom tests. Finally, we'll tackle a particularly difficult issue—namely, how to reduce bias when assessing students with disabilities or students who are English language learners.

Because the other two criteria for evaluating educational tests—reliability and validity—are "good things," we're going to use the expression *absence-of-bias* to describe this evaluative criterion. When bias is absent in tests, this is also a "good thing." Before looking at procedures to promote the absence-of-bias in educational assessment procedures, let's first look more directly at what we're trying to eliminate. In other words, let's look at assessment bias.

As indicated earlier, assessment bias is present when there are elements in an assessment procedure that distort a student's performance merely because of the student's personal characteristics, such as gender, ethnicity, and so on. Most of the time, we think about distortions that tend to lower the scores of students because those students are members of particular subgroups. For example, suppose officials in State *X* installed a high-stakes mathematics test that must be passed before students receive an "honors" diploma. If the mathematics test contained many word problems based on certain competitive sports examples about which boys were more familiar than girls, then girls might perform less well on the test than boys. The lower performance by girls would not occur because girls were less skilled in mathematics, but because they were less familiar with the sports contexts in which the word problems were placed. The mathematics test, therefore, appears to be biased against girls. On the other hand, it could also be said the mathematics test is biased in favor of boys. In the case of assessment bias, what we're worried about is distortions of students' test performances—either unwarranted increases or unwarranted decreases.

Let's try another illustration. Suppose that a scholastic aptitude test featured test items based on five lengthy reading selections, two of which were based on content more likely to be known to members of a particular religious group. If, because of familiarity with the content of the two selections, members of the religious group outperformed others, this would be a distortion in their test performances. There would be an assessment bias in their favor.

If you think carefully about the issue we're considering, you'll realize fairness of testing and assessment bias interfere with the validity of the score-based inferences we draw from our assessment procedures. But, because assessment bias constitutes such a distinctive threat to the validity of test-based interpretations, and a threat that can be directly addressed, it is usually regarded as a separate criterion when evaluating educational tests. To the extent that bias is present, for the groups of students against whom the test is biased, valid score-based interpretations are not apt to be forthcoming.

Let's look, now, at two forms of assessment bias—that is, two ways in which the test performances of individuals in particular groups can be distorted. It was noted earlier in the chapter that assessment bias is present if an educational assessment procedure offends or unfairly penalizes students because of their membership in a gender, racial, ethnic, religious, or similar subgroup. We'll consider both of these forms of assessment bias.

Offensiveness

An assessment procedure is biased if its content (for example, its items) is *offensive* to a subgroup of students. Such **offensiveness** often occurs when negative stereotypes of certain subgroup members are presented in a test. For instance, suppose that in all of an exam's items we saw males portrayed in high-paying and prestigious positions (e.g., attorneys and physicians) and we saw women portrayed in low-paying and unprestigious positions (e.g., housewives and clerks). Because at least some female students will, quite appropriately, be offended by this gender inequality, their resultant distress may lead to less than optimal performances on the exam and, as a consequence, scores that do not accurately represent their capabilities. (Angry women, or angry men, aren't the best test takers.)

Other kinds of offensive content include slurs, blatant or implied, based on stereotypic negatives about how members of particular ethnic or religious groups behave. This kind of offensive content, of course, can distract students in the offended group so they end up focusing more on the offensiveness of a given item than on accurately displaying their own abilities on subsequent items.

Although most of the nation's major test-development agencies now employ item-writing and item-review procedures designed to eliminate such offensive content, one encounters far too many examples of offensive content in less carefully developed teacher-made tests. It is not that teachers deliberately set out to offend any of their students. Rather, many teachers have simply not thought seriously about whether the content of their classroom assessment procedures might cause distress for any of their students. Later in the chapter, we'll consider some practical ways of eradicating offensive content in teachers' classroom assessment procedures.

Unfair Penalization

A second factor contributing to assessment bias is content in a test that may cause *unfair penalization* for a student based on the student's ethnicity, gender, race, religion, and so on. Let's consider for a moment what an "unfair" penalty really is.

Unfair penalization arises when a student's test performance is distorted because of content that, although not offensive, disadvantages the student because of the student's group membership. The previously cited example about girls' unfamiliarity with certain competitive sports would be an illustration of what an unfair penalty would be. As another example, suppose an assessment procedure includes content apt to be known only to children from affluent families. Let's say an assessment procedure is installed to see how well students can "collaboratively problem solve" in groups, and the assessment activity culminates when the teacher gives students a new problem to analyze collaboratively in a group discussion. If the content of the new problem deals with a series of locally presented operas and symphonies likely to have been attended only by those students whose parents can afford such performances' hefty ticket prices, then students from less affluent families will be unfairly penalized because there was probably much less dinner conversation about the local operas and symphonies. Students from lower socioeconomic strata might perform less well on the "collaborative problem solving" assessment enterprise not because they are less skilled at collaborative problem solving, but because they are unfamiliar with the upper-crust content of the particular assessment procedure being employed to gauge students' collaborative problem-solving skills.

Some penalties, of course, are as fair as they can be. If you're a classroom teacher who's generated a test on a unit you've been teaching, and some students perform poorly simply because they didn't pay attention in class or didn't do their homework assignments, their lousy performance on your test is eminently fair. Their "penalty," in fact, simply reeks of fairness. Poor performances on an assessment procedure need not signify the resultant penalty to the student (such as a low grade) is unfair. Many of the students I taught in high school and college richly deserved the low grades I gave them.

Unfair penalization arises only when it is not the student's ability that leads to poor performance but, rather, the student's group membership. If, because of the student's gender, ethnicity, and so on, the content of the test distorts how the student would otherwise have performed, then a solid case of assessment bias is at hand. As was true in the case of offensiveness of test content, we sometimes find classroom teachers who haven't thought carefully about whether their assessment procedures' content gives all students an equal chance to perform well. We'll soon

DECISION TIME

Choose Your Language, Children!

Jaime Jemez teaches mathematics in Wilson Junior High School. He has done so for the past 10 years and is generally regarded as an excellent instructor. In the past few years, however, the student population at Wilson Junior High has been undergoing some dramatic shifts. Whereas there were relatively few Hispanic students in the past, almost 30 percent of the student population is now Hispanic. Moreover, almost half of those students arrived in the United States less than 2 years ago. Most of the newly arrived students in Jaime's classes came from Mexico and Central America.

Because English is a second language for most of these Hispanic students, and because many of the newly arrived students still have a difficult time with written English, Jaime has been wondering if his mathematics examinations are biased against many of the Hispanic students in his classes. Because Jaime reads and writes Spanish fluently, he has been considering whether he should provide Spanish-language versions of his more important examinations. Although such a decision would result in some extra work for him, Jaime believes that language-choice tests would reduce the bias in his assessment procedures for students whose initial language was Spanish.

Jaime is also aware that the demographics of the district are still shifting and that an increasing number of Southeast Asian students are beginning to show up in his classes. He is afraid that if he starts providing Spanish-language versions of his tests, perhaps he will need to provide the tests in other languages as well. However, he is fluent only in Spanish and English.

If you were Jaime, what would your decision be?

consider some ways for classroom teachers to ferret out test content that might unfairly penalize certain of their students.

DISPARATE IMPACT AND ASSESSMENT BIAS

It is sometimes the case that when a statewide, high-stakes test is originally installed, its impact on different ethnic groups will be disparate. For example, African American students or Hispanic American students may perform less well than non-Hispanic White students. Does this *disparate impact* mean the test is biased? Not necessarily. However, if a test has a disparate impact on members of a particular racial, gender, or religious subgroup, this disparate impact certainly warrants further scrutiny to see if the test is actually biased. Disparate impact does not equal assessment bias.

Let me tell you about an experience I had in the late 1970s that drove this point home so I never forgot it. I was working in a southern state to help its state officials develop a series of statewide tests that, ultimately, would be used to deny diplomas to students who failed to pass the twelfth-grade level of the test. Having field-tested all of the potential items for the tests on several thousand children in the state, we had assembled a committee of 25 teachers from throughout the state, roughly half of whom were African American, to review the field-test results. The function of the committee was to see if there were any items that should be discarded. For a number of the items, the African American children in the statewide tryout had performed significantly less well than the other children. Yet, almost any time it was proposed that such items be jettisoned because of such a disparate impact, it was the African American teachers who said, "Our children need to know what's in that item. It deals with important content. Don't you *dare* toss that item out!"

Those African American teachers were saying, in no uncertain terms, that African American children, just as non-African American children, *should* know what was being tested by those items, even if a disparate impact was currently present. The teachers wanted to make sure that if African American youngsters could not currently perform well enough on those items, the presence of the items in the test would allow such deficits to be identified and, as a consequence, to be remediated. The teachers wanted to make sure that *future* disparate impacts would be eliminated.

If an assessment procedure leads to a differential impact on a particular group of students, then it is imperative to discern if the assessment procedure is biased. But if the assessment procedure does not offend or unfairly penalize any student subgroups, then the most likely explanation of disparate impact is prior instructional inadequacies for the low-performing group. In other words, there's nothing wrong with the

test, but there was definitely something wrong with the quality of education previously provided to the subgroup of students who scored poorly on the examination.

It is well known, of course, that genuine equality of education has not always been present in every locale. Thus, it should come as no surprise that some tests will, in particular settings, have a disparate impact on certain subgroups. But this does not necessarily signify the tests are biased. It may well be the tests are helping identify prior inequities in instruction that should be ameliorated.

One of the most commonly encountered factors leading to student's lower than anticipated performance on an exam, particularly a high-stakes exam, is that students have not had an adequate *opportunity to learn*. Opportunity to learn describes the extent to which students have had exposure to the instruction or information that gives them a reasonable chance to master whatever knowledge or skills being assessed by a test. Opportunity to learn simply captures the common-sense notion that if students have not been taught to do something that's to be tested, then those untaught students will surely not shine when testing time arrives.

A relatively recent illustration of a situation in which opportunity to learn was *not* present occurred when education officials in some states closed out the 2013–14 school year by administering newly developed assessments intended to measure students' mastery of a new, often unfamiliar, set of curricular aims—namely, the *Common Core State Standards (CCSS)*. Yet, in at least certain of those states, most teachers had not received sufficient professional development dealing with the *CCSS*. Accordingly, many of those teachers were unable to teach about the new content standards with any instructional effectiveness. As a consequence, many of the state's students ended up not having been taught about the *CCSS* and, unsurprisingly, scored poorly on the new tests. Did those lower than foreseen scores reflect the presence of assessment bias on those new *CCSS*-focused tests? Of course not. What was going on, quite obviously, was not assessment bias but, rather, a clear-cut case of students' trying to tackle a test's targeted content without having been given an opportunity to learn. Teachers must be wary of the opportunity-to-learn issue whenever substantially different content is being assessed by any tests linked to high-stakes decisions.

Let's conclude our consideration of assessment bias by dealing with two strategies for eliminating or at least markedly reducing the extent to which unsuitable content on assessment devices can distort certain students' scores. Such distortions, of course, erode the validity of the score-based interpretations educators arrive at when they use such assessment devices. And rotten interpretations about students' status, of course, usually lead to rotten decisions about those students.

JUDGMENTAL APPROACHES

One particularly useful way to identify any aspects of an assessment procedure that may be biased is to call on content-knowledgeable reviewers to *judgmentally scrutinize* the assessment procedure, item by item, to see if any items offend or unfairly penalize certain subgroups of students. When any important, high-stakes test is developed these days, it is customary to have a bias review panel consider its items in order to isolate and discard any that seem likely to contribute to assessment bias. After seeing how such a procedure is implemented for high-stakes tests, we'll consider how classroom teachers can carry out the essential features of judgmental bias-detection reviews for their own assessment procedures.

Bias Review Panels

For high-stakes tests such as a state's accountability exams, a bias review panel of, say, 15 to 25 reviewers is typically assembled. Each of the reviewers should be conversant with the content of the test being reviewed. For example, if a sixth-grade language arts accountability test were under development, the bias review committee might be comprised mostly of sixth-grade teachers along with a few district-level language arts curriculum specialists or university professors. The panel should be composed exclusively, or almost exclusively, of individuals from the subgroups who might be adversely impacted by the test. In other words, if the test is to be administered to minority students who are Asian American, Native American, African American, and Hispanic American, there should be representatives of each of those groups on the panel. There should also be a mix of male and female panelists so that they can attend to possible gender bias in items.

    After the bias review panel is assembled, its members should be provided with a thorough orientation regarding the overall meaning of fairness in testing and, more specifically, the assessment bias—perhaps along the lines of the discussion earlier in this chapter. Ideally, panelists should be given some guided practice in reviewing several assessment items deliberately designed to illustrate specific deficits—for instance, content that is offensive or content that unfairly penalizes certain subgroups. Discussions of such illustrative items usually help clarify the panel's understanding of assessment bias.

A Per-Item Absence-of-Bias Judgment

After the orientation, the bias review panelists should be asked to respond to a question such as the following for *each* of the test's items:

An Illustrative Absence-of-Bias Question for Bias Review Panelists

Might this item offend or unfairly penalize any group of students on the basis of personal characteristics, such as gender, ethnicity, religion, or race?

Panelists are to respond *yes* or *no* to each item using this question. Note the illustrative question does not ask panelists to judge whether an item *would* offend or unfairly penalize. Rather, the question asks whether an item *might* offend or unfairly penalize. In other words, if there's a *chance* the item might be biased, bias review panelists are to answer *yes* to the absence-of-bias question. Had the item-bias question used *would* instead of *might,* I hope you can see this renders it a less stringent form of per-item scrutiny.

The percentage of *no* judgments per item is then calculated so an average per-item absence-of-bias index (for the whole panel) can be computed for each item and, thereafter, for the entire test. The more *no* judgments panelists supply, the less bias they think is present in the items. If the test is still under development, items are generally discarded that are judged to be biased by several panelists. Because panelists are usually encouraged to indicate (via a brief written comment) why an item appears to be biased, it is often the case that an item will be discarded because of a *single* panelist's judgment if it is apparent this panelist spotted a deficit in the item that had been overlooked by other panelists.

An Overall Absence-of-Bias Judgment

Although having a bias review panel scrutinize the individual items in an assessment device is critical, there's always the chance the *items in aggregate* may be biased, particularly with respect to the degree to which they might offend certain students. For instance, as the bias review panelists consider the individual items, they may find few problems. Yet, when considered as a collectivity, the items may prove to be offensive. Suppose, for example, in an extensive series of mathematics word problems, the individuals depicted were almost always females. Although this gender disproportion was not apparent from panelists' reviews of individual items, it could be discerned from panelists' responses to an overall absence-of-bias question such as the following:

An Illustrative Overall Absence-of-Bias Question for Bias Review Panelists

Considering all of the items in the assessment device you just reviewed, do the items, taken as a whole, offend or unfairly penalize any group of students on the basis of personal characteristics, such as gender, ethnicity, religion, or race?

Similar to the item-by-item judgments of panelists, the percent of *no* responses by panelists to this overall absence-of-bias question can provide a useful index of whether the assessment procedure is biased. As with the individual item judgments, bias review panelists who respond *yes* to an overall absence-of-bias question are usually asked to indicate why. Typically, the deficits identified in response to this overall question can be corrected rather readily. For instance, in the previous example about too many females being described in the mathematics word problems, all that needs to be done is a bit of gender changing (verbally rather than surgically).

In review, then, judgmental scrutiny of an assessment procedure's items, separately or *in toto,* can prove effective in identifying items that contribute to assessment bias. Such items should be modified or eliminated.

EMPIRICAL APPROACHES

If a high-stakes educational test is to be administered to a large number of students, it is typically possible to gather tryout evidence regarding the performance of different groups of students on individual items and then review any items for potential bias for which there are substantial disparities between the performances of different groups. There are a number of different technical procedures for identifying items on which subgroups perform differently. Generally, these procedures are characterized as *differential item functioning (DIF)* procedures because the analyses are used to identify items that function differently for one group (for example, girls) than for another (for example, boys). Numerous DIF analysis procedures are now available for use in detecting potentially biased items.

Even after an item has been identified as a differentially functioning item, this does not automatically mean the item is biased. Recalling our discussion of the difference between assessment bias and disparate impact, it is still necessary to scrutinize a differentially functioning item to see if it is biased or, instead, is detecting the effects of prior instructional inadequacies for a particular group of students such as insufficient opportunity to learn. In most large-scale test-development projects these days, even after all items have been subjected to the judgmental scrutiny of a bias review panel, items identified as functioning differentially are "flagged" for a second look by bias reviewers (for example, by the earlier bias review panel or perhaps by a different bias review panel). Only those items that are, at this point, judgmentally identified as biased are excised from the test.

To reiterate, large numbers of students are required in order for empirical bias-reduction approaches to work. Several hundred responses per item for each subgroup under scrutiny are needed before a reasonably accurate estimate of an item's differential functioning can be made.

BIAS DETECTION IN THE CLASSROOM

If you're an experienced teacher or are preparing to be a teacher, what can you do about assessment bias in your own classroom? I have a deceptively simple but, I believe, accurate answer to this question. The answer is: *Become sensitive to the existence of assessment bias and the need to eliminate it.*

Assessment bias can transform an otherwise fine educational test into one that falls short of what's needed for fairness in testing. Assessment bias really can be a serious shortcoming of your own tests. As indicated earlier, a test that's biased won't allow you to make valid inferences about your students' learning levels. And if your inferences are invalid, who cares if you're making those inferences reliably? Absence-of-bias, in short, is significant stuff.

Okay, let's assume you've made a commitment to be sensitive to the possibility of bias in your own classroom assessments. How do you go about it? I recommend that you always review your own assessments, insofar as you can, from the perspective of the students you have in your classes—students whose experiences will frequently be decisively different from your own. Even if you're a Hispanic American and you have a dozen Hispanic American students, this does *not* mean that their backgrounds parallel yours.

What you need to do is *think seriously* about the impact that differing experiential backgrounds will have on the way students respond to your classroom assessments. You'll obviously not always be able to "get inside the heads" of the many different students you have, but try to.

My first teaching job was in a rural high school in an eastern Oregon town with a population of 1,500 people. I had grown up in a fairly large city and had no knowledge about farming or ranching. To me, a "range" was a gas or electric kitchen appliance on which one cooked meals. In retrospect, I'm certain that many of my classroom tests contained "city" content that might have confused my students. I'll bet anything that many of my early test items unfairly penalized some of the boys and girls who had rarely, if ever, left their farms or ranches to visit more metropolitan areas. And, given the size of our tiny town, almost any place on earth was "more metropolitan." But assessment bias was something I simply didn't think about back then. I hope you will.

Because some teachers are less familiar with some of the newer forms of assessments you'll be reading about in later chapters, particularly performance assessment (in Chapter 8), portfolio assessment (in Chapter 9), and a number of informal assessment procedures to be used as part of the formative-assessment process (in Chapter 12), those types of assessments contain serious potential for assessment bias. To illustrate, most performance assessments call for students to respond to a fairly elaborate task of some sort (such as researching a social issue and presenting an oral report to the class). Given that these tasks sometimes require students to draw heavily on their own experiences, it is imperative to select tasks that present the cherished "level playing field" to all students. You'd certainly not wish to use a performance assessment that gave an up-front advantage to students from more affluent families.

Then there's the problem of how to evaluate students' responses to performance assessments or how to judge the student-generated products in students' portfolios. All too often I have seen teachers evaluate students' responses on the basis of whether those responses displayed "good thinking ability." What those teachers were doing, unfortunately, was creating their own, off-the-cuff version of a group intelligence test—an assessment approach now generally repudiated.

PARENT TALK

Assume that you are White and were raised in a middle-class environment. During your fourth year of teaching, you've been transferred to an inner-city elementary school in which you teach a class of 27 fifth-graders, half of whom are African Americans. Suppose that Mrs. Johnson, a mother of one of your students, telephones you after school to complain about her son's test results in your class. Mrs. Johnson says, "George always got good grades until he came to your class. But on your tests, he always scores low. I think it's because your tests are biased against Black children!"

If I were you, here's how I'd respond to Mrs. Johnson:

"First, Mrs. Johnson, I really appreciate your calling about George's progress. We both want the very best for him, and now that you've phoned, I hope we can work together in his best interest.

"About George's test performance, I realize he hasn't done all that well on most of the tests. But I'm afraid it isn't because of test bias. Because this is my first year in this school, and because about half of my fifth-graders are African American, I was really worried that, as a White person, I *might* be developing tests that were biased against some of my students.

"So, during my first week on the job, I asked Ms. Fleming—another fifth-grade teacher who's African American—if she'd review my tests for possible bias. She agreed and she's been kind enough to review every single test item I've used this year. I try to be careful myself about identifying biased items, and I'm getting pretty good at it, but Ms. Fleming helped me spot several items, particularly at the start of the year, that might have been biased against African American children. I removed or revised all those items.

"What I think is going on in George's case, Mrs. Johnson, is the instruction he's received in the past. I think George is a very bright child, but I know your family transferred to our district this year from another state. I really fear that where George went to school in the past, he may not have been provided with the building-block skills he needs for my class.

"What I'd like to do, if you're willing, is to set up a conference either here at school or in your home, if that's more convenient, to discuss the particular skills George is having difficulty with. I'm confident we can work out an approach, with your assistance, that will help George acquire the skills he needs."

Now, how would you respond to Mrs. Johnson?

Students' responses to performance and portfolio assessments are too often judged on the basis of factors that are more background dependent than instructionally promotable. Assessment bias applies to *all* forms of testing, not merely paper-and-pencil tests.

If you want to expunge bias from your own assessments, try to review *every* item in *every* assessment from the perspective of whether there is anything present in the item that might *offend* or *unfairly penalize* any of your students. If you ever find such potential bias in any of your items, then without delay patch them up or plow them under.

You'll probably never be able to remove *all* bias from your classroom assessments. Biased content has a nasty habit of slipping past even the most bias-conscious classroom teacher. But if you show me 100 teachers who are seriously sensitized to the possibility of assessment bias in their own tests and 100 teachers who've not thought much about assessment bias, there's no doubt in my mind regarding which 100 teachers will create less biased assessments. My doubt-free judgment, of course, might be biased!

ASSESSING STUDENTS WITH DISABILITIES AND ENGLISH LANGUAGE LEARNERS

Assessment bias can blossom in often unforeseen ways when teachers attempt to assess two distinctive categories of children—namely, *students with disabilities* and *English language learners*. In the past, because these two groups of students often received the bulk of their instruction from educational specialists rather than regular classroom teachers, many teachers gave scant attention to the testing of such students. However, largely due to the enactment of far-reaching federal laws, today's classroom teachers need to understand, at the very least, some fundamentals about how to assess children with disabilities as well as English language learners. We'll briefly consider potential assessment bias as it relates to both of these types of students.

Children with Disabilities and Federal Law

Many teachers, when they hear the phrase *children with disabilities* immediately think of children who, because they are mentally retarded, are euphemistically regarded as *special education* students. Such perceptions are way off the mark. Actually, only about 10 percent of children with disabilities are mentally retarded. Fully two thirds of children with disabilities either have specific learning disabilities—almost 80 percent of which arise from students' problems with reading—or impairments in a child's speech or language. There are 13 categories of disability set forth in federal law, including such less-frequent disabilities as autism (2 percent of children with disabilities), emotional disturbance (8 percent), and hearing impairments (1 percent).

Federal law, you see, has triggered substantially reconceptualized views about how to teach and to test students with disabilities. The Education for All Handicapped Children Act (Public Law 94-142) was enacted in 1975 because of (1) a growing recognition of the need to properly educate children who had disabilities and (2) a series of judicial rulings requiring states to provide a suitable education for students with disabilities if those states were providing one for students without disabilities. Usually referred to simply as "P.L. 94-142," this influential law supplied federal funding to states, but only if those states appropriately educated children with disabilities.

Public Law 94-142 also installed the use of an *individualized education program*, or *IEP*, for a student with disabilities. An IEP is the federally prescribed document developed by parents, teachers, and specialized services providers (such as an audiologist) describing how a particular child with disabilities should be educated. An IEP represents a per-child plan that spells out annual curricular aims for the child, indicates how the student's attainment of those goals will be determined, specifies whatever related services are needed by the child, and sets forth any adjustments or substitutions in the assessments to be used with the child. The architects of P.L. 94-142 believed it would encourage many students with disabilities to be educated, to the extent possible, in regular classrooms.

In 1997, P.L. 94-142 was reauthorized and, at the same time, labeled the Individuals with Disabilities Act (IDEA). That reauthorization called for states and districts to identify curricular expectations for special education students that were as consonant as possible with the curricular expectations that had been established *for all other students*. Under IDEA, all states and districts were required to include students with disabilities in their assessment programs—and to publicly report those test results. However, because IDEA of 1997 contained few negative consequences for noncompliance, most of the nation's educators simply failed to comply.

The special education landscape, however, was significantly altered on January 8, 2002, when President George W. Bush affixed his signature to the No Child Left Behind (NCLB) law. Unlike IDEA of 1997, NCLB possessed significantly increased penalties for noncompliance. The act intends to improve the achievement levels of *all* students—including children with disabilities—and to do so in a way that such improvement will be *demonstrated* on state-chosen tests linked to each state's curricular aims. Students' test scores were to improve on a regular basis over a dozen years in order to reflect substantially improved student learning. Even though NCLB allowed states some flexibility in deciding how many more students must earn "proficient or higher" scores each year on that state's accountability tests, if a school failed to make adequate yearly progress (AYP) based on a state's 12-year improvement schedule, then the school was placed on a sanction-laden improvement track.

Importantly, NCLB required adequate yearly progress not only for students overall but also for subgroups reflecting race/ethnicity, the economically disadvantaged, students with limited English proficiency, and *students with disabilities*. Accordingly, if there were sufficient numbers of any of those subgroups in a school, and *one* of those subgroups failed to score high enough to make that subgroup's

AYP targets, then the whole school flopped on AYP. Obviously, the assessed performances of students with disabilities became far more significant to a school's educators than was the case prior to the enactment of NCLB.

In 2004, IDEA was reauthorized once again. At that juncture, however, there was already another significant federal statute on the books dealing with the assessment of students with disabilities—namely, NCLB. Federal lawmakers attempted to shape the reauthorized IDEA so it would be as consistent as possible with the assessment provisions of NCLB that had been enacted two years earlier. Even so, there were important procedural differences between IDEA and NCLB, though one could find few fundamental contradictions between those two laws. Remember that when P.L. 94-142 first trotted onto the scene, one of its most influential contributions was the IEP. Many teachers came to understand that an individualized education program was supposed to be just what it said it was— an *individualized* program for a particular student with disabilities. Thus, the push of IDEA has historically been directed toward an *individualized* approach to instruction and an *individualized* approach to assessing what a student has learned.

Instead of the more student-tailored approach embodied in IDEA, the accountability strategy embodied in NCLB was a far more *group-based* (and *subgroup-based*) approach than the kid-by-kid orientation of IDEA. I thought that a key congressional committee put it well when it observed, "IDEA and NCLB work in concert to ensure that students with disabilities are included in assessment and accountability systems. While IDEA focuses on the needs of the individual child, NCLB focuses on ensuring improved academic achievement for *all* students."[1]

The most important thing teachers need to understand about the instruction and assessment of students with disabilities is that the education of all but a *very* small group of those children must be aimed at precisely *the same curricular targets* as the curricular targets teachers have for all other students. Both NCLB and IDEA required the *same* content standards for *all* children—with no exceptions! However, for students with the most severe cognitive disabilities, it is possible to use different definitions of achievement. Thus, this small group of students can use modified ways to display their performance related to the same content standards. These modifications, under NCLB, took the form of **alternate assessments**. Such alternate assessments were to be used with only that super-small percent of children who suffer from the most severe cognitive disabilities. In other words, whereas the academic content standards must stay the same for all students, it is the academic achievement standards (performance levels) that can differ substantively for children who have the most severe cognitive disabilities.

Because IEPs are central to the assessment of many children with disabilities, I want to deal with the widespread misperception that IEPs are written documents allowing the parents and teachers of children with disabilities to do some serious bar-lowering, but to do so behind closed doors. Some general education teachers are not knowledgeable about the IEP process. To certain teachers, IEPs are born in clandestine meetings in which biased individuals simply soften expectations so that children with disabilities need not pursue the curricular aims identical to those sought for all other children. Perhaps such perceptions were warranted earlier on, but IEP regulations have been seriously modified in recent years. If those who create today's IEPs deliberately aim at anything less than the same content standards being pursued by all students, then such IEPs violate some big-stick federal statutes.

Accommodations

A prominent procedure to minimize assessment bias for students with disabilities is to employ *assessment accommodations*. An *accommodation* is a procedure or practice that permits students with disabilities to have an equitable access to instruction and assessment. The mission of an assessment accommodation is to eliminate or reduce the inference-distorting effects of a student's disabilities. It is not the purpose of accommodations to lower the aspirations educators have for students with disabilities. Typically, but not always, the accommodations provided to a student in an assessment setting are similar to the ones used during instruction for that student.

Although accommodations smack of fairness by providing students with opportunities to circumvent their disabilities, there's a critical limitation on just how much fairness-induction can be provided. Here's the rub: An assessment accommodation must not fundamentally alter the nature of the skills or knowledge being assessed. I can illustrate with respect to the skill of reading. Teachers clearly want children to learn to read—whether those children have disabilities or not. A teacher, however, can't simply look at a student and tell whether that student can read. That's because the ability to read is a *covert* skill. To determine a child's reading ability, teachers need to have a student engage in an *overt* act, such as silently reading a brief short story, then saying aloud—or in writing—what the story was about. A teacher then can, based on the child's *assessed* overt performance, arrive at an inference about the child's reading skills.

However, what if a teacher proposed to use an accommodation for a child with disabilities that called for a short story to be read aloud to the child? This would surely be a meaningful accommodation, and I suppose the child would enjoy hearing a read-aloud story. But suppose the child were then given a written or oral test about the content of the short story. Do you think the child's overt responses to that test would allow a teacher to arrive at a valid inference about the child's reading skills? Of course it wouldn't. Teachers who devise assessment accommodations for children with disabilities must be vigilant so they don't distort the essential nature of the skills or knowledge being measured.

A cracking good analysis of the accommodations needed for the instruction and assessment of students with disabilities was published in 2005 by the Council of Chief State School Officers (CCSSO). If you wish to delve more deeply into the accommodations arena, I recommend that manual highly. I've cited the CCSSO manual in the References at the close of this chapter (see Thompson et al., 2005). In that manual, there is a breakdown of the four common categories of accommodations typically considered for either assessment or instruction: presentation, response, setting, and timing and scheduling.

Authors of the CCSSO *Accommodations Manual* provide a convincing argument that students themselves should be involved, whenever practical, in the selection of their own accommodations. It is pointed out that if students are involved in the selection of their own accommodations, it is more likely that those accommodations will be used subsequently, especially when students reach adolescence and desire greater independence.

Accessibility

During the past decade or so, *accessibility* has become an emerging concept of increasing relevance for assessing students with disabilities—as well as for measuring students with limited English proficiency. Accessibility is intended to minimize assessment bias and therefore increase fairness. Accessibility refers to the notion that all test takers must have an unobstructed opportunity to demonstrate their status with respect to the construct(s) being measured by an educational test. If a student's access to the assessed construct(s) is impeded by skills and/or characteristics unrelated to what's being tested, this will limit the validity of score interpretations for particular uses. And those limitations in validity can affect both individuals and particular subgroups of test takers.

It is generally agreed that because 1997's Individuals with Disabilities Act (IDEA) called for students with disabilities to be given "access to the general curriculum," educators of such children became sensitized to the concept of accessibility. Although the term *access* has, in years past, not been used in this particular way, assessment specialists who work with special populations of students have concluded that the concept of accessibility captures a factor that, for many students, plays a prominent role in determining the fairness of testing.

What does it mean to test developers or classroom teachers that students, whether those students have disabilities or are learning English, must have access to the construct(s) being assessed? Well, for developers of major external exams such as a state's standardized accountability tests or a district's high school graduation test, it means that the test's developers must be continually on guard to make sure there are no features in a test's design that might preclude any student from having a chance to "show what they know"—that is, to demonstrate how they stack up against the construct(s) being measured. And for a teacher's classroom tests, it means the very same thing!

Put differently, both large-scale test developers and teachers who crank out their own tests must be constantly on guard to ensure that their assessments will provide total accessibility to each and every child. Given the wide range of student disabilities and the considerable variety of levels of students' English proficiency encountered in today's schools, this constant quest for accessibility often represents a genuine challenge for the test developers/teachers involved.

Universal Design

An increasingly applauded strategy for increasing accessibility to educational tests is the process of **universal design**. Universal design describes an approach to the building of tests that *from the very outset* of the test-construction process attempts to maximize accessibility for *all* intended test takers. In years past, tests were first built and then—often as an afterthought—attempts were made so that the tests could be made accessible to more students. The motivations for those sorts of after-the-fact accessibility enhancements were, of course, commendable. But after-the-fact attempts to change an already completed assessment instrument are almost certain to be less effective than one might wish.

When approaching test development from a universal-design perspective, however, the maximizing of accessibility governs the test developer's decisions from the very get-go. Test items and tasks are designed with an overriding motive in mind: to minimize construct-irrelevant features that might reduce access for the *complete* array of potential test takers, not merely the typical test takers. Universal design constitutes an increasingly prevalent mind-set on the part of major test developers. It is a mind-set that classroom teachers can—and should—develop for themselves.

English Language Learners

And what about students whose first language is not English? In other words, how should classroom teachers assess such students? First off, we need to do a bit of term-defining, because there are a number of descriptive labels for such youngsters being used these days. **English language learners (ELLs)** represent a diverse, fast-growing student population in the United States and Canada. Included in the ELL group are (1) students whose first language is not English and know little, if any, English; (2) students who are beginning to learn English but could benefit from school instruction; and (3) students who are proficient in English but need additional assistance in academic or social contexts. English language learners also include language minority students (also called "linguistic minority" students) who use a language besides English in the home. The federal government sometimes uses the term **limited English proficient (LEP)** to describe ELL students. Currently, most people, because they believe it more politically correct, describe those students as "English language learners," but it is equally accurate to employ the governmentally favored descriptor of "limited English proficient." I'll be using the ELL label here. (I suppose I should note that during several recent conferences I've attended in which English language learners have been discussed, I found a number of colleagues who work with such students simply referring to them as "language learners." I have no idea whether this label will become a widespread way of identifying such students, but don't be surprised if you occasionally run into it.)

Federal and state laws, if subjected to sufficient political pressure, are capable of being altered almost anytime. As I was wrapping up the writing of this eighth edition of *Classroom Assessment,* two significant assessment provisions of NCLB spelled out the federally required testing of ELL students. But, as noted in Chapter 1, the provisions of this law might change.

I indicated earlier that NCLB is the current reauthorization of a landmark federal 1965 law, the Elementary and Secondary Education Act (ESEA). Sometime soon, we have been told for many years now, another reauthorization of ESEA (or, if you prefer, NCLB) is slated to take place. Given the considerable intensity with which certain provisions of NCLB have been assailed and defended, it seems likely that there may well be substantial changes in the next version of ESEA. So, if you are interested in the assessment requirements of the law insofar as ELLs are concerned, be sure to be attentive to any such alterations. Until any changes take place, however, two NCLB requirements spelled out the kinds of assessments to be used with language-minority students.

First, there is the requirement to determine the degree to which certain subgroups of students—specifically those subgroups identified in NCLB—are making adequate yearly progress. One of these groups consists of "students with limited English proficiency." If there are sufficient numbers of ELL students in a school (or in a district) to yield "statistically reliable information," then a designated proportion of those students must have earned proficient-or-above scores on a state's accountability tests. If enough students don't earn those scores, a school (or district) will be regarded as having failed to make its AYP targets.

Interestingly, because federal officials have allowed states some latitude in deciding on the minimum numbers of students (in a subgroup) needed in order to provide "statistically reliable information," there is considerable variation from state to state in these subgroup minimum numbers. You will easily recognize that if a state had set its minimum numbers fairly high, then fewer schools and districts would be regarded as having failed AYP. This is because low-performing students in a particular subgroup need not be counted in AYP calculations if there were too few students (that is, below state-set minima) in a particular subgroup. Conversely, a state whose subgroup-minima had been set fairly low would find more of its schools or districts flopping on AYP because of one or more subgroups' shortcomings.

Although the state accountability tests administered to ELL students are typically written in English, students who are counted in AYP subgroup analyses were only those who had attended U.S. schools for 3 or more consecutive years. In other words, to satisfy the subgroup analyses required by NCLB, language-minority students had to take the very same tests that all other students took, but were counted for AYP purposes only after having attended U.S. schools for 3 years in a row. (On a case-by-case individual basis, NCLB allowed for a state's academic assessments to be written in another language if this would yield more accurate information about a student's achievement.)

Second, the NCLB contained another assessment requirement related to ELL students. The law called for states to employ separate "academic assessments of English language proficiency" so that, on an annual basis, such tests can measure

ELL students' skills in "oral language, reading, and writing." Because most states did not have such tests on hand (or, if they did, those tests usually measured beginning students' social English skills rather than the now required tests of students' academic English skills), we witnessed substantial test-development activity under way in individual states or, frequently, in test-development consortia from several participating states.

The technical quality of these tests to assess students' English language proficiency, of course, will be the chief determinant regarding whether valid inferences can be made regarding ELL students' mastery of English. Clearly, considerable attention must be given to evaluating the caliber of this emerging collection of assessment instruments.

Lest you think that the assessment of ELL students, once it is addressed seriously because of federal requirements, is going to be easy to pull off, think again. Jamal Abedi, one of the nation's leading authorities on the assessment of ELL students, has reminded us of a half-dozen issues that must be addressed if federal laws are going to accomplish for LEP students what those laws' architects intended (Abedi, 2004). He points to the following concerns:

1. *Inconsistency in ELL classification across and within states.* A variety of different classification criteria are used to identify ELL students among states and even within districts and schools in a state, thus affecting the accuracy of AYP reporting for ELL students.
2. *Sparse ELL populations.* In a large number of states and districts there are too few ELL students to permit meaningful analyses, thus distorting state and federal policy decisions in such settings.
3. *Subgroup instability.* Because a student's ELL status is not stable over time, a school's ELL population represents a moving, potentially unattainable, target. To illustrate, if a given ELL student's mastery of English has improved sufficiently, that student is moved out of the ELL group only to be replaced by a new student whose English proficiency is apt to be substantially lower. Therefore, even with superlative instruction, there is little chance of improving the AYP status of the ELL subgroup from year to year.
4. *Technical quality of AYP-determining assessment tools.* Because studies have shown that assessment instruments constructed for native English speakers have lower reliability and validity when used with ELL populations, results of such tests are likely to be misinterpreted when employed with ELL students.
5. *Lower baseline scores.* Because schools with large numbers of ELL students are likely to have lower baseline scores and thus may have improvement targets that will be unrealistically challenging, such schools may have difficulty in attaining state-set increments in students' achievement levels.
6. *Cut-scores for ELL students.* Unlike the previous version of ESEA in which a student's weaker performance in one subject area could be compensated for by a higher performance in another subject (referred to as a *compensatory*

model), federal statutes may require use of a *conjunctive* model in which students' performances in all assessed subject areas must be acceptable. Students' performances in mathematics are apt to be less dependent on language prowess than their performances in reading/language arts where language demands are higher. This, then, renders the AYP expectations for schools with large ELL populations more challenging than those imposed on schools with fewer ELL students.

Even with all these issues that must be considered when assessing students in the accountability structure of federal assessment-related statutes, Abedi believes the isolation of subgroup performances is "a step in the right direction." He argues that state and federal officials appear to be addressing many of these issues at this time. Abedi regards this as necessary to resolve these problems if genuine fairness is to be attained in the assessment-based accountability focused on ELL students. And this quest means there needs to be some sensible judgments made by teachers. It is decisively *unsmart* to force a child who speaks and reads only Spanish to take an English language test about mathematics and then conclude the child can't do math because the child's test score is low.

The issue of whether teachers should try to make available versions of their tests in non-English languages is, unfortunately, often decided on totally practical grounds. In many settings, teachers may find a dozen or more first languages spoken by their students. In some urban settings, more than 100 first languages other than English are found in a district's students. And, if an attempt is made to create an alternate assessment only in the *most* common language a teacher's students possess, how fair is this to those students whose first languages aren't found in sufficient numbers to warrant the creation of a special test in their native language?

Assessment accommodations, in the form of giving language-minority students more time or the use of dictionaries, can, depending on students' levels of English mastery, often help deal with the measurement of such students. In recent years, several of the larger test-development firms have been experimenting with supplying cartoon-like illustrations of the meaning of key words in some test items. If this more generic approach is successful, it would help address the myriad non-English languages that require language-specific dictionaries or glossaries. Results of early experiments with this sort of pictorial-definition approach are too fragmentary, however, for the immediate application of the approach.

It is difficult to attend any conference on educational assessment these days without finding a number of sessions devoted to the measurement of language minority students or students with disabilities. Clearly, an effort is being made to assess these children in a fashion that is not biased against them. But, just as clearly, the problems of measuring such students with fairness, compassion, and accuracy are nontrivial.

Clearly, the accurate assessment of students whose first language is not English will continue to pose a serious problem for the nation's teachers. To provide equivalent tests in English and all other first languages spoken by students represents an essentially impossible task. The policy issue now being hotly contested in the United States is whether to create equivalent tests for the most numerous of our schools' language-minority students.

When ESEA is reauthorized, it is widely expected that the new version of this 1965 federal statute will deal with the education and assessment of ELL students differently than did NCLB. Please attend to the ELL-related provisions of the reauthorized ESEA when (and if!) it is ever refurbished.

WHAT DO CLASSROOM TEACHERS REALLY NEED TO KNOW ABOUT FAIRNESS?

Classroom teachers need to know that if assessment bias exists, then assessment fairness scampers out the door. Unfairness bias in educational testings is probably less prevalent than it was a decade or two ago because most measurement specialists, after having been sensitized to the presence of assessment bias, now strive to eliminate such biases. However, for the kinds of teacher-developed assessment procedures seen in typical classrooms, systematic attention to bias eradication is much less common.

All classroom teachers *routinely* need to use fairness—and, in particular, absence-of-bias—as one of the evaluative criteria by which they judge their own assessments and those educational assessments developed by others. For instance, if you are ever called on to review the quality of a high-stakes test—such as a district-developed or district-adopted examination whose results will have a meaningful impact on students' lives—be sure that suitable absence-of-bias procedures, both judgmental and empirical, were employed during the examination's development.

But what about your own tests? How much effort should you devote to making sure your tests are fair, and that they don't offend or unfairly penalize any of your students because of personal characteristics such as ethnicity or gender? My answer is that you really do need to devote attention to absence-of-bias for *all* your classroom assessment procedures. For the least significant of your assessment procedures, I suggest you simply heighten your consciousness about bias eradication as you generate the test items or, having done so, as you review the completed test.

For more important examinations, try to enlist the assistance of a colleague to review your assessment instruments. If possible, attempt to secure the help of colleagues from the same subgroups as those represented in your students. For instance, if many of your students are Hispanics (and you aren't), then try to get a Hispanic colleague to look over your test's items to see if there are any that might offend or unfairly penalize Hispanic students. When you enlist a colleague to help you review your tests for potential bias, try to carry out a mini-version of the bias review panel procedures described in the chapter. Briefly describe to your co-workers how you define assessment bias, give them a succinct orientation to the review task, and structure their reviews with absence-of-bias questions such as those seen earlier in the chapter.

But What Does This Have to Do with Teaching?

Decades ago I was asked to serve as an expert witness in a federal court case taking place in Florida. It was known as the *Debra P.* versus *Turlington* case, because Ralph Turlington was the Florida Commissioner of Education and Debra P. was one of nine African American children who were about to be denied high school diplomas because they had not passed a state-administered basic skills test. A class-action lawsuit had been brought against Florida to stop this test-based denial of diplomas.

When I was invited to serve as a witness for the state, I was initially pleased. After all, to be an "expert" witness in a federal court case sounded like a form of instant tenure. So, my first inclination was to agree to serve as a witness. But then I learned that Florida's high school graduation test was having a substantial disparate impact on the state's African American children, far more of whom were going to be denied diplomas than their White counterparts. I pondered whether I wanted to support an assessment program that would surely penalize more minority than majority children.

So, before making up my mind about becoming a witness in the *Debra P.* case, I consulted a number of my African American friends at UCLA and in the Los Angeles Unified School District. "Should I," I asked, "take part in the support of a test that denies diplomas to so many African American youngsters?"

Well, *without exception,* my African American friends urged me to accept the Florida assignment. The essence of their argument was simple. What was going on in Florida, they claimed, was the awarding of "counterfeit" diplomas to African American children. If so many African American youngsters were actually failing the state's basic skills test, then it was quite likely that those children did not possess the necessary basic skills. Yet, even without those basic skills, many of Florida's African American children had *previously* been given high school diplomas that allowed them to graduate *without* the skills they needed. My friends made it clear. As one put it, "Get your tail down to Tallahassee and support any test that shows many African American children are being instructionally shortchanged. You can't fix something if you don't know it's broken."

And that's where bias detection comes in. If teachers can eliminate bias from their own assessments, then any gaps in performance levels of minority and majority students can be attributed to instruction, not shortcomings in a test. Achievement gaps, properly identified, can then be ameliorated instructionally. If there's no recognition of a bona fide gap, then there's little reason for instructional alterations.

(As a postscript, the *Debra P.* case turned out to be an important precedent-setter. It was ruled that a state *can* deny a high school diploma on the basis of a basic skills test, but if the test covers content that students have not had an opportunity to learn, then this violates a student's—that is, a U.S. citizen's—constitutionally guaranteed property rights. I liked the ruling a lot.)

Most importantly, if you personally realize how repugnant all forms of assessment unfairness are, and how assessment bias can distort certain students' performances even if the bias was inadvertently introduced by the test's developer, you'll be far more likely to eliminate assessment bias in your own tests. In education, as in any other field, assessment bias should definitely be *absent*.

The presence of assessment-related federal laws obliges today's teachers to rethink the ways they should test students with disabilities and ELL students. With few exceptions, children with disabilities are to be assessed (and instructed) in relation to the same curricular goals as all other children. This can often be accomplished through the use of accommodations—that is, alterations in presentations, responses, settings, and timing/scheduling. Assessment accommodations, however, must never alter the fundamental nature of the skill or knowledge being assessed. Assessment accommodations can also be used to reduce potential bias associated with the testing of ELL students. Given the enormous number of first languages other than English now found in the nation's schools, financial limitations tend to prevent the development of suitable assessments for many language-minority students.

CHAPTER SUMMARY

This chapter on fairness in testing was, quite naturally, focused on how educators make their tests fair. Assessment bias was described as any element in an assessment procedure that offends or unfairly penalizes students because of personal characteristics, such as their gender and ethnicity. Assessment bias, when present, was seen to distort certain students' performances on educational tests, hence reduce the validity of score-based interpretations about those students. The two chief contributors to assessment unfairness were identified as offensiveness and unfair penalization. The essential features of both of these factors were considered. It was contended that an examination having a disparate impact on a particular subgroup was not necessarily biased, although such a differential impact certainly would warrant further scrutiny of the examination's content to discern if assessment bias was actually present. In many instances, disparate impact from an examination simply indicates that certain groups of students have previously received inadequate instruction or an insufficient opportunity to learn.

Two procedures for identifying unfair—that is, biased—segments of educational assessment devices were described. A *judgmental* approach relies on the considered opinions of properly oriented bias reviewers. Judgmental approaches to bias detection can be formally employed with high-stakes tests or less formally used by classroom teachers. An *empirical* approach that relies chiefly on differential item functioning can also be used, although its application requires large numbers of students. It was recommended that classroom teachers be vigilant in the identification of bias, whether in their own tests or in the tests of others. For detecting bias in their own tests, classroom teachers were urged to adopt a judgmental review strategy consonant with the importance of the assessment procedures involved.

Issues associated with the assessment of ELL students or students with disabilities were identified near the chapter's conclusion. In many cases, assessment accommodations can yield more valid inferences about students with disabilities or who have less conversance with English. In other instances, alternate assessments need to be developed. Neither of these assessment modifications, however, is completely satisfactory in coping with this important assessment problem. Fairness, from an assessment perspective, currently appears to be much more difficult to attain in the case of students with disabilities and ELL students. Two relevant concepts, *accessibility* and *universal design,* that hold promise for assessing such learners were introduced and advocated.

Determining Your Outcome Mastery

The dominant mission of this chapter was for you to acquire a solid understanding of what's meant by *assessment bias*—and, having acquired that understanding, to know how to get rid of it, or at least diminish it dramatically. The Mastery Checks for this chapter, then, assess your attainment of this chief outcome:

> *An understanding of the nature of assessment bias and the procedures by which it can be reduced in both large-scale tests and classroom assessments*

Remember, when teachers construct their own tests, those teachers must constantly fend off unfairness—usually present in the form of assessment bias—because, if they don't, the validity of a teacher's score-based inferences will be reduced or, possibly, completely obliterated.

Complete both the Selected-Response and the Constructed-Response quizzes and think about the feedback you receive for each quiz.

MyEdLab *Selected-Response Check of Outcome Mastery*

MyEdLab *Constructed-Response Check of Outcome Mastery*

After completing both quizzes, go to the Learning Outcome Mastery Determination, where you will decide whether you've mastered the chapter's learning outcome or whether you need further study.

MyEdLab *Learning Outcome Mastery Determination*

References

Abedi, J. (2004). "The No Child Left Behind Act and English language learners: Assessment and accountability issues," *Educational Researcher, 33*, no. 1: 4–14.

Abedi, J. (2008). "Classification system for English language learners: Issues and recommendations," *Educational Measurement: Issues and Practice, 27*, no. 3 (Fall): 17–31.

American Educational Research Association. (2014). *Standards for educational and psychological testing*. Washington, DC: Author.

Pennock-Roman, M., and Rivera, C. (2011). "Mean effects of test accommodations for ELLs and non-ELLs: A meta-analysis of experimental studies," *Educational Measurement: Issues and Practice, 30*, no. 3 (Fall): 10–28.

Rose, M. (2013). "Being careful about character," *Phi Delta Kappan, 95*, no. 2 (October): 44–46.

Solano-Flores, G, Wang, C., Kachchaf, R., Soltero-Gonzalez, L., and Nguyen-Le, K. (2014). "Developing testing accommodations for English language-learners: Illustrations as visual supports for item accessibility," *Educational Assessment, 19*, no. 4: 267–283.

Thompson, S. J., et al. (2005, August). *Accommodations manual: How to select, administer, and evaluate use of accommodations for instruction and assessment of students with disabilities* (2nd ed.). Washington, DC: Council of Chief State School Officers.

Wolf, M. K., Farnsworth, T., and Herman, J. (2008). "Validity issues in assessing English language learners' language proficiency," *Educational Assessment, 13*, nos. 2–3: 80–107.

Endnote

1. U.S. Congressional Committee on Education and the Workforce. (2005, February 17). *IDEA Guide to Frequently Asked Questions* (p. 10). Washington, DC: Author.

6

Selected-Response Tests

The ability to accurately employ
professionally accepted item-
writing guidelines, both general
and item-type specific, when
constructing selected-response
items or evaluating those items
constructed by others

In this and the following four chapters, you will learn how
to construct almost a dozen different kinds of test items you
might wish to use for your own classroom assessments. As
suggested in the preceding chapters, you really need to
choose item types that mesh properly with the inferences
you want to make about students—and to be sure those inferences are directly linked to the educational decisions you
need to make. Just as the child who's convinced that vanilla
is ice cream's only flavor won't benefit from a 36-flavor ice
cream emporium, the more item types you know about, the
more appropriate your selection of item types will be. In
this chapter and the next four, you'll be learning about blackberry-ripple exams
and mocha-mango assessment devices.

Let me level with you regarding what you can really expect after wading
through the exposition about item construction contained in the upcoming chapters. Unless you're a remarkably quick study, you'll probably finish the chapters
and *not* be instantly transformed into a consummately skilled test constructor.
It takes more than reading a set of fairly brief chapters to turn someone into a
capable item developer. But, just as the journey of a thousand miles begins with a
single step, you'll have initiated a tentative trot toward the Test Construction Hall
of Fame. You'll have learned the essentials of how to construct the most common
kinds of classroom assessments.

What you'll need after you complete the five test-construction chapters
is tons of practice in churning out classroom assessment devices. And, if you
remain in teaching for a while, such practice opportunities will surely come
your way. Ideally, you'll be able to get some feedback about the quality of
your classroom assessment procedures from a supervisor or colleague who
is clearheaded and/or conversant with educational measurement. If a competent cohort critiques your test-construction efforts, you'll profit by being able
to make needed modifications in how you create your classroom assessment
instruments.

EXPANDING ELECTRONIC OPTIONS

Once upon a time, when teachers churned out their classroom tests, about the only alternative open to those teachers was reliance on paper to present items that, then, were responded to by students using pencils or pens. Oh, if you head back far enough in history, you might find Egyptian teachers relying on papyrus or pre-history teachers dishing up quizzes on tree bark.

But we have comfortably ensconced (some being more ensconced than others) ourselves into a technological age in which whole classrooms full of students possess laptop computers, electronic tablets, or similar devices that can be employed during instruction *and assessment.* Accordingly, because the availability of such electronically provided assessment options depends almost totally on what's available for use in a particular district or school, some of the test-construction guidelines you will encounter in the following pages may need to be massaged because of electronic limitations in the way a test's items can be written. To illustrate, you'll learn in this chapter how to create "matching" items for a classroom assessment. Well, one of the recommendations to teachers who use such items is that they put everything for a given item on only one page (of paper)—so that the students need not flip back and forth between pages when selecting their answers. But, what if the electronic devices that a teacher's students have been given do not provide sufficient room to follow this all-on-one-page guideline?

Well, in that situation it makes sense for a teacher to arrive at the most reasonable/sensible solution possible. Thus, the test-construction guidelines you'll encounter from here on in this book will be couched almost always in terms suitable for paper-presented tests. If you must create classroom assessments using electronic options that fail to permit implementation of the guidelines presented, just do the best job you can in adapting a guideline to the electronic possibilities at hand. Happily, the use of electronic hardware will typically expand, not truncate, your assessment options.

TEN (DIVIDED BY TWO) ITEM-WRITING COMMANDMENTS

As you can discern from this chapter's title, it's going to describe how to construct selected-response kinds of test items. You'll learn how to create four different varieties of selected-response test items—namely, binary-choice items, multiple binary-choice items, multiple-choice items, and matching items. All four of these selected-response kinds of items can be used effectively by teachers to derive defensible inferences about students' cognitive status—that is, the knowledge and skills teachers typically try to promote in their students.

But no matter whether you're developing selected-response or constructed-response kinds of test items, there are several general guidelines that, if adhered to, will lead to better assessment procedures. Because the original Ten Commandments were stated in fairly stern "Thou shall not" form, and have proven successful in shaping many folks' behavior, I shall now dish out five general item-writing commandments structured along the same lines. If followed, these commandments won't get you into heaven, but they will make your assessment schemes slightly more divine. All five commandments are presented in a box. A subsequent discussion of each commandment will help you understand how to adhere to the five item-writing mandates being discussed. It will help if you refer to each of the following item-writing commandments (guidelines) before reading the discussion of that commandment.

Five General Item-Writing Commandments

1. Thou shall not provide opaque directions to students regarding how to respond to your assessment instruments.
2. Thou shall not employ ambiguous statements in your assessment items.
3. Thou shall not provide students with unintentional clues regarding appropriate responses.
4. Thou shall not employ complex syntax in your assessment items.
5. Thou shall not use vocabulary that is more advanced than required.

Opaque Directions

The first item-writing commandment deals with a topic most teachers haven't thought seriously about—the directions for their classroom tests. Teachers who have been laboring to create a collection of test items typically know the innards of those items very well. Thus, because of the teacher's intimate knowledge not only of the items but also how students are supposed to deal with those items, it is often the case that only sketchy directions are provided to students regarding how to respond to a test's items. Yet, of course, unclear test-taking directions can result in confused test takers. And the responses of confused test takers don't lead to very accurate inferences about those test takers.

Flawed test directions are particularly problematic when students are being introduced to forms of assessment with which they're not very familiar, such as the performance tests I'll be describing in Chapter 8 or the multiple binary-choice tests to be discussed later in this chapter. It is useful to create directions for students early in the game when you're developing an assessment instrument. When generated as a last-minute afterthought, test directions typically turn out to be tawdry.

Ambiguous Statements

The second item-writing commandment deals with ambiguity. In all kinds of classroom assessments, ambiguous writing is to be avoided. If your students aren't really sure about what you mean in the tasks you present to them, the students are apt to misinterpret what you're saying and, as a consequence, come up with incorrect responses even though they might really know how to respond correctly. For example, sentences in which pronouns are used can frequently be unclear about the individual or individuals to whom the pronoun refers. Suppose, in a true–false test item, you asked your students to indicate whether the following statement was true or false: "Leaders of developing nations have tended to distrust leaders of developed nations due to their imperialistic tendencies." Because it is ambiguous regarding whether the pronoun *their* refers to the "leaders of developing nations" or to the "leaders of developed nations," and because the truth or falsity of the statement depends on the pronoun's referent, students are likely to be confused.

Because you will typically be writing your own assessment items, *you* will know what you mean. At least you ought to. However, try to slide yourself, at least figuratively, into the shoes of your students. Reread your assessment items from the perspective of the students, and modify any statements apt to be even a mite ambiguous to those less well-informed students.

Unintended Clues

The third of our item-writing commandments calls for you to *intentionally* avoid something *unintentional*. Well, nobody said that following commandments was going to be easy! What this commandment is trying to sensitize you to is the tendency of test-development novices to inadvertently provide clues to students about appropriate responses. As a consequence, students come up with correct responses even if they don't possess the knowledge or skill being assessed.

For example, inexperienced item writers often tend to make the correct answer to multiple-choice items twice as long as the incorrect answers. Even clucko students will opt for the lengthy response; they get so many more words for their choice. As another example of how inexperienced item writers unintentionally dispense clues, absolute qualifiers such as *never* and *always* are sometimes used for the false items in a true–false test. Because even uninformed students know there are few absolutes in this world, they gleefully (and often unthinkingly) indicate such items are false. One of the most blatant examples of giving unintended clues occurs when writers of multiple-choice test items initiate those items with incomplete statements such as "The bird in the story was an …" and then offer answer options in which only the correct answer begins with a vowel. For instance, even though you never read the story referred to in the previous incomplete statement, if you encountered the following four response options, I bet you'd know the correct answer: A. Falcon, B. Hawk, C. Robin, D. Owl. The article *an* gives the game away.

Unintended clues are seen more frequently with selected-response items than constructed-response items, but even in supplying background information to students for complicated constructed-response items, the teacher must be wary of unintentionally pointing truly unknowledgeable students down the correct-response trail.

Computer-Adaptive Assessment: Its Seductive Allure

Large-scale assessments, such as statewide accountability tests or nationally standardized achievement tests, are definitely different from the classroom tests teachers might, during a dreary weekend, whip up for their students. Despite those differences, the assessment tactics used in large-scale tests should not be totally unknown to teachers. After all, parents of a teacher's students might occasionally toss out questions at a teacher about such tests, and what teacher wants to be seen, when it comes to educational tests, as a no-knowledge ninny?

One of the two multistate assessment consortia (the Smarter Balanced Assessment Consortium) is committed to have its major tests use *computer-adaptive assessment* to measure students' mastery of the *Common Core State Standards (CCSS)* adopted as curricular aims by so many states during 2010 and 2011. Therefore, given the likelihood that students in many states will be tested by computer-adaptive assessments, a brief description of this assessment approach is in order.

Not all assessments involving computers are computer-adaptive. *Computer-based assessments* rely on computers to deliver test items to students. Moreover, students respond to these computer-transmitted items by using a computer. This form of computer-abetted assessment is becoming more and more popular as (1) schools acquire enough computers to make the approach practicable and (2) states and school districts secure sufficient "bandwidth" (whatever that is!) to transmit tests and receive students' responses electronically. Computer-based assessments, as you can see, rely on computers only as delivery and retrieval mechanisms. Computer-adaptive assessment is something quite different.

Here's how computer-adaptive assessment works. Notice, incidentally, the key term *adaptive* in its name. That word is your key to understanding how this approach to educational assessment functions. As a student takes this kind of test, the student is given items of known difficulty levels. Then, based on the student's responses to those initial items, the computer supplies new items whose difficulties mesh with the student's earlier answers. For instance, if a student is answering correctly the early items doled out by the computer, then the next items popping up on the screen will be more difficult ones. Conversely, if the student stumbles on the initially received items, the computer will then provide easier items to the student, and so on. In short, the computer's program constantly *adapts* to the student's responses by providing items matched to the student's assessment-determined level of achievement.

Using this adaptive approach, a student's mastery level regarding whatever the test is measuring can be determined with far fewer items than would typically be the case. This is because, in a typical test, many of the test's items might be too difficult or too easy for a particular student. Accordingly, one of the payoffs of computer-adaptive testing is that it saves testing time—and the stolen instructional minutes that are often snatched away from teachers because of externally imposed assessment obligations.

But there's a limitation of computer-adaptive testing you need to recognize. It stems from the necessity for all the items in such an approach to be measuring a *single variable*, such as students' "mathematical mastery." Because many, many items are needed to make computer-adaptive assessment purr properly, and because the varying difficulties of these items must *all* be linked to what's sometimes referred to as "a unidimensional trait" (such as a child's overall reading prowess), computer-adaptive assessment precludes the possibility of providing student-specific diagnostic data. Too few items dealing with a particular subskill or a body of enabling knowledge can be administered during a student's abbreviated testing time. In other words, whereas computer-adaptive assessment can supply teachers with an efficiently garnered *general fix* on a student's status with respect to what's often a broadly conceptualized curricular aim, it won't reveal a student's specific strengths and weaknesses.

Complex Syntax

Complex syntax, although it sounds like an exotic surcharge on cigarettes and alcohol, is often encountered in the assessment items of neophyte item writers. Even though some teachers may regard themselves as Steinbecks-in-hiding, an assessment instrument is no setting in which to wax eloquent. This fourth item-writing

commandment directs you to avoid complicated sentence constructions and, instead, use very simple sentences. Although esteemed writers such as Thomas Harding and James Joyce are known for their convoluted and clause-laden writing styles, I'll wager they would have been mediocre item writers. Too many clauses, except at Christmas-time, mess up test items. (For readers needing a clue regarding the previous sentence's cryptic meaning, think of a red-garbed guy who brings presents.)

Difficult Vocabulary

Our fifth and final item-writing commandment is fairly straightforward. It indicates that when writing educational assessment items, *you should eschew obfuscative verbiage*. In other words, in almost *any* other words, use vocabulary suitable for the students who'll be taking your tests. Assessment time is not the occasion for you to trot out your best collection of polysyllabic terms or to secure a series of thesaurus-induced thrills. The more advanced the vocabulary level is in your assessment devices, the more likely you'll fail to get a good fix on your students' true status. They will have been laid low by the overblown vocabulary. In the case of the terminology to be used in classroom assessment instruments, simple wins.

In review, you've now seen five item-writing commandments that apply to any kind of classroom assessment device you develop. They certainly apply to tests containing selected-response items. And that's what we'll be looking at in the rest of the chapter. More specifically, you'll be encountering a series of item-writing guidelines to follow when constructing particular kinds of selected-response items. For convenience, we can refer to these guidelines linked to particular categories of items as "item-category guidelines" or "item-specific guidelines." These item-category guidelines are based either on empirical research evidence or on decades of teachers' experience in using such items. If you opt to use any of the item types to be described here in your own classroom tests, try to follow the guidelines for that kind of item. Your tests will typically turn out to be better than if you hadn't.

Here, and in several subsequent chapters, you'll be encountering sets of item-writing, item-revision, and response-scoring guidelines that you'll be encouraged to follow. Are the accompanying guidelines *identical* to the guidelines you're likely to find in other textbooks written about classroom assessment? No, they are not *identical*, but if you were to line up all of the textbooks ever written about classroom testing, you'll find that their recommendations regarding the care and feeding of items for classroom assessment are fundamentally similar.

BINARY-CHOICE ITEMS

A *binary-choice item* gives students only two options from which to select. The most common form of binary-choice item is the *true–false item*. Educators have been using true–false tests probably as far back as Socrates. (True or False: Plato was a type of serving-dish used by Greeks for special meals.) Other variations of binary-choice items would be those in which students must choose between yes–no, right–wrong, correct–incorrect, fact–opinion, and so on.

The virtue of binary-choice items is they are typically so terse that students can respond to many items in a short time. Therefore, it is possible to cover a large amount of content in a brief assessment session. The greatest weakness of binary-choice items is that, because there are only two options, students have a 50-50 chance of guessing the correct answer even if they don't have the foggiest idea of what's correct. If a large number of binary-choice items are used, however, this weakness tends to evaporate. After all, although students might guess their way correctly through a few binary-choice items, they would need to be extraordinarily lucky to guess their way correctly through 30 such items.

Here are five item-category guidelines for writing binary-choice items. A brief discussion of each guideline is provided in the following paragraphs.

Item-Writing Guidelines for Binary-Choice Items

1. Phrase items so that a superficial analysis by the student suggests a wrong answer.
2. Rarely use negative statements, and never use double negatives.
3. Include only one concept in each statement.
4. Have an approximately equal number of items representing the two categories being tested.
5. Keep item length similar for both categories being tested.

Phrasing Items to Elicit Thoughtfulness

Typically, binary items are quite brief, but brevity need not reflect simplistic choices for students. In order to get the most payoff from binary-choice items, you'll want to phrase items so students who approach the items superficially will answer them incorrectly. Thus, if you were creating the items for a true–false test, you would construct statements for your items that were not blatantly true or blatantly false. Blatancy in items rarely leads to accurate inferences about students. Beyond blatancy avoidance, however, you should phrase at least some of the items so if students approach them unthinkingly, they'll choose false for a true statement and vice versa. What you're trying to do is to get students to *think* about your test items and, thereby, give you a better idea about how much good thinking the students can do.

Minimizing Negatives

With binary-choice items, many students have a really difficult time responding to negatively phrased items. For instance, suppose in a true–false test you were asked to decide about the truth or falsity of the following statement: "The League of Nations was not formed immediately after the conclusion of World War II." What the item is looking for as a correct answer to this statement is *true*, because the League of Nations was in existence prior to World War II. Yet, the existence of the *not* in the item really will confuse some students. They'll be apt to answer *false* even if they know the League of Nations was functioning before World War II commenced.

Because I've churned out my share of true–false items over the years, I know all too well how tempting it is to simply insert a *not* into an otherwise true statement. But don't yield to the temptation. Only rarely succumb to the lure of the nagging negative in binary-choice items. Items containing double negatives or triple negatives (if you could contrive one) are obviously to be avoided.

Avoiding Double-Concept Items

The third guideline for binary-choice items directs you to focus on only a single concept in each item. If you are creating a statement for a right–wrong test, and have an item in which half of the statement is clearly right and the other half is clearly wrong, you make it mighty difficult for students to respond correctly. The presence of two concepts in a single item, even if both are right or both are wrong, tends to confuse students and, as a consequence, yields test results apt to produce inaccurate inferences about those students.

Balancing Response Categories

If you're devising a binary-choice test, try to keep an approximately equal number of items representing the two response categories. For example, if it's a true–false test, make sure you have somewhat similar proportions of true and false statements. It's not necessary to have exactly the same number of true and false items. The proportion of true and false items, however, should be roughly the same. This fourth guideline is quite easy to follow if you simply keep it in mind when creating your binary-choice items.

Maintaining Item-Length Similarity

The fifth guideline is similar to the fourth because it encourages you to structure your items so there are no give-away clues associated with item length. If your two response categories are *accurate* and *inaccurate*, make sure the length of the accurate statements is approximately the same as the length of the inaccurate statements. When creating true–false tests, there is a tendency to toss in qualifying clauses for the true statements so those statements, properly qualified, are truly true—but also long! As a result, there's a systematic pattern wherein long statements are true and short statements are false. As soon as students catch on to this pattern, they can answer items correctly without even referring to an item's contents.

In review, we've considered five item-writing guidelines for binary-choice items. If you'll follow those guidelines and keep your wits about you when creating binary-choice items, you'll often find this type of test will prove useful in the classroom. And that's true, not false.

MULTIPLE BINARY-CHOICE ITEMS

A *multiple binary-choice item* is one in which a cluster of items is presented to students, requiring a binary response to each of the items in the cluster. Typically, but not always, the items are related to an initial statement or set of statements. Multiple binary-choice items are formatted so they look like traditional multiple-choice tests. In a multiple-choice test, the student must choose one answer from several options, but in the multiple binary-choice test, the student must make a response for each statement in the cluster. Figure 6.1 is an example of a multiple binary-choice item.

David Frisbie (1992) reviewed research regarding such items and concluded that multiple binary-choice items are (1) highly efficient for gathering student achievement data, (2) more reliable than other selected-response items, (3) able to measure the same skills and abilities as multiple-choice items dealing with comparable content, (4) a bit more difficult for students than multiple-choice tests, and (5) perceived by students to be more difficult but more efficient than multiple-choice items. Frisbie believes that when teachers construct multiple binary-choice items, they must be attentive to all of the usual considerations in writing regular binary-choice items. However, he suggests the following two additional guidelines.

Item-Writing Guidelines for Multiple Binary-Choice Items

1. Separate item clusters vividly from one another.
2. Make certain that each item meshes well with the cluster's stimulus material.

---

figure 6.1 ■ An Illustrative Multiple True-False Item

• • • Suppose that a dozen of your students completed a 10-item multiple-choice test and earned the following number of correct scores:

5, 6, 7, 7, 7, 7, 8, 8, 8, 8, 9, 10

9. The median for your students' scores is 7.5.   (True)

10. The mode for the set of scores is 8.0.   (False)

11. The range of the students' scores is 5.0.   (True)

12. The median is different than the mean.   (False)

Separating Clusters

Because many students are familiar with traditional multiple-choice items, and because each of those items is numbered, there is some danger that students may become confused by the absence of numbers where such numbers are ordinarily found. Thus, be sure to use some kind of formatting system to make it clear a new cluster is commencing. In the illustrative item seen in Figure 6.1, notice that three dots (• • •) have been used to signify the beginning of a new cluster of items. You can use asterisks, lines, boxes, or some similar way of alerting students to the beginning of a new cluster.

Coordinating Items with Their Stem

In multiple-choice items, the first part of the item—the part preceding the response options—is called the *stem*. For multiple binary-choice items, we refer to the first part of the item cluster as the cluster's stem or stimulus material. The second item-writing guideline for this item type suggests you make sure all items in a cluster are, in fact, linked in a meaningful way to the cluster's stem. If they're not, then you might as well use individual binary-choice items rather than multiple binary-choice items.

There's another compelling reason you should consider adding multiple binary-choice items to your classroom assessment repertoire. Unlike traditional binary-choice items, for which it's likely students will need to rely on *memorized* information, that's rarely the case with multiple binary-choice items. It is rare, that is, *if* the stimulus materials contain content that's not been encountered previously by students. In other words, if the stem for a subset of multiple binary-choice items contains material that's new to the student, and if each binary-choice item depends directly on the previously unencountered content, it's dead certain the student will need to function above the mere recollection of knowledge, the lowest level of Bloom's cognitive taxonomy. So, if you make certain your stimulus material for multiple binary-choice items contains new content, those items will surely be more intellectually demanding than the run-of-the-memory true–false item.

In review, we've considered an item type that's not widely used but has some special virtues. The major advantage of multiple binary-choice items is that students can respond to two or three such items in the time it takes them to respond to a single multiple-choice item. Other things being equal, the more items students respond to, the more reliably we can gauge their abilities.

I must confess to a mild bias toward this often overlooked item type because for over 20 years I used such tests as the final examinations in an introductory educational measurement course I taught in the UCLA Graduate School of Education. I'd give my students 20 one- or two-paragraph descriptions of previously unencountered educational measurement situations and then follow up each description with five binary-choice items. In all, then, I ended up with a 100-item final exam that really seemed to sort out those students who knew their stuff from those who didn't. The five items in each cluster were simply statements to which students were to respond *accurate* or *inaccurate*. I could just as appropriately have asked for *true* or *false* responses, but I tried to add a touch of suave to my exams. After all, I was teaching in a *Graduate* School of Education. (In retrospect, my decision seems somewhat silly.) Nonetheless, I had pretty good luck with my 100-item final exams. I used 50-item versions for my midterm exams, and they worked well too. For certain kinds of purposes, I think you'll find multiple binary-choice items will prove useful.

MULTIPLE-CHOICE ITEMS

For a number of decades, the **multiple-choice test item** has dominated achievement testing in the United States and many other nations. Multiple-choice items can be used to measure a student's possession of knowledge or a student's ability to engage in higher levels of thinking. A strength of multiple-choice items is they can contain several answers differing in their *relative* correctness. Thus, the student can be called on to make subtle distinctions among answer options, several of which may be somewhat correct. A weakness of multiple-choice items, as is the case with all selected-response items, is that students need only *recognize* a correct answer. Students need not *generate* a correct answer. Although a fair amount of criticism has been heaped on multiple-choice items, particularly in recent years, properly constructed multiple-choice items can tap a rich variety of student skills and knowledge, and thus can be useful tools for classroom assessment.

The first part of a multiple-choice item, as noted earlier, is referred to as the item's *stem*. The potential answer options are described as **item alternatives**. Incorrect alternatives are typically referred to as **item distractors**. Two common ways of creating multiple-choice items are to use an item stem that is either a direct question or an incomplete statement. With younger students, the direct-question approach is preferable. Using either direct-question stems or incomplete-statement stems, a multiple-choice item can ask students to select either a correct answer or, instead, to select a best answer.

In Figure 6.2 there are examples of a direct-question item requesting a best-answer response (indicated by an asterisk) and an incomplete-statement item requesting a correct-answer response (also indicated by an asterisk).

Let's turn now to a consideration of item-category guidelines for multiple-choice items. Because of the widespread use of multiple-choice items over the past half-century, there are quite a few experience-sired suggestions regarding how to create such items. Here, you'll find five of the more frequently cited item-specific recommendations for constructing multiple-choice items.

figure 6.2 ■ Illustrative Multiple-Choice Items

Direct-Question Form (best-answer version)

Which of the following modes of composition would be most effective in explaining to someone how a bill becomes a law in this nation?

      A. Narrative
* B. Expository
      C. Persuasive
      D. Descriptive

Incomplete-Statement Form (correct-answer version)

Mickey Mouse's nephews are named

      A. Huey, Dewey, and Louie.
      B. Mutt and Jeff.
      C. Larry, Moe, and Curly.
* D. Morty and Ferdie.

Item-Writing Guidelines for Multiple-Choice Items

1. The stem should consist of a self-contained question or problem.
2. Avoid negatively stated stems.
3. Do not let the length of alternatives supply unintended clues.
4. Randomly assign correct answers to alternative positions.
5. Never use "all-of-the-above" alternatives, but do use "none-of-the-above" alternatives to increase item difficulty.

Stem Stuffing

A properly constructed stem for a multiple-choice item will present a clearly described task to the student so the student can then get to work on figuring out which of the item's options is best (if it's a best-answer item) or correct (if it's a correct-answer item). A poorly constructed stem for a multiple-choice item will force the student to read one or more of the alternatives in order to figure out what the item is getting at. In general, therefore, it's preferable to load as much of the item's content as possible into the stem. Lengthy stems and terse alternatives are, as a rule, much better than skimpy stems and long alternatives. You might try reading the stems of your multiple-choice items without any of the alternatives to see if the stems (either direct questions or incomplete statements) make sense all by themselves.

Knocking Negatively Stated Stems

It has been alleged, particularly by overly cautious individuals, that "one robin does not spring make." Without debating the causal relationship between seasonal shifts and feathered flyers, in multiple-choice item writing we could say with confidence that "one negative in an item stem does not confusion unmake." Negatives are strange commodities. A single *not*, tossed casually into a test item, can make students crazy. Besides, because *not* is such a tiny word, and might be overlooked by students, a number of students (who didn't see the *not*) may be trying to ferret out the best alternative for a positively stated stem that, in reality, is negative.

For example, let's say you wanted to do a bit of probing of your students' knowledge of U.S. geography and phrased the stem of a multiple-choice item such as this: "Which one of the following cities is located in a state west of the Mississippi River?" If your alternatives were: A. San Diego, B. Pittsburgh, C. Boston, and D. Atlanta, students would have little difficulty in knowing how to respond. Let's say, however, that you decided to add a dollop of difficulty by using the same alternatives but tossing in a *not*. Now your item's stem might read something like this: "Which one of the following cities is not located in a state east of the Mississippi River?" For this version of the item, the student who failed to spot the *not* (this, in psychometric circles, is known as not-spotting) would be in big trouble.

By the way, note in both stems, the student was asked to identify which *one* of the following answers was correct. If you leave the *one* out, a student might have interpreted the question to mean there were two or more cities being sought.

If there is a compelling reason for using a negative in the stem of a multiple-choice item, be sure to highlight the negative with italics, boldface type, or underscoring so that students who are not natural not-spotters will have a fair chance to answer the item correctly.

Attending to Alternative Length

Novice item writers often fail to realize that the length of a multiple-choice item's alternatives can give away what the correct answer is. Let's say choices A, B, and C say blah, blah, blah, but choice D says blah, blah, blah, blah, blah, and blah. The crafty student will be inclined to opt for choice D not simply because one gets many more blahs for one's selection, but because the student will figure out the teacher has given so much attention to choice D that there must be something special about it.

Thus, when you're whipping up your alternatives for multiple-choice items, try either to keep all the alternatives about the same length or, if this isn't possible, to have at least two alternatives be of approximately equal length. For instance, if you were using four-alternative items, you might have two fairly short alternatives and two fairly long alternatives. What you want to avoid, of course, is having the correct alternative be one length (either short or long) while the distractors are all another length.

Incidentally, the number of alternatives is really up to you. Most frequently, we see multiple-choice items with four or five alternatives. Because students can guess correct answers more readily with fewer alternatives, three alternatives are not seen all that often except with younger students. Having more than five alternatives puts a pretty heavy reading load on the student. I've usually employed four alternatives on my own multiple-choice tests, but in a few instances, the nature of the test's content has led me to use three or five alternatives.

Assigning Correct Answer Positions

A fourth guideline for writing multiple-choice items is to make sure you scatter your correct answers among your alternatives so students don't "guess their way to high scores" simply by figuring out your favorite correct answer spot is, for instance, choice D or perhaps choice C. Many novice item writers are reluctant to put the correct answer in the choice-A position because they believe it gives away the correct answer too early. Yet, the choice-A position deserves its share of correct answers too. Absence-of-bias should also apply to answer-choice options.

As a rule of thumb, if you have four-alternative items, try to assign roughly 25 percent of your correct answers to each of the four positions. It may be necessary to do some last-minute shifting of answer positions in order to achieve what is essentially a random assignment of correct answers to the available positions. But always do a last-minute check on your multiple-choice tests to see you haven't accidentally overbooked your correct answers too heavily in a particular answer-choice position.

Dealing with "of-the-above" Alternatives

Sometimes a beginning item writer who's trying to come up with four (or five) reasonable alternatives will toss in a none-of-the-above or an all-of-the-above alternative simply as a "filler" alternative. But both of these options must be considered more carefully.

The fifth guideline for this item type says quite clearly you should never use the all-of-the-above alternative. Here's why. Let's say you're using a five-option type of multiple-choice item and you want to set up the item so the fifth option (choice E), "all of the above," would be correct. This indicates the first four answers, choices A through D, must all be correct. The problem with such an item is that even a student who only knows two of the first four alternatives are correct will be able to select the all-of-the-above response because if any two responses are correct, choice E is the only possible best answer. Even worse, some students will read only the first alternative, see that it is correct, mark choice A on their response sheet, and move on to the next test item without going over the full array of alternatives for the item. For either of these reasons, you should never use an all-of-the-above alternative in your multiple-choice items.

What about the none-of-the above alternative? The guideline indicates it should be used when you wish to increase an item's difficulty. You should do so only when the presence of the none-of-the-above alternative will help you make the kind of test-based inference you want to make. To illustrate, let's say you want to find out how well your students can perform basic mathematical operations such as multiplying and dividing. Moreover, you want to be confident your students can really perform the computations either "in their heads," by using scratch paper, or by employing an appropriate app with their cell phones or digital tablets. Now, if you use only four-alternative multiple-choice items, there's a real likelihood certain students won't be able to perform the actual mathematical operations, but may be able to select by estimation the answer that is most reasonable. After all, *one* of the four options *has* to be correct. Yet, simply by adding the none-of-the-above option (as a fourth or fifth alternative), students can't be sure the correct answer is silently sitting there among the item's alternatives. To determine whether the correct answer is *really* one of the alternatives for the item, students will be obliged to perform the required mathematical operation and come up with the actual answer. In essence, when the none-of-the-above option is added, the task presented to the student more closely approximates the task the teacher is interested in. A student's chance of guessing the correct answer to a multiple-choice item is markedly less likely when a none-of-the-above option shows up in the item.

Here's a little wrinkle on this guideline you might find useful. Be a bit careful about using a none-of-the-above option for a *best-answer* multiple-choice item. Care is warranted because there are wily students waiting out there who'll parade a series of answers for you they regard as better than the one option you think is a winner. If you can cope with such carping, there's no problem. If you have a low carping-coping threshold, however, avoid none-of-the-above options for most—if not all—of your best-answer items.

In review, we've taken a cursory look at five guidelines for the creation of multiple-choice items. There are other more subtle suggestions for creating such items, but if you combine these guidelines with the five general item-writing commandments discussed earlier in the chapter, you'll have a good set of ground rules for devising decent multiple-choice items. As with all the item types I've been describing, there's no substitute for oodles of practice in item writing that's followed by collegial or supervisorial reviews of your item-writing efforts. It is said that Rome wasn't built in a day. Similarly, in order to become a capable constructor of multiple-choice items, you'll probably need to develop more than one such test—or even more than two.

DECISION TIME

Multiple-Guess Test Items?

For all six years that he has taught, Leroy Larson has worked with fifth-graders. Although Leroy enjoys all content areas, he takes special pride in his reading instruction because he believes his students enter the sixth grade with dramatically improved comprehension capabilities. Leroy spends little time trying to promote his students' isolated reading skills but, instead, places great emphasis on having students "construct their own meanings" from what they have read.

All of Leroy's reading tests consist exclusively of four-option, multiple-choice items. As Leroy puts it, "I can put together a heavy-duty multiple-choice item when I put my mind to it." Because he has put his mind to it many times during the past six years, Leroy is quite satisfied that his reading tests are as good as his reading instruction.

At the most recent open house night at his school, however, a group of five parents registered genuine unhappiness with the exclusive multiple-choice makeup of Leroy's reading tests. The parents had obviously been comparing notes prior to the open house, and Mrs. Davies (the mother of one of Leroy's fifth-graders) acted as their spokesperson. In brief, Mrs. Davies argued that multiple-choice tests permitted even weak students to "guess their way to good scores." "After all," Mrs. Davies pointed out, "do you want to produce good readers or good guessers?"

Surprised and somewhat shaken by this incident, Leroy has been rethinking his approach to reading assessment. He concludes he can (1) stick with his tests as they are, (2) add some short-answer or essay items to his tests, or (3) replace all of his multiple-choice items with open-ended items. As he considers these options, he realizes that he has given himself a multiple-choice decision!

 If you were Leroy, what would your decision be?

MATCHING ITEMS

A *matching item* consists of two parallel lists of words or phrases requiring the student to match entries on one list with appropriate entries on the second list. Entries in the list for which a match is sought are referred to as *premises*. Entries in the list from which selections are made are referred to as *responses*. Usually, students are directed to match entries from the two lists according to a specific kind of association described in the test directions. Figure 6.3 is an example of a matching item.

Notice in Figure 6.3's illustrative matching item that both lists are *homogeneous*. All of the entries in the column at the left (the premises) are U.S. military

figure 6.3 ■ An Illustrative Matching Item

Directions: On the line to the left of each military conflict listed in Column A, write the letter of the U.S. president in Column B who was in office when that military conflict was concluded. Each name in Column B may be used no more than once.

Column A

_____ 1. World War I

_____ 2. World War II

_____ 3. Korea

_____ 4. Vietnam

_____ 5. First Persian Gulf

Column B

A. Bush (the father)

B. Clinton

C. Eisenhower

D. Johnson

E. Nixon

F. Roosevelt

G. Truman

H. Wilson

conflicts and all of the entries in the column at the right (the responses) are names of U.S. presidents. Homogeneity is an important attribute of properly constructed matching items.

An advantage of matching items is that their compact form takes up little space on a printed page or on a computer screen, thus making it easy to tap a good deal of information efficiently. Matching items can also be easily scored by simply holding a correct-answer template next to the list of premises where students are to supply their selections from the list of responses. A disadvantage of matching items is, as with binary-choice items, they sometimes encourage students' memorization of low-level factual information that, in at least some instances, is of debatable utility. The illustrative matching item is a case in point. Although it's relatively easy to create matching items such as this, is it really important to know which U.S. chief executive was in office when a military conflict was concluded? That's the kind of issue you'll be facing when you decide what kinds of items to include in your classroom assessments.

Typically, matching items are used as *part* of a teacher's assessment instruments. It's pretty difficult to imagine a major classroom examination consisting exclusively of matching items. Matching items don't work well when teachers are trying to assess relatively distinctive ideas, because matching items require pools of related entries to insert into the matching format.

Let's consider a half-dozen guidelines you should think about when creating matching items for your classroom assessment instruments. The guidelines are presented here.

> ### Item-Writing Guidelines for Matching Items
>
> 1. Employ homogeneous lists.
> 2. Use relatively brief lists, placing the shorter words or phrases at the right.
> 3. Employ more responses than premises.
> 4. Order the responses logically.
> 5. Describe the basis for matching and the number of times responses may be used.
> 6. Place all premises and responses for an item on a single page/screen.

Employing Homogeneous Entries

As noted earlier, each list in a matching item should consist of homogeneous entries. If you really can't create a homogeneous set of premises and a homogeneous set of responses, you shouldn't be mucking about with matching items.

Going for Relative Brevity

From the student's perspective, it's much easier to respond to matching items if the entries in both lists are relatively few in number. About 10 or so premises should be the upper limit for most matching items. The problem with longer lists is that students spend so much time trying to isolate the appropriate response for a given premise, they may forget what they're attempting to find. Very lengthy sets of premises or responses are almost certain to cause at least some students difficulty in responding because they'll lose track of what's being sought. It would be far better to take a lengthy matching item with 24 premises and split it into three 8-premise matching items.

In addition, to cut down on the reading requirements of matching items, be sure to place the list of shorter words or phrases at the right. In other words, make the briefer entries the responses. In this way, when students are scanning the response lists for a matching entry, they'll not be obliged to read too many lengthy phrases or sentences.

Loading Up on Responses

A third guideline for the construction of matching items is to make sure there are at least a few extra responses. Otherwise, if the numbers of premises and responses are identical, the student who knows, say, 80 percent of the matches to the premises may be able to figure out the remaining matches by a process of elimination. A few extra responses reduce this likelihood substantially. Besides, these sorts of responses are inexpensive.

PARENT TALK

Assume that you've been using a fair number of multiple-choice items in your classroom examinations. Benito's parents, Mr. and Mrs. Olmedo, have set up a 15-minute conference with you during a Back-to-Classroom Night to talk about Benito's progress.

When they arrive, they soon get around to the topic in which they are most interested—namely, your multiple-choice test items. As Mr. Olmedo puts it, "We want our son to learn to use his mind, not his memory. Although my wife and I have little experience with multiple-choice tests because almost all of our school exams were of an essay nature, we believe multiple-choice tests measure only what Benito has memorized. He has a good memory, as you've probably found out, but we want more for him. Why are you using such low-level test items?"

If I were you, here's how I'd respond to Mr. Olmedo's question:

"I appreciate your coming in to talk about Benito's education and, in particular, the way he is being assessed. And I also realize that recently there has been a good deal of criticism of multiple-choice test items. More often than not, such criticism is altogether appropriate. In far too many cases, because multiple-choice items are easy to score, they're used to assess just about everything. And, all too often, those kinds of items do indeed ask students to do little more than display their memorization skills.

"But this doesn't need to be the case. Multiple-choice items, if they are carefully developed, can assess a wide variety of truly higher-order thinking skills. In our school, all teachers have taken part in a series of staff-development workshop sessions in which every teacher learned how to create *challenging* multiple-choice items that require students to display much more than memory." (At this point, I'd whip out a few examples of demanding multiple-choice items used in my own tests and then go through them, from stem to alternatives, showing Mr. and Mrs. Olmedo what I meant. If I *didn't* have any examples of such items from my tests, I'd think seriously about the legitimacy of Benito's parents' criticism.)

"So, although there's nothing wrong with Benito's acquiring more memorized information, and a small number of my multiple-choice items actually do test for such knowledge, the vast majority of the multiple-choice items that Benito will take in my class call for him to employ that fine mind of his.

"That's what you two want. That's what I want."

Now, how would you respond to Mr. and Mrs. Olmedo's concerns?

Ordering Responses

So that you'll not provide unintended clues to students regarding which responses go with which premises, it's a good idea in matching items to order the responses in some sort of logical fashion—for example, alphabetical or chronological sequence. Notice that the names of the U.S. presidents are listed alphabetically in the illustrative matching item in Figure 6.3.

Describing the Task for Students

The fifth guideline for the construction of matching items suggests the directions for an item always make explicit the basis on which the matches are to be made and, at the same time, the number of times a response can be used. The more clearly students understand how they're supposed to respond, the more accurately they'll respond, and the more validly you'll be able to make score-based inferences about your students.

Formatting Items to Avoid Page Flipping

The final guideline for this item type suggests that you make sure all premises and responses for a matching item are on a single page. Not only does this eliminate the necessity for massive, potentially disruptive page turning by students, but it will also decrease the likelihood students will overlook correct answers merely because they were on the "other" page.

In review, matching items, if employed judiciously, can efficiently assess your students' knowledge. The need to employ homogeneous lists of related content tends to diminish the applicability of this type of selected-response item. Nonetheless, if you are dealing with content that can be addressed satisfactorily by such an approach, you'll find matching items a useful member of your repertoire of item types.

WHAT DO CLASSROOM TEACHERS REALLY NEED TO KNOW ABOUT SELECTED-RESPONSE TESTS?

If you engage in any meaningful amount of assessment in your own classroom, it's quite likely you'll find that selected-response items will be useful. Selected-response items can typically be used to ascertain students' mastery of larger domains of content than is the case with constructed-response kinds of test items. Although it's often thought selected-response items must, of necessity, measure only lower-order kinds of cognitive capabilities, inventive teachers can create selected-response options to elicit very high levels of cognitive skills from students.

As for the four types of items treated in the chapter, you really need to understand enough about each kind to help you decide whether one or more of those item types would be useful for a classroom assessment task you have in mind. If

But What Does This Have to Do with Teaching?

In this chapter, not only have you become acquainted with varied types of test items but you have also learned how to construct them properly. Why, you might ask, does a classroom teacher need to possess such a resplendent repertoire of item types? After all, if a student knows that Abraham Lincoln was assassinated while attending a play, the student could satisfactorily display such knowledge in a variety of ways. A good old true–false item or a nifty multiple-choice item would surely do the necessary assessing.

Well, that's quite true. But what you need to recall, *from a teaching perspective,* is that students ought to master the skills and knowledge they're being taught so thoroughly they can display such mastery in a good many ways, not just one. A cognitive skill that's been learned *well* by a student will be a cognitive skill that can be displayed in all sorts of ways, whether via selected-response items or constructed-response items.

And this is why, when you *teach* children, you really need to be promoting their generalizable mastery of whatever's being taught. Consistent with such a push for generalizable mastery, you will typically want to employ varied assessment approaches. If you gravitate toward only one or two item types (that is, if you become "Multiple-Choice Molly" or "True-False Teddy"), then your students will tend to learn things only in a way that meshes with your favored item type.

Eons ago, when I was preparing to be a teacher, my teacher education professors advised me to employ different kinds of items "for variety's sake." Well, classroom teachers aren't putting on a fashion show. Variety for its own sake is psychometrically stupid. But variety of assessment approaches as a deliberate way of promoting and measuring students' *generalizable mastery* of what's been taught—this is psychometrically suave.

you do decide to use binary-choice, multiple binary-choice, multiple-choice, or matching items in your own tests, then you'll find the sets of item-writing guidelines for each item type will come in handy.

In Chapter 12, you will learn how to employ selected-response items as part of the formative-assessment process. Rather than complete reliance on paper-and-pencil versions of these items, you will see how to employ such items in a variety of less formal ways. Yet, in honesty, even if you adhere to the chapter's five general item-writing commandments and the set of guidelines for a particular type of item, you'll still need practice in constructing selected-response items such as those considered here. As was suggested several times in the chapter, it is exceedingly helpful if you can find someone with measurement moxie, or at least an analytic mind, to review your test-development efforts. It's difficult in any realm to improve if you don't get feedback about the adequacy of your efforts. That's surely true with classroom assessment.

Try to entice a colleague or supervisor to look over your selected-response items to see what needs to be strengthened. However, even without piles of practice, if you adhere to the item-writing guidelines provided in the chapter, your selected-response tests won't be all that shabby.

The most important thing to learn from this chapter is that there are four use-ful *selected*-response procedures for drawing valid inferences about your students' status. The more assessment options you have at your disposal, the more appro-priately you'll be able to assess those student variables in which you're interested.

CHAPTER SUMMARY

The chapter was initiated with a presentation of five item-writing commandments that pertain to both constructed-response and selected-response items. The five admonitions directed teachers to avoid unclear directions, ambiguous statements, unintentional clues, complex syntax, and hypersophisticated vocabulary.

In turn, then, consideration was given to the four most common kinds of selected-response test items—namely, binary-choice items, multiple binary-choice items, multiple-choice items, and matching items. For each of these four item types, after a brief description of the item type and its strengths and weaknesses, a set of item-writing guidelines was presented. These four sets of guidelines were presented on pages 157, 159, 162, and 168. Each guideline was briefly discussed. Readers were encouraged to consider the four item types when deciding on an answer to the how-to-assess-it question.

Determining Your Outcome Mastery

Chapter 6 is the first of five chapters focused on item construction. As a reminder, here is the chapter's chief outcome:

> *The ability to accurately employ professionally accepted item-writing guidelines, both general and item-type specific, when constructing selected-response items or evaluating those items constructed by others*

Now that you've finished the chapter, you should be better able to create selected-response classroom assessments that you can use in your own class-room to arrive at valid interpretations about what your students know and can do. This is an altogether worthwhile aspiration. Good testing contributes to good teaching.

However, as a practical matter, the current capabilities of digital technology make it difficult to comprehensively gauge your ability to construct test items.

In this chapter, therefore, and in several other chapters as well, your ability to identify strengths and weaknesses in items written by others will function as a surrogate to represent your own item-construction prowess. This assessment tactic rests on the eminently reasonable assumption that if you can spot the shortcomings in other people's selected-response items, you'll be more likely to spot the shortcomings in your own selected-response items.

Complete both the Selected-Response and the Constructed-Response quizzes and think about the feedback you receive for each quiz.

MyEdLab *Selected-Response Check of Outcome Mastery*

MyEdLab *Constructed-Response Check of Outcome Mastery*

After completing both quizzes, go to the Learning Outcome Mastery Determination, where you will decide whether you've mastered the chapter's learning outcome or whether you need further study.

MyEdLab *Learning Outcome Mastery Determination*

References

Brookhart, S. M., and Nitko, A. J. (2014). *Educational assessment of students* (7th ed.). Boston: Pearson.

Frisbie, D. A. (1992). "The multiple true-false format: A status review," *Educational Measurement: Issues and Practice, 11,* no. 4 (Winter): 21–26.

Holler, E. W., Gareis, C. R., Martin, J., Clouser, A., and Miller, S. (2008). "Teacher-made assessments: Getting them right," *Principal Leadership, 9,* no. 1 (September): 60–64.

Waugh, C. K., and Gronlund, N. (2013). *Measurement and assessment in teaching* (10th ed.). Columbus, OH: Pearson.

Constructed-Response Tests

You're going to learn about constructed-response tests in this chapter. To be really truthful, you're going to learn about only two kinds of *paper-and-pencil* constructed-response items—namely, short-answer items and essay items (including students' written compositions). Although I suspect you already know that "you can't tell a book by its cover," now you've discovered that a chapter's title doesn't always describe its contents accurately. Fortunately, as far as I know, there are no state or federal "truth-in-chapter-entitling" laws.

You might be wondering why your ordinarily honest, never-fib author has descended to this act of blatant mislabeling. Actually, it's just to keep your reading chores more manageable. In an earlier chapter, you learned that student-constructed responses can be obtained from a wide variety of item types. In this chapter, we'll be looking at two rather traditional forms of constructed-response items, both of them paper-and-pencil in nature. In the next chapter, the focus will be on *performance tests,* such as those that arise when we ask students to make oral presentations or supply comprehensive demonstrations of complex skills in class. After that, in Chapter 9, we'll be dealing with portfolio assessment and how portfolios are used for assessment purposes.

Actually, all three chapters could be lumped under the single description of *performance assessment* or *constructed-response measurement* because anytime you assess your students by asking them to respond in other than a make-a-choice manner, the students are *constructing;* that is, they are *performing.* It's just that if I'd loaded all of this performance assessment stuff in a single chapter, you'd have thought you were experiencing a month-long TV mini-series. Yes, it was my inherent concern for your well-being that led me to disregard accuracy when titling this chapter.

The major payoff of all constructed-response items is they elicit student responses more closely approximating the kinds of behavior students must display in real life. After students leave school, for example, the demands of daily living almost never require them to choose responses from four nicely arranged alternatives. And when was the last time, in normal conversation, you were obliged to render a flock of true–false judgments about a set of statements? Yet, you may well be asked to make a brief oral presentation to your fellow teachers or to a parent group, or you may be asked to write a brief report for the school newspaper about your students' field trip to City Hall. Constructed-response tasks unquestionably coincide more closely with nonacademic tasks than do selected-response tasks.

As a practical matter, if the nature of a selected-response task is sufficiently close to what might be garnered from a constructed-response item, then you may wish to consider a selected-response assessment tactic to be a reasonable surrogate for a constructed-response assessment tactic. Selected-response tests are clearly much more efficient to score. And, because almost all the teachers I know are busy folks, time-saving procedures are not to be scoffed at. Yet, there will be situations when you'll want to make inferences about your students' status when selected-response tests just won't fill the bill. For instance, if you wish to know what kind of a cursive writer Jamal is, then you'll have to let Jamal write cursively. A true–false test about *i* dotting and *t* crossing just doesn't cut it.

Given the astonishing technological advances we see every other week, what today is typically a paper-and-pencil test is apt, tomorrow, to be some sort of digitized assessment linked to some sort of outer-space satellite. Computer-dispensed exams may become quite commonplace for teachers to develop themselves. However, because such a digital-assessment derby does not yet surround us, in this chapter the guidelines and illustrations will tend to reflect what most teachers currently do, that is, paper-and-pencil assessment. Happily, most of the guidelines you will encounter in the chapter apply with equal force to either paper-and-pencil or electronically dispensed assessments.

SHORT-ANSWER ITEMS

The first kind of constructed-response item we'll look at is the ***short-answer item***. These types of items call for students to supply a word, a phrase, or a sentence in response to either a direct question or an incomplete statement. If an item asks students to come up with a fairly lengthy response, it would be considered an essay item, not a short-answer item. If the item asks students to supply only a single word, then it's a *really* short-answer item.

Short-answer items are suitable for assessing relatively simple kinds of learning outcomes such as those focused on students' acquisition of knowledge. If crafted carefully, however, short-answer items can measure substantially more challenging kinds of learning outcomes. The major advantage of short-answer items is that students need to *produce* a correct answer, not merely recognize it from a set of selected-response options. The level of partial knowledge that might allow a student to respond correctly to a choose-the-best-response item won't be sufficient when the student is required to produce a correct answer to a short-answer item.

The major drawback with short-answer items, as is true with all constructed-response items, is that students' responses are difficult to score. The longer the responses sought, the tougher it is to score them accurately. And inaccurate scoring, as we saw in Chapter 3, leads to reduced reliability—which, in turn, reduces the validity of the test-based interpretations we make about students—which, in turn, reduces the quality of the decisions we base on those interpretations. Educational measurement is much like the rest of life—it's simply loaded with trade-offs. When classroom teachers choose constructed-response tests, they must be willing to trade some scoring accuracy (the kind of accuracy that comes with selected-response approaches) for greater congruence between constructed-response assessment strategies and the kinds of student behaviors about which inferences are to be made.

Here, you will find five straightforward item-writing guidelines for short-answer items. Please look them over, and then I'll briefly amplify each guideline by describing how it works.

Item-Writing Guidelines for Short-Answer Items

1. Usually employ direct questions rather than incomplete statements, particularly for young students.
2. Structure the item so that a response should be concise.
3. Place blanks in the margin for direct questions or near the end of incomplete statements.
4. For incomplete statements, use only one or, at most, two blanks.
5. Make sure blanks for all items are equal in length.

Using Direct Questions Rather than Incomplete Statements

For young children, the direct question is a far more familiar format than the incomplete statement. Accordingly, such students will be less confused if direct questions are employed. Another reason short-answer items should employ a direct-question format is that the use of direct questions typically forces the item writer to phrase the item so less ambiguity is present. With incomplete-statement formats, there's often too much temptation simply to delete words or phrases from statements the teacher finds in textbooks. To make sure there isn't more than one correct answer to a short-answer item, it is often helpful if the item writer first decides on the correct answer and then builds a question or incomplete statement designed to elicit a *unique* correct response from knowledgeable students.

Nurturing Concise Responses

Responses to short-answer items, as might be inferred from what they're called, should be *short*. Thus, no matter whether you're eliciting responses that are words, symbols, phrases, or numbers, try to structure the item so a brief response is clearly sought. Suppose you conjured up an incomplete statement item such as this: "An animal that walks on two feet is _____." There are all sorts of answers a student might legitimately make to such an item. Moreover, some of those responses could be fairly lengthy. Now note how a slight restructuring of the item constrains the student: "An animal that walks on two feet is technically classified as _____." By the addition of the phrase "technically classified as," the item writer has restricted the appropriate responses to only one—namely, "biped." If your short-answer items are trying to elicit students' phrases or sentences, you may wish to place word limits on each, or at least indicate in the test's directions that only a *short* one-sentence response is allowable for each item.

Always try to put yourself, mentally, inside the heads of your students and try to anticipate how they are apt to interpret an item. What this second guideline suggests is that you massage an item until it truly lives up to its name—that is, until it becomes a *bona fide* short-answer item.

Positioning Blanks

If you're using direct questions in your short-answer items, place the students' response areas for all items near the right-hand margin of the page, immediately after the item's questions. By doing so, you'll have all of a student's responses nicely lined up for scoring. If you're using incomplete statements, try to place the blank near the end of the statement, not near its beginning. A blank positioned too early in a sentence tends to perplex the students. For instance, notice how this too-early blank can lead to confusion: "The _____ is the governmental body that, based on the United States Constitution, must ratify all U.S. treaties with foreign nations." It would be better to use a direct question or to phrase the item as follows: "The governmental body that, based on the United States Constitution, must ratify all U.S. treaties with foreign nations is the _____."

Limiting Blanks

For incomplete-statement types of short-answer items, you should use only one or two blanks. Any more blanks and the item is labeled a "Swiss-cheese item," or an item with holes galore. Here's a Swiss-cheese item to illustrate the confusion that a profusion of blanks can make in what is otherwise a decent short-answer item: "After a series of major conflicts with natural disasters, in the year _____, the explorers _____ and _____, accompanied by their _____, discovered _____." The student who could supply correct answers to such a flawed short-answer item should also be regarded as a truly successful explorer.

Inducing Linear Equality

Too often in short-answer items, a beginning item writer will give away the answer by varying the length of the answer blanks so that short lines are used when short answers are correct and long lines are used when lengthier answers are correct. This practice tosses unintended clues to students and so should be avoided. In the interest of linear egalitarianism, not to mention decent item writing, keep all blanks for short-answer items equal in length. Be sure, however, the length of the answer spaces provided is sufficient for students' responses—in other words, not so skimpy that students have to cram in their answers in an illegible fashion.

Okay, let's review. Short-answer items are the most simple form of constructed-response items, but they can help teachers measure important skills and knowledge. Because such items seek students' constructed rather than selected responses, they can be employed to tap some genuinely higher-order skills. Although students' responses to short-answer items are more difficult to score than are their answers to selected-response items, the scoring of such items isn't impossible. That's because short-answer items, by definition, should elicit only *short* answers.

ESSAY ITEMS: DEVELOPMENT

The essay item is surely the most commonly used form of constructed-response assessment item. Anytime teachers ask their students to churn out a paragraph or two on what the students know about Topic X or to compose an original composition describing their "Favorite Day," an *essay item* is being used. Essay items are particularly useful in gauging a student's ability to synthesize, evaluate, and compose. Such items have a wide variety of applications in most teachers' classrooms.

A special form of the essay item is the *writing sample*—when teachers ask students to generate a written composition in an attempt to measure students' composition skills. Because the procedures employed to construct items for such writing samples and, thereafter, for scoring students' compositions, are so similar to the procedures employed to create and score responses to any kind of essay item, we'll treat writing samples and other kinds of essay items all at one time in this chapter. You'll find it helpful, however, to remember that the requirement to have students generate a writing sample is, in reality, a widely used type of *performance test*. We'll dig more deeply into performance tests in the following chapter.

For assessing certain kinds of complex learning outcomes, the essay item is the hands-down winner. It clearly triumphs when you're trying to see how well students can create original compositions. Yet, there are a fair number of drawbacks associated with essay items, and if you're going to consider using such items in your own classroom, you ought to know the weaknesses as well as the strengths of this item type.

One difficulty with essay items is that they're more difficult to write—at least write properly—than is generally thought. I must confess that as a first-year high

DECISION TIME

Forests or Trees?

Allison Allen is a brand-new English teacher assigned to work with seventh-grade and eighth-grade students at Dubois Junior High School. Allison has taken part in a state-sponsored summer workshop that emphasizes "writing as a process." Coupled with what she learned while completing her teacher education program, Allison is confident that she can effectively employ techniques such as brainstorming, outlining, early drafts, peer critiquing, and multiple revisions. She assumes that her students will acquire not only competence in their composition capabilities but also confidence about their possession of those capabilities. What Allison's preparation failed to address, however, was how to grade her students' compositions.

Two experienced English teachers at Dubois Junior High have gone out of their way to help Allison get through her first year as a teacher. Mrs. Miller and Ms. Stovall have both been quite helpful during the early weeks of the school year. However, when Allison asked them one day during lunch how she should judge the quality of her students' compositions, two decisively different messages were given.

Ms. Stovall strongly endorsed *holistic* grading of compositions—that is, a general appraisal of each composition as a whole. Although Ms. Stovall bases her holistic grading scheme on a set of explicit criteria, she believes a single "gestalt" grade should be given so that "one's vision of the forest is not obscured by tree-counting."

Arguing with equal vigor, Mrs. Miller urged Allison to adopt *analytic* appraisals of her students' compositions. "By supplying your students with a criterion-by-criterion judgment of their work," she contended, "each student will be able to know precisely what's good and what isn't." (It was evident during the fairly heated interchanges that Mrs. Miller and Ms. Stovall had disagreed about this topic in the past.) Mrs. Miller concluded her remarks by saying, "Forget about that forest-and-trees metaphor, Allison. What we're talking about here is clarity!"

 If you were Allison, how would you decide to judge the quality of your students' compositions?

school teacher, I sometimes conjured up essay items while walking to school and then slapped them up on the chalkboard so that I created almost instant essay exams. At the time, I thought my essay items were pretty good. Such is the pride of youth and the product of ignorance. I'm glad I have no record of those items. In retrospect, I assume they were pretty putrid. I now know that generating a really good essay item is a tough task—a task not accomplishable while strolling to school. You'll see this is true from the item-writing rules to be presented shortly. It takes time to create a solid essay item. You'll need to find time to construct suitable essay items for your own classroom assessments.

The most serious problem with essay items, however, is the difficulty teachers have in reliably scoring students' responses. Let's say you use a six-item essay test to measure your students' ability to solve certain kinds of problems in social studies. Suppose that, by some stroke of measurement magic, all your students' responses could be transformed into typed manuscript form so you could not tell which response came from which student. Let's say you were asked to score the complete set of responses *twice*. What do you think is the likelihood your two sets of scores would be consistent? Well, experience suggests that most teachers aren't able to produce very consistent results when they score students' essay responses. The challenge in this instance, of course, is to *increase* the reliability of your scoring efforts so you're not distorting the validity of the score-based inferences you want to make on the basis of your students' responses.

Creating Essay Items

Because the scoring of essay responses (and students' compositions) is such an important topic, you'll soon be getting a set of guidelines on how to score responses to such items. The more complex the nature of students' constructed responses become, as you'll see in the next two chapters, the more attention you'll need to lavish on scoring. You can't score responses to items that you haven't written, however, so let's look at the five guidelines for the construction of essay items.

Item-Writing Guidelines for Essay Items

1. Convey to students a clear idea regarding the extensiveness of the response desired.
2. Construct items so the student's task is explicitly described.
3. Provide students with the approximate time to be expended on each item as well as each item's value.
4. Do not employ optional items.
5. Precursively judge an item's quality by composing, mentally or in writing, a possible response.

Communicating the Desired Extensiveness of Students' Responses

It is sometimes thought that if teachers decide to use essay items, students have total freedom of response. On the contrary, teachers can structure essay items so students produce (1) barely more than they would for a short-answer item or, in contrast, (2) extremely lengthy responses. The two types of essay items reflecting this distinction in the desired extensiveness of students' responses are described as restricted-response items and extended-response items.

A *restricted-response item* decisively limits the form and content of students' responses. For example, a restricted-response item in a health education class might ask students the following: "Describe the three most common ways HIV, the AIDS virus, is transmitted. Take no more than 25 words to describe each method of transmission." In this example, the number of HIV transmission methods was specified, as was the maximum length for each transmission method's description.

In contrast, an *extended-response item* provides students with far more latitude in responding. Here's an example of an extended-response item from a social studies class: "Identify the chief factors contributing to the U.S. government's financial deficit during the past two decades. Having identified those factors, decide which factors, if any, have been explicitly addressed by the U.S. legislative and/or executive branches of government in the last five years. Finally, critically evaluate the likelihood that any currently proposed remedies will bring about significant reductions in the U.S. national debt." A decent response to such an extended-response item not only should get high marks from the teacher but might also be the springboard for a student's successful career in politics.

One technique teachers commonly use to limit students' responses is to provide a certain amount of space on the test paper, in their students' response booklets, or in the available response area on a computer screen. For instance, the teacher might direct students to "Use no more than two sheets (both sides) in your blue books to respond to each test item." Although the space-limiting ploy is an easy one to implement, it really disadvantages students who write in a large-letter, scrawling fashion. Whereas such large-letter students may only be able to cram a few paragraphs onto a page, those students who write in a small, scrunched-up style may be able to produce a short novella in the same space. Happily, when students respond to a computer-administered test "in the space provided," we can preclude their shifting down to a tiny, tiny font that might allow them to yammer on near endlessly.

This first guideline asks you to think carefully about whether the inference at issue that you wish to make about your students is best serviced by students' responses to (1) more essay items requiring shorter responses or (2) fewer essay items requiring extensive responses. Having made that decision, then be sure to convey to your students a clear picture of the degree of extensiveness you're looking for in their responses.

Describing Students' Tasks

Students will find it difficult to construct responses to tasks if they don't understand what the tasks are. Moreover, students' responses to badly understood tasks are almost certain to yield flawed inferences by teachers. The most important part of an essay item is, without question, the description of the *assessment task*. It is the task students respond to when they generate essays. Clearly, then, poorly described assessment tasks will yield many off-target responses that, had the student truly understood what was being sought, might have been more appropriate.

There are numerous labels used to represent the assessment task in an essay item. Sometimes it's simply called the *task*, the *charge,* or perhaps the *assignment*.

In essay items that are aimed at eliciting student compositions, the assessment task is often referred to as a *prompt*. No matter how the assessment task is labeled, if you're a teacher who is using essay items, you must make sure the nature of the task is really set forth clearly for your students. Put yourself, at least hypothetically, in the student's seat and see if, with the level of knowledge possessed by most of your students, the nature of the assessment task is really apt to be understood.

To illustrate, if you wrote the following essay item, there's little doubt your students' assessment task would have been badly described: "In 500 words or less, discuss democracy in Latin America." In contrast, notice in the following item how much more clearly the assessment task is set forth: "Describe how the checks and balances provisions in the U.S. Constitution were believed by the Constitution's framers to be a powerful means to preserve democracy (300–500 words)."

Providing Time-Limit and Item-Value Guidance

When teachers create an examination consisting of essay items, they often have an idea regarding which items will take more of the students' time. But students don't know what's in the teacher's head. As a consequence, some students will lavish loads of attention on items the teacher thought warranted only modest effort, yet devote little time to items the teacher thought deserved substantial attention. Similarly, sometimes teachers will want to weight certain items more heavily than others. Again, if students are unaware of which items count most, they may toss reams of rhetoric at the low-value items and have insufficient time to give more than a trifling response to the high-value items.

To avoid these problems, there's quite a straightforward solution—namely, letting students in on the secret. If there are any differences among items in point value or in the time students should spend on them, simply provide this information in the directions or, perhaps parenthetically, at the beginning or end of each item. Students will appreciate such clarifications of your expectations.

Avoiding Optionality

It's fairly common practice among teachers who use essay examinations to provide students with a certain number of items and then let each student choose to answer fewer than the number of items presented. For example, the teacher might allow students to "choose any three of the five essay items presented." Students, of course, really enjoy such an assessment procedure because they can respond to items for which they're well prepared and avoid those items for which they're inadequately prepared. Yet, other than inducing student glee, this optional-items classroom assessment scheme has little going for it.

When students select different items from a menu of possible items, they are actually responding to different examinations. As a consequence, it is impossible to judge their performances on some kind of common scale. Remember, as a classroom teacher you'll be trying to make better educational decisions about your students by relying on test-based interpretations regarding those students. It's tough enough to make a decent test-based interpretation when you have only one test to consider. It's infinitely more difficult to make such interpretations when you are faced with a medley of different tests because you allow your students to engage in a mix-and-match measurement procedure.

In most cases, teachers rely on an optional-items procedure with essay items when they're uncertain about the importance of the content measured by their examinations' items. Such uncertainty gives rise to the use of optional items because the teacher is not clearheaded about the inferences (and resulting decisions) for which the examination's results will be used. If you spell out those inferences (and decisions) crisply, prior to the examination, you will usually find you'll have no need for optional item selection in your essay examinations.

Previewing Students' Responses

After you've constructed an essay item for one of your classroom assessments, there's a quick way to get a preliminary fix on whether the item is a winner or loser. Simply toss yourself, psychologically, into the head of one of your typical students and then anticipate how such a student would respond to the item. If you have time, and are inclined to do so, you could try writing a response that the student might produce to the item. More often than not, because you'll be too busy to conjure up such fictitious responses in written form, you might try to compose a mental response to the item on behalf of the typical student you've selected. An early mental run-through of how a student might respond to an item can often help you identify deficits in the item because, when you put yourself, even hypothetically, on the other side of the teacher's desk, you'll sometimes discover shortcomings in items you otherwise wouldn't have identified. Too many times I've seen teachers give birth to a set of essay questions, send them into battle on examination day, and only then discover that one or more of the items suffers severe genetic deficits. Mental previewing of likely student responses can help you detect such flaws while there's still time for repairs.

In review, we've looked at five guidelines for creating essay items. If you'll remember that all of these charming little collections of item-specific recommendations should be adhered to *in addition to* the five general item-writing commandments set forth in Chapter 6 (see page 152), you'll probably be able to come up with a pretty fair set of essay items. Then, perish the thought, you'll have to score your students' responses to those items. That's what we'll be looking at next.

ESSAY ITEMS: SCORING STUDENTS' RESPONSES

If you'll recall what's to come in future chapters, you'll be looking at how to evaluate students' responses to performance assessments in Chapter 8 and how to judge students' portfolios in Chapter 9. In short, you'll be learning much more about how to evaluate your students' performances on constructed-response assessments.

Thus, to spread out the load a bit, in this chapter we'll be looking only at how to score students' responses to essay items (including tests of students' composition skills). You'll find that many of the suggestions for scoring students' constructed responses you will encounter will also be applicable when you're trying to judge your students' essay responses. But just to keep matters simple, let's look now at recommendations for scoring responses to essay items.

Guidelines for Scoring Responses to Essay Items

1. Score responses holistically and/or analytically.
2. Prepare a tentative scoring key in advance of judging students' responses.
3. Make decisions regarding the importance of the mechanics of writing prior to scoring.
4. Score all responses to one item before scoring responses to the next item.
5. Insofar as possible, evaluate responses anonymously.

Choosing an Analytic and/or Holistic Scoring Approach

During the past few decades, the measurement of students' composition skills by having students generate actual writing samples has become widespread. As a consequence of all this attention to students' compositions, educators have become far more skilled regarding how to evaluate students' written compositions. Fortunately, classroom teachers can use many of the procedures that have been identified and refined while educators scored thousands of students' compositions during statewide assessment extravaganzas.

A fair number of the lessons learned about scoring students' writing samples apply quite nicely to the scoring of responses to any kind of essay item. One of the most important of the scoring insights picked up from this large-scale scoring of students' compositions is that almost any type of student-constructed response can be scored either *holistically* or *analytically*. That's why the first of the five guidelines suggests you make an early decision whether you're going to score your students' responses to essay items using a holistic approach or an analytic approach or, perhaps, using a combination of the two scoring approaches. Let's look at how each of these two scoring strategies works.

A *holistic scoring* strategy, as its name suggests, focuses on the essay response (or written composition) as a whole. At one extreme of scoring rigor, the teacher can, in a fairly unsystematic manner, supply a "general impression" overall grade to each student's response. Or, in a more systematic fashion, the teacher can isolate, in advance of scoring, those evaluative criteria that should be attended to in order to arrive at a single, overall score per essay. Generally, a score range of four to six points is used to evaluate each student's response. (Some scoring schemes have a few more points, some a few less.) A teacher, then, after considering whatever factors should be attended to in a given item, will give a score to each student's response. Here is a set of evaluative criteria teachers might use in holistically scoring a student's written composition.

Illustrative Evaluative Criteria to Be Considered When Scoring Students' Essay Responses Holistically

For scoring a composition intended to reflect students' writing prowess:

- Organization
- Communicative Clarity
- Adaptation to Audience
- Word Choice
- Mechanics (spelling, capitalization, punctuation)

And now, here are four evaluative factors a speech teacher might employ in holistically scoring a response to an essay item used in a debate class.

Potential Evaluative Criteria to Be Used When Scoring Students' Essay Responses in a Debate Class

For scoring a response to an essay item dealing with rebuttal preparation:

- Anticipation of Opponent's Positive Points
- Support for One's Own Points Attacked by Opponents
- Isolation of Suitably Compelling Examples
- Preparation of a "Spontaneous" Conclusion

When teachers score students' responses holistically, they do *not* dole out points-per-criterion for a student's response. Rather, the teacher keeps in mind evaluative criteria such as those set forth in the previous two boxes. The speech teacher, for instance, while looking at the student's essay response to a question regarding how someone should engage in effective rebuttal preparation, will not necessarily penalize a student who overlooks one of the four evaluative criteria. The response as a whole may lack one thing, yet otherwise represent a really wonderful response. Evaluative criteria such as those illustrated here simply dance

figure 7.1 ▪ An Illustrative Guide for Analytically Scoring a Student's Written Composition

Factor	Unacceptable (0 points)	Satisfactory (1 point)	Outstanding (2 points)
1. Organization	_____	✓	_____
2. Communicative Clarity	_____	_____	✓
3. Audience Adaptation	_____	✓	_____
4. Word Choice	_____	_____	✓
5. Mechanics	_____	✓	_____

Total Score = __7__

around in the teacher's head when the teacher scores students' essay responses holistically.

In contrast, an *analytic scoring* scheme strives to be a fine-grained, specific point-allocation approach. Suppose, for example, instead of using a holistic method of scoring students' compositions, a teacher chose to employ an analytic method of scoring students' compositions. Under those circumstances, a scoring guide such as the example in Figure 7.1 might be used by the teacher. Note, for each evaluative criterion in the guide, the teacher must award 0, 1, or 2 points. The lowest overall score for a student's composition, therefore, would be 0, whereas the highest overall score for a student's composition would be 10 (that is, 2 points × 5 criteria).

The advantage of an analytic scoring system is it can help you identify the specific strengths and weaknesses of your students' performances and, therefore, you can communicate such diagnoses to students in a pinpointed fashion. The downside of analytic scoring is that a teacher sometimes becomes so attentive to the subpoints in a scoring system that, almost literally, the forest (overall quality) can't be seen because of a focus on individual trees (the separate scoring criteria). In less metaphoric language, the teacher will miss the communication of the student's response "as a whole" because of excessive attention to a host of individual evaluative criteria.

One middle-of-the-road scoring approach can be seen when teachers initially grade all students' responses holistically and then return for an analytic scoring of only those responses that were judged, overall, to be unsatisfactory. After the analytic scoring of the unsatisfactory responses, the teacher then relays more fine-grained diagnostic information to those students whose unsatisfactory responses were analytically scored. The idea underlying this sort of hybrid approach is that the students who are most in need of fine-grained feedback are those who, on the basis of the holistic evaluation, are performing less well.

This initial guideline for scoring students' essay responses applies to the scoring of responses to all kinds of essay items. As always, your decision about whether to opt for holistic or analytic scoring should flow directly from your intended use of the test results. Putting it another way, your choice of scoring approach will depend on the educational decision linked to the test's results. (Is this beginning to sound somewhat familiar?)

Devising a Tentative Scoring Key

No matter what sort of approach you opt for in scoring your students' essay responses, you'll find it will be useful to develop a tentative scoring key for responses to each item *in advance* of actually scoring students' responses. Such tentative scoring schemes are almost certain to be revised on the basis of your scoring of actual student papers, but that's to be anticipated. If you wait until you commence scoring your students' essay responses, there's too much likelihood you'll be unduly influenced by the responses of the first few students whose papers you grade. If those papers are atypical, the resultant scoring scheme is apt to be unsound. It is far better to think through, at least tentatively, what you really hope students will supply in their responses and then modify the scoring key if unanticipated responses from students suggest that alterations are requisite.

If you don't have a tentative scoring key in place, there's a great likelihood you'll be influenced by such factors as a student's vocabulary or writing style even though, in reality, such variables may be of little importance to you. Advance exploration of the evaluative criteria you intend to employ, either holistically or analytically, is a winning idea when scoring responses to essay items.

Let's take a look at what a tentative scoring key might look like if employed by a teacher in a U.S. History course. The skill being promoted by the teacher is a genuinely high-level one that's reflected in the following curricular aim:

> *When presented with a description of a current real-world problem in the United States, the student will be able to (1) cite one or more significant events in American history that are particularly relevant to the presented problem's solution, (2) defend the relevance of the cited events, (3) propose a solution to the presented problem, and (4) use historical parallels from the cited events to support the proposed solution.*

As I indicated, this is no rinky-dink low-level cognitive skill. It's way, way up there in its cognitive demands on students. Now, let's suppose our hypothetical history teacher routinely monitors students' progress related to this skill by having students respond to similar problems either orally or in writing. The teacher presents a real-world problem. The students, aloud or in an essay, try to come up with a suitable four-part response.

In Figure 7.2 you'll see an illustrative tentative scoring key for evaluating students' oral or written responses to constructed-response items measuring their

figure 7.2 ▪ An Illustrative Tentative Scoring Key for a High-Level Cognitive Skill in History

Students' Subtasks	Tentative Point Allocation		
	Weak Response	*Acceptable Response*	*Strong Response*
1. Citation of Pertinent Historical Events	0 pts.	5 pts.	10 pts.
2. Defense of the Cited Historical Events	0 pts.	10 pts.	20 pts.
3. Proposed Solution to the Presented Problem	0 pts.	10 pts.	20 pts.
4. Historical Support of Proposed Solution	0 pts.	20 pts.	40 pts.

Total Points Possible = <u>90 pts.</u>

mastery of this curricular aim. As you can discern, in this tentative scoring key, greater weight has been given to the fourth subtask—namely, the student's provision of historical parallels to support the student's proposed solution to the real-world problem the teacher proposed. Much less significance was given to the first subtask of citing pertinent historical events. This, remember, is a *tentative* scoring key. Perhaps when the history teacher begins scoring students' responses, it will turn out that the first subtask is far more formidable than the teacher originally thought, and the fourth subtask seems to be handled without much difficulty by students. At that point, based on the way students are actually responding, this hypothetical history teacher surely ought to do a bit of score-point juggling in the tentative scoring key before applying it in final form to the appraisal of students' responses.

Deciding Early about the Importance of Mechanics

Few things influence scorers of students' essay responses as much as the mechanics of writing employed in the response. If the student displays subpar spelling, chaotic capitalization, and poor punctuation, it's pretty tough for a scorer of the student's response to avoid being influenced adversely. In some instances, of course, mechanics of writing certainly do play a meaningful role in scoring students' performances. For instance, suppose you're scoring students' written responses to a task of writing an application letter for a position as a reporter for a local newspaper. In such an instance, it is clear that mechanics of writing would be pretty important when judging the students' responses. But in a chemistry class, perhaps the teacher cares less about such factors when scoring students' essay responses to a problem-solving task. The third guideline simply suggests you make up your mind about this issue early in the process so, if mechanics aren't all that important to you, you don't let your students' writing mechanics subconsciously influence the way you score their responses.

Scoring One Item at a Time

If you're using an essay examination with more than one item, be sure to score all your students' responses to one item, then score all their responses to the next item, and so on. Do *not* score all responses of a given student and then go on to the next student's paper. There's too much danger a student's responses to early items will unduly influence your scoring of their responses to later items. If you score all responses to item number 1 and then move on to the responses to item number 2, you can eliminate this tendency. In addition, the scoring will actually go a bit quicker because you won't need to shift evaluative criteria between items. Adhering to this fourth guideline will invariably lead to more consistent scoring and hence to more accurate response-based inferences about your students. There'll be more paper shuffling than you might prefer, but the increased accuracy of your scoring will be worth it. (Besides, you'll be getting a smidge of psychomotor exercise.)

PARENT TALK

The mother of one of your students, Jill Jenkins, was elected to your district's school board 2 years ago. Accordingly, anytime Mrs. Jenkins wants to discuss Jill's education, you are understandably "all ears."

Mrs. Jenkins recently stopped by your classroom to say that three of her fellow board members have been complaining there are too many essay tests being given in the district. The three board members contend that such tests, because they must be scored "subjectively," are neither reliable nor valid.

Because many of the tests you give Jill and her classmates are essay tests, Mrs. Jenkins asks you if the three board members are correct.

 If I were you, here's how I'd respond to Jill's mom. (Oh yes, because Mrs. Jenkins is a board member, I'd simply ooze politeness and professionalism while I responded.)

"Thanks for giving me an opportunity to comment on this issue, Mrs. Jenkins. As you've already guessed, I truly believe in the importance of constructed-response examinations such as essay tests. The real virtue of essay tests is that they call for students to *create* their responses, not merely *recognize* correct answers, as students must with other types of tests such as multiple-choice exams.

"The three school board members are correct when they say it is more difficult to score constructed-response items consistently than it is to score selected-response items consistently. And that's a shortcoming of essay tests. But it's a shortcoming that's more than compensated for by the far greater *authenticity* of the tasks presented to students in almost all constructed-response tests. When Jill writes essays during my major exams, this is much closer to what she'll be doing in later life than choosing the best answer from four options. In real life, people aren't given four-choice options. Rather, they're required to generate a response reflecting their views. Essay tests give Jill and her classmates a chance to do just that.

"Now, let's talk briefly about consistency and validity. Actually, Mrs. Jenkins, it is important for tests to be scored consistently. We refer to the consistency with which a test is scored as its *reliability*. And if a test isn't reliable, then the interpretations about students we make based on test scores aren't likely to be valid. It's a technical point, Mrs. Jenkins, but it isn't a *test* that's valid or invalid; it's a score-based inference about students that may or may not be valid. As your board colleagues pointed out, some essay tests are not scored very reliably. But essay tests *can* be scored reliably and they *can* yield valid inferences about students.

"I hope my reactions have been helpful. I'll be happy to show you some of the actual essay exams I've used with Jill's class. And I'm sure the District Superintendent, Dr. Stanley, can supply you with additional information."

 Now, how would you respond to Mrs. Jenkins?

Striving for Anonymity

Because I've been a teacher, I know all too well how quickly teachers can identify their students' writing styles, particularly those students who have especially distinctive styles, such as the "scrawlers," the "petite letter-size crew," and those who dot their *i*'s with half-moons or cross their *t*'s with lightning bolts. Yet, insofar as you can, try not to know whose responses you're scoring. One simple way to help in that effort is to ask students to write their names on the reverse side of the last sheet of the examination in the response booklet. Try not to peek at the students' names until you've scored all of the exams.

I used such an approach for three decades of scoring graduate students' essay examinations at UCLA. It worked fairly well. Sometimes I was really surprised because students who had appeared to be knowledgeable during class discussions displayed just the opposite on the exams, while several Silent Sarahs and Quiet Quentins came up with really solid exam performances. I'm sure if I had known whose papers I had been grading, I would have been improperly influenced by my classroom-based perceptions of different students' abilities. I am not suggesting that you shouldn't use students' classroom discussions as part of your evaluation system. Rather, I'm advising you that classroom-based perceptions of students can sometimes cloud your scoring of essay responses. This is one strong reason for you to strive for anonymous scoring.

In review, we've considered five guidelines for scoring students' responses to essay examinations. If your classroom assessment procedures involve any essay items, you'll find these five practical guidelines will go a long way in helping you come up with consistent scores for your students' responses. And consistency, as you learned in Chapter 3, is something that makes psychometricians mildly euphoric.

In the next two chapters you'll learn about two less common forms of constructed-response items. You'll learn how to create and score performance assessments and to use students' portfolios in classroom assessments. You'll find what we've been dealing with in this chapter will serve as a useful springboard to the content of the next two chapters.

WHAT DO CLASSROOM TEACHERS REALLY NEED TO KNOW ABOUT CONSTRUCTED-RESPONSE TESTS?

At the close of a chapter dealing largely with the nuts and bolts of creating and scoring written constructed-response tests, you probably expect to be told you really need to internalize all those nifty little guidelines so, when you spin out your own short-answer and essay items, you'll elicit student responses you can score accurately. Well, that's not a terrible aspiration, but there's really a more important insight you need to walk away with after reading the chapter. That insight, not surprisingly, derives from the central purpose of classroom assessment—namely, to

? But What Does This Have to Do with Teaching?

A teacher wants students to learn the stuff that's being taught—to learn it well. And one of the best ways to see if students have really acquired a cognitive skill or have truly soaked up scads of knowledge is to have them display what they've learned by *generating* answers to constructed-response tests. A student who has learned something well enough to toss it out from scratch, rather than choosing from presented options, clearly has learned it pretty darn well.

But, as this chapter has pointed out, the creation and scoring of really first-rate constructed-response items, especially anything beyond short-answer items, requires serious effort from a teacher. And if constructed-response items aren't really first-rate, then they are not likely to help a teacher arrive at valid interpretations about students' correct knowledge and/or skills. Decent constructed-response tests take time to create and to score. And that's where this kind of classroom assessment runs smack into a teacher's instructional-planning requirements.

A classroom teacher should typically reserve constructed-response assessments for a modest number of really *significant* instructional outcomes. And, remember, a teacher's assessments typically exemplify the outcomes the teacher wants most students to master. It's better to get students to master three to five really *high-level* cognitive skills, adroitly assessed by excellent constructed-response tests, than it is to have students master a litany of low-level outcomes. In short, choose your constructed-response targets with care. Those choices will have curricular and instructional implications.

Putting it another way, if you, as a classroom teacher, want to determine whether your students have the skills and/or knowledge that can be best measured by short-answer or essay items, then you need to refresh your memory regarding how to avoid serious item construction or response scoring errors. A review of the guidelines presented on pages 176, 180, and 184 should give you the brushup you need. Don't believe you are obligated to use short-answer or essay items simply because you now know a bit more about how to crank them out. If you're interested in the extensiveness of your students' *knowledge* regarding Topic Z, it may be far more efficient to employ fairly low-level selected-response kinds of items. If, however, you really want to make inferences about your students' abilities to perform the kinds of tasks represented by short-answer and essay items, then the guidelines provided in the chapter should be consulted.

draw accurate inferences about students' status so you can make more appropriate educational decisions. What you really need to know about short-answer items and essay items is that you should use them as part of your classroom assessment procedures if you want to make the sorts of inferences about your students that those students' responses to such items would support.

CHAPTER SUMMARY

After a guilt-induced apology for the chapter's mislabeling, we started off with a description of short-answer items accompanied by a set of guidelines (page 176) regarding how to write short-answer items. Next, we took up essay items and indicated that, although students' written compositions constitute a particular kind of essay response, most of the recommendations for constructing essay items and for scoring students' responses were the same, whether measuring students' composition skills or skills in subject areas other than language arts. Guidelines were provided for writing essay items (page 180) and for scoring students' responses to essay items (page 184). The chapter concluded with the suggestion that much of the content to be treated in the following two chapters, because those chapters also focus on constructed-response assessment schemes, will also relate to the creation and scoring of short-answer and essay items.

Determining Your Outcome Mastery

This chapter focused on how to write constructed-response items and, after having written them, how to score students' responses to such items. The chapter presented a set of item-specific guidelines for writing essay and short-answer items and for scoring responses to essay items. The goal for readers was to understand the chapter's guidelines well enough so that any violations of those guidelines can be readily spotted. Accordingly, the chief outcome was stated as:

> *A sufficient understanding of generally approved guidelines for creating constructed-response items, and scoring students' responses to them, so that errors in item construction and response scoring can be identified.*

In general, teachers who understand the chapter's item-development and response-scoring guidelines are likely to develop tests with better items and score students' responses more accurately.

Complete both the Selected-Response and the Constructed-Response quizzes and think about the feedback you receive for each quiz.

MyEdLab *Selected-Response Check of Outcome Mastery*

MyEdLab *Constructed-Response Check of Outcome Mastery*

After completing both quizzes, go to the Learning Outcome Mastery Determination, where you will decide whether you've mastered the chapter's learning outcome or whether you need further study.

MyEdLab *Learning Outcome Mastery Determination*

References

Downing, S. M., and Haladyna, T. M. (Eds.). (2006). *Handbook of test development.* Mahwah, NJ: Erlbaum.

Humphry, S. M., and Heldsinger, S. A. (2014). "Common structural design features of rubrics may represent a threat to validity," *Educational Researcher, 43,* no. 5 (June/July): 253–263.

Miller, M. D., and Linn, R. (2012). *Measurement and assessment in teaching* (11th ed.). Columbus, OH: Pearson.

Nitko, A. J., and Brookhart, S. M. (2014). *Educational assessment of students* (7th ed.). Upper Saddle River, NJ: Prentice-Hall/Merrill Education.

Stiggins, R. J., and Chappuis, J. (2012). *An introduction to student-involved assessment FOR learning* (6th ed.). Upper Saddle River, NJ: Prentice-Hall.

Wiliam, D. (2014). "The right questions, the right way," *Educational Leadership, 71,* no. 6 (March): 16–19.

8

Performance Assessment

CHIEF CHAPTER OUTCOME

A sufficiently broad under-standing of performance assessment to distinguish between accurate and inaccurate statements regarding the nature of performance tests, the identification of such tests' tasks, and the scoring of students' performances

During the early 1990s, a good many educational policy-makers became enamored with *performance assessment*, which is an approach to measuring a student's status based on the way the student completes a specified task. Theoreti-cally, of course, when the student chooses between *true* and *false* for a binary-choice item, the student is completing a task, although an obviously modest one. But the propo-nents of performance assessment have measurement schemes in mind that are meaningfully different from binary-choice or multiple-choice tests. Indeed, it was a dis-satisfaction with traditional paper-and-pencil tests that caused many educators to travel eagerly down the perfor-mance-testing trail.

WHAT IS A PERFORMANCE TEST?

Before digging into what makes performance tests tick and how you might use them in your own classroom, we'd best explore the chief attributes of such an assessment approach. Even though all educational tests, as noted earlier, require students to perform in some way, when most educators talk about performance tests, they are thinking about assessments in which the student is required to con-struct an original response. More often than not, an examiner (such as the teacher) *observes* the process of construction so that observation of the student's perfor-mance and judgment of that performance are required. More than four decades ago, Fitzpatrick and Morrison (1971) observed that "there is no absolute distinc-tion between performance tests and other classes of tests." They pointed out that the distinction between performance assessments and more conventional tests is chiefly the degree to which the examination simulates the criterion situation—that is, the extent to which the examination approximates the kind of student behav-iors about which we wish to make inferences.

Suppose, for example, a teacher who had been instructing students in the process of collaborative problem solving wanted to see whether students had acquired this collaborative skill. The *inference* at issue centers on the extent to which each student has mastered the skill. The *educational decision* on the line might be whether particular students need additional instruction or, instead, whether it's time to move on to other curricular aims. The teacher's real interest, then, is in how well students can work with other students to arrive collaboratively at solutions to problems. In Figure 8.1, you will see there are several assessment procedures that could be used to get a fix on a student's collaborative problem-solving skills. Yet, note that the two selected-response assessment options (numbers 1 and 2) don't really ask students to construct anything. For the other three constructed-response assessment options (numbers 3, 4, and 5), however, there are clear differences in the degree to which the task presented to the student coincides with the class of tasks called for by the teacher's curricular aim. Assessment Option 5, for example, is obviously the closest match to the behavior called for in the curricular aim. Yet, Assessment Option 4 is surely more of a "performance test" than is Assessment Option 1.

figure 8.1 ▪ A Set of Assessment Options That Vary in the Degree to Which a Student's Task Approximates the Curricularly Targeted Behavior

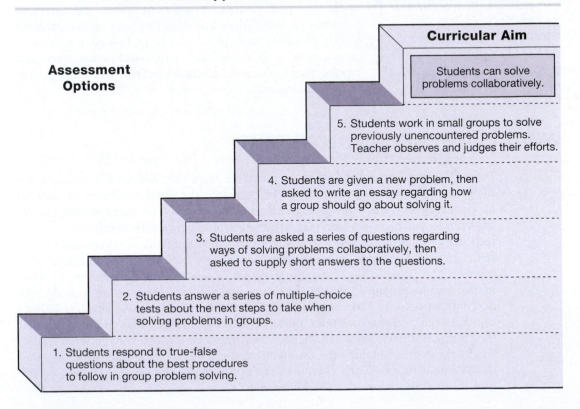

Curricular Aim

Students can solve problems collaboratively.

Assessment Options

5. Students work in small groups to solve previously unencountered problems. Teacher observes and judges their efforts.

4. Students are given a new problem, then asked to write an essay regarding how a group should go about solving it.

3. Students are asked a series of questions regarding ways of solving problems collaboratively, then asked to supply short answers to the questions.

2. Students answer a series of multiple-choice tests about the next steps to take when solving problems in groups.

1. Students respond to true-false questions about the best procedures to follow in group problem solving.

It should be apparent to you, then, that different educators will be using the phrase *performance assessment* to refer to very different kinds of assessment approaches. Many teachers, for example, are willing to consider short-answer and essay tests a form of performance assessment. In other words, those teachers essentially equate performance assessment with any form of constructed-response assessment. Other teachers establish more stringent requirements in order for a measurement procedure to be described as a performance assessment. For example, some performance-assessment proponents contend that genuine performance assessments must possess at least three features:

- *Multiple evaluative criteria.* The student's performance must be judged using more than one **evaluative criterion.** To illustrate, a student's ability to speak Spanish might be appraised on the basis of the student's accent, syntax, and vocabulary.
- *Prespecified quality standards.* Each of the evaluative criteria on which a student's performance is to be judged is clearly explicated in advance of judging the quality of the student's performance.
- *Judgmental appraisal.* Unlike the scoring of selected-response tests in which electronic computers and scanning machines can, once programmed, carry on without the need of humankind, genuine performance assessments depend on human judgments to determine how acceptable a student's performance really is.

Looking back to Figure 8.1, it is clear that if the foregoing three requirements were applied to the five assessment options supplied, Assessment Option 5 would qualify as a performance test, and Assessment Option 4 probably would as well, but the other three assessment options wouldn't qualify under a definition of performance assessment requiring the incorporation of multiple evaluative criteria, prespecified quality standards, and judgmental appraisals.

A good many advocates of performance assessment would prefer that the tasks presented to students represent real-world rather than school-world kinds of problems. Other proponents of performance assessment would be elated simply if more school-world measurement was constructed response rather than selected response in nature. Still other advocates of performance testing want the tasks in performance tests to be genuinely *demanding*—that is, way up the ladder of cognitive difficulty. In short, proponents of performance assessment often advocate different approaches to measuring students on the basis of how they perform.

In light of the astonishing advances we now see every few weeks in the sorts of computer-delivered stimuli for various kinds of assessment—performance tests surely included—the potential nature of performance-test tasks seems practically unlimited. For example, the possibility of digitally simulating a variety of authentic performance-test tasks provides developers of performance tests with an ever-increasing range of powerful performance assessments.

You'll sometimes encounter educators who use other phrases to describe performance assessment. For example, they may use the term **authentic assessment** (because the assessment tasks more closely coincide with real-life, nonschool tasks) or *alternative assessment* (because such assessments constitute an alternative to traditional, paper-and-pencil tests). In the next chapter, we'll be considering *portfolio assessment,* which is a particular type of performance assessment and should not be considered a synonymous descriptor for the performance-assessment approach to educational measurement.

We now turn to the twin issues that are at the heart of performance assessments: *selecting appropriate tasks* for students and, once the students have tackled those tasks, *judging the adequacy of students' responses.*

IDENTIFYING SUITABLE TASKS FOR PERFORMANCE ASSESSMENT

Performance assessment typically requires students to respond to a small number of more significant tasks rather than respond to a large number of less significant tasks. Thus, rather than answering 50 multiple-choice items on a conventional chemistry examination, students who are being assessed via performance tasks may find themselves asked to perform an actual experiment in their chemistry class and then prepare a written interpretation of the experiment's results and an analytic critique of the procedures they used. From the chemistry teacher's perspective, instead of seeing how students respond to the 50 "mini-tasks" represented in the multiple-choice test, an estimate of each student's status must be derived from a student's response to a single, complex task. Given the significance of each task used in a performance-testing approach to classroom assessment, it is apparent that great care must be taken in the selection of performance-assessment tasks. Generally speaking, classroom teachers will either have to (1) generate their own performance test tasks or (2) select performance test tasks from the increasing number of tasks available from educators elsewhere.

Inferences and Tasks

Consistent with the frequently asserted message of this book about classroom assessment you are currently reading, the chief determinants of how you assess your students are (1) the inference—that is, the interpretation—you want to make about those students and (2) the decision that will be based on the inference. For example, suppose you're a history teacher and you've spent a summer at a lakeside cabin meditating about curricular matters (which, in one lazy setting or another, is the public's perception of how most teachers spend their vacations). After three months of heavy curricular thought, you have concluded that what you really want to teach your students is for them to be able to apply historical lessons of the past to the solution of current and future problems that, at least to some extent, parallel the problems of the past. You have decided to abandon your week-long, 1,500-item true–false final examination that your stronger students

DECISION TIME

Grow, Plants, Grow!

Francine Floden is a third-year biology teacher in Kennedy High School. Because she has been convinced by several of her colleagues that traditional paper-and-pencil examinations fail to capture the richness of the scientific experience, Francine has decided to base almost all of her students' grades on a semester-long performance test. As Francine contemplates her new assessment plan, she decides that 90 percent of the students' grades will stem from the quality of their responses to the performance test's task; 10 percent of the grades will be linked to classroom participation and a few short true-false quizzes administered throughout the semester.

The task embodied in Francine's performance test requires each student to design and conduct a 2-month experiment to study the growth of three identical plants under different conditions and then prepare a formal scientific report describing the experiment. Although most of Francine's students carry out their experiments at home, several students use the shelves at the rear of the classroom for their experimental plants. A number of students vary the amount of light or the kind of light received by the different plants, but most students modify the nutrients given to their plants. After a few weeks of the two-month experimental period, all of Francine's students seem to be satisfactorily under way with their experiments.

Several of the more experienced teachers in the school, however, have expressed their reservations to Francine about what they regard as "overbooking on a single assessment experience." The teachers suggest to Francine that she will be unable to draw defensible inferences about her students' true mastery of biological skills and knowledge based on a single performance test. They urged her to reduce dramatically the grading weight for the performance test so that, instead, additional grade-contributing examinations can be given to the students.

Other colleagues, however, believe Francine's performance-test approach is precisely what is needed in courses such as biology. They recommend she "stay the course" and alter "not one whit" of her new assessment strategy.

If you were Francine, what would your decision be?

refer to as a "measurement marathon" and your weaker students refer to by using a rich, if earthy, vocabulary. Instead of true–false items, you are now committed to a performance-assessment strategy and wish to select tasks for your performance tests to help you infer how well your students can draw on the lessons of the past to illuminate their approach to current and/or future problems.

In Figure 8.2, you will see a graphic depiction of the relationships among (1) a teacher's key curricular aim, (2) the inference that the teacher wishes to draw about each student, and (3) the tasks for a performance test intended to secure

figure 8.2 ■ **Relationships among a Teacher's Key Curricular Aim, the Assessment-Based Inference Derivative from the Aim, and the Performance-Assessment Tasks Providing Evidence for the Inference**

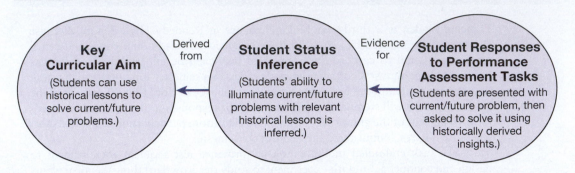

data to support the inference that the teacher wants to make. As you will note, the teacher's curricular aim provides the source for the inference. The assessment tasks yield the evidence needed for the teacher to arrive at defensible inferences regarding the extent to which students can solve current or future problems using historical lessons. To the degree that students have mastered the curricular aim, the teachers will make a decision about how much more instruction, if any, is needed.

The Generalizability Dilemma

One of the most serious difficulties with performance assessment is, because students respond to fewer tasks than would be the case with conventional paper-and-pencil testing, it is often more difficult to generalize accurately about what skills and knowledge are possessed by the student. To illustrate, let's say you're trying to get a fix on your students' ability to multiply pairs of double-digit numbers. If, because of your instructional priorities, you can devote only a half-hour to assessment purposes, you could require the students to respond to 20 such multiplication problems in the 30 minutes available. (That's probably more problems than you'd need, but I'm trying to draw a vivid contrast for you.) From a student's responses to 20 multiplication problems, you can get a pretty fair idea about what kind of double-digit multiplier the student is. As a consequence of the student's performance on a *reasonable sample* of items representing the curricular aim, you can conclude "Javier really knows how to multiply those sorts of problems," or "Fred really couldn't multiply double-digit multiplication problems if his life depended on it." It is because you have adequately sampled the kind of student performance (to which you wish to make an inference) that you can confidently make inferences about your students' abilities to solve similar sorts of multiplication problems.

With only a 30-minute assessment period available, however, if you moved to a more elaborate kind of performance test, you might only be able to have students respond to one big-bopper item. For example, if you presented a multiplication-focused mathematics problem involving the use of manipulatives, and wanted your students to derive an original solution and then describe it in writing, you'd be lucky if your students could finish the task in a half hour. Based on this single task, how confident would you be in making inferences about your students' abilities to perform comparable multiplication tasks?

And this, as you now see, is the rub with performance testing. Because students respond to fewer tasks, the teacher is put in a trickier spot when it comes to deriving accurate interpretations about students' abilities. If you use only one performance test, and a student does well on the test, does this signify the student *really* possesses the category of skills the test was designed to measure, or did the student just get lucky? On the other hand, if a student messes up on a single-performance test, does this signify the student *really* doesn't possess the assessed skill, or was there a feature in this particular performance test that misled the student who, given other tasks, might have performed wonderfully?

As a classroom teacher, you're faced with two horns of a classic measurement dilemma. Although performance tests often measure the kinds of student abilities you'd prefer to assess (because those abilities are in line with really worthwhile curricular aims), the inferences you make about students on the basis of their responses to performance tests must be made with increased caution. As with many dilemmas, there may be no perfect way to hop this one's two horns. But there is, at least, a way of dealing with the dilemma as sensibly as you can. In this instance, the solution strategy is to devote great care to the selection of the tasks embodied in your performance tests. Among the most important considerations in selecting such tasks is to choose tasks that optimize the likelihood of accurately generalizing about your students' capabilities. If you really keep generalizability at the forefront when you select/construct performance-test tasks, you'll be able to make the strongest possible performance-based inferences about your students' capabilities.

Factors to Consider When Evaluating Performance-Test Tasks

We've now looked at what many measurement specialists regard as the most important factor you can consider when judging potential tasks for performance assessments—*generalizability*. Let's look at a list of seven such factors you might wish to consider, whether you select a performance-test task from existing tasks or, in contrast, create your own performance-test tasks.

Evaluative Criteria for Performance-Test Tasks

- *Generalizability.* Is there a high likelihood the students' performance on the task will generalize to comparable tasks?
- *Authenticity.* Is the task similar to what students might encounter in the real world as opposed to encounter only in school?

- *Multiple foci.* Does the task measure multiple instructional outcomes instead of only one?
- *Teachability.* Is the task one that students can become more proficient in as a consequence of a teacher's instructional efforts?
- *Fairness.* Is the task fair to all students—that is, does the task avoid bias based on such personal characteristics as students' gender, ethnicity, or socioeconomic status?
- *Feasibility.* Is the task realistically implementable in relation to its cost, space, time, and equipment requirements?
- *Scorability.* Is the task likely to elicit student responses that can be reliably and accurately evaluated?

Whether you're developing your own tasks for performance tests or selecting such tasks from an existing collection, you may wish to apply some but not all the factors listed here. Personally, I would usually try to apply all seven factors, although I can see how one might, on occasion, dump the *authenticity* criterion or the *multiple foci* criterion. In some instances, for example, school tasks rather than real-world tasks might be suitable for the kinds of inferences a teacher wishes to reach, hence the authenticity criterion may not be relevant. And even though it is economically advantageous to measure more than one outcome at one time, particularly considering the time and effort that goes into almost any performance test, there may be instances in which a single educational outcome is sufficiently important so it warrants a solo performance test. More often than not, though, a really good task for a performance test will satisfy most, if not all seven, of the evaluative criteria presented here.

Performance Tests and Teacher Time

Back in Chapter 1, I promised that if you completed this book with a reasonable degree of attentiveness, you'd become a better teacher. Now I have another promise for you. I promise to be *honest* about the measurement mysteries we're probing together. And this brings me to an important consideration regarding performance testing. In brief, it takes time!

Think for a moment about the time that you, as the teacher, need to give to (1) the selection of suitable tasks, (2) the development of an appropriate scheme for scoring students' responses, and (3) the actual scoring of students' responses. Talk to any teacher who's already used many classroom performance tests and you'll learn it takes a ton of time to use performance assessment.

So what I want to suggest is that there's one additional factor you should throw into your decision-making about performance assessment. It is the *significance of the skill* you're using the performance test to assess. Because you'll almost certainly have time for only a handful of such performance tests in your teaching, make sure that every performance test you use is linked to a truly significant skill you're trying to have your students acquire. If performance assessments aren't based on genuinely demanding skills, you'll soon stop using them because, to be truthful, they'll be more trouble than they're worth.

THE ROLE OF RUBRICS

Performance assessments invariably are based on constructed-response measurement procedures in which students generate rather than select their responses. Student-constructed responses must be scored, however, and it's clearly much tougher to score constructed responses than to score selected responses. The scoring of constructed responses centers on the *evaluative criteria* one calls on to determine the adequacy of students' responses. Let's turn our attention now to the evaluative criteria we use to decide whether students' responses to performance tests are splendid or shabby.

A *criterion*, according to most people's understanding, is a standard on which a decision or judgment can be based. In the case of scoring students' responses to a performance test's task, you're clearly trying to make a judgment regarding the adequacy of the student's constructed response. The specific criteria to be used in making that judgment will obviously influence the way you score a student's response. For instance, if you were scoring a student's written composition on the basis of organization, word choice, and communicative clarity, you might arrive at very different scores than if you had scored the composition on the basis of spelling, punctuation, and grammar. The evaluative criteria used when scoring students' responses to performance tests (or their responses to any kind of constructed-response item) really control the whole assessment game.

Referring to my previously mentioned compulsion to fall back on my five years of Latin studies in high school and college, I feel responsible for explaining that the Latin word *criterion* is singular and the Latin word *criteria* is plural. Unfortunately, so many of today's educators mix up these two terms that I don't even become distraught about it anymore. However, now that you know the difference, if you find any of your colleagues erroneously saying "the criteria is" or "the criterion were," you can display an ever so subtle, yet altogether condescending, smirk.

The scoring procedures for judging students' responses to performance tests are usually referred to these days as *scoring rubrics* or, more simply, **rubrics**. A rubric that's used to score students' responses to a performance assessment has, at minimum, three important features:

- *Evaluative criteria.* These are the factors to be used in determining the quality of a student's response.
- *Descriptions of qualitative differences for all evaluative criteria.* For each evaluative criterion, a description must be supplied so qualitative distinctions in students' responses can be made using the criterion.
- *An indication of whether a holistic or analytic scoring approach is to be used.* The rubric must indicate whether the evaluative criteria are to be applied collectively in the form of *holistic* scoring or on a criterion-by-criterion basis in the form of *analytic* scoring.

The identification of a rubric's evaluative criteria, as might be guessed, is probably the most important task for rubric developers. If you're creating a rubric for a performance test you wish to use in your own classroom, be careful not to come up with a lengthy laundry list of evaluative criteria a student's response should satisfy. Personally, I think when you isolate more than three or four evaluative criteria per rubric, you've identified too many. If you find yourself facing more than a few evaluative criteria, simply *rank each criterion in order of importance* and then chop off those listed lower than the very most important ones.

The next job you'll have is deciding how to *describe in words* what a student's response must be in order to be judged wonderful or woeful. The level of descriptive detail you apply needs to work *for you*. Remember, you're devising a scoring rubric for your own classroom, not a statewide or national test. Reduce the aversiveness of the work down by employing brief descriptors of quality differences you can use when teaching and, if you're instructionally astute, your students can use as well.

Finally, you'll need to decide whether you'll make a single, overall judgment about a student's response by considering all of the rubric's evaluative criteria as an amalgam (holistic scoring) or, instead, award points to the response on a criterion-by-criterion basis (analytic scoring). The virtue of holistic scoring, of course, is it's quicker to do. The downside of holistic scoring is it fails to communicate to students, especially low-performing students, what their shortcomings are. Clearly, analytic scoring yields a greater likelihood of diagnostically pinpointed scoring and sensitive feedback than does holistic scoring. Some classroom teachers have attempted to garner the best of both worlds by scoring all responses holistically and then analytically rescoring (for feedback purposes) all responses of low-performing students.

Because most performance assessments call for fairly complex responses from students, there will usually be more than one evaluative criterion employed to score students' responses. For each of the evaluative criteria chosen, a numerical scale is typically employed so that for each criterion, a student's response might be assigned a specified number of points—for instance, 0 to 6 points. Usually, these scale points are accompanied by verbal descriptors; sometimes they aren't. For instance, in a 5-point scale, the following descriptors might be used: 5 = Exemplary, 4 = Superior, 3 = Satisfactory, 2 = Weak, 1 = Inadequate. If no verbal descriptors are used for each score point on the scale, a scheme such as the following might be employed:

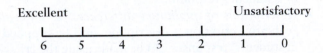

In some cases, the scoring scale for each criterion is not numerical; that is, it consists only of verbal descriptors such as "exemplary," "adequate," and so on. Although such verbal scales can be useful with particular types of performance tests, their disadvantage is that scores from multiple criteria cannot be added together in order to produce a meaningful overall score.

The heart of the intellectual process in isolating suitable evaluative criteria is to get to the essence of what the most significant factors are that distinguish acceptable from unacceptable responses. In this instance, as in many others, less is more. A few truly important criteria are preferable to a ton of trifling criteria. Go for the big ones. If you need help in deciding what criteria to employ in conjunction with a particular performance test, don't be reluctant to ask colleagues to toss in their ideas regarding what *significant* factors to use (for a given performance test) in order to discriminate between super and subpar responses.

In this chapter you'll be presented with scoring rubrics that can serve as useful models for your own construction of such rubrics. In those illustrative scoring rubrics, you'll see that great care has been taken to isolate a small number of instructionally addressable evaluative criteria. The greatest payoff from a well-formed scoring rubric is in its contribution to improved instruction.

AN ILLUSTRATIVE PERFORMANCE-TEST TASK

To give you a better idea about the kinds of tasks that might be used in a performance test and the way you might score a student's responses, let's take a look at an illustrative task for a performance test. The task presented on the next page in Figure 8.3 is intended to assess students' mastery of an oral communications skill.

WRETCHED AND THE RAPTUROUS RUBRICS

Unfortunately, many educators believe a rubric is a rubric is a rubric. Not so. Rubrics differ dramatically in their instructional worth. I'll now describe two types of rubrics that are sordid and one type that's super.

Task-Specific Rubrics

Some rubrics are created so their evaluative criteria are linked only to the particular task embodied in a specific performance test. These are called *task-specific rubrics*. Such a rubric does little to illuminate instructional decision-making because it implies that students' performances on the constructed-response test's specific task are what's important. They're not! What's important is the student's ability to perform well on the *class of tasks* that can be accomplished by using the skill being measured in the assessment. If students are taught to shine only on the single task represented in a performance test, but not on the full range of comparable tasks, students lose out. If students learn to become good problem solvers, they'll be able to solve all sorts of problems—not merely the one problem embodied in a particular performance test.

figure 8.3 ■ **Task Description and Sample Tasks for a One-on-One Oral Communication Performance Assessment**

An Oral Communication Performance Test

Introduction

There are numerous kinds of speaking tasks students must perform in everyday life, both in school and out of school. This performance assessment focuses on some of these tasks—namely, describing objects, events, and experiences; explaining the steps in a sequence; providing information in an emergency; and persuading someone.

In order to accomplish a speaking task, the speaker must formulate and transmit a message to a listener. This process involves deciding what needs to be said, organizing the message, adapting the message to the listener and situation, choosing language to convey the message and, finally, delivering the message. The effectiveness of the speaker may be rated in terms of how well the speaker meets the requirement of the task.

Sample Tasks

Description Task: Think about your favorite class or extracurricular activity in school. Describe to me everything you can about it so I will know a lot about it. (How about something like a school subject, a club, or a sports program?)

Emergency Task: Imagine you are home alone and you smell smoke. You call the fire department and I answer your call. Talk to me as if you were talking on the telephone. Tell me everything I would need to know to get help to you. (Talk directly to me; begin by saying hello.)

Sequence Task: Think about something you know how to cook. Explain to me, step by step, how to make it. (How about something like popcorn, a sandwich, or scrambled eggs?)

Persuasion Task: Think about one change you would like to see made in your school, such as a change in rules or procedures. Imagine I am the principal of your school. Try to convince me the school should make this change. (How about something like a change in the rules about hall passes or the procedures for enrolling in courses?)

Source: Based on assessment efforts of the Massachusetts Department of Education.

So, to provide helpful instructional illumination—that is, to assist the teacher's instructional decision-making—a rubric's evaluative criteria dare not be task specific. Instead, those criteria must be rooted in the skill itself. Let me illustrate by considering an evaluative criterion frequently employed in rubrics used to judge students' written communication skills—namely, the evaluative criterion of *organization*. Presented here is a task-specific evaluative criterion that might be used in a scoring rubric to judge the quality of a student's response to the following task:

> "Compose a brief narrative essay, of 400 to 600 words, describing what happened during yesterday's class session when we were visited by the local firefighters who described a fire-exit escape plan for the home."
>
> **A task-specific evaluative criterion for judging the organization of students' narrative essays:** Superior essays will (1) commence with a recounting of the particular rationale for home fire-escape plans the local firefighters provided, then (2) follow up with a description of the six elements in home-safety plans in the order those elements were presented, and (3) conclude by citing at least three of the life–death safety statistics the firefighters provided at the close of their visit. Departures from these three organizational elements will result in lower evaluations of essays.

Suppose you're a teacher who has generated or been given this task-specific evaluative criterion. How would you organize your instruction? If you really tried to gain instructional guidance from this evaluative criterion, you'd be aiming your instruction directly at a particular task—in this case, a narrative account of the firefighters' visit to your class. You'd have to teach your students to commence their narrative essays with a rationale when, in fact, using a rationale for an introduction might be inappropriate for other sorts of narrative essays. Task-specific evaluative criteria do not help teachers plan instructional sequences that promote their students' abilities to *generalize* the skills they acquire. Task-specific criteria are just what they are touted to be—specific to one task.

During recent years, I've had an opportunity to review a number of rubrics that classroom teachers are trying to employ. From an instructional perspective, most of these rubrics don't pass muster. Many of the rubrics are task specific. Such task-specific rubrics may make it easier to score students' constructed responses. For *scoring* purposes, the more specific evaluative rubrics are, the better. But task-specific rubrics do *not* provide teachers with the kinds of *instructional* insights rubrics should.

You'll not be surprised to learn that when the nation's large testing firms set out to score thousands of students' responses to performance tasks, they almost always employ task-specific rubrics. Such task-focused scoring keeps down costs. But, of course, the results of such scoring give teachers few instructional insights.

Hypergeneral Rubrics

Another variety of scoring rubric that will not help teachers plan their instruction is referred to as a *hypergeneral rubric*. Such a rubric is one in which the evaluative criteria are described in exceedingly general and amorphous terms. The evaluative criteria are so loosely described that, in fact, teachers' instructional plans really aren't benefited. For example, using the previous example of a task calling for students to write a narrative essay, a hypergeneral evaluative criterion for organization might resemble the following one:

> **A hypergeneral evaluative criterion for judging the organization of students' narrative essays:** *Superior* essays are those in which the essay's content has been arranged in a genuinely excellent manner, whereas *inferior* essays are those displaying altogether inadequate organization. An *adequate* essay is one representing a lower organizational quality than a superior essay, but a higher organizational quality than an inferior essay

You may think I'm putting you on when you read the illustrative hypergeneral evaluative criterion just given. But I'm not. I've seen many such hypergeneral scoring rubrics. These rubrics ostensibly clarify how teachers can score students' constructed responses, but really these vague rubrics do little more than loosely redefine such quality descriptors as *superior, proficient,* and *inadequate.* Hypergeneral rubrics often attempt to draw distinctions among students' performances no more clearly than among students' performances in earning grades of A through F. Hypergeneral rubrics provide teachers with no genuine benefits for their instructional planning because such rubrics do not give the teacher meaningfully clarified descriptions of the criteria to be used in evaluating the quality of students' performances.

Unfortunately, Robert Marzano, one of our field's most respected analysts of educational research, has taken a stance regarding scoring guides that seems to endorse the virtues of the kinds of hypergeneral rubrics I am currently trying to revile. Marzano (2008, pp. 10–11) has urged educators to develop rubrics for each curricular aim at each grade level using a generic rubric that can be "applied to all content areas." However, for a rubric to be applicable to *all* content areas, it must obviously be so general and imprecise that much of its *instructional* meaning is likely to have been leached from the rubric.

The midpoint (anchor) of Marzano's hypergeneral rubric calls for no major errors or omissions on the student's part regarding the simple or complex content and/or the procedures taught. If errors or omissions are present in either the content or procedures taught, these deficits lead to lower evaluations of the student's performance. If the student displays "in-depth inferences and applications" that go beyond what was taught, then higher evaluations of the student's performance are given. Loosely translated, these generic rubrics tell teachers that a student's "no-mistakes" performance is okay, a "some-mistakes" performance is less acceptable, and a "better-than-no-mistakes" performance is really good.

When these very general rubrics are applied to the appraisal of students' mastery of particular curricular goals, such rubrics' level of generality offers scant instructional clarity to teachers about what's important and what's not. I have enormous admiration for Bob Marzano's contributions through the years, and I count him as a friend. In this instance, I fear my friend is pushing for a sort of far-too-general scoring guide that won't help teachers do a better instructional job.

Skill-Focused Rubrics

Well, because I've now denigrated task-specific rubrics and sneered at hypergeneral rubrics, it's only fair for me to trot out the type of rubric that really can illuminate a teacher's instructional planning. Such scoring guides can be described as *skill-focused rubrics* because they really are conceptualized around the skill that is (1) being measured by the constructed-response assessment and (2) being pursued instructionally by the teacher. It is my conviction, based on discussions with many teachers who have used a variety of scoring rubrics, that teachers who create a skill-focused scoring rubric prior to their instructional planning will almost always devise a better instructional sequence than will teachers who don't.

For an example of an evaluative criterion you'd encounter in a skill-focused rubric, look over the following illustrative criterion for evaluating the organization of a student's narrative essay:

> **A skill-focused evaluative criterion for judging the organization of students' narrative essays:** Two aspects of organization will be employed in the appraisal of students' narrative essays—namely, *overall structure* and *sequence*. To earn maximum credit, an essay must embody an overall structure containing an introduction, a body, and a conclusion. The content of the body of the essay must be sequenced in a reasonable manner—for instance, in a chronological, logical, or order-of-importance sequence.

Now, when you consider this evaluative criterion from an instructional perspective, you'll realize a teacher could sensibly direct instruction by (1) familiarizing students with the two aspects of the criterion—that is, overall structure and sequence; (2) helping students identify essays in which overall structure and sequence are, or are not, acceptable; and (3) supplying students with gobs of guided and independent practice in writing narrative essays possessing the desired overall structure and sequence. The better students become in being able to employ this double-barreled criterion in their narrative essays, the better those students will be at responding to a task such as the illustrative one we just saw about the local firefighters' visit to the classroom. This skill-focused evaluative criterion for *organization,* in other words, can generalize to a wide variety of narrative-writing tasks, not just an essay about visiting fire-folk.

And even if teachers do not create their own rubrics—for instance, if rubrics are developed by a school district's curriculum or assessment specialists—those teachers who familiarize themselves with skill-focused rubrics in advance of instructional planning will usually plan better instruction than will teachers who aren't familiar with a skill-focused rubric's key features. Skill-focused rubrics make clear what a teacher should emphasize instructionally when the teacher attempts to promote students' mastery of the skill being measured. Remember, although students' acquisition of knowledge is an important curricular aspiration for teachers, assessment of students' knowledge can obviously be accomplished by procedures other than the use of performance tests.

Let me now set out five rubric rules I encourage you to follow if you're creating your own skill-focused scoring rubric—a rubric you should generate *before* you plan your instruction.

Rule 1: Make sure the skill to be assessed is significant. It takes time and trouble to generate skill-focused rubrics. It also takes time and trouble to score students' responses by using such rubrics. Make sure the skill being promoted instructionally, and scored via the rubric, is worth all this time and trouble. Skills that are scored with skill-focused rubrics should represent demanding accomplishments by students, not trifling ones.

Teachers ought not be ashamed to be assessing their students with only a handful of performance tests, for example. It makes much more sense to measure a modest number of truly important skills properly than to do a shoddy job in measuring a shopping-cart full of skills.

Rule 2: Make certain all the rubric's evaluative criteria can be addressed instructionally. This second rule calls for you always to "keep your instructional wits about you" when generating a rubric. Most importantly, you must scrutinize every potential evaluative criterion in a rubric to make sure you can actually teach students to master it.

This doesn't oblige you to adhere to any particular instructional approach. Regardless of whether you are wedded to the virtues of direct instruction, indirect instruction, constructivism, or any other instructional strategy, what you must be certain of is that students can be *taught* to employ appropriately *every* evaluative criterion used in the rubric.

Rule 3: Employ as few evaluative criteria as possible. Because people who start thinking seriously about a skill will often begin to recognize a host of nuances associated with the skill, they sometimes feel compelled to set forth a veritable litany of evaluative criteria. But for instructional purposes, as for most other purposes, less almost always turns out to be more. Try to focus your instructional attention on three or four evaluative criteria; you'll become overwhelmed if you try to promote students' mastery of a dozen evaluative criteria.

Rule 4: Provide a succinct label for each evaluative criterion. The instructional yield of a skill-focused rubric can be increased simply by giving each evaluative criterion a brief explanatory label. For instance, suppose you were trying to improve your students' oral presentation skills. You might employ a skill-focused rubric for oral communication containing four evaluative criteria—namely, *delivery, organization, content,* and *language.* These one-word, easy-to-remember labels will help remind you *and your students* of what's truly important in judging mastery of the skill being assessed.

Rule 5: Match the length of the rubric to your own tolerance for detail. I've spent a fair amount of time worrying about this particular rule because much of my early experience in generating skill-focused rubrics dealt with the creation of lengthy scoring rubrics for high-stakes statewide or districtwide assessments. Such detailed rubrics were intended to constrain scorers so their scores would be in agreement. But I've discovered that many classroom teachers consider fairly long, rather detailed rubrics to be altogether off-putting. Whereas those teachers might be willing to create and/or use a one-page rubric, they would regard a six-page rubric as reprehensible. More recently, therefore, I've been recommending much shorter rubrics—rubrics that never exceed one or two pages.

Of course, not all teachers are put off by very detailed rubrics. Some teachers, in fact, find that abbreviated rubrics just don't do an adequate job for them. Such detail-prone teachers would rather work with rubrics that specifically spell out just what's involved when differentiating between quality levels regarding each evaluative criterion. I've therefore come to the conclusion that rubrics should be built to match the detail preferences of the teachers involved. Teachers who believe in brevity should create brief rubrics, and teachers who believe in detail should create lengthier rubrics. If school districts (or publishers) are supplying rubrics to teachers, I recommend both a short and a long version be provided. Let teachers decide on the level of detail that best meshes with their own tolerance/need for detail.

So far, skill-focused rubrics have been touted in this chapter as the most useful for promoting students' mastery of really high-level skills. Such advocacy has been present because of the considerable instruction contributions that can be made by skill-focused rubrics.

But please do not feel obliged to carve out a skill-focused rubric every time you find yourself needing a rubric. There will be occasions when your instruction is not aimed at high-level cognitive skills, but you still want your students to achieve what's being sought of them. To illustrate, you might want to determine your students' mastery of a recently enacted federal law—a law that will have a significant impact on how American citizens elect their legislators. Well, suppose you decide to employ a constructed-response testing strategy for assessing your students' understanding of this particular law. More specifically, you want your students to write an original, explanatory essay describing how certain of the law's components might substantially influence U.S. elections. Because, to evaluate your students' essays, you'll need some sort of scoring guide to assist you, what sort of rubric should you choose? Well, in that sort of situation, it is perfectly acceptable to employ a task-specific rubric rather than a skill-focused rubric. If there is no powerful, widely applicable cognitive skill being taught (and assessed), then the scoring can properly be focused on the particular task involved rather than on a more generally usable skill.

To supply a close-to-home example, each of the chapters in *Classroom Assessment* contains a constructed-response Outcome Mastery at the end of each chapter. Readers are asked to score their own responses by considering (1) an illustrative response to the Outcome Mastery's task and (2) several suggested evaluative criteria that could be used in a rubric to score a reader's response to the chapter's task. If you consider those per-chapter evaluative criteria as components of a possible rubric, you will discern that they will lead to a task-specific rubric rather than a skill-focused one. What's being sought in this book is your mastery of particular content in each chapter. Particularistic curricular targets will almost always lead to the use of task-specific rather than skill-focused rubrics. It is okay if they do.

Lights ... Action ... Computers!

Two major educational assessment consortia were established in 2010: the Partnership for the Assessment of Readiness for College and Careers (PARCC) and the Smarter Balanced Assessment Consortium (SBAC). Early on, both of those federally funded collaboratives promised that a meaningful number of computer-based performance tests would be included in the assessments they intended to develop for the 2014–15 school year. The SBAC tests were, in fact, used during the 2014–2015 school year; the PARCC tests were administered one year later during the 2015–2016 school year. These performance tests were designed to take full advantage of technological advances in the presentation and scoring of computer-governed test items. Leaders of both SBAC and PARCC were confident that, because they intended to employ computer-controlled items for their new assessments, and could require students to respond to those items on computers, it would be possible to present test-takers with more challenging, yet authentic, kinds of performance tests.

American educators have now had an opportunity to review the performance tests generated by PARCC and SBAC, so teachers and administrators in many states are forming their own judgments about the merits of those assessments. From the perspective of the item-writers who must construct computer-enhanced performance assessments, it is an exciting opportunity to create assessments simply swathed in *verisimilitude* (the appearance or semblance of truth). Indeed, creating such items may be only slightly more exciting to those item-writers than being able to dress up their conversations by tossing in an occasional "verisimilitude."

However, glitter alone won't help a guitar produce good music. Educators will need to apply the same levels of evaluative scrutiny to fancy computer-generated performance tests that they previously applied to performance tests served up in paper-and-ink test booklets. That is, can we base valid interpretations about a student's mastery of a worthwhile curricular aim on a student's interaction with one of these glitzy, computer-governed performance tests? If the tests do, as hoped, provide evidence regarding a student's status related to a worthwhile curricular aim, can teachers determine what sort of instructional support is needed by a student whose performance-test efforts are flawed? If a computer-based performance test is loaded with sparkle and spangles, yet turns out to be merely an intelligence test, was that performance test really worth building?

When you try to decide how much confidence you should give to inferences based on your students' performance-test results, this is where good, hard thinking needs to prevail. Do not defer, automatically, to the results of assessments based on flashy, computer-managed test results. Instead, think through carefully—for yourself—just what's going on when students are asked to complete an innovative performance test. Then, thinking about "what's going on" when arriving at a score-base inference, decide for yourself whether to trust the evidence staring you in the face.

RATINGS AND OBSERVATIONS

Once you've selected your evaluative criteria, you then need to apply them reliably to the judgment of students' responses. If the nature of the performance test task calls for students to create some sort of *product,* such as a written report of an experiment carried out in a biology class, then at your leisure you can rate the product's quality in relation to the criteria you've identified as important. For example, if you had decided on three criteria to use in evaluating students' reports of biology experiments, and could award from 0 to 4 points for each criterion, then you could leisurely assign from 0 to 12 points for each written report. The more clearly you understand what each evaluative criterion is, and what it means to award a different number of points on whatever scale you've selected, the more accurate your scores will be. Performance tests that yield student products are easier to rate because you can rate students' responses when you're in the mood.

It is often the case with performance tests, however, that the student's performance takes the form of some kind of *behavior.* With such performance tests, it will usually be necessary for you to observe the behavior as it takes place. To illustrate, suppose that you are an elementary school teacher whose fifth-grade students have been carrying out fairly elaborate social studies projects culminating in 15-minute oral reports to classmates. Unless you have the equipment to videotape your students' oral presentations, you'll have to observe the oral reports and make judgments about the quality of a student's performance as it occurs. As was true when scores were given to student products, in making evaluative judgments about students' behavior, you will apply whatever criteria you've chosen and assign what you consider to be the appropriate number of points on the scales you are using.

For some observations, you'll find it sensible to make instant, on-the-spot quality judgments. For instance, if you are judging students' social studies reports on the basis of (1) content, (2) organization, and (3) presentation, you might make observation-based judgments on each of those three criteria as soon as a report is finished. In other cases, your observations might incorporate a delayed evaluative approach. For instance, let's say that you are working with students in a speech class on the elimination of "filler words and sounds," two of the most prominent of which are starting a sentence with "well" and interjecting frequent "uh"s into a presentation. In the nonevaluative phase of the observation, you could simply count the number of "well"s and "uh"s uttered by a student. Then, at a later time, you could decide on a point allocation for the criterion "avoids filler words and sounds." Putting it another way, systematic observations may be set up so you make immediate or delayed allocations of points for the evaluative criteria you've chosen. If the evaluative criteria involve qualitative factors that must be appraised more judgmentally, then on-the-spot evaluations and point assignments are typically the way to go. If the evaluative criteria involve more quantitative factors, then a "count now and judge later" approach usually works better.

SOURCES OF ERROR IN SCORING STUDENT PERFORMANCES

When scoring student performances, there are three common sources of error that can contribute to inaccurate inferences. First, there is the *scoring scale*. Second, there are the *scorers* themselves who may bring a number of bothersome biases to the enterprise. Finally, there are errors in the *scoring procedure*—that is, the process by which the scorers employ the scoring scale.

Scoring-Instrument Flaws

The major defect with most scoring instruments is the lack of descriptive rigor with which the evaluative criteria to be used are described. Given this lack of rigor, ambiguity exists in the interpretations scorers make about what the scoring criteria mean. This typically leads to a set of unreliable ratings. For example, if teachers are to rate students on the extent to which students are "controlling," some teachers may view this as a positive quality and some may view it as a negative quality. Clearly, an inadequately clarified scoring form can lead to all sorts of "noise" in the scores provided by teachers.

Procedural Flaws

Among common problems with scoring students' responses to performance tests, we usually encounter demands on teachers to rate too many qualities. Overwhelmed scorers are scorers rendered ineffectual. Teachers who opt for a large number of evaluative criteria are teachers who have made a decisively inept opt. Care should be taken that no more than three or four evaluative criteria are to be employed in evaluations of students' responses to your performance assessments. Generally speaking, the fewer evaluative criteria used, the better.

Teachers' Personal-Bias Errors

If you recall Chapter 5's consideration of assessment bias, you'll remember that bias is clearly an undesirable commodity. Teachers, albeit unintentionally, are frequently biased in the way they score students' responses. Several kinds of personal-bias errors are often encountered when teachers score students' constructed responses. The first of these, known as *generosity error*, occurs when a teacher's bias leads to higher ratings than are warranted. Teachers with a proclivity toward generosity errors see good even where no good exists.

At the other extreme, some teachers display *severity errors*. A severity error, of course, is a tendency to underrate the quality of a student's work. When a pupil's product deserves a "good," a teacher suffering from this personal-bias error will award it only an "average" or even a "below average."

But What Does This Have to Do with Teaching?

Teachers are busy people. (This profound recognition will not come as a surprise to anyone who really knows what a teacher's life is like.) But busy people who are apt to survive in their task-buffeted lives will typically try to manage their multiple responsibilities efficiently. Busy people who are teachers, therefore, need to make sure they don't expend their finite reservoir of energy unwisely. And that's where caution needs to be exerted with respect to the use of performance tests. Performance testing, you see, can be so very *seductive*.

Because performance tests are typically focused on measuring a student's mastery of real-world, significant skills, such tests are appealing. If you're an English teacher, for example, wouldn't you rather see whether your students possess composition skills by having them whip out actual "written-from-scratch" compositions than having them spot punctuation problems in multiple-choice items? Of course you would.

But although the allure of performance assessment is considerable, you should never forget that *it takes time!* And the time-consumption requirements of performance testing can readily eat into a teacher's daily 24-hour allotment. It takes time for teachers to come up with defensible tasks for performance tests, to devise suitable rubrics for scoring students' responses, and to actually score those responses. Performance assessment takes time. But, of course, proper performance testing not only helps teachers aim their instruction in the right directions; it also allows students to recognize the skill(s) being promoted.

So, the trick is to select judiciously the cognitive skills you will measure via performance tests. Focus on a small number of truly significant skills. You'll be more likely to maintain your instructional sanity if you employ only a handful of high-level performance tests. Too many performance tests can quickly put a teacher over the edge.

Another sort of personal-bias error is known as *central-tendency error*. This describes a tendency for teachers to view everything as being "in the middle of the scale." Very high or very low ratings are avoided by such folks. They prefer the warm fuzziness of the mean or the median. They tend to regard midpoint ratings as inoffensive and they therefore dispense midpoint ratings almost thoughtlessly.

A particularly frequent error arises when a teacher's overall impression of a student influences how the teacher rates that student with respect to an individual criterion. This error is known as *halo effect*. If a teacher has a favorable attitude toward a student, that student will receive a host of positive ratings (deserved or not) on a number of individual criteria. Similarly, if a teacher has an unfavorable attitude toward a student, the student will receive a pile of negative ratings on all sorts of separate criteria.

One way to minimize halo effect, at least a bit, is occasionally to reverse the order of the high and low positions on the scoring scale so the teacher cannot *unthinkingly* toss out a whole string of positives (or negatives). What you really need to do to avoid halo effect when you're scoring students' responses is to remember it's always lurking in the wings. Try to score a student's responses on each evaluative criterion by using that specific criterion, not a contaminated general impression of the student's ability.

WHAT DO CLASSROOM TEACHERS REALLY NEED TO KNOW ABOUT PERFORMANCE ASSESSMENT?

Performance assessment has been around for a long, long while. Yet, in recent years, a growing number of educators have become strong supporters of this form of assessment because it (1) represents an alternative to traditional paper-and-pencil tests and (2) is often more authentic—that is, reflective of tasks people routinely need to perform in the real world. One of the things you need to understand about performance assessment is that it differs from more conventional assessment chiefly in the degree the assessment task matches the skills and/or knowledge about which you wish to make inferences. Because performance tasks often coincide more closely with high-level cognitive skills than do paper-and-pencil tests, more accurate interpretations can often be derived about students. Another big plus for performance tests is they establish assessment targets that, because such targets often influence the teacher's instruction, can have a positive impact on instructional activities.

You need to realize, however, that because performance tasks require a fair chunk of time from students, the teacher is often faced with making rather shaky generalizations on the basis of relatively few student performances. It's also important for you to recognize that the development of defensible performance tests is difficult cerebral work. It takes rigorous thinking to identify suitable tasks for performance tests and then isolate appropriate evaluative criteria and spell out the scoring scale for each criterion. And, of course, once the test and its associated scoring procedures are in place, you still have to score students' performances—an operation that invariably takes much more time than is required to score a ream of answers to selected-response items.

The chapter's final admonitions regarding the biases that teachers bring to the scoring of students' responses to performance tests should serve as a reminder. If you employ performance tests frequently in your classrooms, you'll need to be careful at every step of the process—from the original conception and birthing of a performance test down to the bias-free scoring of students' responses.

PARENT TALK

The vice president of your school's Parent Advisory Council has asked you to tell him why so many of your school's teachers are now assessing students with performance tests instead of the more traditional paper-and-pencil tests.

 If I were you, here's how I'd respond:

"The reason that most of us are increasingly relying on performance tests these days is that performance tests almost always measure higher-level student skills. With traditional tests, too many of our teachers found they were inadvertently assessing only the students' abilities to memorize facts.

"In recent years, educators have become far more capable of devising really *demanding* performance tests that require students to display genuinely high-level intellectual skills—skills that are way, way beyond memorization. We've learned how to develop the tests *and* how to score students' responses using carefully developed scoring rules that we refer to as *rubrics*.

"Please stop by my classroom and I'll show you some examples of these demanding performance tests. We're asking more from our students, and we're getting it."

 Now, how would you respond to the vice president of the Parent Advisory Council?

CHAPTER SUMMARY

Although this chapter dealt specifically with performance assessment, a number of the points made in the chapter apply with equal force to the scoring of any type of constructed-response items such as those used in essay tests or short-answer tests. After defining performance tests as a measurement procedure in which students create original responses to an assessment task, it was pointed out that performance tests differ from more conventional tests primarily in the degree the test situation approximates the real-life situation to which inferences are made.

The identification of suitable tasks for performance assessments was given considerable attention in the chapter because unsuitable tasks will surely lead to unsatisfactory performance assessments. Seven evaluative criteria were supplied for performance test tasks: (1) generalizability, (2) authenticity, (3) multiple foci, (4) teachability, (5) fairness, (6) feasibility, and (7) scorability. Particular emphasis was given to selecting tasks about which defensible inferences could be drawn regarding students' generalized abilities to perform comparable tasks.

The significance of the skill to be assessed via a performance task was stressed. Next, *evaluative criteria* were defined as the factors by which the acceptability of a student's performance is judged. The evaluative criteria constitute the most important features of a *rubric* that's employed to score student responses. The significance of selecting suitable evaluative criteria was emphasized. Once the criteria have been identified, a numerical scoring scale, usually consisting of three to six score points, is devised for each evaluative criterion. The evaluative criteria are applied to student performances in the form of ratings for student products or observations for student behaviors.

Distinctions were drawn among *task-specific, hypergeneral,* and *skill-focused rubrics.* Deficits in the former two types of rubrics render them less appropriate for supporting a teacher's classroom instructional effort. A skill-focused rubric, however, can markedly enhance a teacher's instruction.

Determining Your Outcome Mastery

The intent of this chapter was to promote an overall understanding of performance testing and how it can be used to help engender higher-order skills on the part of students. The chapter addressed three questions: (1) What is performance assessment? (2) What should its tasks be? (3) How should students' responses to those tasks be scored?

Look back at the chapter's chief intended learning outcome:

> *A sufficiently broad understanding of performance assessment to distinguish between accurate and inaccurate statements regarding the nature of performance tests, the identification of such tests' tasks, and the scoring of students' performances*

You should now be sufficiently familiar with what's involved in performance testing—its strengths, its weaknesses, and how it works—so you can arrive at a more defensible decision about the degree to which you will use performance assessment in your own teaching.

To help you discern whether you have attained mastery of this outcome, complete both the Selected-Response and the Constructed-Response quizzes and think about the feedback you receive for each quiz.

MyEdLab *Selected-Response Check of Outcome Mastery*

MyEdLab *Constructed-Response Check of Outcome Mastery*

After completing both quizzes, go to the Learning Outcome Mastery Determination, where you will decide whether you've mastered the chapter's learning outcome or whether you need further study.

MyEdLab *Learning Outcome Mastery Determination*

References

Boyd-Batstone, P. (2007). *Anecdotal records assessment: An observational tool with a standards-based focus.* Norwood, MA: Christopher-Gordon.

Fitzpatrick, R., and Morrison, E. J. (1971). "Performance and product evaluation." In E. L. Thorndike (Ed.), *Educational Measurement* (pp. 237–270). Washington, DC: American Council on Education.

Glickman-Bond, J., and Rose, K. (2006). *Creating and using rubrics in today's class-rooms: A practical guide.* Norwood, MA: Christopher-Gordon.

Marzano, R. J. (2008). *Vision document.* Bloomington, IN: Marzano Research Laboratory.

Waugh, C. K., and Gronlund, N. (2013). *Measurement and assessment in teaching* (10th ed.). Columbus, OH: Pearson.

Wormeli, R. (2008, September). "Show what you know," *Principal Leadership,* 9, no. 1: 48–52.

9

Portfolio Assessment

CHIEF CHAPTER OUTCOME

An understanding not only of the distinctive relationship between measurement and instruction inherent in portfolio assessment, but also the essentials of a seven-step process teachers can use to install portfolio assessment

"Assessment should be a part of instruction, not apart from it" is a point of view most proponents of portfolio assessment would enthusiastically endorse. Portfolio assessment, a contemporary entry in the educational measurement derby, has captured the attention of many educators because it represents a clear alternative to more traditional forms of educational testing.

A *portfolio* is a systematic collection of one's work. In education, portfolios refer to systematic collections of students' work. Although the application of portfolios in education has been a relatively recent phenomenon, portfolios have been widely used in a number of other fields for many years. Portfolios, in fact, constitute the chief method by which certain professionals display their skills and accomplishments. For example, portfolios are traditionally used for this purpose by photographers, artists, journalists, models, architects, and so on. Although many educators tend to think of portfolios as collections of written works featuring "words on paper," today's almost literal explosion of technological devices makes it possible for students to assemble their work in a variety of electronically retained forms rather than as a sheaf of hand-written papers in a manila folder. An important feature of portfolios is that they must be updated as a person's achievements and skills grow.

Portfolios have been warmly embraced by those educators who regard traditional assessment with less than enthusiasm. In Table 9.1, for example, a chart presented by Tierney, Carter, and Desai (1991) indicates what those three proponents of portfolios believe are the differences between *portfolio assessment* and assessment based on standardized testing.

table 9.1 ■ **Differences in Assessment Outcomes between Portfolios and Standardized Testing Practices**

Portfolio	Testing
Represents the range of reading and writing students are engaged in	Assesses students across a limited range of reading and writing assignments which may not match what students do
Engages students in assessing their progress and/or accomplishments and establishing ongoing learning goals	Mechanically scored or scored by teachers who have little input
Measures each student's achievement while allowing for individual differences between students	Assesses all students on the same dimensions
Represents a collaborative approach to assessment	Assessment process is not collaborative
Has a goal of student self-assessment	Student assessment is not a goal
Addresses improvement, effort, and achievement	Addresses achievement only
Links assessment and teaching to learning	Separates learning, testing, and teaching

Source: Material from *Portfolio Assessment in the Reading-Writing Classroom,* by Robert J. Tierney, Mark A. Carter, and Laura E. Desai, published by Christopher-Gordon Publishers, Inc. © 1991, used with permission of the publisher.

CLASSROOM PORTFOLIO ASSESSMENT VERSUS LARGE-SCALE PORTFOLIO ASSESSMENT

Classroom Applications

Most advocates of portfolio assessment believe the real payoffs for such assessment approaches lie in the individual teacher's classroom, because the relationship between instruction and assessment will be strengthened as a consequence of students' continuing accumulation of work products in their portfolios. Ideally, teachers who adopt portfolios in their classrooms will make the ongoing collection and appraisal of students' work a central focus of the instructional program rather than a peripheral activity whereby students occasionally gather up their work to convince a teacher's supervisors or students' parents that good things have been going on in class.

Here's a description of how an elementary teacher might use portfolios to assess students' progress in social studies, language arts, and mathematics. The teacher, let's call him Phil Pholio, asks students to keep three portfolios, one in each of those three subject fields. In each portfolio, the students are to place their early and revised work products. The work products are always dated so Mr. Pholio, as well as the students themselves, can see what kinds of differences in quality take place over time. For example, if effective instruction is being provided, there should be discernible improvement in the caliber of students' written compositions, solutions to mathematics problems, and analyses of social issues.

Three or four times per semester, Mr. Pholio holds 15- to 20-minute portfolio conferences with each student about the three different portfolios. The other, non-conferencing students take part in small-group and independent learning activities while the portfolio conferences are conducted. During a conference, the participating student plays an active role in evaluating his or her own work. Toward the close of the school year, students select from their regular portfolios a series of work products that not only represent their best final versions but also indicate how those final products were created. These selections are placed in a display portfolio featured at a spring open-school session designed for parents. Parents who visit the school are urged to take their children's display portfolios home. Mr. Pholio also sends portfolios home to parents who are unable to attend the open-school event.

There are, of course, many other ways to use portfolios effectively in a classroom. Phil Pholio, our phictitious (sic) teacher, employed a fairly common approach, but a variety of alternative procedures could also work quite nicely. The major consideration is that the teacher uses portfolio *assessment* as an integral aspect of the *instructional* process. Because portfolios can be tailored to a specific student's evolving growth, the ongoing diagnostic value of portfolios for teachers is immense.

Who Is Evaluating Whom?

Roger Farr, a leader in language arts instruction and assessment, contends that the real payoff from proper portfolio assessment is that students' *self-evaluation* capabilities are enhanced. Thus, during portfolio conferences the teacher encourages students to come up with personal appraisals of their own work. The conference, then, becomes far more than merely an opportunity for the teacher to dispense an "oral report card." On the contrary, students' self-evaluation skills are nurtured not only during portfolio conferences but also throughout the entire school year. For this reason, Farr strongly prefers the term *working portfolios* rather than *showcase portfolios* because he believes self-evaluation is nurtured more readily in connection with ongoing reviews of products not intended to impress external viewers.

For self-evaluation purposes, it is particularly useful to be able to compare earlier work with later work. Fortunately, even if a teacher's instruction is downright abysmal, students grow older and, as a consequence of maturation, tend to get better at what they do in school. If a student is required to review three versions of a student's written composition (a first draft, a second draft, and a final draft), self-evaluation can be fostered by encouraging the student to make comparative judgments of the three compositions based on appropriate evaluative criteria. As anyone who has done much writing knows, written efforts tend to get better with time and revision. Contrasts of later versions with earlier versions can prove illuminating from an appraisal perspective and, because students' self-evaluation is so critical to their future growth, from an instructional perspective as well.

Large-Scale Applications

It is one thing to use portfolios for classroom assessment; it is quite another to use portfolios for large-scale assessment programs. Several states and large school districts have attempted to install portfolios as a central component of a large-scale accountability assessment program—that is, a program in which student performances serve as an indicator of an educational system's effectiveness. To date, the results of efforts to employ portfolios for accountability purposes have not been encouraging.

In large-scale applications of portfolio assessments for accountability purposes, students' portfolios are judged either by the students' regular teachers or by a cadre of specially trained scorers (often teachers) who carry out the scoring at a central site. The problem with specially trained scorers and central-site scoring is that it typically costs much more than can be afforded. Some states, therefore, have opted to have all portfolios scored by students' own teachers who then relay such scores to the state department. The problem with having regular teachers score students' portfolios, however, is that such scoring tends to be too unreliable for use in accountability programs. Not only have teachers usually not been provided with thorough training about how to score portfolios, but there is also a tendency for teachers to be biased in favor of their own students. To cope with such problems, sometimes teachers in a school or district evaluate their students' portfolios, but then a random sample of those portfolios are scored by state officials as an "audit" of the local scoring's accuracy.

One of the most visible of the statewide efforts to use portfolios on every pupil has been a performance assessment program in the state of Vermont. Because substantial national attention has been focused on the Vermont program, and because it has been evaluated independently, many policymakers in other states have drawn on the experiences encountered in the Vermont Portfolio Assessment Program. Unfortunately, independent evaluators of Vermont's statewide efforts to use portfolios found that there was considerable unreliability in the appraisals given to students' work. And, if you harken back to Chapter 3's quick dip into the importance of reliability, it's tough to draw valid inferences about students' achievements if the assessments of those achievements are not made with consistency.

But, of course, this is a book about classroom assessment, not large-scale assessment. It certainly hasn't been shown definitely that portfolios do *not* have a place in large-scale assessment. What has been shown, however, is that there are significant obstacles to be surmounted if portfolio assessment is going to make a meaningful contribution to large-scale educational accountability testing.

DECISION TIME

Does Self-Evaluation Equal Self-Grading?

After a midsummer, schoolwide three-day workshop on the Instructional Payoffs of Classroom Portfolios, the faculty at Rhoda Street Elementary School have agreed to install student portfolios in all classrooms for one or more subject areas. Maria Martinez, an experienced third-grade teacher in the school, has decided to try out portfolios only in mathematics. She admits to her family (but not to her fellow teachers) that she's not certain she'll be able to use portfolios properly with her students.

Because she has attempted to follow the guidelines of the National Council of Teachers of Mathematics, Maria stresses mathematical problem solving and the integration of mathematical understanding with content from other disciplines. Accordingly, she asks her students to place in their mathematics portfolios versions of their attempts to solve quantitative problems drawn from other subjects. Maria poses these problems for her third-graders and then requires them to prepare an initial solution strategy and to revise that solution at least twice. Students are directed to put all solutions (dated) in their portfolios.

Six weeks after the start of school, Maria sets up a series of 15-minute portfolio conferences with her students. During the three days on which the portfolio conferences are held, students who are not involved in a conference move through a series of learning stations in other subject areas where they typically engage in a fair amount of peer critiquing of each other's responses to various kinds of practice exercises.

Having learned during the summer workshop that the promotion of students' self-evaluation is critical if students are to get the most from portfolios, Maria devotes the bulk of her 15-minute conferences to students' personal appraisals of their own work. Although Maria offers some of her own appraisals of most students' work, she typically allows the student's self-evaluation to override her own estimates of a student's ability to solve each problem.

Because it will soon be time to give students their 10-week grades, Maria doesn't know whether to base the grades on her own judgments or on students' self-appraisals.

 If you were Maria, what would you decide to do?

KEY INGREDIENTS IN CLASSROOM PORTFOLIO ASSESSMENT

Although there are numerous ways to install and sustain portfolios in a classroom, you will find that the following seven-step sequence provides a reasonable template for getting under way with portfolio assessment. Taken together, these seven activities capture the key ingredients in classroom-based portfolio assessment.

1. *Make sure your students "own" their portfolios.* In order for portfolios to represent a student's evolving work accurately, and to foster the kind of self-evaluation so crucial if portfolios are to be truly educational, students must perceive portfolios to be collections of their own work and not merely temporary receptacles for products you ultimately grade. You will probably want to introduce the notion of portfolio assessment to your students (assuming portfolio assessment isn't already a schoolwide operation and your students aren't already familiar with the use of portfolios) by explaining the distinctive functions of portfolios in the classroom.

2. *Decide on what kinds of work samples to collect.* Various kinds of work samples can be included in a portfolio. Obviously, such products will vary from subject to subject. In general, a substantial variety of work products is preferable to a limited range of work products. However, for portfolios organized around students' mastery of a particularly limited curricular aim, it may be preferable to include only a single kind of work product. Ideally, you and your students can collaboratively determine what goes in the portfolio.

3. *Collect and store work samples.* Students need to collect the designated work samples as they are created, place them in a suitable container (a folder or notebook, for example), and then store the container in a file cabinet, storage box, or some suitably safe location. You may need to work individually with your students to help them decide whether particular products should be placed in their portfolios. The actual organization of a portfolio's contents depends, of course, on the nature of the work samples being collected.

4. *Select criteria by which to evaluate portfolio work samples.* Working collaboratively with students, carve out a set of criteria by which you and your students can judge the quality of your students' portfolio products. Because of the likely diversity of products in different students' portfolios, the identification of evaluative criteria will not be a simple task. Yet, unless at least rudimentary evaluative criteria are isolated, the students will find it difficult to evaluate their own efforts and, thereafter, to strive for improvement. The criteria, once selected, should be described with the same sort of clarity we saw in the previous chapter regarding how to employ a rubric's evaluative criteria when judging students' responses to performance test tasks.

5. *Require students to evaluate continually their own portfolio products.* Using the agreed-on evaluative criteria, be sure your students routinely appraise their own work. Students can be directed to evaluate their work products holistically, analytically, or using a combination of both approaches. Such self-evaluation can be made routine by requiring each student to complete brief evaluation slips on $3' \times 5'$ cards on which they identify the major strengths and weaknesses of a given product and then suggest how the product could be improved. Be sure to have your students date such self-evaluation sheets so they can keep track of modifications in their self-evaluation skills. Each completed self-evaluation sheet should be stapled or paper-clipped to the work product being evaluated.

6. *Schedule and conduct portfolio conferences.* Portfolio conferences take time. Yet, these interchange sessions between teachers and students regarding students' work are really pivotal in making sure portfolio assessment fulfills its potential. The conference should not only evaluate your students' work products but should also help them improve their self-evaluation abilities. Try to hold as many of these conferences as you can. In order to make the conferences time efficient, be sure to have students prepare for the conferences so you can start right in on the topics of most concern to you and the student.

7. *Involve parents in the portfolio assessment process.* Early in the school year, make sure your students' parents understand what the nature of the portfolio assessment process is you've devised for your classroom. Insofar as is practical, encourage your students' parents/guardians periodically to review their children's work samples as well as their children's self-evaluation of those work samples. The more active parents become in reviewing their children's work, the stronger the message will be to the child that the portfolio activity is really worthwhile. If you wish, you may have students select their best work for a showcase portfolio or, instead, simply use the students' working portfolios.

These seven steps reflect only the most important activities teachers might engage in when creating assessment programs in their classrooms. There are obviously all sorts of variations and embellishments possible.

There's one situation in which heavy student involvement in the portfolio process may not make instructional sense. This occurs in the early grades when, in the teacher's judgment, those little tykes are not developmentally ready to take a meaningful hand in a full-blown portfolio self-evaluation extravaganza. Any sort of educational assessment ought to be *developmentally appropriate* for the students who are being assessed. Thus, for students who are in early primary grade levels, a teacher may sensibly decide to employ only *showcase* portfolios to display a child's accomplishments to the child and the child's parents. *Working* portfolios, simply bristling with student-evaluated products, can be left for later. This is, clearly, a teacher's call.

Purposeful Portfolios

There are numerous choice-points you'll encounter if you embark on a portfolio assessment approach in your own classroom. The first one ought to revolve around *purpose*. Why is it that you are contemplating a meaningful prance down the portfolio pathway?

Assessment specialists typically identify three chief purposes for portfolio assessment. The first of these is *documentation of student progress* wherein the major function of the assembled work samples is to provide the student, the teacher, and the student's parents with evidence about the student's growth—or lack of it. These are the *working* portfolios that provide meaningful opportunities for self-evaluation by students.

Pointing out that students' achievement levels ought to influence teachers' instructional decisions, Anderson (2003, p. 44) concludes that "the information should be collected as near to the decision as possible (e.g., final examinations are administered in close proximity to end-of-term grades). However, if decisions are to be based on learning, then a plan for information collection over time must be developed and implemented." The more current any documentation of students' progress is, the more accurate such documentation is apt to be.

From an *instructional* perspective, the really special advantage of portfolio assessment is that its recurrent assessment of the student's status with respect to mastery of a demanding skill provides both teachers and students assessment-informed opportunities to make any needed adjustments in what they are currently doing. Later in Chapter 12, we will be considering the instructional dividends of the formative-assessment process. Well, because of its periodic, recurring assessment of students' evolving skill-mastery, portfolio assessment practically forces teachers to engage in a classroom instructional process closely resembling formative assessment.

A second purpose of portfolios is to provide an opportunity for *showcasing student accomplishments*. Stiggins (2003) describes portfolios that showcase students' best work as *celebration portfolios,* and he contends celebration portfolios are especially appropriate for the early grades. In portfolios intended to showcase student accomplishments, students typically select their best work and reflect thoughtfully on its quality.

One midwest teacher I know always makes sure students include the following elements in their showcase portfolios:

- A letter of introduction to portfolio reviewers
- A table of contents
- Identification of the skills or knowledge being demonstrated
- A representative sample of the student's best work
- Dates on all entries
- The evaluative criteria (or rubric) being used
- The student's self-reflection on all entries

The inclusion of student self-reflections about ingredients of portfolios is a pivotal ingredient in showcase portfolios. Some portfolio proponents contend that a portfolio's self-evaluation by the student helps the learner learn better and permits the reader of the portfolio to gain insights about how the learner learns.

A final purpose for portfolios is *evaluation of student status*—that is, the determination of whether students have met previously determined quality levels of performance. McMillan (2013) points out that when portfolios are used for this purpose, there must be greater standardization about what should be included in a portfolio and how the work samples should be appraised. Typically, teachers select the entries for this kind of portfolio, and considerable attention is given to scoring so any rubrics employed to score the portfolios will yield consistent results even if different scorers are involved. For portfolios being used to evaluate student status, there is usually less need for self-evaluation of entries—unless such self-evaluations are themselves being evaluated by others.

Well, we've peeked at three purposes underlying portfolio assessment. Can one portfolio perform all three functions? My answer is a somewhat shaky *yes*. But if you were to ask me whether one portfolio can perform all three functions *well*, you'd get a rock-solid *no*. The three functions, though somewhat related—rather like second cousins—are fundamentally different.

That's why your very first decision if you're going to install portfolios in your classroom is to decide on the *primary purpose* of the portfolios. You can then determine what the portfolios should look like and how students should prepare them.

Scripture tells us that "no man can serve two masters." (The authors of that scriptural advice, clearly insensitive to gender equality, were not implying that females are more capable of double-master serving.) Similarly, one kind of portfolio cannot blithely satisfy multiple functions. Some classroom teachers rush into portfolio assessment because they've heard about all of the enthralling things that portfolios can do. But one kind of portfolio cannot easily fulfill all three functions. Pick your top-priority purpose and then build your portfolio assessment to satisfy this purpose.

Work-Sample Selection

For a teacher just joining the portfolio party, another key decision hinges on the identification of the work samples to be put into the portfolios. All too often, teachers who are novices at portfolio assessment will fail to think divergently enough about the kinds of entries that should constitute a portfolio's chief contents.

But divergency is not necessarily a virtue when it comes to the determination of a portfolio's contents. You shouldn't search for varied kinds of work samples simply for the sake of variety. What's important is that the particular kinds of work samples to be included in the portfolio will allow you to derive valid inferences about the skills and/or knowledge you're trying to have your students master. It's far better to include a few kinds of *inference-illuminating* work samples than to include a galaxy of work samples, many of which do not contribute to your interpretations regarding students' knowledge or skills.

Appraising Portfolios

As indicated earlier in the chapter, students' portfolios are almost always evaluated by the use of a rubric. The most important ingredients of such a rubric are its evaluative criteria—that is, the factors to be used in determining the quality of a particular student's portfolio. If there's any sort of student self-evaluation to be done, and such self-evaluation is almost always desirable, then it is imperative that students have access to, and thoroughly understand, the rubric that will be used to evaluate their portfolios.

As you'll see when we treat formative assessment in Chapter 12, for certain applications of formative assessment, students must definitely understand the rubrics (and those rubrics' evaluative criteria). However, for *all* forms of portfolio assessment, students' familiarity with rubrics is imperative.

Here's one quick-and-dirty way to appraise any sort of portfolio assessments you might install in your classroom. Simply ask yourself whether your students' portfolios have substantially increased the accuracy of the inferences you make regarding your students' skills and knowledge. If your answer is *yes*, then portfolio assessment is a winner for you. If your answer is *no*, then pitch those portfolios without delay—or guilt. But wait! If your answer resembles "I'm not sure," then you really need to think this issue through rigorously. Classroom assessment is supposed to contribute to more valid inferences from which better instructional decisions can be made. If your portfolio assessment program isn't *clearly* doing those things, you may need to make some serious changes in that program.

THE PROS AND CONS OF PORTFOLIO ASSESSMENT

You must keep in mind that portfolio assessment's greatest strength is that it can be tailored to the individual student's needs, interests, and abilities. Yet, portfolio assessment suffers from the drawback faced by all constructed-response measurement. Students' constructed responses are genuinely difficult to evaluate, particularly when those responses vary from student to student.

As was seen in Vermont's Portfolio Assessment Program, it is quite difficult to come up with consistent evaluations of different students' portfolios.

Sometimes the scoring guides devised for use in evaluating portfolios are so terse and so general as to be almost useless. They're akin to Rorschach ink-blots in which different scorers see in the scoring guide what they want to see. In contrast, some scoring guides are so detailed and complicated that they simply overwhelm scorers. It is difficult to devise scoring guides that embody just the right level of specificity. Generally speaking, most teachers are so busy they don't have time to create elaborate scoring schemes. Accordingly, many teachers (and students) find themselves judging portfolios by using fairly loose evaluative criteria. Such criteria tend to be interpreted differently by different people.

Another problem with portfolio assessment is it takes time—loads of time—to carry out properly. Even if you're very efficient in reviewing your students' portfolios, you'll still have to devote many hours both in class (during portfolio conferences) and outside of class (if you also want to review your students' portfolios by yourself). Proponents of portfolios are convinced the quality of portfolio assessment is worth the time such assessment takes. You at least need to be prepared for the required investment of time if you decide to undertake portfolio assessment. And teachers will definitely need to receive sufficient training to learn how to carry out portfolio assessment well. Any

But What Does This Have to Do with Teaching?

Portfolio assessment almost always fundamentally changes a teacher's approach to instruction. A nifty little selected-response test, or even a lengthy constructed-response exam, can usually be tossed into a teacher's ongoing instructional program without significantly altering how the teacher goes about teaching. But that's not so with portfolio assessment. Once a teacher hops aboard the portfolio bus, there's a long and serious ride in the offing.

Portfolio assessment, if it's properly focused on helping children improve by being able to evaluate their own work samples, becomes a continuing and *central* component of a teacher's instructional program. Work samples have to be chosen, scoring rubrics need to be developed, and students need to be taught how to use those rubrics to monitor the evolving quality of their efforts. Portfolio assessment, therefore, truly dominates most instructional programs in which it is employed.

The first thing you need to do is decide whether the knowledge and skills you are trying to have your students master (especially the skills) lend themselves to portfolio assessment. Will there be student work samples that, because they permit you to make accurate interpretations about your students' evolving skill mastery, could provide the continuing focus for portfolio assessment?

Some content lends itself delightfully to portfolio assessment. Some doesn't. During my first year as a high school teacher, I taught two English courses and a speech class. Because my English courses focused on the promotion of students' composition skills, I think that a portfolio assessment might have worked well in either English course. My students and I could monitor their improvements in being able to write.

But I don't think I would have been able to use portfolios effectively in my speech class. At that time, television itself had just arrived on the West Coast, and videotaping was unknown. Accordingly, my speech students and I wouldn't have had anything to toss in their portfolios.

The first big question you need to ask yourself when it comes to portfolio assessment is quite simple: Is this powerful but time-consuming form of assessment right for what I'm trying to teach?

teachers who set out to do portfolio assessment by simply stuffing student stuff into folders built for stuff stuffing will end up wasting their time and their students' time. Meaningful professional development is a must if portfolio assessment is to work well. If several teachers in a school will be using portfolio assessment in their classes, this would be a marvelous opportunity to establish a *teacher learning community* in which, on a continuing basis during the year, portfolio-using teachers meet to share insights and work collaboratively on common problems.

On the plus side, however, most teachers who have used portfolios agree portfolio assessment provides a way of documenting and evaluating growth happening in a classroom in ways standardized or written tests cannot. Portfolios have the potential to create authentic portraits of what students learn. I agree with Stiggins (2007) when he points out that for portfolios to merge effectively with instruction, they must have a story to tell. Fortunately, this story can be made compatible with improved student learning.

Most of the teachers I've talked with who use portfolio assessments are primarily enamored with two payoffs. They believe that the *self-evaluation* it fosters in students is truly important in guiding students' learning over time. They also think the *personal ownership* students experience regarding their own work, and the progress they experience, makes the benefits of portfolio assessment outweigh its costs.

WHAT DO CLASSROOM TEACHERS REALLY NEED TO KNOW ABOUT PORTFOLIO ASSESSMENT?

As noted at the beginning of this four-chapter excursion into item types, the more familiar you are with different kinds of test items, the more likely you will be to select an item type that best provides you with the information you need in order to draw suitable inferences about your students. Until recently, portfolios haven't been viewed as a viable assessment option by many teachers. These days, however, portfolio assessment clearly is a legitimate weapon in a teacher's assessment arsenal.

You need to realize, if portfolio assessment is going to constitute a helpful adjunct to your instructional program, portfolios will have to become a central, not tangential, part of what goes on in your classroom. The primary premise in portfolio assessment is that a particularized collection of a student's *evolving* work will allow both the student and you to determine the student's progress. You can't gauge the student's progress if you don't have frequent evidence of the student's efforts.

It would be educationally unwise to select portfolio assessment as a one-time measurement approach to deal with a short-term instructional objective. Rather, it makes more sense to select some key curricular aim, such as the student's ability to write original compositions, and then monitor this aspect of the student's learning throughout the entire school year. It is also important for you to recall that although portfolio assessment may prove highly valuable for classroom instruction and measurement purposes, at this juncture there is insufficient evidence it can be used appropriately for large-scale assessment.

A number of portfolio assessment specialists believe the most important dividend from portfolio assessment is the increased abilities of students to evaluate their own work. If this becomes one of your goals in a portfolio assessment approach,

PARENT TALK

Suppose that Mr. and Mrs. Holmgren, parents of your student, Harry, stopped by your classroom during a back-to-school night to examine their son's portfolio. After spending almost 30 minutes going through the portfolio and skimming the portfolios of several other students, they speak to you—not with hostility, but with genuine confusion. Mrs. Holmgren sums up their concerns nicely with the following comments: "When we stopped by Mr. Bray's classroom earlier this evening to see how our daughter, Elissa, is doing, we encountered a series of extremely impressive portfolios. Elissa's was outstanding. To be honest, Harry's portfolio is a lot less polished. It seems that he's included everything he's done in your class, rough drafts as well as final products. Why is there this difference?"

 If I were you, here's how I'd respond to Harry's parents:

"It's really good that you two could take the time to see how Harry and Elissa are doing. And I can understand why you're perplexed by the differences in Elissa's and Harry's portfolios. You see, there are *different* kinds of student portfolios, and different portfolios serve different purposes.

"In Mr. Bray's class, and I know this because we often exchange portfolio tips with one another during regular meetings of our teacher learning community, students prepare what are called *showcase* portfolios. In such portfolios, students pick their very best work to show Mr. Bray and their parents what they've learned. I think Mr. Bray actually sent his students' showcase portfolios home about a month ago so you could see how well Elissa is doing. For Mr. Bray and his students, the portfolios are collections of best work that, in a very real sense, celebrate students' achievements.

"In my class, however, students create *working* portfolios in which the real emphasis is on getting students to make progress and to evaluate this progress *on their own*. When you reviewed Harry's portfolio, did you see how each entry is dated and how he had prepared a brief self-reflection of each entry? I'm more interested in Harry's seeing the improvement he makes than in anyone seeing polished final products. You, too, can see the striking progress he's made over the course of this school year.

"I'm not suggesting that my kind of portfolio is better than Mr. Bray's. Both have a role to play. Those roles, as I'm sure you'll see, are quite different."

 Now, how would you respond to Mr. and Mrs. Holmgren?

you must be certain to nurture such self-evaluation growth deliberately via portfolios instead of simply using portfolios as convenient collections of work samples.

The seven key ingredients in portfolio assessment that were identified in the chapter represent only one way of installing this kind of assessment strategy.

Variations of those seven suggested procedures are not only possible but also to be encouraged. The big thing to keep in mind is that portfolio assessment offers your students and you a way to particularize your evaluation of each student's growth over time. And, speaking of time, it's only appropriate to remind you it takes substantially more time to use a portfolio assessment approach properly than to score a zillion true–false tests. If you opt to try portfolio assessment, you'll have to see whether, *in your own instructional situation,* it yields sufficient educational benefits to be worth the investment you'll surely need to make in it.

CHAPTER SUMMARY

After defining portfolios as systematic collections of students' work, contrasts were drawn between portfolio assessment and more conventional testing. It was suggested that portfolio assessment was far more appropriate for an individual teacher's classroom assessment than for large-scale accountability assessments.

An emphasis on self-assessment was suggested as being highly appropriate for portfolio assessment, particularly in view of the way portfolios can be tailored to an *individual* student's evolving progress. Seven steps were then suggested as key ingredients for classroom teachers to install and sustain portfolio assessment in their classroom: (1) establish student ownership, (2) decide on what work samples to collect, (3) collect and score work samples, (4) select evaluative criteria, (5) require continual student self-evaluations, (6) schedule and conduct portfolio conferences, and (7) involve parents in the portfolio assessment process.

Three different functions of portfolio assessment were identified—namely, documentation of student progress, showcasing student accomplishments, and evaluation of student status. Teachers were urged to select a primary purpose for portfolio assessment.

The chapter was concluded with an identification of plusses and minuses of portfolio assessment. It was emphasized that portfolio assessment represents an important measurement strategy now available to today's classroom teachers.

Determining Your Outcome Mastery

Let's look, once more, at the chief intended learning outcome for this chapter:

An understanding not only of the distinctive relationship between measurement and instruction inherent in portfolio assessment, but also the essentials of a seven-step process teachers can use to install portfolio assessment.

It's expected that you will be in a position to decide if you want to investigate portfolio assessment more deeply or, beyond that, if you might give it a try in your own instructional endeavors.

The Mastery Checks assess your understanding of the powerful instructional payoffs derived from portfolio assessment when it functions as a central component of a teacher's instructional process and also the seven-step procedure for installing portfolio assessment in your own teaching. This chapter-endorsed sequence is, to be sure, not the only way of carrying out portfolio assessment. However, the seven steps in the sequence do represent an experience-derived way of making portfolio assessment purr.

Complete both the Selected-Response and the Constructed-Response quizzes and think about the feedback you receive for each quiz.

MyEdLab *Selected-Response Check of Outcome Mastery*

MyEdLab *Constructed-Response Check of Outcome Mastery*

After completing both quizzes, go to the Learning Outcome Mastery Determination, where you will decide whether you've mastered the chapter's learning outcome or whether you need further study.

MyEdLab *Learning Outcome Mastery Determination*

References

Anderson, L. W. (2003). *Classroom assessment: Enhancing the quality of teacher decision making.* Mahwah, NJ: Erlbaum.

Andrade, H. (2007/2008). "Self-assessment through rubrics," *Educational Leadership,* 65, no. 4 (December/January): 60–63.

McMillan, J. H. (2013). *Classroom assessment: Principles and practice for effective standards-based instruction* (6th ed.). Boston: Allyn and Bacon.

Miller, M. D., and Linn, R. (2012). *Measurement and assessment in teaching* (11th ed.). Columbus, OH: Pearson.

Stiggins, R. J. (2007). *Student-involved classroom assessment for learning* (5th ed.). Upper Saddle River, NJ: Prentice-Hall.

Stiggins, R. J., and Chappuis, J. (2011). *An introduction to student-involved classroom assessment for learning* (6th ed.). Boston: Pearson.

Tierney, R. J., Carter, M. A., and Desai, L. E. (1991). *Portfolio assessment in the reading-writing classroom.* Norwood, MA: Christopher-Gordon.

Affective Assessment

Affective variables, most educators concede, are important. Students' attitudes toward learning, for example, play a major role in how much learning those students subsequently pursue. The values students have regarding truthfulness and integrity shape their daily conduct. And students' self-esteem, of course, influences almost everything they do. There's little doubt that the affective status of students should concern all educators.

In truth, however, few classroom teachers give explicit attention to influencing their students' attitudes and values. Even fewer classroom teachers actually try to assess the affective status of their students. Certainly, a teacher may observe a student's sour demeanor and conclude he's "out of sorts" or she's "a mite depressed," but how many times have you heard about a teacher who tried to gather *systematic* evidence regarding students' attitudes and interests? Unfortunately, systematic assessment of affect is pretty uncommon.

This chapter will address the issue of affective assessment by providing you with general insights regarding the assessment of students' attitudes, interests, and values. Thereafter, the chapter will give you some practical, step-by-step procedures for gauging students' status regarding a number of educationally important affective variables.

WHY ASSESS AFFECT?

One question you might be asking yourself is, Why assess attitudes at all? Many teachers, particularly those who teach older students, believe that their only educational mission is to increase students' knowledge and skills. Affect, such teachers believe, simply doesn't fall into their proper sphere of influence. However, students who learn to perform mathematics like magicians yet abhor mathematics certainly aren't apt to apply the mathematics they've learned. Students who can compose outstanding essays, but believe they are "really rotten writers," won't spend much time volitionally churning out essays.

The Importance of Affect

I'd like to get my own bias regarding this issue out on the table so you don't think I'm trying to subliminally influence you. I personally believe affective variables are often more significant than cognitive variables. How many times, for example, have you seen people who weren't all that intellectually "gifted" still succeed because they were highly motivated and hard working? Conversely, how many times have you seen truly able people simply veer away from challenges because they did not consider themselves worthy? Day in and day out, we see the enormous impact people's affective status has on them. Affect is every bit as important as cognitive ability.

Have you ever seen a group of kindergarten students troop off to school loaded with enthusiasm and gumption, only to encounter those same students a few years later and see that a fair number were disenchanted with school and down on themselves? Well, I have. And what's going on with such children is surely taking place in the affective realm. When most kindergartners start school, they are enthused about school and themselves. However, after failing to be successful for a year or two, many of those formerly upbeat children carry around decisively lowered self-concepts. They've tried and been found wanting. Such negative attitudes about self and school will typically influence all of a child's subsequent education. Yet, because few teachers try to assess their students' affective status, most teachers don't know what their students' attitudes, interests, and values really are. This situation needs to change.

Spurring Affectively Focused Instruction

Even if there were no such thing as externally imposed "educational accountability" whereby students' performances on high-stakes tests serve as indicators of educational effectiveness, what's on achievement tests would still influence the stuff teachers teach. When I was a high school teacher, I knew what kinds of items I had on my final exams. (That is, I knew in the second year of teaching, after I'd whipped out my first-year final exams only minutes before my students needed to take those exams.) Because I wanted my students to do well on my final exams, I made reasonably sure I spent at least some instructional time on the content covered by the final examinations.

It's the same with affective assessment. Let's say you've installed a fairly straightforward pretest–posttest evaluation design to assess changes in your students' responses to an affective inventory regarding whether they are interested in the subject(s) you're teaching. Your recognition that there will be a formal pretest–posttest assessment of students' subject-matter interest will, as surely as school buses run late, influence you to provide instruction so your students will, in fact, become more positive about the subject(s) you're teaching.

DECISION TIME

Where Went Wonder?

Lance Larson has decided to try to get an accurate reading of his kindergarten students' attitudes toward school. Although he has worked with kindergartners for the past four years, only recently has Lance become convinced of the importance of student affect.

Because he is dealing with very young children, most of whom can't read when they arrive at Mission Elementary School, Lance uses an orally administered, anonymously completed inventory for which he reads a question to the students and they are to respond by circling either a smiling face or a frowning face. Students respond to one question, and then another, after Lance tells them to "Answer by the bird," "Answer by the star," and so on.

At the end of the first week of school, students' responses to Lance's inventory indicated they really liked school. In fact, 100 percent of the children responded that they couldn't wait to find out what new things they would learn at school each day. However, three months later, a re-administration of the same inventory showed students' attitudes toward school seemed to have taken a nosedive. Well over half of his kindergartners indicated they no longer looked forward to coming to school. Almost 75 percent, in fact, indicated they were often bored in class. Lance was alarmed.

If you were Lance, what would you decide to do?

In other words, the presence of affective postinstruction measurement will incline you to include affectively focused activities in your instruction. In a sense, you're saying to yourself—and anyone else you care to have understand your instructional planning—that affective outcomes are important enough for you to formally assess them. You can be assured that what's important enough to be assessed, even if it's measured in your classroom and nowhere else in the world, is likely to influence your instruction. As I confessed earlier, I think affectively focused instruction deals with the kinds of outcomes that are some of the most important we teach.

It has been said *we measure what we treasure*. Well, if we really think affective outcomes are worth promoting, we darn well ought to measure them.

Monitoring Students' Status

In addition to serving as an end-of-instruction target, affective assessment devices, if administered regularly, help teachers determine if modifications in their instructional program are warranted. For example, let's say you're a physics teacher and you want to get a fix on how enthused your students are about continuing their study of physics in college. Ideally, you'd like a fair number of your students to get fairly ecstatic over the raptures of future physics coursework. Suppose, each month, you employ a brief self-report attitudinal inventory focused on the likelihood of students' pursuing future physics instruction. For illustrative purposes, let's assume that in September, 60 percent of your students registered an interest in taking college physics courses and in October about 65 percent indicated such an interest. In November, however, interest in future physics courses plummeted so only 25 percent of your students signified any interest in college physics. This is a clear message to you that something went on in late October or early November to really turn off your budding Nobel Laureates. A review of your instructional program during that period and some serious effort on your part to generate more interest in postsecondary physics would seem to be warranted. As you can see, periodic monitoring of your students' affective status can assist you in seeing what sorts of shifts in your instructional program might be needed.

In review, there are a number of reasons classroom teachers should devote at least a segment of their assessment program to the measurement of students' affect. If you don't believe your students' attitudes, interests, and values are important, of course, you'll not agree with the views I've expressed. But if you do think student affect is significant, you'll want to learn what kinds of affective variables to assess and how to assess them. That's coming up shortly.

THE OTHER SIDE OF THE ARGUMENT

Before turning to the nuts and bolts of affective assessment, I need to point out that not all citizens share my view regarding the importance of affective assessment and instruction. Particularly during the past decade we have seen the emergence of vocal individuals who have taken strong positions against public schools' offering anything other than traditional academic (cognitive) education. Usually representing religious or conservative constituencies, these critics have argued it is the job of the family and church to promote values in children, and any attempt by the schools to systematically modify students' attitudes or values should cease.

I agree with these critics that if any attention to affective outcomes is to be given, it must be focused only on those affective consequences that would be close to universally approved. For example, I regard the promotion of students' positive attitudes toward learning as an affective aspiration almost everyone would support. Similarly, I can't really imagine there are too many people who wouldn't want the schools to nurture students' self-esteem. Yet, I would hate to see educators dabbling with any controversial attitudes or values—those that a vast majority of parents wouldn't want their children to possess.

If you decide to devote some of your classroom assessment/instruction time to affective targets, you'll clearly need to consider carefully the legitimacy of the targets you select. And even if you do so, you should recognize there will be some people who may disapprove of such affective education regardless of the care with which you select your affective curricular aims.

WHICH AFFECTIVE VARIABLES SHOULD BE ASSESSED?

A Closer Look at Affect

Before discussing the sorts of variables that you, as a classroom teacher, might wish to assess, let's spend just a moment looking at the nature of *affect* itself. The reason such affective variables as students' attitudes, interests, and values are important to us is that those variables typically influence students' future behavior. If you think about this for a bit, you'll realize we don't really care very much, in the abstract, whether students' attitudes toward learning are positive. The reason we want to promote positive attitudes toward learning is because students who have positive attitudes toward learning today will be inclined to pursue learning in the future.

The affective status of students lets us see how students are predisposed to behave subsequently. If we find that students believe healthy bodies are important, those students will be predisposed to maintain their own bodily health in the future. If we find that students have positive attitudes toward persons from other ethnic groups, then in the future such students will be predisposed to behave appropriately toward persons from other ethnic groups. As seen in Figure 10.1, current affective status predicts future behavior.

Do attitudes predict future behavior perfectly? Of course not. But suppose there are 100 third-graders who display very negative attitudes toward violence as a way of settling disputes, and there are 100 third-graders who believe violence is an altogether suitable way of resolving disputes. Probabilistically, in the future there are likely to be fewer violent dispute-resolution behaviors from the first 100 third-graders than from the second. Affective assessment, therefore, allows teachers to get a far-better-than-chance fix on the behavioral dispositions of their students. That's why affective assessment is so important.

As you know, schools have historically focused on cognitive variables. And that's probably the way it's always going to be. Thus, if you are interested in giving some attention to affect in your own classroom, you'll need to select your affective foci judiciously. That's what we'll deal with next. We'll look at attitudes first and then consider interests and values.

figure 10.1 ■ **The Relationship between Current Affect and Future Behavior Wherein an Individual's Affective Status Predicts That Individual's Future Behavior**

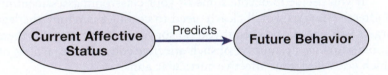

Potential Attitudinal Targets

There are all sorts of possible attitudinal targets for a teacher's instruction. Here are a few of the attitudes most commonly endorsed by teachers as reasonable attitudinal targets:

- *Positive attitudes toward learning.* Students should regard the act of learning positively. Students who are positive today about learning will tend to be tomorrow's learners.
- *Positive attitudes toward self.* Self-esteem is the attitude on which most people's personal worlds turn. Although children's self-esteem is probably influenced more by parents and nonschool events than by teachers, what happens in the classroom can have a significant impact on children's self-esteem.
- *Positive attitudes toward self as a learner.* Self-esteem as a learner is an affective variable over which educators have substantial influence. If students believe they are capable of learning, they will tend to learn.
- *Appropriate attitudes toward those who differ from us.* The more tolerant and accepting students are toward members of other ethnic, gender, national, racial, or religious groups, the more likely those students will behave properly toward such individuals in the future.

There are numerous other subject-specific kinds of attitudes teachers will want to foster. For example, many teachers who deal with language arts will want to enhance students' heightened confidence as writers—that is, students' more positive attitudes toward their own composition capabilities. Science teachers will want to foster students' curiosity. Health education teachers will wish to promote students' accurate perceptions of their vulnerability to health risks such as sexually transmitted diseases. Depending on your own instructional responsibilities, you'll discover there are usually several attitudinal assessment contenders you'll want to consider.

Potential Interest Targets

Students' interests represent another set of potential targets. Clearly, if you're a high school chemistry teacher, you'd like at least some of your students to develop an interest in chemistry. Similarly, teachers of U.S. government would prefer that their students become interested in governmental affairs rather than regard such topics as repugnant. Here, then, are a few illustrations of the kinds of interest targets teachers might consider for possible assessment:

- *Subject-related interests.* Students should regard the subject matter taught (for example, mathematics) as more interesting at the end of instruction than they did when instruction began. At the very least, students should be no less interested in the subject being taught as a consequence of the teacher's instruction.

- *Interest in reading.* Because of the enormous impact students' reading prowess has on their subsequent lives, we'd like students to be interested in reading and, indeed, enjoy it. Children who read because of their interest will—almost whether they want to or not—become good readers.
- *Interest in emerging technology.* As the world becomes increasingly dependent on technological advances, students who are interested in these sorts of technological improvements are more apt to learn about computers and, as a consequence, be able to utilize such technological tools.

To get a fix on possible interest-focused affective targets that might be suitable for assessment in your particular teaching situation, simply give a good, hard think to the things you'd like to see your students, as a consequence of what goes on in your classroom, become more interested in. It's just that straightforward.

Potential Value Targets

There are all sorts of values to which people subscribe that the schools should have nothing to do with. Most educators agree that political values and religious values, for example, should not be dealt with instructionally in the schools. Whether students turn out to be liberals or conservatives is really none of a teacher's business. And, historically, there's been a long tradition in the United States of separating church and state. Teachers, therefore, certainly shouldn't be advocating acceptance of particular religions or rejection of others. Well, then, what sorts of values are sufficiently meritorious and noncontroversial so they could serve as the targets for classroom attention? Here are a few to consider:

- *Honesty.* Students should learn to value honesty in their dealing with others.
- *Integrity.* Students should firmly adhere to their own code of values—for example, moral or artistic values.
- *Justice.* Students should subscribe to the view that all citizens should be the recipients of equal justice from governmental law enforcement agencies.
- *Freedom.* Students should believe that democratic nations must provide the maximum level of freedom to their citizens.

Although these kinds of values may seem to be little more than lofty, flag-waving endorsements of goodness, you may still wish to consider them and similar values for potential effective assessment in your own classroom. If there really are significant values you would like your students to embrace, and those values fall properly in the sphere of what schools should be about, then the possibility of including such values in a classroom assessment program may have real appeal for you.

Don't try to assess too many affective variables. You'd be surprised how quickly you can become overwhelmed with the time required to gather such data, and the time needed to make sense of the data you collect. This is another "less is more" setting in which you should try to get a fix on only a few of the affective dimensions you regard as most important for your students.

Here's an issue you'll need to consider if you decide to assess your students' affect with regard to one or more of the sorts of variables just described. Put simply, it calls for an answer to the following question: Should I let my students know—early on—what affective targets I have selected for them? When we think about cognitive curricular aims, it is universally agreed that there is a positive impact on learning when—early on—the teacher informs students about the nature of the intended learning outcomes. However, with regard to affective curricular aims, the picture is less clear. If students know, in advance, what kinds of affective variables are being sought, will this knowledge have a positive or negative impact on students' acquisition of the affect being sought? The answer to this question almost always depends on the particular affective aim being sought and the students involved. Each teacher must answer this question for each affective target being sought.

HOW SHOULD AFFECT BE ASSESSED IN CLASSROOMS?

The assessment of affect can be carried out at varying levels of complexity and sophistication. To illustrate, in psychological experiments designed to get a fix on children's honesty, researchers have utilized trained accomplices who contrive elaborate situations in which a child can or cannot cheat; then the researchers observe the child's behavior through one-way mirrors in order to draw inferences about the child's tendencies to be honest or dishonest in situations where the attractiveness of the temptations vary. I know few teachers who have the time or inclination to engage in very elaborate assessment of their students' affective status, although I suspect those teachers would know how to use one-way mirrors advantageously.

As a practical matter, the classroom assessment of student affect must be relatively easy to pull off, or it simply isn't going to happen. Teachers are too busy to carry out the galaxy of responsibilities they already face each day. Accordingly, in this chapter I'm only going to set out for you a single, readily accomplishable procedure to assess your students' attitudes and values. If you wish to consider more elaborate and time-demanding ways of measuring your students' affect, there are several excellent volumes cited in the References section at the end of this chapter. The books by Anderson and Bourke (2000) and by Webb and others (1981) are particularly thought provoking.

SELF-REPORT ASSESSMENT

You can get a decent fix on students' affective status by asking them to complete *self-report inventories*. If you set up the assessment situation so students can respond in a truly anonymous fashion, the data derived from self-report instruments can really be useful to you. Just as importantly, the use of straightforward self-report devices won't be so onerous you become disenchanted with such measurement. Anderson and Bourke (2000) provide a compelling argument in favor of self-report affective measurement by educators.

Likert Inventories

Because of its ready applicability to a variety of affective assessment targets, the approach to attitudinal measurement introduced many years ago by Rensis Likert (1903–1981) is the most widely used. You've probably responded to *Likert inventories* many times in your life. They consist of a series of statements to which you register your agreement or disagreement. For example, you are given a statement such as "Reading this book about classroom assessment represents one of the finest professional experiences of my career." You then choose from a set of options to decide whether you agree or disagree with the statement. The usual options, at least for adults, are *strongly agree, agree, uncertain, disagree,* and *strongly disagree.* (I am altogether confident you would have opted for the *strongly agree* response regarding the previous illustrative statement about this book's impact on your professional life.)

Clearly, depending on the age of the students you're teaching, you'll need to make adjustments in the statements used and in the number and/or phrasing of the response options. For example, with very young children you might need to use brief statements containing very simple words. You might even have to read the statements aloud. Older students might be able to handle the five-choice agreement scale just described, but for younger students you'll most likely want to drop down to three response options (for instance, *agree, don't know,* and *disagree*) or even two response options (perhaps *yes* and *no*). You'll be the best judge of the language level to be used with the students you teach. In general, err in the direction of less-demanding rather than more-demanding language. Incidentally, you could probably win a few faculty-lounge trivia contests by quizzing your colleagues about Likert's first name. Face it, Rensis is not a widely used moniker!

The essence of this sort of measurement, of course, boils down to the way students who complete an inventory respond to a collection of negative and positive statements about the same affective variable. This being so, the statements in a Likert inventory or, indeed, any affective inventory, must be created with considerable care. To illustrate, dare not be *too* positive or *too* negative so no student will ever agree (or disagree) with it. Take a look at the two statements about school given here and then decide which statement would elicit a greater *range* of agreement in students' responses:

- *Every day in every way, school is always the most enjoyable part of my day.* (Strongly Agree, Agree, Not Sure, Disagree, Strongly Disagree)
- *Even though I occasionally find school disagreeable, most of the time I enjoy it.* (Strongly Agree, Agree, Not Sure, Disagree, Strongly Disagree)

The initial statement is so "goody-goody" that few students are apt to agree with it. In contrast, the second statement has sufficient qualifiers ("occasionally" and "most of the time") so there will most likely be students who will agree with it and also students who will disagree with it. You need to be certain your inventory's statements are constructed so they are neither *too* positive nor *too* negative.

Even though Likert inventories have been around for more than three-quarters of a century (Likert, 1932), I rarely recommend a traditional Likert inventory these days to assess students' affect. As you now see, a Likert inventory is focused on a *single* affective variable. Thus, Likert inventories require a substantial amount of inventory-development energy from the teacher, and I find most teachers are interested in several, rather than only one, affective variable. Accordingly, I urge teachers to employ assessment devices that can simultaneously get at several affective variables, not just one. Let me describe how to build the kind of affective inventory I think will have the most utility for you in your own classroom. As you will see, the assessment strategy being used in this procedure is essentially the same as the one used in a traditional Likert inventory, but focused on more than a solitary affective variable.

Multifocus Affective Inventories

A *multifocus affective inventory* is an assessment device that attempts to collect information about a number of students' affective dispositions. Such inventories must, therefore, reduce the number of statements (items) dealing with a particular affective variable. So, whereas a traditional Likert inventory might devote 10 to 20 items to a single affective dimension, a multifocus affective inventory might contain items measuring only 5 or 6 affective dimensions, but assess each one of those with just a few items.

The trade-off is obvious. Will two items dealing with, for example, a student's "interest in science" yield inferences as accurate as a 10-item inventory devoted only to that same affective dimension? Of course not. The key question, however, is the following: Does a teacher really *require* 10 items on an inventory in order to arrive at a sufficiently valid inference regarding a classroom full of students' interest in history? I don't think so.

Remember, all educational measurement devices are much less precise than typically thought by educators and noneducators alike. Affective assessment is no exception. This issue boils down to the following question: If you're trying to get a fix on the affective status of an entire class of students, what's the minimum number of items (statements) you'll be willing to rely on? Having dealt with this issue in my own classes more than a few times, for me the answer turns out to be *two*. That's right; I think I can garner sufficient insights from my students' responses to two affect-related items—one stated positively and one stated negatively—to come up with an actionable inference about my students' affect.

If you regard two items per affective focus as being too skimpy, then you might bump that number up to four items per affective focus. By doing so, of course, this will either (1) reduce the number of affective dimensions you can address in an inventory or (2) make your inventory so long that students, having seen the numerous upcoming responses they must supply, will often race rapidly through such a lengthy inventory and, thereby, reduce the thoughtfulness of their responses to all of the items. You'll get a better idea about how to create a multifocus affective inventory if I supply you with a step-by-step construction procedure—along with an illustrative inventory of this type.

Building a Multifocus Affective Inventory

Here, then, is a five-step process for creating multifocus affective inventories suitable for classroom use.

1. *Select the affective variables to measure.* In recognition that you will be devoting only a small number of items to each affective variable you choose, you'll need to identify the educationally significant attitudes, interests, or values about which you will ask students to respond.

2. *Determine how many items to allocate to each affective variable.* You must include an equal number of positive *and* negative statements for each affective variable you choose. For openers, start with a minimum of two items per variable. Then, if you decide you need to add more items per variable, increase the number of items in multiples of two. For instance, with two items per affective variable, you would use one positively phrased statement and one negatively phrased statement. For four items per affective variable, you would use two positive statements and two negative statements. In a given affective inventory, incidentally, there is no need to devote an identical number of items to each affective variable being assessed. So you might attempt to measure several variables with two items per variable, but allocate four items to other variables being measured in the same inventory. The choice regarding numbers of items you'll need hinges on your judgment regarding the minimum number of items necessary to yield reasonably accurate inferences about a student group's affective status with respect to a particular affective variable.

3. *Create a series of positive and negative statements related to each affective variable.* The statements in a multifocus affective inventory are similar to those used in Likert inventories. Yet, because you are attempting to gauge your students' affective dispositions with only a few items, even greater care should be taken to craft the statements so they are apt to elicit differential responses from students. All of these statements (items) should be scattered randomly throughout the inventory—that is, not placed in any sort of identifiable groups related to a particular affective dimension.

4. *Determine the number and phrasing of students' response options.* At this point you need to determine whether you'll use three, four, or five response options for students to register agreement/disagreement with the inventory's statements. You'll also need to decide whether you're using the traditional Likert responses (such as "strongly agree") or some sort of alternative responses (such as "true for me").

5. *Create clear directions for the inventory and an appropriate presentation format.* Directions for affective inventories should be given more attention than is usually allotted by those who develop typical classroom achievement tests. Students are often unfamiliar with these sorts of affective assessment devices and, therefore, need to understand what they're being asked to do. Be certain to include (a) lucid directions about how to respond; (b) at least one sample item; (c) a request for students to supply anonymous, honest responses; and (d) a reminder there are no right or wrong answers to the inventory's items.

Please refer to the illustrative multifocus affective inventory presented in Figure 10.2. This inventory was developed for use with students in grades 4 through 6 and was intended to allow teachers to get a fix on students' sentiments regarding three subject areas (science, mathematics, and social studies) as well as three im-

figure 10.2 ■ **An Illustrative Multifocus Affective Inventory for Students in Grades 4–6**

SCHOOL AND ME

Directions: Please indicate how much the statements in this inventory are true for you. Some of the statements are positive and some are negative. Decide whether each statement is true *for you*. There are no right or wrong answers, so answer honestly. Do not write your name on the inventory. Only make X marks.

Here is a sample:

Response (one per statement)

	True for me.	Not true for me.	I'm not sure.
I like to go to the movies.	☒	☐	☐

When you are finished, a student will collect your inventory and place it and all other completed inventories in a sealed envelope that will be taken by the student directly to the principal's office. Thank you for your help.

Response (one per statement)

Statements	True for me.	Not true for me.	I'm not sure.
1. In general, I like school a lot.	☐	☐	☐
2. I like to learn about scientific things.	☐	☐	☐
3. I can write good reports and stories.	☐	☐	☐
4. I don't like to read.	☐	☐	☐
5. I don't like to speak in front of the class.	☐	☐	☐
6. I think that doing mathematics is fun.	☐	☐	☐
7. I like when we learn about social studies.	☐	☐	☐
8. I don't want to grow up to be a scientist.	☐	☐	☐
9. I really don't like to write very much.	☐	☐	☐
10. I like to read books when I have the time.	☐	☐	☐
11. I usually enjoy speaking in front of other students.	☐	☐	☐
12. I don't like to do mathematics problems.	☐	☐	☐
13. When we do social studies in school, I don't like it.	☐	☐	☐
14. Overall, I don't enjoy school very much.	☐	☐	☐

portant skills students need to acquire (reading, writing, and making oral presentations). In addition, the inventory seeks students' responses regarding school in general. In all, then, the 14-item inventory in Figure 10.2 tries to tap seven affective variables by using two items per variable.

Spend just a few moments looking at the items in the Figure 10.2 inventory. Note, for instance, each positively phrased statement regarding a particular variable is balanced by a counterpart statement that's phrased negatively. To illustrate, Statement 5 is a negative statement about giving oral reports, but Statement 11 is a positive statement regarding that same skill. Note also the two statements for each variable need *not* be mirror-image contradictions such as "I like school" versus "I don't like school."

Multifocus affective inventories are scored in the same way Likert inventories are scored: Points are awarded for students' agreement with positive statements and also for students' disagreement with negative statements. So, for example, let's say there were five level-of-agreement options available, ranging from strong agreement to strong disagreement in an inventory using only two items per affected variable. You would assign a maximum of five points per item (for strong agreement with a positive item or strong disagreement with a negative item) and a minimum of one point per item (for strong agreement with a negative item or strong disagreement with a positive item). Thus, focusing on a pair of items dealing with, for instance, students' interest in science, the scores on this two-item pair could range from a high of 10 to a low of 2.

Perhaps you are uncomfortable about arriving at inferences for an entire class of students based on only two items. But the purpose of this sort of assessment is to give *you* insights regarding your students' affect. If the inference you come up with based on only a pair of items is way out of whack with your own best judgment about your students' affective learnings, then treat the two-item data with a slug of suspicion. *You* are always the decision-maker in your class. I promise you that insights based even on two-item inventories—administered to a whole group of students—will often prove useful to you.

The Importance of Genuine Anonymity

In order for you to draw accurate inferences about your students' affective status based on their responses to self-report inventories, it is clearly necessary for students to *respond truthfully* to your affective inventories. Unfortunately, many students tend to provide what are referred to as **socially desirable responses** to affective self-report devices. In other words, many students are inclined to respond in the way they think society (in this case, you) wants them to respond. Students are particularly apt to provide socially desirable responses if they believe the teacher can trace their responses. Consequently, to increase the likelihood that students will respond honestly to your affective inventories, it is imperative you not only make all students' responses anonymous but you also employ as many procedures as possible so most students regard their responses as truly untraceable.

Among the more simple but effective *anonymity-enhancement procedures* you might want to consider are these:

1. *Directions.* Make sure the directions for your affective inventories stress the importance of honest answers and that students are not to put their names on their inventories.
2. *Response restrictions.* Set up your inventories so the *only* form of student response is to be check marks, circling of preferred answers, and so on. Because students believe the teacher may figure out who supplied which inventory by recognizing students' handwriting, don't permit any handwriting whatsoever on affective inventories. If you are desperate to give students an opportunity to supply written comments, then supply your students with totally separate forms on which they can make written comments.
3. *Collection.* Install a procedure whereby students deposit their completed inventories in a collection box, or have a student (not one thought to be your "pet" student) collect the completed inventories. Announce *before* students start to fill out the inventories that one of these collection methods will be employed.

As you can see, you must try to make sure your students really don't think there's any way to trace their responses back to them. Even under those circumstances, this doesn't ensure that students will respond truthfully. However, well-conceived anonymity-enhancement techniques increase the odds that students will respond honestly.

In recent years, we often encounter attempts to secure students' responses to affectively oriented inventories by completing anonymous, computer-collected online inventories. Such inventories, given the magic of computers, can actually be anonymous—that is, a student's responses cannot be traced back to the student. What worries me, however, is whether students who fill out a computer-delivered inventory *believe* their responses are truly anonymous. The more likely that students believe their electronic responses are traceable back to them, the greater will be the social desirability of their answers.

When to Assess Affect

When should classroom teachers assess their students' affective status? Well, for openers, it seems important to set up at least a preinstruction and a postinstruction measure of students' attitudes, interests, and/or values. Thus, for elementary teachers teaching students in self-contained classrooms, an affective assessment at the start of the school year and again at its close will allow teachers to discern any meaningful changes in students' affect. Ideally, however, teachers can engage in occasional "affective dip sticking" to monitor students' affect. For example, every couple of months, a teacher might measure students' self-esteem as learners as

PARENT TALK

"You're messing with my child's head," was the first comment you heard from Mrs. Jillian, Paul's mother, when she telephoned you at school during your after-school planning period. Mrs. Jillian then continued by saying she had heard from Paul that you were getting students to fill out "attitude tests" that try to find out "whether kids have the right attitudes." Mrs. Jillian concluded by asking, "How dare you delve into Paul's value and attitudes! Isn't this something his dad and I should be influencing?"

 If I were you, here's how I'd respond to Mrs. Jillian:

"I agree completely with you, Mrs. Jillian, about whose right it is to influence Paul's values and attitudes. That responsibility is yours and Mr. Jillian's. But I have a hunch you may not have a clear picture of what I'm trying to do in Paul's class. Let me explain.

"As you may know, children at Paul's age often become disinterested in certain subjects, especially mathematics and science. What I've been trying to do is determine ways I can help improve or sustain my students' interest in science and mathematics. I've been administering *anonymous* attitude inventories related to math and science on a pretest and posttest basis—that is, in the fall and in the spring. But I'm not using the results of those anonymous inventories to influence the attitudes or values of Paul or any other child. What I'm trying to do is figure out how my own teaching can engender more interest, from the entire class, in science and mathematics.

"I would *never* try to influence a value or attitude that falls within your family's purview. But I'm sure you'd like Paul, and the other students in his class, to regard science and mathematics positively, not negatively. Whether the children eventually pursue careers related to science or mathematics will, of course, be up to them and their families."

Now, how would you respond to Mrs. Jillian?

well as their attitudes regarding learning. If these occasional assessments suggest inappropriate affective changes are occurring, the teacher may wish to modify affect-related aspects of the instructional program.

In the next section of the chapter, you'll discover that you can often *sample* your students' affective status rather than measure all students' affective status. Thus, some of the suggested affective dip sticking might be carried out only with a portion of your students.

WHAT KINDS OF INFERENCES ARE AT STAKE IN AFFECTIVE ASSESSMENT?

When teachers use cognitively oriented tests, they typically make inferences—that is, interpretations about individual students. If, for instance, Harvey Haley earns a high score on a mathematics test, the teacher makes an inference about Harvey's possession of certain mathematics skills and knowledge. Teachers need to make inferences about individual students in order to make decisions about how to provide suitable instruction for those students.

Teachers also aggregate students' individual scores on achievement tests to arrive at group-focused inferences. For example, if most students in a history class performed poorly on a start-of-the-term achievement pretest, yet most students earned top scores on a comparable posttest administered near the term's conclusion, the teacher would conclude that the students, as a group, had learned substantially more about history.

It's different with affect. Whereas cognitive tests (and, in most cases, psychomotor tests) are measures of students' *optimum performance,* affective inventories strive to measure students' *typical performance.* Remember that when students complete most affective devices, those results don't count toward the students' grades, so self-report assessment offers students a wonderful opportunity to distort their responses. Thus, there's a strong likelihood that at least some students won't respond honestly. As a consequence, inferences about the affective status of *individual* students (based on a student's responses to an affective inventory) are risky.

Besides, instructional decisions about individual students based on affective assessment devices are rare. If Harry Helms knows history well, but happens to hate it, few teachers would give Harry a low grade in history based on his disdain for "dead folks' foolishness."

In contrast, however, teachers often make *instructional* decisions about what goes on in class based on aggregated affective data. Assuming that there will be a small number of students who supply inaccurate responses, it is still reasonable to assume that the total collectivity of students' responses will permit meaningful *group-focused inferences.* And those are the kinds of inferences you should be making when you use affective assessment instruments. Because I've already pointed out that affective inventories must be administered anonymously, you've surely recognized that getting a fix on a particular student's affective status is literally impossible. Anonymity is, after all, anonymity.

However, there's another good reason for arriving at only group-focused affective inferences. Even if you were to use all sorts of anonymity-enhancement procedures when you administer any affective inventory, some students will *still* not respond honestly. Certain students will be fearful of offending you in any way, even though cloaked by anonymity, and thus will respond more positively than they would if they were being completely truthful. Interestingly, however, there are also some students who will

But What Does This Have to Do with Teaching?

I know very few teachers who don't believe, at some level, that student affect is important. Most teachers realize that if students learn to detest schooling, it's unlikely those students will wind up near the top of any academic sweepstakes. Most chemistry teachers want their students to groove on chemistry. Most math teachers want their students to get mildly ecstatic over the relationships nestled in the theorem tumbled onto by Pythagoras some 2,500 years ago. Yet, although most teachers recognize that students' interests, attitudes, and values are important, few teachers deliberately strive to promote appropriate affect in their students.

One of the reasons for this neglect of affect is that students' affective dispositions often get lost in the curricular roads today's teachers must travel. There is so much knowledge and so many skills that society wants today's students to master. And the current accountability pressures for teachers to boost students' test scores have made it even less likely teachers will have time to promote positive student affect. It's easy to see how affect gets overlooked, even by teachers who recognize its importance. And that's where affective assessment arrives to save the day. Even if a teacher uses only one self-report inventory, at the start of a term and at its conclusion, the *presence* of this assessment instrument will almost certainly incline the teacher to think about the degree to which any classroom activities are being directed toward the promotion of appropriate affective outcomes.

Affective assessment instruments, even a 10-item self-report inventory, will sensitize the teacher to affect's importance. And such sensitized teachers will typically devote at least *some* effort to the promotion of the kinds of student attitudes, interests, and values that—far more than the cognitive content we cram into their heads—will surely influence their lives.

use their anonymity cloaks as an opportunity to "get even" with you for your real or imagined shortcomings. Such students will then toss more negativity your way than they really feel. Will these too-positive or too-negative responses cancel each other out perfectly? Of course not. But they will do at least *some* cancelling out and, as a consequence, should allow you to put greater confidence in your students' *average* response as a reflection of the entire group's affective status.

Affective assessment devices are simply too crude to permit individual-focused inferences. In aggregate, however, you ought to be able to make some very solid judgments about how your students, as a group, are affectively disposed. This is why, in some cases, you can collect affective data from only, say, half of your class yet still make a fairly accurate inference about the group based on responses from that 50-percent sample. Sample-based, en route affective assessment of your students, especially as a way of coming up with dip-stick inferences about that group of students, really works quite well.

WHAT DO CLASSROOM TEACHERS REALLY NEED TO KNOW ABOUT AFFECTIVE ASSESSMENT?

The most important thing you need to know about affective assessment is that if you don't measure your students' affective status in a systematic fashion, you're far less likely to emphasize affect instructionally. Moreover, without systematic affective assessment, you're not apt to have a very decent fix on the affective consequences, possibly unintentional, that you're having on your students.

If you do decide to engage in some affective measurement in your own classes, you'll be much better off if you rely on fairly straightforward self-report instruments (Likert inventories or multifocus affective inventories) rather than trying to employ some exotic affective measurement strategies that are both time-consuming and, at the same time, yield inferences of arguable validity. You also need to know affective assessment devices are too imprecise to allow you to make inferences about individual students. Group-focused inferences are as far as you should go in the affective realm.

There's one other thing teachers ought to recognize about the assessment of affect—namely, that most teachers do not possess even a foggy notion about how to promote affect *instructionally*. If teachers actually decide to measure important student affect, they'll typically need some solid professional-development support to learn how to alter students' attitudes, values, and interests. There are a number of instructional techniques for doing so, but most teachers are unaware of those affective-focused instructional procedures. Here's where a **professional learning community**—that is, a group of educators who meet periodically to deal with topics such as "affective instructional techniques"—would be especially useful.

Looking back, then, at the description of affective assessment as it might be carried out by a typical classroom teacher, it is possible to isolate three key features that, if present, can lead toward more valid interpretations of students' affective status. Those three features are reliance on (1) *self-report inventories* to be completed by students under conditions of (2) *actual and perceived anonymity* leading to (3) *group-focused inferences* rather than individual inferences about students' current affective status. If teachers can satisfy all three of these procedural requirements, then the resultant inferences about students' affect will have a heightened likelihood of being valid Given the likely impact that assessing students' affect will have on what and how a teacher teaches, the instructional dividends of affective assessment were underscored. The chapter was concluded with a reminder that the validity of inferences drawn from affective assessment depends directly on a teacher's forming group-focused inferences about students' affect using self-report inventories to which students respond with real *and* perceived anonymity.

CHAPTER SUMMARY

This chapter was initiated by an unabashed endorsement of the instructional importance of affect and, as a consequence, the importance of assessing students' affective status. It was suggested that the use of affective assessment in classrooms would incline teachers to address affective goals instructionally. It was also argued that if teachers monitor their students' affective status, instructional modifications can be made whenever inappropriate or insufficient affective shifts in students are occurring. Affective variables were described as important predictors of individuals' future behaviors because people's affective status reveals their behavioral predispositions. It was also pointed out, however, that there are vocal groups whose members oppose instructional attention to affect.

Regarding the kinds of affective variables to assess in one's classroom, a series of potential attitudinal, interest, and value foci were presented. Teachers were urged to select only a few highly meaningful affective variables rather than so many as to induce affective overwhelm.

Self-report assessment procedures were recommended as the most practical way to gather affective data in classrooms. Multifocus affective inventories were recommended over Likert inventories on the practical ground that Likert inventories assess only a single affective dimension. Teachers are, it was argued, usually interested in more than one affective variable. A five-step process for constructing multifocus affective inventories was described. Anonymity was identified as an indispensable component of appropriate affective assessment. Several anonymity-enhancement procedures were presented. It was also suggested that affective assessments be made prior to and at the conclusion of instruction as well as in the form of occasional affective dip sticking.

The nature of assessment-based affective inferences was also explored. It was argued the imprecision of affective assessment devices should incline teachers to make group-focused inferences rather than inferences about individual students.

Determining Your Outcome Mastery

You should now be familiar with the instructional impact that affective assessment can exert and be able to recognize how classroom teachers can create and administer affective assessments resulting in valid inferences about students' affect. Review the chapter's chief learning outcome:

An understanding of the potential instructional dividends of affective assessment and what's necessary for teachers to draw valid inferences about their students' affect—namely, the use of anonymity-cloaked self-report inventories leading to inferences about groups of students, not individuals

This outcome is dominantly cognitive in nature—your understanding of how affective assessment can have a positive impact on a teacher's classroom instruction. To be candid, however, an intended *affective* outcome for the chapter also lurks in these pages—to incline you, if you're a teacher or a teacher-in-preparation, to consider affective assessment in your own classroom.

To assess whether you've achieved the chief outcome, complete both the Selected-Response and the Constructed-Response quizzes and think about the feedback you receive for each quiz.

MyEdLab *Selected-Response Check of Outcome Mastery*

MyEdLab *Constructed-Response Check of Outcome Mastery*

After completing both quizzes, go to the Learning Outcome Mastery Determination, where you will decide whether you've mastered the chapter's learning outcome or whether you need further study.

MyEdLab *Learning Outcome Mastery Determination*

References

Anderson, L. W., and Bourke, S. F. (2000). *Assessing affective characteristics in the schools* (2nd ed.). Mahwah, NJ: Erlbaum.

Aschbacher, P. R., Ing, M., and Tsai, S. M. (2013). "Boosting student interest in science," *Phi Delta Kappan, 95,* no. 2 (October): 47–51.

Chamberlin, S. A. (2010). "A review of instruments created to assess affect in mathematics," *Journal of Mathematics Education, 3,* no. 1 (June): 167–182.

Likert, R. (1932). "A technique for the measurement of attitudes," *Archives of Psychology, 140*: 1–55.

Preble, B., and Taylor, L. (2008/2009). "School climate through students' eyes," *Educational leadership, 66,* no. 4 (December/January): 35–40.

Webb, E. J., Campbell, D. T., Schwartz, R. D., Sechreat, L., and Grove, J. B. (1981). *Nonreactive measures in the social sciences* (2nd ed.). Boston: Houghton Mifflin.

Weissberg, R. P., and Cascarino, J. (2013). "Academic learning + social-emotional learning = national priority," *Phi Delta Kappan, 95,* no. 2 (October): 8–13.

11

Improving Teacher-Developed Assessments

Sufficient comprehension of both judgmental and empirical test-improvement procedures so that accurate decisions can be made about the way teachers are employing these two test-improvement strategies

If you've ever visited the manuscript room of the British Museum, you'll recall seeing handwritten manuscripts authored by some of the superstars of English literature. It's a moving experience. Delightfully, the museum presents not only the final versions of famed works by such authors as Milton and Keats but also the early drafts of those works. It is somewhat surprising and genuinely encouraging to learn those giants of literature didn't get it right the first time. They had to cross out words, delete sentences, and substitute phrases. Many of the museum's early drafts are genuinely messy, reflecting all sorts of rethinking on the part of the author. Well, if the titans of English literature had to revise their early drafts, is it at all surprising that teachers usually need to spruce up their classroom assessments?

This chapter is designed to provide you with several procedures by which you can improve the assessment instruments you develop. I can promise that if you use the chapter's recommended procedures, your tests will get better. Yet, they'll probably never make it to the British Museum—unless you carry them in when visiting.

There are two general improvement strategies to be described in this chapter. First, you'll learn about *judgmental item-improvement* procedures in which the chief means of sharpening your tests is human judgment—your own and that of others. Second, you'll be considering *empirical item-improvement* procedures based on students' responses to your assessment procedures. Ideally, if time permits and your motivation abounds, you can use both forms of test-improvement procedures for your own classroom assessment devices.

But I really need to give you a heads-up regarding the upcoming *empirical item-repair procedures. What you'll recognize when you get into that section is there are *numbers* in it. (There's even a formula or two.) When encountering this material, perhaps you'll conclude I've tricked you—lulled you into a sense of non-numeric complacency for 10 chapters—then blindsided you with a quagmire of quantitative esoterica. But that's not so. Don't be intimidated by the last half of the chapter's quantitative stuff. It truly constitutes a fairly Mickey-Mouse level of number-nudging. Just take it slow and easy. You'll survive surprisingly well. I promise.

JUDGMENTALLY BASED IMPROVEMENT PROCEDURES

Human judgment, although it sometimes gets us in trouble, is a remarkably useful tool. Judgmental approaches to test improvement can be carried out quite systematically or, in contrast, rather informally. Judgmental assessment-improvement strategies differ chiefly according to who is supplying the judgments. There are three sources of test-improvement judgments you should consider—those supplied by (1) yourself, (2) your colleagues, and (3) your students. We'll consider each of these potential judgment sources separately.

Judging Your Own Assessment Instruments

Let's suppose you've created a 70-item combination short-answer and multiple-choice examination for a U.S. government class and, having administered it, you want to improve the examination for your next year's class. We'll assume that during item development you did a reasonable amount of in-process sharpening up of the items so they represented what, at the time, was your best effort. Now, however, you have an opportunity to revisit the examination to see if its 70 items are all that marvelous. It's a good thing to do.

Let's consider another kind of assessment. Suppose you have devised what you think are pretty decent directions for your students to follow when preparing portfolios or when responding to tasks in a performance test. Even if you regard those directions as suitable, it's always helpful to review such directions after a time to see if you can now detect shortcomings that, when you had originally prepared the set of directions, escaped your attention.

As you probably know from other kinds of writing, it is almost always the case that if you return to one of your written efforts after it has had time to "cool off," you're likely to spot deficits that, in the heat of the original writing, weren't apparent to you. However, beyond a fairly casual second look, you will typically be able to improve your assessment procedures even more if you approach this test-improvement task systematically. To illustrate, you could use specific review criteria when you judge your earlier assessment efforts. If a test item or a set of directions falls short on any criterion, you should obviously do some modifying. Presented here are five review criteria you might wish to consider if you set out systematically to improve your classroom assessment procedures:

- *Adherence to item-specific guidelines and general item-writing commandments.* When you appraise your assessment procedures, it will be useful to review briefly the general item-writing commandments supplied earlier (in Chapter 6) as well as the particular item-writing guidelines provided for the specific kind of item(s) you've developed. If you now see violations of the principles set forth in either of those two sets of directives, fix the flaws.
- *Contribution to score-based inference.* Recall that the real reason teachers assess students is in order to arrive at score-based interpretations about the status of students. Therefore, it will be helpful for you to reconsider each aspect of a previously developed assessment procedure to see whether it does, in fact, really contribute to the kind of inference you wish to draw about your students.
- *Accuracy of content.* There's always the possibility that previously accurate content has now been superseded or contradicted by more recent content. Be sure to see if the content you included earlier in the assessment instrument is still accurate and that your answer key is still correct.
- *Absence of content lacunae.* This review criterion gives me a chance to use one of my favorite words, the plural form of *lacuna* which, incidentally, means a *gap*. Although *gaps* would have done the job in this instance, you'll admit *gaps* look somewhat tawdry when stacked up against *lacunae*. (This, of course, is a norm-referenced contrast.)

  Hindsight is a nifty form of vision. Thus, when you take a second look at the content coverage represented in your assessment instrument, you may discover you originally overlooked some important content. This review criterion is clearly related to an earlier review criterion regarding the assessment's contribution to the score-based inference that you want to make. Any meaningful lacunae in content will obviously reduce the accuracy of your inference.
- *Fairness.* Although you should clearly have tried to eradicate any bias in your assessment instruments when you originally developed them, there's always the chance you overlooked something. Undertake another bias review just to make certain you've been as attentive to bias elimination as you possibly can be.

I can personally attest to a case of bias blindness when I authored a textbook on educational evaluation in the seventies. Recognizing that a number of women at the time were beginning to take offense at authors' use of masculine pronouns when referring to unnamed individuals (for example, "The student lost *his* lunch"), I had assiduously written the textbook so that all my illustrative make-believe people were plural. I never had to use *his* or *her* because I could always use *their*. After churning out the last chapter, I was smugly proud of my pluralization prowess. Yet, having been so attentive to a pronoun issue that might offend some women, I blithely included a cartoon in the book that showed scantily clad females cavorting before male members of a school board. Talk about dumb! If only I'd taken a serious second look at the book before it hit the presses, I might have spotted my insensitive error. As it was, because the cartoon appeared in all copies of the first edition (not the second!), I received more than a few heated, and quite deserved, complaints from readers—both male and female!

I'm not suggesting you fill out an elaborate rating form for each of these five review criteria—with each criterion requiring a numerical rating. Rather, I'm recommending that you seriously think about these five criteria before you tackle any judgmental review of a previously developed assessment instrument.

Collegial Judgments

If you are working with a colleague whose judgment you trust, it's often helpful to ask this person to review your assessment procedures. To get the most mileage out of such a review, you'll probably need to provide your co-worker with at least a brief description of review criteria such as the five previously cited ones—that is, (1) adherence to item-specific guidelines and general item-writing commandments, (2) contribution to score-based inference, (3) accuracy of content, (4) absence of content gaps lacunae, and (5) fairness. You will need to describe to your colleague the key inference(s) you intend to base on the assessment procedure. It will also be useful to your colleague if you identify the decisions that will, thereafter, be influenced by your inferences about students.

I've found that collegial judgments are particularly helpful to teachers who employ many performance tests or who use portfolio assessments. Most of the empirically based improvement procedures you'll be learning about later in the chapter are intended to be used with more traditional sorts of items such as those found in multiple-choice exams. For portfolio assessment and performance tests, judgmental approaches will often prove more useful.

Remember, if *you* are the creator of the portfolio assessment or performance tests you're setting out to improve, you're apt to be biased in their favor. After all, parents usually adore their progeny. What you need is a good, hard, *nonpartisan* review of what you've been up to assessment-wise.

To do a thorough job of helping you review your assessment approaches, of course, your colleague will need to put in some time. In fairness, you'll probably feel obliged to toss in a *quid pro quo* or two whereby you return the favor by reviewing your colleague's tests (or by resolving a pivotal personal crisis in your colleague's private life). If your school district is large enough, you might also have access to some central-office supervisorial personnel who know something about assessment. Here's a neat opportunity to let them earn their salaries—get them to review your assessment procedures. It is often asserted that another pair of eyes can help improve almost any written document. This doesn't necessarily mean the other pair of eyes see accurately while yours are in need of contact lenses. You should listen to what other reviewers say, but be guided by your own judgments about the virtues of their suggestions.

Student Judgments

When teachers set out to improve assessment procedures, a rich source of data is often overlooked because teachers typically fail to secure advice from their students. Yet, because students have experienced test items in a most meaningful context,

figure 11.1 ■ An Illustrative Item-Improvement Questionnaire for Students

Item-Improvement Questionnaire for Students

1. If any of the items seemed confusing, which ones were they?
2. Did any items have more than one correct answer? If so, which ones?
3. Did any items have no correct answers? If so, which ones?
4. Were there words in any items that confused you? If so, which ones?
5. Were the directions for the test, or for particular subsections, unclear? If so, which ones?

more or less as an executionee experiences a firing squad, student judgments can provide useful insights. Student reactions can help you spot shortcomings in particular items and in other features of your assessment procedures such as a test's directions or the time you've allowed for completing the test.

The kinds of data secured from students will vary, depending on the type of assessment procedure being used, but questions such as those on the item-improvement questionnaire in Figure 11.1 can profitably be given to students after they have completed an assessment procedure. Although the illustrative questionnaire in Figure 11.1 is intended for use with a selected-response type of test, only minor revisions would be needed to make it suitable for a constructed-response test, a performance test, or a portfolio assessment system.

It is important to let students finish a test prior to their engaging in such a judgmental exercise. If students are asked to *simultaneously* play the roles of test takers and test improvers, they'll probably botch up both tasks. No student should be expected to serve two such functions, at least at the same time.

Simply give students the test as usual, collect their answer sheets or test booklets, and provide them with new, blank test booklets. *Then* distribute a questionnaire asking students to supply per-item reactions. In other words, ask students to play examinees and item reviewers, but to play these roles consecutively, not simultaneously.

Now, how do you treat students' reactions to test items? Let's say you're a classroom teacher and a few students come up with a violent castigation of one of your favorite items. Do you automatically buckle by scrapping or revising the item? Of course not; teachers are made of sterner stuff. Perhaps the students were miffed about the item because they didn't know how to answer it. One of the best ways for students to escape responsibility for a dismal test performance is to assail the test itself. Teachers should anticipate a certain amount of carping from low-scoring students.

Yet, after allowing for a reasonable degree of complaining, student reactions can sometimes provide useful insights for teachers. A student-castigated item may, indeed, deserve castigation. To overlook students as a source of judgmental test-improvement information, for either selected-response or constructed-response items, would clearly be an error.

To review, then, judgmentally based test-improvement procedures can rely on the judgments supplied by you, your colleagues, or your students. In the final analysis, you will be the decision-maker regarding whether to modify your assessment procedures. Nonetheless, it is typically helpful to have others react to your tests.

EMPIRICALLY BASED IMPROVEMENT PROCEDURES

In addition to judgmentally based methods of improving your assessment procedures, there are improvement approaches based on the empirical data students supply when they respond to the assessment instruments you've developed. Let's turn, then, to the use of student-response data in the improvement of assessment procedures. A variety of empirical item-improvement techniques have been well honed over the years. We will consider the more traditional item-analysis procedures first, turning later to a few more recent wrinkles for using student data to improve a teacher's classroom assessments procedures.

Most of the procedures employed to improve classroom assessments on the basis of students' responses to those assessments rely on numbers. And I recognize there are some readers of this text (*you* may be one) who are definitely put off by numbers. I sometimes believe there is a secret cult among teachers and prospective teachers who have taken a "tremble pledge"—that is, a vow to tremble when encountering any numerical value larger than a single digit (a number larger than 9). If you are one of these mathphobics, I beg you to stay calm because the numbers you'll be encountering in this and later chapters will really be Simple-Simon stuff. Tremble not. It'll be pain free. Just work through the easy examples and you'll survive with surprising ease.

Difficulty Indices

One useful index of an item's quality is its *difficulty*. The most commonly employed item-difficulty index, often referred to simply as a *p value,* is calculated as follows:

$$\text{Difficulty } p = \frac{R}{T}$$

where R = the number of students responding correctly (right) to an item.
T = the total number of students responding to the item.

To illustrate, if 50 students answered an item, and only 37 of them answered it correctly, then the p value representing the item's difficulty would be

$$\text{Difficulty } p = \frac{37}{50} = .74$$

It should be clear that such p value can range from 0 to 1.00, with higher p values indicating items that more students answered correctly. For example, a p value of .98 would signify an item answered correctly by almost all students. Similarly, an item with a p value of .15 would be one that most students (85 percent) missed.

The p value of an item should always be viewed in relationship to the student's chance probability of getting the correct response. For example, if a binary-choice item is involved, *on the basis of chance alone*, students should be able to answer the item correctly half of the time, and thus the item would have a p value of .50. On a four-option multiple-choice test, a .25 p value by chance alone would be expected.

Educators sometimes err by referring to items with high p values (for instance, p values of .80 and above) as "easy" items, while items with low p values (of, say, .20 and below) are described as "difficult" items. Those descriptions may or may

not be accurate. Even though we typically refer to an item's *p* value as its *difficulty* index, the actual difficulty of an item is tied to the instructional program surrounding it. If students are especially well taught, they may perform excellently on a complex item that, by anyone's estimate, is a tough one. Does the resulting *p* value of .95 indicate the item is easy? No. The item's complicated content may have simply been taught effectively. For example, almost all students in a pre-med course for prospective physicians might correctly answer a technical item about the central nervous system that almost all "people off the street" would answer incorrectly. A *p* value of .96 based on the pre-med students' performances would not render the item intrinsically easy.

Item-Discrimination Indices

For tests designed to yield norm-referenced inferences, one of the most powerful indicators of an item's quality is the **item-discrimination index**. In brief, an *item-discrimination index* typically tells us how frequently an item is answered correctly by those who perform well on the total test. Fundamentally, an item-discrimination index reflects the relationship between students' responses for the total test and their responses to a particular test item. One approach to computing an item-discrimination statistic is to calculate a correlation coefficient between students' total test scores and their performance on a particular item.

A *positively discriminating item* indicates an item is answered correctly more often by those who score well on the total test than by those who score poorly on the total test. A *negatively discriminating item* is answered correctly more often by those who score poorly on the total test than by those who score well on the total test. A *nondiscriminating item* is one for which there's no appreciable difference in the correct response proportions of those who score well or poorly on the total test. This set of relationships is summarized in the following chart. (Remember that < and > signify *less than* and *more than*, respectively.)

Type of Item	Proportion of Correct Responses on Total Test
Positive Discriminator	High Scorers > Low Scorers
Negative Discriminator	High Scorers < Low Scorers
Nondiscriminator	High Scorers = Low Scorers

In general, teachers would like to discover that their items are positive discriminators because a positively discriminating item tends to be answered correctly by the most knowledgeable students (those who scored high on the total test) and incorrectly by the least knowledgeable students (those who scored low on the total test). Negatively discriminating items indicate something is awry, because the item tends to be missed more often by the most knowledgeable students and answered correctly more frequently by the least knowledgeable students.

Now, how do you go about computing an item's discrimination index? Increasingly, these days, teachers can send off a batch of machine-scorable answer sheets (for selected-response items) to a district-operated assessment center where electronic machines have been taught how to spit out p values and item-discrimination indices. Teachers can also carry out such analyses themselves. The following four steps can be employed for the analysis of classroom assessment procedures:

1. *Order the test papers from high to low by total score.* Place the paper having the highest total score on top, and continue with the next highest total score sequentially until the paper with the lowest score is placed on the bottom.
2. *Divide the papers into a high group and a low group, with an equal number of papers in each group.* Split the groups into upper and lower halves. If there is an odd number of papers, simply set aside one of the middle papers so the number of papers in the high and low groups will be the same. If there are several papers with identical scores at the middle of the distribution, then randomly assign them to the high or low distributions so the number of papers in the two groups is identical. The use of 50-percent groups has the advantage of providing enough papers to permit reliable estimates of upper and lower group performances.
3. *Calculate a p value for each of the high and low groups.* Determine the number of students in the high group who answered the item correctly and then divide this number by the number of students in the high group. This provides you with p_h. Repeat the process for the low group to obtain p_l.
4. *Subtract p_l from p_h to obtain each item's discrimination index (D).* In essence, then, $D = p_h - p_l$.

Suppose you are in the midst of conducting an item analysis of your midterm examination items. Let's say you split your class of 30 youngsters' papers into two equal upper-half and lower-half papers. All 15 students in the high group answered item 42 correctly, but only 5 of the 15 students in the low group answered it correctly. The item discrimination index for item 42, therefore, would be $1.00 - .33 = .67$.

Now, how large should an item's discrimination index be in order for you to consider the item acceptable? Ebel and Frisbie (1991) offer the experience-based guidelines in Table 11.1 for indicating the quality of items to be used for making norm-referenced interpretations. If you consider their guidelines as approximations, not absolute standards, they'll usually help you decide whether your items are discriminating satisfactorily.

An item's ability to discriminate is highly related to its overall difficulty index. For example, an item answered correctly by all students has a total p value of 1.00. For that item, the p_h and p_l are also 1.00. Thus, the item's discrimination index is zero ($1.00 - 1.00 = 0$). A similar result would ensue for items in which the overall p value was zero—that is, items no student had answered correctly.

table 11.1 ■ Guidelines for Evaluating the Discriminating Efficiency of Items

Discrimination Index	Item Evaluation
.40 and above	Very good items
.30–.39	Reasonably good items, but possibly subject to improvement
.20–.29	Marginal items, usually needing improvement
.19 and below	Poor items, to be rejected or improved by revision

Source: Ebel, R.L. and Frisbie, D.A. (1991) *Essentials of Educational Measurement* (5th ed.). Englewood Cliffs, NJ: Prentice Hall.

With items that have very high or very low p values, it is thus less likely substantial discrimination indices can be obtained. Later in the chapter you will see this situation has prompted proponents of criterion-referenced interpretations of tests (who often hope almost all postinstruction responses from students will be correct) to search for alternative ways to calculate indices of item quality.

In looking back at the use of item-discrimination indices to improve a test's items, it is important to understand that these indices, as their name signifies, were designed to *discriminate*. That is, such indices have been employed to help spot items that do a good job in contributing sufficient variation to students' total-test scores so those total-test scores can be accurately compared with one another. Educators in the United States have been using most educational tests to do this sort of discriminating between high-scorers and low-scorers for almost a century. To make the kind of norm-referenced, comparative interpretations that have historically been the chief function of U.S. educational testing, we needed to refine a set of test-improvement procedures suitable for sharpening the accuracy of our comparative score-interpretations. Item-discrimination indices help us to locate the optimal items for contrasting students' test performances.

But although it is certainly appropriate to employ educational tests in an effort to come up with norm-referenced interpretations of students' performances, there are educational settings in which a test's comparative function should be overshadowed by its instructional function. In those more instructionally oriented settings, traditional item-discrimination indices may be quite *inappropriate*. To illustrate, suppose a mathematics teacher decides to get her students to become skilled in the use of a really demanding mathematical procedure. (We can call it Procedure X.) Well, when the teacher gave her students a test containing Procedure X items early in the year, students' performances on the items were rather scattered, and the resulting item-discrimination indices for all the Procedure X items looked quite acceptable—between .30 and .60. However, at the end of the school year, after an awesomely wonderful instructional job by our plucky math teacher, almost every student answered almost every Procedure X item correctly. The p values for every one of those items was .95 or above! As a consequence of this almost nonexistent

DECISION TIME

To Catch a Culprit: Teacher or Test?

Susan Stevens teaches sixth-grade social studies in Exeter Middle School. During the seven years she has taught at Exeter, Susan has always spent considerable time in developing what she refers to as "credible classroom assessments." She really has put in more than her share of weekends working to create crackerjack examinations.

This last spring, however, Susan completed an extension course on educational testing. In the course she learned how to compute discrimination analyses of her test items. As a consequence, Susan has been subjecting all of her examinations to such analyses this year.

On one of her examinations containing mostly selected-response items, Susan discovered to her dismay that 4 of the test's 30 items turned out to have negative discriminators. In other words, students who performed well on the total test answered the 4 items incorrectly more often than students who didn't do so well on the total test. To her surprise, all 4 negatively discriminating items dealt with the same topic—that is, relationships among the legislative, judicial, and executive branches of the U.S. government.

Susan's first thought was to chuck the 4 items because they were clearly defective. As she considered the problem, however, another possibility occurred to her. Because all 4 items were based on the same instructional content, perhaps she had confused the stronger students with her explanations.

> *If you were Susan and wanted to get to the bottom of this issue so you could decide whether to overhaul the items or the instruction, how would you proceed?*

variation in her students' Procedure X item performances, those items produced particularly low item-discrimination indices—much lower than those regarded as acceptable. Were those Procedure X items flawed? Do they need to be revised or replaced? Of course not! The "culprit" in this caper is simply the teacher's excellent instruction. If almost all students score perfectly on a related set of test items because their teacher has done a spectacular instructional job teaching whatever those items measure, does this make the items unacceptable? Obviously not.

Item-discrimination indices, therefore, are often quite inappropriate for evaluating the quality of items in teacher-made tests if those tests are being employed chiefly for instructional purposes. Be wary of unthinkingly submitting your classroom assessments to a medley of traditional item-improvement procedures—empirical or judgmental—that do not mesh with the purpose for which the test was originally created. For norm-referenced measurement missions, item-discrimination indices have much to commend them; for criterion-referenced assessment, the results of item-discrimination procedures are often misleading.

table 11.2 ■ A Typical Distractor-Analysis Table

Item No. 28	Alternatives				
$(p = .50, D = -.33)$	A	B*	C	D	Omit
Upper 15 students	2	5	0	8	0
Lower 15 students	4	10	0	0	1

Distractor Analyses

For a selected-response item that, perhaps on the basis of its p value or its discrimination index, appears to be in need of revision, it is necessary to look deeper. In the case of multiple-choice items, we can gain further insights by carrying out a *distractor analysis* in which we see how the high and low groups are responding to the item's distractors.

Presented in Table 11.2 is the information typically used when conducting a distractor analysis. Note that the asterisk in Table 11.2 indicates that choice B is the correct answer to the item. For the item in the table, the difficulty index *(p)* was .50 and the discrimination index *(D)* was $-.33$. An inspection of the distractors reveals there appears to be something in alternative D that is enticing the students in the high group to choose it. Indeed, while over half of the high group opted for choice D, not a single student in the low group went for choice D. Alternative D needs to be reviewed carefully.

Also note that alternative C is doing nothing at all for the item. No student selected choice C. In addition to revising choice D, therefore, choice C might be made a bit more appealing. It is possible, of course, particularly if this is a best-answer type of multiple-choice item, that alternative B, the correct answer, needs a bit of massaging as well. For multiple-choice items in particular, but also for matching items, a more intensive analysis of student responses to individual distractors can frequently be illuminating. In the same vein, careful scrutiny of students' responses to essay and short-answer items can typically supply useful insights for revision purposes.

ITEM ANALYSIS FOR CRITERION-REFERENCED MEASUREMENT

When teachers use tests intended to yield criterion-referenced interpretations, they typically want most students to score well on those tests after instruction has occurred. In such instances, because postinstruction p values may approach 1.0, traditional item-analysis approaches will often yield low discrimination indices. Accordingly, several alternative approaches to item analysis for criterion-referenced measurement have been devised in recent years.

PARENT TALK

Suppose a parent of one of your students called you this morning, before school, to complain about his son's poor performance on your classroom tests. He concludes his grousing by asking you, "Just how sure are you the fault is in Tony and not in your tests?"

 If I were you, here's how I'd respond to the parent:

"I'm glad you called about your son's test results because I'm sure we both want what's best for Tony, and I want to be sure I'm making the instructional decisions that will be best for him.

"The way I use my classroom tests is to try to arrive at the most accurate conclusion I can about how well my students have mastered the skills and knowledge I'm trying to teach them. It's very important, then, that the conclusions I reach about students' skill levels are valid. So, every year I devote systematic attention to the improvement of each of my major exams. You'll remember that it was on the last two of these exams that Tony scored so badly.

"What I'd like to do is show you the exams I've been giving my students and the data I use each year to improve those exams. Why don't we set up an after-school or, if necessary, an evening appointment for you and your wife to look over my classroom assessments and the evidence I've been compiling over the years to make sure my tests help me make valid inferences about what Tony and the rest of my students are learning?"

 Now, how would you respond to this parent?

Two general item-analysis schemes have been employed thus far, depending on the kinds of student groups available. Both of these item-analysis schemes are roughly comparable to the item-discrimination indices used with tests that yield norm-referenced inferences. The first approach involves the administration of the test to *the same group of students* prior to and following instruction. A disadvantage of this approach is that the teacher must wait for instruction to be completed before securing the item-analysis data. Another problem is that the pretest may be *reactive,* in the sense that its administration sensitizes students to certain items so students' posttest performance is actually a function of the instruction *plus* the pretest's administration.

Using the strategy of testing the same groups of students prior to and after instruction, we can employ an item discrimination index calculated as follows:

$$D_{ppd} = p_{post} - p_{pre}$$

where p_{post} = proportion of students answering the item correctly on posttest.
p_{pre} = proportion of students answering the item correctly on pretest.

The value of D_{ppd} (discrimination based on the pretest–posttest difference) can range from -1.00 to $+1.00$, with high positive values indicating an item is sensitive to instruction.

For example, if 41 percent of the students answered item 27 correctly in the pretest and 84 percent answered it correctly on the posttest, then item 27's D_{ppd} would be $.84 - .41 = .43$. A high positive value would indicate the item is sensitive to the instructional program you've provided to your students. Items with low or negative D_{ppd} values would be earmarked for further analysis because such items are not behaving the way one would expect them to behave if instruction were effective. (It is always possible, particularly if many items fail to reflect large posttest-minus-pretest differences, that the instruction being provided was not so very wonderful.)

The second approach to item analysis for criterion-referenced measurement is to locate two *different groups of students*, one of which has already been instructed and one of which has not. By comparing the performance on items of instructed and uninstructed students, you can pick up some useful clues regarding item quality. This approach has the advantage of avoiding the delay associated with pretesting and posttesting the same group of students and also of avoiding the possibility of a re-active pretest. Its drawback, however, is that you must rely on human judgment in the selection of the "instructed" and "uninstructed" groups. The two groups should be fairly identical in all other relevant respects (for example, in intellectual ability) but different with respect to whether or not they have been instructed. The isolation of two such groups sounds easier than it usually is. Your best bet would be to prevail on a fellow teacher whose students are studying different topics than yours.

If you use two groups—that is, an instructed group and an uninstructed group—one of the more straightforward item discrimination indices is D_{uigd} (discrimination based on uninstructed versus instructed group differences). This index is calculated as follows:

$$D_{uigd} = p_i - p_u$$

where p_i = proportion of instructed students answering an item correctly.
p_u = proportion of uninstructed students answering an item correctly.

The D_{uigd} index can also range in value from -1.00 to $+1.00$. To illustrate its computation, if an instructed group of students scored 91 percent correct on a particular item, while the same item was answered correctly by only 55 percent of an uninstructed group, then D_{uigd} would be $.91 - .55 = .36$. Interpretations of D_{uigd} are similar to those used with D_{ppd}.

As suggested earlier, clearly there are advantages associated with using both judgmental and empirical approaches to improving your classroom assessment procedures. Practically speaking, classroom teachers have only so much energy to expend. If you can spare a bit of your allotted energy to spiff up your assessment instruments, you'll usually see meaningful differences in the quality of those instruments.

But What Does This Have to Do with Teaching?

Because of the demands on most teachers' time, the typical teacher really doesn't have time to engage in unbridled test-polishing. So, as a practical matter, very few teachers spend *any* time trying to improve their classroom assessments. It is all too understandable.

But there are two approaches to item improvement described in this chapter, one of which, a judgmentally based strategy, doesn't burn up much time at all. It's a judgmental approach to item improvement that represents a realistic item-improvement model for most classroom teachers.

Whereas teachers should understand the basics of how a test can be made better by using empirical data based on students' responses, they'll rarely be inclined to use such data-based strategies for improving items unless a test is thought to be a super-important one.

During the 29 years that I taught courses in the UCLA Graduate School of Education, the *only* tests that I ever subjected to empirical item-improvement analyses were my midterm and final exams in courses I taught year after year. Oh, to be sure, I applied judgmental improvement techniques to most of my other tests, but the only tests I did a full-throttle, data-based improvement job on were the one or two most important tests for an oft-taught course.

My fear is that the apparent complexity of empirical item-improvement efforts might even dissuade you from routinely employing *judgmental* item-improvement procedures. Don't let it. Even if you *never* use students' data to sharpen your classroom tests, those tests will almost surely still need sharpening. Judgmental approaches will help do the job.

WHAT DO CLASSROOM TEACHERS REALLY NEED TO KNOW ABOUT IMPROVING THEIR ASSESSMENTS?

You ought to know that teacher-made tests can be improved as a consequence of judgmental and/or empirical improvement procedures. Judgmental approaches work well with either selected-response or constructed-response kinds of test items. Empirical item-improvements have been used chiefly with selected-response tests and hence are more readily employed with such test items. You should realize that most of the more widely used indices of item quality, such as discrimination indices, are intended for use with test items in norm-referenced assessment approaches, and may have less applicability to your tests if you employ criterion-referenced measurement strategies. Finally, you must understand that because educators have far less experience in using (and improving) performance assessments and portfolio assessments, there isn't really a delightful set of improvement procedures available for those assessment strategies—other than good, solid judgment.

CHAPTER SUMMARY

A focus on two strategies for improving assessment procedures was seen in this chapter. It was suggested that, with adequate time and motivation, teachers could use judgmental and/or empirical methods of improving their assessments.

Judgmentally based improvement procedures were described for use by teachers, teachers' colleagues, and students. Five review criteria for evaluating assessment procedures were presented for use by teachers and their colleagues: (1) adherence to item-specific guidelines and general item-writing commandments, (2) contribution to score-based inferences, (3) accuracy of content, (4) absence of content lacunae, and (5) fairness. A set of possible questions to ask students about test items was also provided.

Two empirical item-improvement indices described in the chapter were p values and item-discrimination indices. A step-by-step procedure for determining item-discrimination values was described. Designed chiefly for use with norm-referenced measurement, item-discrimination indices do not function well when large numbers of students respond correctly (or incorrectly) to the items involved. Distractor analyses have proven highly useful in the improvement of multiple-choice items because the effectiveness of each item's alternatives can be studied. Finally, two indices of item quality for criterion-referenced measurement were described. Although roughly comparable to the kind of item-discrimination indices widely used with norm-referenced measurement, the two indices for criterion-referenced assessment can be used in settings where many effectively taught students perform well on examinations.

Determining Your Outcome Mastery

Let's look, once more, at the chapter's chief intended outcome. It is intended that you have attained:

> *sufficient comprehension of both judgmental and empirical test-improvement procedures so that accurate decisions can be made about the way teachers are employing these two test-improvement strategies.*

In other words, you should have sufficient understanding of a collection of effective test-improvement tactics that you are able not only to describe the key features of those tactics but also to identify shortcomings in their implementation by other teachers—and yourself.

To gather evidence of your mastery, complete both the Selected-Response and the Constructed-Response quizzes and think about the feedback you receive for each quiz.

MyEdLab *Selected-Response Check of Outcome Mastery*

MyEdLab *Constructed-Response Check of Outcome Mastery*

After completing both quizzes, go to the Learning Outcome Mastery Determination, where you will decide whether you've mastered the chapter's learning outcome or whether you need further study.

MyEdLab *Learning Outcome Mastery Determination*

References

Downing, Steven M., and Haladyna, T. M. (Eds.). (2006). *Handbook of test development*. Mahwah, NJ: Erlbaum.

Ebel, R. L., and Frisbie, D. A. (1991). *Essentials of educational measurement* (5th ed.). Englewood Cliffs, NJ: Prentice-Hall.

Miller, M. D., and Linn, R. (2012). *Measurement and assessment in teaching* (11th ed.). Columbus, OH: Pearson.

Thorndike, Robert M., and Thorndike-Christ, T. (2010). *Measurement and evaluation in psychology and education* (8th ed.). Boston: Allyn and Bacon.

Waugh, C. K., and Gronlund, N. (2012). *Measurement and assessment in teaching* (11th ed.). Columbus, OH: Pearson.

12

Formative Assessment

CHIEF CHAPTER OUTCOME

An understanding of research-ratified formative assessment's essence sufficient for identifying teachers' proper and improper implementations of the formative-assessment process

Suppose there were a really convincing collection of research evidence showing that a particular *assessment-based* instructional strategy helped students learn more and learn it better. Suppose further, because this assessment-based instructional strategy helped students learn more and learn it better, teachers who used this research-supported strategy became demonstrably more successful.

Because both of those two suppositions are stone-cold true, wouldn't it seem that most of today's teachers would be using this assessment-based instructional strategy in their classrooms? Yet, at the moment, most teachers aren't. In this chapter, you'll discover why.

ASSESSMENT THAT TRANSFORMS TEACHING

The assessment-based instructional strategy to be treated in this chapter is *formative assessment*, and you'll learn what it is and what it isn't. You'll also learn why, when abundant evidence is at hand indicating formative assessment works—and works well—this potent process is not more widely employed by teachers. As you read further in the chapter, see if you can figure out—on your own—why far fewer teachers are currently employing formative assessment than one might think. That's right, think of the chapter as a condensed mystery novel in which your task is to understand what formative assessment is, discover how it can improve a teacher's effectiveness, and then come up with an accurate answer to the following question: *Why is formative assessment, a research-ratified instructional strategy, not more widely used in our schools?*

Early on, however, I want to get my personal preference out there in plain sight so you can interpret my chapter-chatter accurately. I am a definite believer in formative assessment. I think research evidence aplenty exists showing us that formative assessment, if used by teachers, helps kids learn better. Based on this belief, I desperately want to see formative assessment used more extensively in our schools. As you continue to read, whether you are an experienced teacher or an in-preparation teacher, you'll sometimes find me touting the merits of formative assessment. This is because I think formative assessment constitutes a potent process that *all* educators should be touting.

What Is Formative Assessment?

Let's look at the definition of formative assessment and then poke briefly into this definition's key elements:

> *Formative assessment is a planned process in which assessment-elicited evidence of students' status is used by teachers to adjust their ongoing instructional procedures or by students to adjust their current learning tactics.*

A process, not a test. Perhaps what's most important in this definition is that formative assessment is a *process* rather than a *test*. Moreover, it is a *planned* process. So, during a teachers' lounge conversation, if one of your colleagues were to describe a particular test as "a formative test," you now know that, according to the previous definition, your colleague would be mistaken. Formative assessment is not a test but, instead, a carefully conceived process wherein the results of assessments are used by teachers or students to improve what they are doing. The process of collecting such assessment-based evidence, and then using this evidence to make any needed adjustments, is at the very heart of the formative-assessment process. If you prefer, you can accurately think of formative assessment as an *instructional strategy.* It's a strategy for using assessment-elicited evidence to enhance teachers' instruction and to improve students' learning. It is, most definitely, not a particular type of test.

As you will soon see, thoughtful planning needs to take place early in the formative-assessment process—a process that's definitely not a spur-of-the-moment undertaking. Teachers, of course, make on-the-spot changes all the time. For example, in the midst of what a teacher believes will be a lucid explanation of a particular concept, if the teacher sees that most students look totally confused, the teacher might sensibly make an instant decision to start the explanation over again, and try to improve its clarity. Spontaneous instructional changes of this sort are fine, and they'll often improve instruction. Such on-the-spot instructional changes should be encouraged. They just aren't formative assessment. Formative assessment is a process requiring some serious up-front planning if it is going to work as well as the research evidence says it can work.

Terminological Lineage

The "formative" part of the formative-assessment label traces its ancestry to a distinction first drawn by Scriven (1967) almost five decades ago. Scriven's separation of formative and summative functions, however, was related to educational *evaluation,* not to assessment. As you will see, the gist of that evaluation-related distinction has been retained when today's educators contrast formative and summative *assessment*. Scriven argued that *summative evaluation* took place when educators appraised the worth of a fully mature, completed instructional program such as a published collection of self-study history booklets. In contrast, *formative evaluation* occurred when educators appraised the worth of a yet malleable instructional program—for example, a set of under-construction instructional materials still in the tryout-and-revision stage of development. Summative evaluation is employed to inform *go/no-go decisions* about a program, whereas formative evaluation is used to make *improvement decisions* regarding a program. These evaluation-related meanings of the adjectives *formative* and *summative* have carried over to today when those two labels are applied to the use of educational assessments.

Summative assessment takes place when educators collect test-based evidence to inform decisions about already completed instructional activities such as when statewide accountability tests are administered each spring to determine the instructional effectiveness of a state's schools during the soon-to-be-completed school year. As another example of summative assessment, we can think of the final examination a teacher administers to her students, the purpose of that exam being chiefly to help the teacher assign an appropriate grade to her students based on how much those students have learned during a semester or school year. The decision riding on results of the student's performance on the final exam is not an instructional-improvement decision but, rather, a decision about what grade the teacher should dispense to her students.

In contrast to summative assessment, formative assessment focuses on improving the way teachers are teaching something and the way students are learning something. Formative assessment has a "make-better" measurement mission, whereas summative assessment tries to answer the "instructional-quality" question.

Although a given test may be employed in connection with a summative assessment function, it is possible (if the test is properly crafted) for this very same test to be used also as part of the formative-assessment process. In other words, *tests*, all by themselves, are neither formative nor summative. It is the *use* to which a given test's results are put that makes the assessment part of the formative-assessment process or, instead, finds it contributing to a summative-assessment decision. Of course, if educators specifically build a test to fulfill a particular function, such as the improvement of a teacher's instruction, then the test will more likely be suited for a formative measurement mission than for a summative measurement mission. You'll soon see examples of how to build tests so they contribute optimally to the formative-assessment process.

Assessment-Based Evidence

Getting back to the definition of formative assessment, a central feature of the formative-assessment process is the collection of *evidence* from students via some sort of assessment procedure. This evidence-gathering activity need not rely on formal exams such as paper-and-pencil tests or, these days, computer-presented tests. Although time-honored test tactics are typically time honored because, over time, they have worked well enough to be retained, you will soon be seeing several more innovative ways of collecting evidence regarding students' mastery of particular skills or knowledge. The assessment-elicited evidence referred to in the definition of formative assessment can be obtained by a wide variety of assessment ploys, not merely traditional assessment procedures.

Adjustments

If you take a careful look at the definition of formative assessment, you'll see that the evidence elicited by assessment procedures is used either by *teachers* to adjust their ongoing *instruction* or by *students* to adjust their current *learning tactics* (the procedures students are using in an effort to learn what they are supposed to be learning). Formative assessment, therefore, is a process involving teachers and/ or students—not merely teachers. Instructional adjustments are made by teachers regarding their ongoing—that is, *current*—instruction, not instruction aimed at a subsequent group of students. Similarly, the adjustments by students in how they're trying to learn something are those adjustments made with respect to their current learning tactics, not those learning tactics to be used in later classes. Formative assessment, although planned in advance, is a "right now" process focused on shaping up what's currently being taught and learned.

It is not a silly idea, of course, for teachers to assess their current students at the close of instruction to see how well those students have learned, and then for those teachers to make changes in next year's or next term's instruction. No, making such changes represents instructional savvy. Assessing the impact of this year's instruction on students in order to make improvement-focused adjustments in next year's instruction is a smart way for teachers to operate. But those make-better adjustments, if they do not center on a teacher's *current* collection of students, are not part of the formative-assessment process.

A Distinctive Way of Thinking about Instruction

Definitions, even carefully crafted ones, often can't capture the richness of what's being defined. As you look again at the definition of formative assessment, what may not come through is that the formative-assessment process represents a decidedly *distinctive* instructional strategy, a strategy in which teachers and students routinely employ assessments to come up with the evidence to let them know whether adjustments are called for in what's going on in class. Formative assessment is, at bottom, a strategy in which the most important decisions about instruction or learning are made based on students' current *assessed* achievement status. If you, as a teacher-in-training or an already experienced teacher, decide to employ formative assessment in your own classes, I promise that you'll end up thinking about instruction in a manner profoundly different from the way most teachers have traditionally conceived of teaching. Formative assessment can, indeed, transform the way a teacher teaches.

Is Formative Assessment the Same as "Assessment *for* Learning"?

In the past several years, some educators have become excited about the potential instructional dividends of swapping a three-letter preposition for a two-letter preposition. I know it's difficult to imagine any sort of preposition-exchanging that's capable of generalizing even a tiny bit of educational excitement but, trust me, it has.

I'm referring to the notion of assessment *for* learning that's being recommended instead of the more traditional way of thinking about assessment—namely, assessment *of* learning. You see, when most educators have thought about assessment in years past, those educators saw assessment chiefly as a way of figuring out how much their students have learned. Clearly, the time-honored way of regarding testing was to conceive of it as assessment *of* learning. But, increasingly, we find prominent instructional specialists arguing that if teachers are ever to get the most instructional mileage out of their classroom testing, then the way to regard such testing is to view it as a vehicle to enhance instructional effectiveness or, with only a simple preposition-flip, to view it as assessment *for* learning.

Incidentally, assessment *for* learning is not supposed to replace all instances of assessment *of* learning. There are many situations in education when we really do want to find out what kids know and what they don't know. That's assessment *of* learning, and it's not a bad thing. However, there should be many more occasions when we see assessment *for* learning dominating an instructional scene. But before getting into some of the ways assessment *for* learning can be installed in a teacher's classroom, let me clarify for you where this feisty little phrase came from in the first place.

In the United States, the expression "assessment *for* learning" is often mistakenly attributed to Richard Stiggins (2007) or to Paul Black and Dylan Wiliam (1998a), even though all three of these individuals always deny paternity regarding their fathering of the phrase. Because Dylan Wiliam is an able colleague and a good friend, and is associated with the Assessment Reform Group in England where many people think the phrase emerged, I asked Dylan if he would be willing to sleuth the origin of assessment *for* learning. (Sherlock Holmes, after all, was British.) Dylan agreed, and what he came up with you'll find in the following paragraph.

The earliest use of the phrase "assessment for learning" appears to have been in a paper presented by a Brit, Mary James (1992), at a New Orleans conference of the Association for Supervision and Curriculum Development. Three years later, the phrase was used by Ruth Sutton of England as the title of a book she wrote (Sutton, 1995). However, the first explicit contrast of assessment *for* learning with assessment *of* learning seems to have occurred in the third edition of a book by Gipps and Stobart (1997) where their first chapter is entitled "Assessment of Learning" and their second chapter is entitled "Assessment for Learning." This prepositional distinction was brought to a wider audience two years later by England's Assessment Reform Group in a guide for policymakers (Broadfoot et al., 1999).

So, thanks to Dylan's dogged Sherlocking, we now have an idea where this fine formulation came from. It is apparent that most, if not all, of the early thinking on this issue came to the United States from Great Britain. So, in addition to the debt we owe the Brits for tea, scones, and the Beatles, we now have something in the assessment realm for which we should be grateful.

For all practical purposes, the phrases *formative assessment* and *assessment for learning* can be seen as essentially interchangeable. However, not everyone who employs either one of these two descriptors always does so properly. As you'll see in a moment, the research evidence supporting the use of formative assessment is compelling. But that evidence does not support *any old* approach that someone decides to label as either formative assessment or assessment for learning.

Regrettably, we now find test publishers hawking all sorts of assessment products using the label "formative assessment." Lorrie Shepard, a leading U.S. assessment expert, has become particularly vexed with what she regards as test vendors' corruption, for marketing purposes, of an otherwise powerful assessment concept. As Shepard (2006) points out:

> *The research-based concept of formative assessment, closely grounded in classroom instructional processes, has been taken over (hijacked) by commercial test publishers and used instead to refer to formal testing systems called benchmark or interim assessment systems.*

What Formative Assessment Isn't

As you look back at the definition of formative assessment, you can discern that some applications of educational assessment would obviously not satisfy the definition's requirements. For instance, when annual accountability tests are administered at the close of a school year to evaluate a state's schools, this would clearly not be an instance of formative assessment.

And you've already learned that a test itself is not formative assessment. Tests are used to collect information that can lead teachers or students to adjust what they are currently doing. But tests, all by themselves, are not formative assessment.

You've also seen that formative assessment is a *planned* process, not a collection of off-the-cuff alterations in what's going on in class. Although teachers make instant, unplanned changes in their instructional activities, such changes do not make what's going on formative assessment. Careful thought must be given to what sorts of changes might be made, what sorts of evidence might be collected related to those changes, and what kinds of assessment devices might be used to secure this evidence. Don't let a colleague tell you, "I already use formative assessment because I can tell from my students' comments and their facial expressions whether I need to make any instructional adjustments." Such adjustments simply aren't formative assessment.

Moreover, as you saw earlier from Shepard's comment, formative assessment is most definitely *not* what commercial companies happen to call their products. As she noted, some vendors are now peddling assessment materials they describe by using labels such as the following: "interim assessments" and "benchmark assessments." Other vendors are calling the very same types of tests "formative." Commercial companies, of course, can call their products pretty much what they want to—barring violations of registered trademarks. But, as you'll soon see, just because a commercial product is called *formative assessment* by vendors, or even by a group of well-intentioned educators who have built their own test, this mislabeling does not make that product automatically mesh with the kind of empirical research evidence undergirding the formative-assessment process.

When does a teacher use formative assessment? Is it a once-in-a-while activity or an every-single-minute activity? Well, different educators may have different answers to such questions, but I hope most teachers will use the formative-assessment process selectively. To be blunt, properly conceived formative assessment demands a heap of hard thinking on the teacher's part, not to mention the necessary collection of assessment evidence from students. Formative assessment has the clear potential to prove burdensome to teachers and, therefore, dissuade them from using it. But, as you'll soon see, formative assessment helps students learn. If it's not used, then students will be instructionally short-changed. Accordingly, teachers should use formative assessment judiciously—not constantly—as they promote students' mastery of truly significant curricular aims.

What this judicious use of formative assessment would translate to, in practice, is that teachers will typically be using the formative-assessment process as they pursue students' attainment of really challenging outcomes. Such outcomes, because they tend to be higher-order cognitive competencies, will typically take some time to teach, perhaps several weeks or even a full semester or school year. It just doesn't make much sense for teachers to direct the powerful formative-assessment process at a student's mastery of, say, a set of memorized information that can be taught successfully in a couple of days. I am not knocking the importance of students' acquisition of knowledge. Possession of knowledge is a marvelous accomplishment for a student. But, more often than not, one's knowledge is employed in that person's use of higher-order cognitive skills. Because such skills take a hefty hunk of time to teach, formative assessment often works best when it is employed by teachers as they promote their students' mastery of these really significant curricular aims.

As I indicated, not everyone may agree with me on this issue, and some proponents of formative assessment would prefer that the process be used by teachers day-in and day-out. If you decide to employ formative assessment in your own classes, this will be your choice. I urge you not to overuse it—that is, not to use it so much that you become disinclined to use it at all.

FORMATIVE ASSESSMENT RESEARCH SUPPORT

Certain actions should be taken whether or not there is research evidence supporting those actions. A mother should protect her child even if she has not read a definitive research-rooted article in *Pediatrics* attesting to the wisdom of a particular protective action. Similarly, we hold the door open for an overloaded supermarket shopper because it's the proper thing to do—despite our not having reviewed empirical evidence supporting the positive consequences of such door-opening behavior. Common sense, not research evidence, often inclines people to do the right thing.

Let's think for a moment about formative assessment, an approach to instructional decision-making in which a teacher uses along-the-way assessment evidence from students as a guide to whether any instructional adjustments are needed. Formative assessment is an instructional strategy that, on the face of it, makes a sack full of sense. Because teachers are human beings, and human beings often make mistakes, formative assessment simply asks a teacher to monitor students' progress to see whether the teacher's instructional decisions were good ones. Thus, if instructional changes are needed, those changes can be made. Teachers invariably try to "get it right the first time." But, of course, many times an original instructional design will be substantially less than perfect. By monitoring students' status to see how instruction is working, less than wonderful instruction can be

altered so it becomes more wonderful. Similarly, if students are given evidence regarding their own progress in learning whatever they're supposed to be learning, then those students can determine whether their learning tactics need to be adjusted. In almost any sort of instructional setting, formative assessment would make sense even if not one dollop of empirical research were at hand to support its effectiveness.

But such research has, in fact, been carried out. It's much more than a dollop, and it's quite persuasive. So, in addition to a common-sense rationale supporting formative assessment as a classroom instructional strategy, teachers now have ample empirical evidence on hand to confirm the commonsensical.

The Black and Wiliam Research Review

Paul Black and Dylan Wiliam are two British researchers who, in 1998, published a remarkably important review of almost 10 years' worth of empirical research dealing with classroom assessment (Black and Wiliam, 1998a). Entitled "Assessment and Classroom Learning," their rather technical review appeared in the March 1998 issue of the journal *Assessment in Education* and, frankly, attracted only modest attention from U.S. educators. However, in October of the same year, these two authors published a follow-up article in the more widely read *Phi Delta Kappan* (Black and Wiliam, 1998b) not only summarizing their earlier review of research evidence but also describing policy implications of that evidence. In contrast to the March article's almost nonexistent impact on the thinking of American educators, the October essay in the *Kappan* garnered considerable attention. It was Black and Wiliam's March review of classroom assessment research, however, that provided the chief empirical underpinnings of today's formative assessment. As a consequence, let's first look at how these two British researchers went about their review, and then see what they concluded from their analyses.

Basing their review on almost 10 years of research about classroom assessment, Black and Wiliam used two earlier extensive reviews (Crooks, 1988; Natriello, 1987) as the springboards for their own work. Employing a conception of formative assessment essentially similar to the definition presented earlier in this chapter, Black and Wiliam first identified more than 680 research publications appearing to be potentially relevant to their inquiry. From those possibilities, they isolated approximately 250 reports as suitable for further scrutiny and, having reviewed each one carefully, incorporated its results in their synthesis of this considerable body of research.

What is particularly refreshing in this review is the transparency with which the two reviewers describe the criteria they used to decide whether or not to include a specific investigation in their conclusions and, if so, how much weight to ascribe to its results. To be candid, in research reviews of this sort, attention must always be given to the stringency of the analytic procedures employed by the reviewers. The Black and Wiliam 1998 review of classroom assessment research is impressive not only for its analytic rigor but also for its forthright description of the many interpretative quandaries faced during the review, and the procedures chosen to deal with those issues.

Based on the comprehensive study of published research, what did these two British investigators conclude? Well, the following quotation is, for all current teachers and all prospective teachers, worth at least two or three re-readings:

> *The research reported here shows conclusively that formative assessment does improve learning. (Black and Wiliam, 1998a, p. 61)*

Are those learning improvements something substantial or something trifling? Black and Wiliam (1998a) concluded that the student gains in learning triggered by formative assessment were "amongst the largest ever reported for educational interventions" (p. 61). Let's look at this last conclusion for a moment. First off, we need to take seriously any assertion containing the term *amongst*. (Even in print, British people seem so convincingly credible.) But, more importantly, please note that formative assessment, when used by teachers in their classrooms, is capable of causing student gains as great as any ever reported for educational interventions. We are not talking here about tiny improvements in kid learning. No, on the contrary, these are whopping gains that formative assessment can bring about in students' achievement.

One conclusion reached by Black and Wiliam that makes their work especially relevant to teachers' day-to-day instruction is their finding that formative assessment is truly robust. In other words, if formative assessment is installed by teachers, *it is nearly certain to work.* As Black and Wiliam observe, "Significant gains can be achieved by many different routes, and initiatives here are not likely to fail through neglect of delicate and subtle features" (1998a, p. 61). In their review, Black and Wiliam supply numerous examples of research investigations in which it is apparent that formative assessment makes a meaningful contribution to students' learning. Sometimes the studies being reviewed focused on teachers' adjustments of their instruction; sometimes the reviewed reports dealt with students' adjustments of their own learning tactics. As Black and Wiliam observe:

> *However, the consistent feature across the variety of these examples is that they all show that attention to formative assessment can lead to significant learning gains. Although there is no guarantee that it will do so irrespective of the context and the particular approach adopted, we have not come across any report of negative effects following on an enhancement of formative practice. (1998a, p. 17)*

It is apparent that the 1998 research review by Black and Wiliam placed a potent pedagogical truth smack in the hands of educators: Formative assessment works, and it works big time! Moreover, the formative-assessment process seems to work particularly well for low-performing learners (who, because of their lower levels of performance, have greater room for growth).

But even though there was some interest in the 1998 *Kappan* summary of the March 1998 research review, it was not until the enactment of No Child Left Behind (NCLB) that U.S. educators turned their attention seriously to the instructional recommendations provided by these two British scholars. This was because NCLB's 2002 enactment called for U.S. educators to boost students' scores on accountability tests substantially, moving toward a point where, in 2014, all students in U.S. public schools would achieve "proficient or better" scores on NCLB-required state exams. Faced with this nontrivial challenge, many American educators recalled the 1998 *Kappan* article in which it had been pointed out that formative assessment could boost students' achievement, and by a lot—not just a little.

Well, it did not require a huge inferential leap for numerous U.S. educators to conclude that if students' in-classroom learning could be improved by formative assessment, why would not those same improvements splash over onto students' performances on NCLB accountability tests? And thus was ushered in what soon became a sometimes frenzied advocacy of formative assessment by certain educational leaders. Formative assessment was being touted as an NCLB salvation-strategy. Numerous educational administrators really believed that if they could only get enough of their teachers to use formative assessment ("whatever 'formative assessment' is"), then students' scores on NCLB tests would go up sufficiently for educators to dodge NCLB failure. It should be noted that in their review of the 250 classroom assessment studies, Black and Wiliam do not indicate formative assessment will boost students' scores on external accountability tests sufficiently for educators to avoid accountability-test failures.

Wrapping up this quick look at the empirical evidence underlying formative assessment, it is difficult to consider the Black and Wiliam synthesis of classroom assessment research without concluding that the formative-assessment process represents a particularly potent way for assessment to bolster the caliber of teachers' instruction. Even reviewers (for example, Kingston and Nash, 2011) who urge caution in our interpretation of relevant research conclude that the positive effects of the formative-assessment process are both clear and practically meaningful. Let's now look at the fundamental framework around which formative assessment can be carried out.

LEARNING PROGRESSIONS AS FRAMEWORKS

We can begin by turning to what some readers might regard as a topic more suited for a book about instruction than a book about assessment. But don't forget that the text you're currently reading is about *classroom* assessment, and the major activity that goes on in classrooms is *instruction*. Indeed, it is because formative assessment is an assessment-based way of making a teacher's *instruction* better that I hope you'll find the upcoming topic particularly pertinent to what might go on in your own classroom.

What Is a Learning Progression?

You've seen that formative assessment is basically a process in which assessment evidence is used by teachers or students to adjust what they are doing. Well, when is this assessment evidence to be collected? Clearly, teachers can't be collecting assessment evidence from kids every few minutes. After all, the really big job facing teachers is to *teach* students, not *test* students. At what points, then, during an instructional sequence should students be assessed so teachers (or the students themselves) can decide whether adjustments are in order? The answer to this significant question revolves around teachers' reliance on a ***learning progression.*** Here's what a learning progression is:

A learning progression is a sequenced set of building blocks—that is, subskills or bodies of enabling knowledge—it is thought students must master en route to mastering a more remote, target curricular aim.

In plain language, a learning progression is an ordered sequence of the stuff a student must learn in order to achieve a significant curricular outcome. Because the construction of a learning progression requires an expenditure of time and energy from a teacher, the "significant curricular outcome" being sought will typically deal with students' mastery of a high-level cognitive skill, the kind of skill apt to take a meaningful amount of time to teach. Examples of such skills might be a student's ability to (1) design a defensible scientific investigation, (2) write a powerful persuasive essay, or (3) select and compute the most effective statistical indicators to accurately represent a set of empirical data. Thus, the use of learning progressions and, indeed, the use of the formative-assessment process itself, is often focused on the pursuit of significant curricular aims.

Let's briefly consider the key components of the preceding definition of learning progressions. First off, the purpose of a learning progression is to identify what students need to master on their way to mastering a more remote, *target curricular aim.* This aim, as already noted, is usually a higher-order cognitive skill. In order for students to master such a target curricular aim, students will almost always first need to master one or more en route, lesser curricular aims. These lesser aims are called *building blocks,* and they consist either of *bodies of enabling knowledge* or *cognitive subskills.*

To illustrate, if the target curricular aim being sought were for students to be able to write a clear expository (explanatory) essay, then one building block might be for the student to know (that is, to have memorized) the important mechanical conventions of spelling, punctuation, and grammar. By knowing and adhering to those conventions, the student's essay is more likely to be clear than if the student's essay were laden with errors of spelling, punctuation, and grammar. So, an *enabling knowledge* building block in a learning progression aimed at a student's skill in writing clear expository essays might be the student's knowledge of mechanical conventions.

Another building block in this instance might be a cognitive *subskill*. Such a subskill might be the student's ability to effectively organize the information to be presented in an expository essay so the essay's readers would most readily understand what was being explained. The appropriate organization of an essay's content, then, might be a second building block for this learning progression.

One of the most common errors teachers make in developing a learning progression is to include too many building blocks. That's right, the more conversant a teacher becomes with the subskills and knowledge a student must possess in order to master a target curricular aim, the greater is the teacher's tendency to toss in more and more building blocks. This is surely understandable, for the more we know about something, the more attentive we become to its nuances. Yet, as you will soon see, students' mastery of *each* building block in a learning progression must be assessed. With too many building blocks in a learning progression, this assessment obligation often gets out of hand. It makes more sense to focus on a modest number of building blocks that are *truly requisite* for a student's mastery of the target curricular aim than to focus on a larger number of building blocks that are *arguably* requisite. In learning progressions, as in many realms of life, less is most definitely more.

Finally, the building blocks in a learning progression should be sequenced in the order it is believed students can most effectively master those building blocks on the way to mastering the target curricular aim. This sequence of building blocks is the one that the persons who are developing a learning progression believe is the most sensible. Although there are several intuitively reasonable guidelines for this sequencing of building blocks, such as "transmit knowledge before asking students to apply such knowledge," the actual sequence of building blocks in a learning progression is really up to the persons who are building the progression. Here's where a teacher's pedagogical prowess comes into play, for a teacher must analyze the *optimal* order in which students should try to master en route knowledge and subskills.

Consider Figure 12.1 for a moment and you will see one way a learning progression can be represented graphically. Note that, in this instance, the target curricular aim is represented by a rectangle, the two bodies of enabling knowledge are signified by squares, and the solo subskill is depicted by a circle. If you generate your own learning progressions, of course, you can employ any symbols that suit you. Learning progressions can be displayed horizontally as well as vertically. Again, graphic representations are up to those who are trying to represent the learning progression. But most educators report that having access to some sort of graphic depiction of a learning progression helps them comprehend the relationships among the progression's building block and its target curricular aim.

Recalling that formative assessment rests on the use of assessment-elicited evidence for teachers (or students) to make adjustment decisions, when teachers identify the key building blocks they believe their students must master en route to the attainment of a target curricular aim, those teachers have thereby determined *when to assess* their students. If every building block is regarded as genuinely

figure 12.1 ■ Graphic Depiction of a Typical Learning Progression

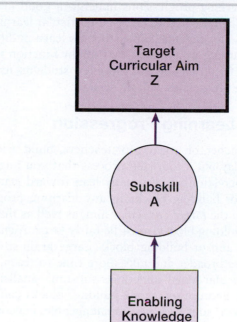

requisite for the student's advancement toward curricular-aim mastery, then it is apparent a teacher will need to see if each building block has, in fact, been mastered. The formative-assessment process revolves around assessments and the adjustment decisions associated with every building block in a learning progression. Clearly, this is why learning progressions are regarded as the guiding framework for formative assessment.

Teachers should know, however, that a learning progression is *not* unerringly accurate. In few instances are we are able to subject learning progressions to the tryout-revision cycles that would empirically confirm their accuracy. Rather, learning progressions usually represent the best estimate that educators have made about what things students must master on their way to mastery of a significant curricular aim—and what constitutes a sensible instructional sequence for those things. Most learning progressions undergo a good many modifications as they are developed, then used. And, finally, a particular learning progression is unlikely to work well for all students. Some students learn in different, seemingly mysterious ways. A learning progression that might function marvelously for most students will often flop for a few. For those few students, meaningful modifications in "their" learning progression will be needed.

Building a Learning Progression

How does a teacher, or a group of teachers, build a learning progression? In a moment I will lay out a four-step process that you might try, but when it comes to learning progressions, I personally lean toward lean. That is, I prefer only a small number of building blocks in any learning progression. This means that the grain-size of the target curricular aim, as well as the grain-size of the learning progression's building blocks, must be fairly large. A *grain-size* refers to the scope of a curricular aim or building block. Large grain-size building blocks (or curricular aims) are broader and take more time to teach. Large grain-size building blocks (or curricular aims) sometimes subsume smaller chunks of knowledge or lesser subskills. Because too many building blocks can clutter up the formative-assessment process so it becomes unmanageable, I encourage you to opt for fairly large grain-size building blocks and, as a result, create a learning progression that doesn't contain too many building blocks.

Here, then, are four steps to be followed in creating the kind of learning progression to serve as the formative-assessment framework for a fairly significant target curricular aim—typically a powerful cognitive skill students are supposed to master.

Step 1: Acquire a thorough understanding of the target curricular aim. Don't even think about building a learning progression unless you first have a fuzz-free fix on the nature of the target curricular aim itself. You can't come up with appropriate building blocks unless you completely comprehend the essence of the outcome being sought. One of the best ways to understand the nature of that target curricular aim is to become familiar with the assessment procedure (or procedures) to be employed in measuring students' mastery of the aim. If you are the person who will build that assessment procedure (or has already built it), then you surely have a good idea of what the target curricular aim actually consists of. If, however, others have built the end-of-instruction assessment(s), be sure you understand it (them) completely. Tests "operationalize" curricular aims—that is, tests constitute the operations that students must display in order to convince us they've mastered a curricular aim.

Step 2: Identify all requisite precursory subskills and bodies of enabling knowledge. This second step is really the toughest of our four-step process. In this second step, you need to think through what students really must know and be able to do if they are going to be successful in mastering the target curricular aim. The most influential word in this second step is *requisite*. This second step is an effort to isolate all "must-know" subskills and knowledge. This second step is not a time to identify "nice-to-know" subskills and knowledge. To keep the number of building blocks manageable, it is sometimes necessary for several lesser subskills or bodies of enabling knowledge to be coalesced into larger grain-sizes. But the focus in this second step must be the isolation of what is truly *necessary* for students to have mastered on their way to mastery of the target curricular aim.

Step 3: Determine the measurability of each preliminarily identified building block.   So far, you will have identified—in Step 2—the building blocks you deem to be necessary precursors to a student's mastery of the target curricular aim. In this third step, you must make certain that you can realistically collect evidence of students' mastery of each building block. The heart of the formative-assessment process is to find out how students are progressing with respect to each building block, and this means measuring students' status with respect to all the building blocks in the learning progression. Thus, if you can't—in a practical manner—assess students' mastery of each building block, then you ought to dump the unmeasurable ones. We'll consider several informal ways of assessing students' building-block mastery later in the chapter.

Step 4: Arrange all the building blocks in an instructionally sensible sequence.   This final step calls for you to think through what sort of sequence makes the most sense from an instructional perspective and then place the learning progression's building blocks in that order. As noted before, teachers rarely have time to try these sequences out to make sure a given sequence is working properly, and it is often necessary to rearrange the sequences after the learning progression has been used a time or two. However, this is the point at which a teacher's instructional acumen is needed. Simply sequence the learning progression's building blocks in the order that a teacher should most appropriately tackle each of those building blocks.

Because formative assessment is a planned process in which students are periodically assessed and, if necessary, adjustments are made, the importance of learning progressions cannot be overestimated. If you decide to employ formative assessment in your own classes, devoting time to the generation of a defensible learning progression for your most significant curricular aims will be time well spent.

I should note that in certain other nations—for instance, Australia and New Zealand—most educators think of learning progressions as much more elongated sequences of students' likely learning sequences. For example, a group of educators might describe the step-by-step progression of skills and knowledge over a course of several years that a student would typically accomplish en route to a sophisticated mastery of a given subject. Such long-term views of learning progressions can be useful to teachers, particularly in devising the kinds of shorter-duration learning progressions described in this chapter.

So far, in this chapter's look at formative assessment, we've considered what formative assessment is, its research base, and the role of learning progressions as frameworks for formative assessment. Now it's time to see how formative assessment can work in classrooms.

ALTERNATIVE IMPLEMENTATION APPROACHES

One of the most encouraging conclusions emerging from Black and Wiliam's (1998a) influential review of classroom assessment studies is that the formative-assessment process is remarkably robust. That is, a teacher who uses it is likely to boost students' learning, irrespective of the particular manner in which the teacher employs formative assessment. As long as the teacher focuses on the collection of assessment evidence from students so that, based on such evidence, either the teacher or the teacher's students can make decisions about adjusting what they're doing, formative assessment works.

But, realistically, many teachers will need more fine-grained guidance regarding how to play the formative assessment game successfully. Thus, in this section of the chapter, three different approaches to the implementation of formative assessment will be briefly described. If you are interested in learning more about any of these three approaches, separate books are available about all three. Hopefully, as you continue to read, you will recognize that formative assessment is akin to a cake capable of being sliced successfully—that is, implemented successfully, in several different ways. As long as formative assessment's implementation centers on assessed evidence of students' status, and the appropriateness of making adjustments based on this evidence, almost any reasonable approach to formative assessment is likely to work well.

A Four-Levels Approach

Remember: Formative assessment is a process that can be used either by teachers to adjust how they're teaching or by students to adjust how they're trying to learn something. Having two potential sets of actors in the formative-assessment drama can, as you might guess, engender confusion. Moreover, because different teachers will surely be using formative assessment in a variety of ways and at varying levels of intensity, this too can cause a clump of confusion.

So, in a head-on assault against confusion for those who try to implement formative assessment, one way for you to think about formative assessment is not as a single entity but, rather, as a *Levels Approach*. Here, then, are brief descriptions of four distinguishable variations of formative assessment:

Four Levels of Formative Assessment

Level 1: Teachers' Instructional Adjustments

In this first level of formative assessment, teachers collect assessment-elicited evidence that they use when deciding whether to adjust their current or immediately upcoming instructional activities.

Level 2: Students' Learning-Tactic Adjustments

A second level of formative assessment takes place when students use assessment-elicited evidence about their own skills or knowledge to decide whether to adjust how they're currently trying to learn something.

Level 3: Classroom Climate Shift

In a melding of Level 1 formative assessment and Level 2 formative assessment, we see a fundamental transformation so that a traditional, comparison-oriented classroom becomes a learning-dominated classroom in which the chief purpose of classroom assessment is not to grade students but, rather, to improve the quality of both teachers' instruction and students' learning.

Level 4: Schoolwide Implementation

In this level of implementation, the expanded use of formative assessment is promoted at the school or district level—chiefly through professional development strategies and/or teacher learning communities. Level 4 formative assessment can be employed to encourage teachers' use of one (or more) of the other three levels of formative assessment.

Although these four levels are meaningfully distinctive, they are not necessarily incremental. In other words, it is possible (but rather unlikely) for a teacher to adopt Level 2 formative assessment (where students are adjusting their own learning tactics) without the teacher's having already adopted Level 1 formative assessment (where teachers are adjusting their instruction). And, realistically, Level 3 formative assessment, where there is a substantial change in the atmosphere of a classroom, would be impossible to pull off if the teacher does not install Level 1 *and* Level 2 formative assessment. This is because Level 3 formative assessment requires substantial shifts in the conduct of *both* teachers and students. But Level 4 formative assessment (schoolwide implementation) definitely doesn't require the installation of all three of the other levels.

What actually goes on in classrooms where each of these four levels of formative assessment is being used? Well, one way for you to understand the nature of the Levels Approach is to consider Figure 12.2 in which the different levels are depicted along with the chief activities typically taking place within each level. (In passing, I should note that although I find most educators in North America concerned with the Level 1 aspects of formative assessment—that is, the teacher's instructional adjustments—in many other parts of the world, greater attention is given to Level 2 formative assessment—that is, helping students take greater responsibility for their own learning.)

Please note in Figure 12.2 that below the four levels of formative assessment, learning progressions underlie the whole works. This is because the four levels are carried out against a guiding framework in which a learning progression's sequenced building blocks help the teacher decide *when* to collect assessment evidence from students. A well-conceived learning progression, as indicated earlier, is integral to the effective implementation of formative assessment.

figure 12.2 ■ **Four Levels of Formative Assessment**

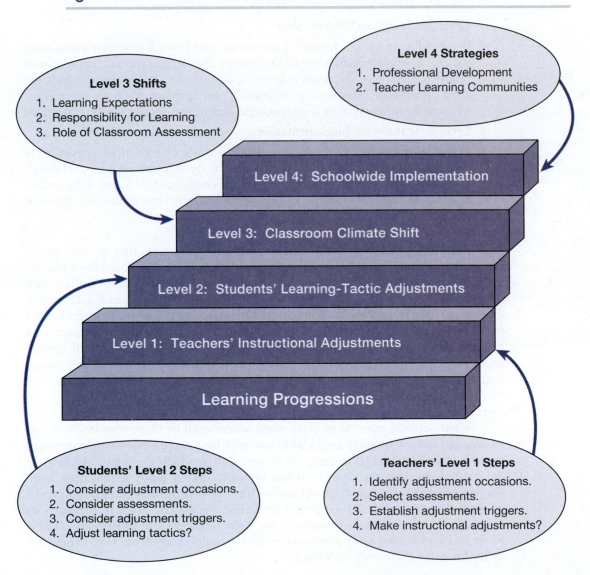

DECISION TIME

To Go Formative or Not?

Reggie Rawlins teaches fifth-grade students in a rural county school in an eastern Washington county fairly close to Spokane. He has recently completed an online master's degree in educational leadership, and found one of the more interesting courses in that program was, to his surprise, a class dealing with educational measurement.

In that course, Reggie acquired two insights that have caused him more than a little discomfort. One of those insights was that the classroom formative-assessment process, when used by teachers, will help students learn what they are supposed to be learning. Although Reggie does not currently use formative assessment with his fifth-graders, he realizes that if he chose to do so, he could employ at least some level of it in his class for the upcoming school year.

On the other hand, he also learned that certain statewide accountability tests, because of the way they have been constructed, are unlikely to detect even substantial improvements in students' classroom learning. Indeed, one of Reggie's online classmates presented an oral report near the end of the measurement class indicating that the specific accountability test then used in his own midwest state would not reveal when classroom instructional improvements were actually occurring.

As Reggie ponders the situation, he sees that if he were to implement formative assessment in his class, then his students would surely be likely to learn more. However, those improvements in students' learning might not show up on the state's annual accountability tests. Moreover, Reggie learned—especially from the anecdotal accounts of teachers who had used formative assessment themselves—that adoption of this approach invariably requires a meaningful expenditure of energy on the teacher's part. Given that, if he used formative assessment with his fifth-graders, his anticipated classroom improvements might not show up on "the big tests." Reggie is not sure whether he should use formative assessment next year or not.

➤ *If you were Reggie and were faced with this situation, what would your decision be?*

In a separate book about formative assessment (Popham, 2008), I have presented—for teachers' consideration—the formative-assessment process as this four-levels approach. If you think you wish to explore in more detail how these four levels of formative assessment actually function, you might wish to explore what's in that analysis. With the Levels Approach to formative assessment, as will be true of other ways of tackling formative assessment, a teacher may choose to use one or more segments of the approach.

A Five-Applications Approach

This second approach to formative assessment hinges heavily on timing—that is, *when* a teacher collects assessment evidence regarding students' status and *when* a teacher or student makes adjustment decisions. I've written a second book about formative assessment structured around this *applications approach* to formative assessment (Popham, 2011). You may wish to consider that text if you regard this way of thinking about formative assessment as potentially useful. Here, then, are descriptions of five applications of the formative-assessment process.

Five Applications of Formative Assessment

1. *Immediate Instructional Adjustments*   In this initial application of formative assessment, a teacher collects assessment evidence, analyzes this evidence, and then decides on the spot—immediately—whether to alter instruction in the next few moments. Two ways for the teacher to collect assessment evidence for this application are available: (1) *teacher-administered assessments* such as brief during-lesson quizzes wherein students supply answers to multiple-choice questions by displaying lettered cards or (2) *student-reported levels of understanding* such as when students signify how well they comprehend a topic by the use of green/yellow/red cards or plastic cups. For this particular application of formative assessment, the teacher needs to have an instructional adjustment standing "at the ready" in case students' assessment data indicate an immediate alteration in instruction is needed.

2. *Near-Future Instructional Adjustments*   A near-future instructional adjustment involves the teachers' collecting assessment evidence, perhaps via during-lesson tests or end-of-lesson "exit tickets" by which students display on slips of paper (handed to the teacher on the way out of the classroom) what they learned during a class session. If the assessment evidence indicates that an instructional adjustment is warranted, the teacher delivers such an adjustment during the next few class sessions. One advantage of this formative-assessment application is that a teacher need not have an "at the ready" instructional adjustment on hand. Thus, if the assessment evidence collected from students indicates no instructional adjustment is needed, the teacher will not have wasted time preparing an instructional approach that's destined to languish—unused. Conversely, if it turns out that students' assessment evidence indicates an instructional adjustment appears to be necessary, the teacher will have a day or two to prepare what will, with forethought, be an *effective* instructional adjustment.

3. *Last-Chance Instructional Adjustments*   This third formative-assessment application is employed only when students are about to be administered a particularly high-stakes examination of some sort, such as a high school graduation test, a grade-to-grade promotion test, or an especially significant accountability test on which a school staff's competence will be

evaluated. While there is still sufficient time to install some meaningful final-hours of instruction for students, instruction can be more effectively targeted because of the diagnostic information obtained from the administration of an exam that is sufficiently similar to the upcoming test to be accurately characterized as a "dress-rehearsal exam." Based on the instructional insights about students' weaknesses yielded by the dress-rehearsal exam, more tailored instruction focused on students' shortcomings can precede the approaching high-stakes test, thereby leading to students' improved performances.

4. *Learning-Tactic Adjustments*   This fourth application of formative assessment is essentially identical to Level 2 in the previously described Levels Approach to formative assessment. Assessment evidence is collected from students and then made available to those students so that, if the students wish to do so, they can alter their learning tactics—in other words, the ways they are trying to learn whatever they are supposed to be learning. As in Level 2 of the Levels Approach, the thrust of this application is to transform students into more autonomous learners than we typically see in our classrooms. Because most students will have scant experience in monitoring their own learning status, and making decisions about whether to (and how to) adjust their learning tactics, students will need substantial support in their use of this formative-assessment application.

5. *Classroom Climate Shifts*   In this fifth application we see a formative-assessment application that is the same as the third level of the Levels Approach—namely, an implementation procedure where both the teacher and the students are relying on evidence collected from ongoing classroom assessments to decide whether any adjustments (either in a teacher's instructional procedures or in students' learning tactics) are warranted. Because of a concerted "everyone participates" strategy, changes in the classroom orientation are sought so that (a) responsibility for learning is shared by all, (b) there is an expectation that every student will be a successful learner, and (c) classroom assessments will be used chiefly for learning enhancement rather than for student grading.

The five applications just described are displayed graphically in Figure 12.3.

As when teachers implement formative assessment by employing the previously described Levels Approach, a teacher need not use all five variations of the Applications Approach. Indeed, a teacher might give formative assessment a try by using only one version of the very first application—that is, by making immediate instructional-adjustment decisions employing students' self-reported levels of understanding as represented by their use of colored cups or cards. The advantage of both the Levels Approach and the Applications Approach is that they provide teachers with options regarding the fervor with which they wish to embrace formative assessment. Teachers' "baby steps" are usually welcomed by proponents of these approaches to formative assessment. Let's turn, now, to a final implementa-

figure 12.3 ■ **Five Applications of Formative Assessment**

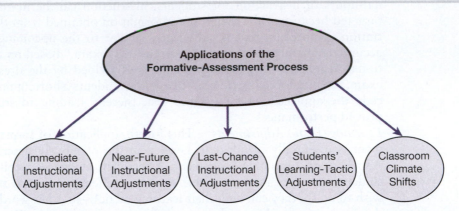

tion approach whereby teachers can, ever so gingerly, give formative assessment a ride around the block.

A Five-Strategies Approach

A third way of splitting up the formative-assessment process as seen in Figure 12.3 has been introduced by Dylan Wiliam and his colleagues (Leahy, Thompson, and Wiliam, 2005). That's right, Wiliam is the same British bloke who, along with his countryman Paul Black, set the formative-assessment bonfire afire with their 1998 review of classroom assessment research (Black and Wiliam, 1998a). In contrast to the two previously described implementation models—the Levels Approach and the Applications Approach—we can characterize this third conceptualization of formative assessment as a *Strategies Approach*. Wiliam has refined this approach, and he described its nuances in a volume devoted to his view of the formative-assessment process (Wiliam, 2011). If you wish to learn more about this Strategies Approach, be sure to refer to that book. It is loaded with particularly practical implementation procedures.

Wiliam believes that all teaching boils down to three essential *processes* and three *roles* by the individuals involved. As he sees it, the three key processes are (1) finding out where students are in their learning, (2) finding out where they are going, and (3) finding out how to get there. The three roles involved in this enterprise are those of (1) teacher, (2) learner, and (3) peer. When Wiliam crosses the three processes with the three roles, he arrives at a three-by-three, nine-cell matrix. By doing a deft bit of coalescing to those nine cells, he ends up with five key strategies of formative assessment that constitute this third attempt to subdivide the formative-assessment process into more teacher-palatable clumps. Here, briefly, is a description of each of the five strategies in this approach, first described by Leahy and associates in 2005.

Five Strategies of Formative Assessment

1. *Clarifying, sharing, and understanding learning intentions and criteria for success* Wiliam believes it incontestable that if students understand the nature of what they are intended to learn, they will learn it better than if they had no idea about what learning is being sought. Communicating a set of learning intentions to students, however, is often more reflective of the teacher's artistry than a teacher's adherence to a set of scientifically validated communication techniques regarding how to get students to understand what's being asked of them. Wiliam thinks learning intentions should be stated in language comprehensible to the student, not in the sorts of "official language" that might be found in formal curricular documents. Moreover, when students are given the criteria by which the success of their performances will be judged, those success criteria should be applicable to the full range of tasks a student might be asked to accomplish, not merely the specific task included in a particular examination.

2. *Engineering effective classroom discussions, activities, and learning tasks that elicit evidence of learning* Because eliciting evidence of students' learning is a quintessential element of the formative-assessment process, this second strategy in Wiliam's approach is particularly important, and he describes a wide array of both formal and informal techniques by which teachers (and students themselves) can gather evidence about students' learning. Such evidence, then, can be used to make inferences—hopefully valid ones—regarding students' learning status. For example, by including in classroom discussions a number of key questions that, when responded to by all students as part of an en route ungraded quiz, the teacher can discern how well students have mastered significant knowledge or subskills that are precursive to students' mastery of a major curricular aim. Teachers must possess a wide array of evidence-eliciting techniques to make this second strategy effective.

3. *Providing feedback that moves learning forward* Providing students with feedback based on their performances on assessments is widely regarded as an instructionally useful activity. However, as Wiliam makes clear, not all feedback has a positive impact on students' learning. Indeed, ill-conceived feedback can harm, not help, students' learning. Wiliam, who has reviewed research evidence regarding feedback through the years, concluded, "If I had to reduce all of the research on feedback into one simple overarching idea, at least for academic subjects in school, it would be this: feedback should cause thinking" (2011, p. 127). In about 40 percent of empirical studies, as he points out, feedback has a negative effect on learning. This suggests, clearly, that feedback must be carefully conceived; it must direct students' attention to "what's next" rather than how well a student performed on an already completed assessment. Well-designed feedback, an imperative for successful formative assessment, must engender in students a cognitive reaction rather

than an emotional reaction—and this cognitive response must be aimed at the student's future activities.

4. *Activating learners as instructional resources for one another* Although substantial research evidence attests to the power of collaborative and cooperative learning, such procedures are encountered far less frequently in today's classrooms than one would expect. In this fourth strategy, activating students as learning resources for one another is regarded as a remarkably important way to enhance the potency of formative assessment. Almost always involving some form of peer assessment or peer tutoring, a wide range of these techniques should be in the teacher's tool kit. Peer assessment, geared toward improvement rather than evaluation, can be especially powerful. However, both peer assessment and peer tutoring can have considerable benefits for the students who are *supplying* the assistance rather than *receiving* it, for those students providing assistance are obliged to internalize learning intentions and success criteria in the context of another student's work.

5. *Activating students as the owners of their own learning* Although teachers have a significant role to play in structuring the situations in which learning takes place, it is only learners who create learning. This final strategy is based on the premise that, to the extent students are better able to manage their own learning, the more likely is it that they will learn well. A teacher who sets out to help students reflect critically on their own learning will discover that this aspiration, although difficult, is attainable for all students. But because reflecting on one's own learning is often emotionally charged, developing students' management skills for fostering *genuine* ownership of their learning takes time—particularly with students who have a history of failing.

As you can see, the Wiliam's Strategy Approach shares features of the two implementation models described earlier—the Levels Approach and the Applications Approach. What all three approaches are intended to do is provide a framework for teachers who wish to employ the formative-assessment process. If you wish to consider doing so, you will find the following treatments of formative assessment useful: For the Levels Approach, see Popham (2008); for the Applications Approach, see Popham (2011); and for the Strategies Approach, see Wiliam (2011). Because there is nothing inherently contradictory among all three of these implementation models, some teachers might find it useful to choose elements of two, or even all three, of the approaches.

Before bidding farewell to the diverse ways in which formative assessment can be implemented, let's not lose sight of the fundamental reason for the positive impact on instruction that the formative-assessment process almost always yields. At bottom, formative assessment looks at the progress toward *ends* (or outcomes) as a way of deciding whether *means* (or inputs) need to be changed. Such a basic ends-means model is so "old hat" that it may, to some educators, seem unworthy of attention. Nonetheless, reliance on an ends-mean model underlies much of society's progress over the centuries. Unquestionably, use of an ends-means paradigm will make teachers' instruction better. Human beings who guide their future actions by evaluating the outcomes of their past actions will invariably be more successful than will human beings who don't. This truth certainly applies to teachers whenever they make their instructional decisions.

The formative-assessment process starts off by having teachers identify the ends—that is, the curricular targets they want their students to accomplish. Then, during ongoing instruction, students are periodically assessed to see whether they are mastering the building blocks (subskills and knowledge) they'll need in order to achieve the target curricular aims. If the results of such en route assessment indicate that progress is satisfactory, no adjustments are required by either the teacher or by the teacher's students. If students are *not* progressing as well as had been hoped, however, then the teacher makes an adjustment in the instructional means and/or the students make adjustments in how they are trying to learn.

That's the essence of formative assessment—the incarnation of an ends-means strategy in which assessment-elicited evidence allows teachers and/or students to decide whether what they are doing (the *means)* needs to be changed so that the curricular targets (the *ends*) can be better achieved. The essence of formative assessment is no more complicated than that!

WHY THE DELAY?

At the outset of this chapter, you were asked to figure out why formative assessment, an assessment-based instructional strategy boasting all sorts of research support, is not more widely used in our schools. Now it's time to come up with an answer to that question. Why do *you* think we don't currently see formative assessment flourishing in most of the nation's classrooms?

There is no right answer to this important question, but I think I can identify at least three reasons why we seem to be dawdling in the implementation of formative assessment. Let's see how my answers mesh with those you may have come up with on your own as you were reading the chapter.

One deterrent to our greater use of formative assessment is educators' *considerable misunderstanding about the nature of formative assessment.* Large numbers of educators think of formative assessment as a test, not a process. It's tough to get substantial benefits in kid learning if teachers think some sort of magic-bullet test is going to help them transform a tawdry instructional sequence into a terrific one. Another form of misunderstanding occurs when educators believe formative assessment is intended to help only *teachers* adjust what they are up to, not to help *students* alter their learning tactics. The Black and Wiliam research review (1998a) makes it clear that if students are actively involved in the learning

PARENT TALK

Suppose one of your better students, Mary Ruth Green, brings in a note from her parents, expressing concern that your classes seem to be organized to "teach to the test, not educate students." Mr. and Mrs. Green ask you to call them at home so they can, using their speaker phone, both discuss this concern with you.

 If I were you, here's what I'd say on the phone to Mary Ruth's parents:

"Thanks for raising this issue. It's an important concern, and because we all want what's best for Mary Ruth, I'm pleased to be able to explain how we're using tests in my class.

"Actually, I do use tests to influence my instruction. But the tests really only *represent* the skills and knowledge I'm trying to get Mary Ruth and her classmates to learn. I use the tests to help me plan my instruction and to make an interpretation about whether students are mastering what the test represents. In this way, I'll know whether more instruction is needed on particular topics.

"Please be assured, I am definitely not teaching to particular test items. All of the items on my tests, in fact, have never been seen before by the students. But those items do reflect the knowledge and skills my class is supposed to promote for students.

"You'll also realize that half of Mary Ruth's grade is based on the portfolio assessment system we use. I think the portfolio work samples, when blended with the test results, give me an even better picture of my students' progress."

Now, how would you respond to Mr. and Mrs. Green?

process, and are given the assessment data to manage their own learning tactics, those students will display superior achievements to those displayed by students who are uninvolved in the learning process and who do not monitor their own ongoing progress. A misunderstood formative-assessment process is unlikely to be widely adopted because those educational leaders who are encouraging teachers to employ formative assessment will end up advocating with imprecision that which they themselves do not understand.

Nor do most of the nation's assessment companies help out in this regard. Many, but certainly not all, testing vendors have developed their own for-purchase assessment products they hawk as the way to boost students' scores on high-stakes accountability tests. Such companies have no interest in helping teachers understand that, according to the research evidence now at our disposal, it is formative assessment *as an evidence-informed, classroom monitoring/adjustment process* that has been shown to be effective—not a collection of prefabricated, off-the-shelf assessment systems. Thus, some self-interested assessment firms are contributing directly to misunderstandings about formative assessment on the part of many educators.

A second roadblock to educators' greater use of formative assessment is the inherent difficulty of getting people to change their ways. Most of today's educators have been educating students for more than a few minutes. And, during the years those educators have been doing their jobs, they have adopted certain instructional behaviors that, in their estimate, work! Almost all teachers think what they're doing helps their students. Otherwise, most teachers would not be doing those things. Now, because of most teachers' firm beliefs that what they have been doing will benefit students, you can see how difficult it is to get those teachers to adopt something fundamentally different. And, be assured, even Level 1 formative assessment is fundamentally different from the way most teachers typically approach their instruction. Moreover, both Level 2 and Level 3 formative assessment constitute particularly dramatic breaks from instruction as usual. So, another factor slowing down teachers' acceptance of a research-proven classroom strategy that works is, simply, human beings' reluctance to alter their established behavior.

Finally, despite the fact that formative assessment can improve students' achievement, and improve it dramatically, this improved achievement may not show up on many external accountability tests. In Chapter 15 you will learn why this is so, but in a nutshell preview of that chapter's message, certain kinds of external accountability tests are basically unable to accurately measure the quality of instruction students receive. Insofar as this is true, teachers who might be doing a crackerjack instructional job by using formative assessment may discover that, despite what their classroom tests demonstrate is considerable improvements in their students' achievements, those improvements simply don't show up on the high-stakes tests being used in that locale to evaluate schools. Disillusioned with such results, some teachers will understandably back away from using what seems to be an ineffectual formative-assessment process. After you read Chapter 15, you will see why this is so.

These, then, are three reasons I believe formative assessment is not more widely employed in our schools: (1) misunderstandings regarding formative assessment, (2) teachers' tendencies to resist altering their current conduct, and (3) the failure of many external accountability tests to accurately mirror the improvements occurring in the classrooms of teachers who use formative assessment. You may arrive at different conclusions about why we are not currently surrounded by swarms of teachers who rely on formative assessment to deliver the best possible instruction to their students. But these are my best guesses.

Whatever obstacles exist to the greater use of formative assessment, we need to overcome those impediments. We must do whatever is necessary so that formative assessment will be used far more widely in our nation's classrooms. Formative assessment works, and it works to help students learn. Accordingly, we need much more of it.

WHAT DO CLASSROOM TEACHERS REALLY NEED TO KNOW ABOUT FORMATIVE ASSESSMENT?

What a teacher really needs to know about formative assessment depends almost completely on what the teacher intends to do with formative assessment. If teachers don't intend to use formative assessment in their own classrooms, then there's much less such teachers must know about it. A "non-user" teacher, however, should still know what formative assessment is—and what it isn't. It's especially important these days, even for non-using teachers, to understand the essential nature of formative assessment. This is because, as a member of a school's faculty, such teachers can help forestall their colleagues' sometimes unthinking adoption of commercial products that, though praised by those products' publishers, have essentially no evidence to support their use. If a non-user teacher has a general understanding of what the research basis underlying formative assessment actually is, then research-free claims of effectiveness for commercial products can be contrasted with the kind of evidence Black and Wiliam (1998a) have assembled to show that classroom assessment, if used formatively, can benefit students. Summing up, even teachers who don't intend to use formative assessment should know what it is, what it isn't, and the nature of its research support.

On the other hand, if a teacher intends to actually use formative assessment, then what that teacher needs to know is substantially greater. For openers, a would-be user of formative assessment must obviously understand what formative assessment is and what it isn't. Any prospective user of formative assessment must surely grasp the nature of formative assessment as a process in which assessment-elicited evidence allows teachers to adjust their instruction and students to adjust their learning tactics—if such adjustments are warranted. Potential users of formative assessment must also recognize how, by dividing formative assessment into different levels or applications, teachers can understand this potent process more accurately.

Teachers who intend to use formative assessment must be thoroughly conversant with the structure of learning progressions, and the role those progressions play in the formative-assessment process. Unless a teacher is fortunate enough to stumble onto an already-developed learning progression for the same target curricular aim a teacher has chosen, then the teacher should be able to build a brand-new learning progression from scratch.

Finally, depending on the level(s) or application(s) of formative assessment a teacher hopes to employ, a prospective user of formative assessment ought to be reasonably conversant with the major activities associated with those approaches.

But What Does This Have to Do with Teaching?

Formative assessment is not the same thing as teaching. On the contrary, formative assessment is an assessment-rooted process capable of making teaching better. It may be useful for educators to think of formative assessment as a *companion activity* whose one and only *raison d'être* is to improve the quality of teaching. It does so by providing the assessment-based evidence that informs selected instructional decisions a teacher should make.

Accordingly, formative assessment must, of necessity, be a *classroom-based* process. Formative assessment doesn't take place in a principal's office or at a school district's central offices. Formative assessment occurs in a particular classroom taught by a particular teacher, and it is based on assessment evidence collected from that teacher's current students. To the extent that anyone tries to make formative assessment an activity occurring outside what goes on in a given teacher's classroom, those efforts really cannot be supported by the existing research base that so strongly undergirds the use of classroom-based formative assessment.

Teaching consists of the instructional activities a teacher chooses to employ, and those activities are chosen on the basis of conscious decisions made by the teacher. One category of such instructional decisions can be accurately characterized as *adjustment decisions*—that is, decisions regarding whether preplanned instruction should be adjusted by a teacher and, if so, in what ways. Well, those adjustment decisions are precisely the ones that the formative-assessment process is intended to inform. If formative assessment is employed properly, teachers' adjustment decisions will be better and, as a consequence, kids will be better educated.

What does formative assessment have to do with teaching? *Everything!*

CHAPTER SUMMARY

Formative assessment was defined, at the chapter's outset, as a planned process in which assessment-elicited evidence of students' status is used by teachers to adjust their ongoing instructional procedures or by students to adjust their current learning tactics. Because a teacher's understanding of this conception of formative assessment is essential, considerable attention was given to describing the key components of the definition.

The second emphasis of the chapter was on the research evidence underlying the formative-assessment process. The Black and Wiliam (1998a) review of almost a decade's worth of classroom assessment investigations currently supplies the bulk of evidence usually called on to support the effectiveness of formative assessment. Based on 250 solid studies drawn from almost 700 such studies, Black and Wiliam concluded the empirical evidence they studied "shows conclusively that formative assessment does improve learning." Moreover, the improvements in students' learning attributed to formative assessment were among the largest ever reported for educational interventions. Finally, Black and Wiliam pointed out that the formative-assessment process is so robust it can be employed by teachers in diverse ways, yet still work well.

Considerable attention was given in the chapter to learning progressions—the sequenced sets of building blocks students must master en route to mastering a more remote, target curricular aim. The building blocks in a learning progression are either (1) bodies of enabling knowledge or (2) cognitive subskills. Learning progressions function as the frameworks for the formative-assessment process because assessments of students' building-block mastery supply the evidence for teachers (or students) to decide whether to make adjustments. Suggestions were provided regarding how to build a learning progression for a selected curricular aim.

Three alternate ways of conceptualizing the formative-assessment process were then presented. A *four-application approach* consisted of the following levels: (1) Teachers' Instructional Adjustments, (2) Students' Learning-Tactic Adjustments, (3) Classroom Climate Shift, and (4) Schoolwide Implementation. A *five-applications approach* featured (1) Immediate Instructional Adjustments, (2) Near-Future Instructional Adjustments, (3) Last-Chance Instructional Adjustments, (4) Learning-Tactic Adjustments, and (5) Classroom Climate Shifts. Finally, a *five-strategies approach* was set forth featuring the following strategies: (1) Clarifying, sharing, and understanding learning intentions and criteria for success; (2) Engineering effective classroom discussions, activities, and learning tasks that elicit evidence of learning; (3) Providing feedback that moves learning forward; (4) Activating learners as instructional resources for one another; and (5) Activating students as the owners of their own learning.

The chapter was concluded with some speculation regarding why it is that this research-supported, assessment-rooted process is not more widely used by teachers. It was contended that the reluctance of many teachers to adopt formative assessment is due to (1) educators' misunderstandings about formative assessment, (2) teachers' natural reluctance to alter their current behaviors, and (3) the inability of many accountability tests to accurately measure classroom improvements attributable to formative assessment.

Determining Your Outcome Mastery

In this chapter an attempt was made to promote your recognition of what it is that makes formative assessment so instructionally beneficial. As a reminder, here is the chapter's chief outcome:

> *An understanding of research-ratified formative assessment's essence sufficient for identifying teachers' proper and improper implementations of the formative-assessment process*

If you truly comprehend the nature of formative assessment, you will be more likely to identify instances in which teachers (real teachers, fictitious teachers, or you) are effectively or ineffectively employing the formative-assessment process.

Complete both the Selected-Response and the Constructed-Response quizzes and think about the feedback you receive for each quiz.

MyEdLab *Selected-Response Check of Outcome Mastery*

MyEdLab *Constructed-Response Check of Outcome Mastery*

After completing both quizzes, go to the Learning Outcome Mastery Determination, where you will decide whether you've mastered the chapter's learning outcome or whether you need further study.

MyEdLab *Learning Outcome Mastery Determination*

References

Black, P., and Wiliam, D. (1998a). "Assessment and classroom learning," *Assessment in Education: Principles, Policy and Practice, 5*, no. 1: 7–73.

Black, P., and Wiliam, D. (1998b). "Inside the black box: Raising standards through classroom assessment," *Phi Delta Kappan, 80*, no. 2: 139–148.

Broadfoot, P. M., Daugherty, R., Gardner, J., Gipp, C. V., Harlen, W., James, M., and Stobart, G. (1999). *Assessment for Learning: Beyond the Black Box.* Cambridge, UK: University of Cambridge School of Education.

Brookhart, S. M. (2013). "Develop a student-centered mind-set for formative assessment," *Voices from the Middle, 21*, no. 2 (December): 21–25.

Crooks, T. (1988). "The impact of classroom evaluation practices on students," *Review of Educational Research, 58*, no. 4: 438–481.

Duckor, B. (2014). "Formative assessment in seven good moves," *Educational Leadership, 71*, no. 6 (March): 28–33.

Fisher, D., and Frey, N. (2015). *Checking for understanding* (2nd ed.). Alexandria, VA: ASCD.

Gipps, C. V., and Stobart, G. (1997). *Assessment: A teacher's guide to the issues* (3rd ed.). London, UK: Hodder and Stroughton.

Heritage, M. (2010). *Formative assessment: Making it happen in the classroom.* Thousand Oaks, CA: Corwin.

Kingston, N., and Nash, B. (2011). "Formative assessment: A meta-analysis and a call for research," *Educational Measurement: Issues and Practice, 30*, no. 4 (Winter): 28–37.

James, M. (1992). *Assessment for learning.* Paper presented at the Annual Conference of the Association for Supervision and Curriculum Development.

Leahy, S., Thompson, C. L. M., and Wiliam, D. (2005). "Classroom assessment—Minute by minute, day by day," *Educational Leadership, 63*, no. 3 (November): 18–24.

Masters, G., and Forster, M. (1996). *Progress maps.* Melbourne: Australian Council for Educational Research.

Natriello, G. (1987). "The impact of evaluation processes on students," *Educational Psychologist, 22*, no. 2: 155–175.

Popham, W. J. (2008). *Transformative assessment.* Alexandria, VA: ASCD.

Popham, W. J. (2011). *Transformative assessment in action.* Alexandria, VA: ASCD.

Scriven, M. (1967). "The methodology of evaluation." In R. W. Tyler, R. M. Gagne, and M. Scriven (Eds.), *Perspectives of curriculum evaluation*, Volume I (pp. 39–83). Chicago: Rand McNally.

Shepard, L. (2006). *Can benchmark assessments be formative? Distinguishing formative assessment from formative program evaluation.* A presentation during the National Large-Scale Assessment Conference, Council of Chief State School Officers, San Francisco, CA.

Stiggins, R. J. (2007). *Student-involved classroom assessment for learning* (5th ed.). Upper Saddle River, NJ: Prentice-Hall.

Stiggins, R., and Popham, W. J. (2008). *Assessing students' affect related to assessment for learning.* Washington, DC: The Council of Chief State School Officers.

Sutton, R. (1995). *Assessment for learning.* Salford, UK: RS Publications.

Tomlinson, C. A. (2014). "The bridge between today's lesson and tomorrow's," *Educational Leadership, 71*, no. 6 (March): 10–15.

Wiliam, D. (2011). *Embedded formative assessment.* Bloomington, IN: Solution Tree.

Making Sense Out of Standardized Test Scores

Classroom teachers need to be able to interpret the results not only of their own assessment procedures but also of the various kinds of standardized tests that are frequently administered to students. Teachers need to be able to interpret such test results so they can base classroom instructional decisions on those results and also be able to respond accurately when students' parents raise such questions as, "What does my child's grade-equivalent score of 7.4 really mean?" or "When my child's achievement test results are at the 97th percentile, is that three percentiles from the top or the bottom?"

This chapter focuses on the task of making sense out of students' performances on standardized achievement and aptitude tests. One of the kinds of tests under consideration will be the achievement tests (for instance, in mathematics or reading) developed and distributed by commercial testing companies. Achievement tests are also developed and administered by state departments of education in connection with statewide assessment programs in such subjects as social studies, sciences, mathematics, reading, and writing. These state tests often employ reporting procedures akin to those used with commercially distributed standardized achievement tests.

And, even though I've desperately tried to avoid numbers larger than 9, in this chapter you'll encounter a few that are, indeed, larger. Don't be dismayed. Simply go through the examples, one step at a time, and you'll emerge from the chapter a finer human being. The numbers in this chapter will be easier to deal with than might be thought at first glance.

These days, standardized tests (especially standardized *achievement* tests) are often misused. In Chapter 15 you'll learn why it is unwise to try to evaluate educators' effectiveness on the basis of students' scores on many such tests. Nonetheless, standardized tests *do* have an important, educationally useful role to play. This chapter focuses on the appropriate uses of standardized tests.

Thise chapter will be wrapped up with a consideration of two aptitude tests that have a whopping impact on students' lives. You'll be looking at the two examinations that often become determiners to a student's continued education. That's right, we'll be dealing with the two most widely used college entrance exams: the SAT and the ACT.

If you're a current or would-be secondary school teacher, you'll immediately recognize the need for you to know about the SAT and the ACT. After all, many of your students will soon be taking one or both of these tests. But if you're an elementary teacher, or are preparing to be one, you might be thinking, "What do college entrance exams have to do with me?" Well, all teachers—elementary and secondary—ought to understand at least the most significant facts about these two examinations. Even teachers of primary-grade kids will find parents asking questions such as, How can we get our child really ready for those in-the-future, important college entrance tests? Every teacher should be familiar with any really significant information associated with the teaching profession. Thus, because most students and their parents will, at some point, want to know more about college entrance exams, I think every single teacher—and even married ones—should know the basic SAT and ACT facts you'll learn about in this chapter.

STANDARDIZED TESTS

A *standardized test* is a test, designed to yield either norm-referenced or criterion-referenced inferences, that is administered, scored, and interpreted in a standard, predetermined manner. Almost all *nationally* standardized tests are distributed by commercial testing firms. Most such firms are for-profit corporations, although there are a few not-for-profit measurement organizations, such as the Educational Testing Service (ETS), that distribute nationally standardized tests. Almost all nationally standardized tests, whether focused on the measurement of students' aptitude or achievement, are chiefly intended to provide norm-referenced interpretations.

Standardized achievement tests have also been developed in a number of states under the auspices of state departments of education. In many instances, these state-acquired standardized tests may have been acquired from one of the two major assessment consortia—Partnership for the Assessment of Readiness for College and Careers (PARCC) or Smarter Balanced Assessment Consortium (SBAC)—or even from smaller consortia of only a few collaborating states. These statewide tests (clearly intended to be administered, scored, and interpreted in a standard, predetermined fashion) have usually been installed to satisfy a legislative mandate that establishes an educational accountability program of some sort. In certain instances, important decisions about individual students are made on the basis of a student's test performance. In many states, for example, if a student does not pass a prescribed statewide basic skills examination by the end of high school, the student is not awarded a diploma, even though the student has satisfied all other curricular requirements. In other cases, although no contingencies for individual students depend on how a student performed on a test, results of student

DECISION TIME

Which Test to Believe

Each spring in the Big Valley Unified School District, students in grades 5, 8, 10, and 12 complete nationally standardized achievement tests in reading and mathematics as well as a nationally standardized test described by its publishers as "a test of the student's cognitive aptitude." Because William White teaches eighth-grade students in his English classes, he is given the task of answering any questions raised by his eighth-graders' parents about the test results.

He is faced with one fairly persistent question from most parents, particularly those parents whose children scored higher on the aptitude test than on the achievement test. For example, Mr. and Mrs. Wilkins (Wanda's parents) put the question like this: "If Wanda scored at the 90th percentile on the aptitude test and only at the 65th percentile on the achievement test, does that mean she's not logging enough study time? Putting it another way," they continued, "should we really believe the aptitude tests results or the achievement test's results? Which is Wanda's 'true' test performance?"

➤ *If you were William and had to decide how to answer the questions posed by Wanda's parents, what would your answers be?*

tests are publicized by the media on a district-by-district or school-by-school basis. The test results thus serve as an indicator of local educators' effectiveness, at least in the perception of many citizens. These state-sired standardized achievement tests are generally intended to yield criterion-referenced interpretations. Educational aptitude tests are rarely, if ever, developed by state departments of education.

Although standardized tests have traditionally consisted almost exclusively of selected-response items, in recent years the developers of standardized tests have attempted to incorporate a certain number of constructed-response items in their tests. Standardized tests, because they are intended for widespread use, are developed with far more care (and cost) than is possible in an individual teacher's classroom. Even so, the fundamentals of test development you've learned about in earlier chapters are routinely employed when standardized tests are developed. In other words, the people who create the items for such tests attempt to adhere to the same kinds of item-writing and item-improvement precepts you've learned about. The writers of multiple-choice items for standardized tests worry, just as you should, about inadvertently supplying students with clues that give away the correct answer. The writers of short-answer items for standardized tests try to avoid, just as you should, the inclusion of ambiguous language in their items.

There are, of course, staggering differences in the level of effort associated with the construction of standardized tests and the construction of classroom tests.

A commercial testing agency may assign a flotilla of item writers and a fleet of item editors to a new test-development project, whereas you'll be fortunate if you have a part-time teacher's aide or, possibly, a malleable spouse to proofread your tests to detect typographical errors.

GROUP-FOCUSED TEST INTERPRETATION

Although the bulk of this chapter will be devoted to a consideration of score-reporting mechanisms used to describe an individual student's performance, you'll sometimes find you need to describe the performance of your students as a group. To do so, you'll typically compute some index of the group of scores' *central tendency,* such as when you determine the group's **mean** or **median** performance. For example, you might calculate the *mean raw score* or the *median raw score* for your students. A **raw score** is simply the number of items a student answers correctly. The *mean,* as you probably know, is the arithmetic average of a set of scores. For example, the mean of the scores 10, 10, 9, 8, 7, 6, 3, 3, and 2 would be 6.4 (that is, summing the nine scores and then dividing that sum by 9). The *median* is the midpoint of a set of scores. For the nine scores in the previous example, the median would be 7 because this score divides the group into two equal parts. Means and medians are useful ways to describe the point at which the scores in a set of scores are centered.

In addition to describing the central tendency of a set of scores (via the mean and/or median), it is also helpful to describe the *variability* of the scores—that is, how spread out the scores are. One simple measure of the variability of a set of students' scores is the **range**. The range is calculated by simply subtracting the lowest student's score from the highest student's score. To illustrate, suppose the highest test score by students in your class was a 49 correct out of 50 earned by Hortense (she always tops your tests; it is surprising she missed one). Suppose further that the lowest score of 14 correct was, as usual, earned by Ed. The range of scores would be 35—that is, Hortense's 49 minus Ed's 14.

Because only two scores influence the range, it is less frequently used as an index of test score variability than is the standard deviation. A **standard deviation** is a kind of average. More accurately, it's the average difference between the individual scores in a group of scores and the mean of that set of scores. The larger the size of the standard deviation, the more spread out are the scores in the **distribution**. (That's a posh term to describe a set of scores.) Presented here is the formula for computing a standard deviation for a set of scores:

$$\text{Standard Deviation (S.D.)} = \sqrt{\frac{\Sigma(X - M)^2}{N}}$$

where: $\Sigma(X - M)^2$ = the sum of the squared raw scores *(X)* − the mean *(M)*

N = number of scores in the distribution

figure 13.1 ■ Two Fictitious Sets of Tests Scored with Equal Means but Different Standard Deviations

More Homogeneous Scores:

3, 4, 4, 5, 5, 5, 5, 6, 6, 7

Mean = 5.0

$$S.D. = \sqrt{\frac{12}{10}} = 1.1$$

More Heterogeneous Scores:

0, 1, 2, 4, 5, 5, 6, 8, 9, 10

Mean = 5.0

$$S.D. = \sqrt{\frac{102}{10}} = 3.2$$

Here's a step-by-step description of how you compute a standard deviation using this formula. First, compute the mean of the set of scores. Second, subtract the mean from each score in the distribution. (Roughly half of the resulting values, called *deviation scores,* will have positive values and half will have negative values.) Third, square each of these deviation scores. This will make them all positive. Fourth, add the squared deviation scores together. Fifth, divide the resulting sum by the number of scores in the distribution. Sixth, and last, take the square root of the results of the division you did in the fifth step. The square root that you get is the standard deviation. Not too tough, right?

To illustrate the point that larger standard deviations represent more spread in a distribution of scores than smaller standard deviations, take a look at the two fictitious sets of scores on a 10-item short-answer test presented in Figure 13.1. Both sets of scores have a mean of 5.0. The distribution of scores at the left is much more homogeneous (less spread out) than the distribution of scores at the right. Note the standard deviation for the more homogeneous scores is only 1.1, whereas the standard deviation of the more heterogeneous scores is 3.2. The larger the standard deviation, therefore, the more distant, on average, will be the distribution's scores from the distribution's mean.

You may have occasions to describe the scores of an entire group of the students you teach. Those descriptions might portray your students' performances on standardized tests or on teacher-made tests. If you get at all comfortable with means and standard deviations, those two indices usually provide a better picture of a score distribution than do the median and range. But if you think means and standard deviations are statistical gibberish, then go for the median (midpoints are easy to identify) and range (ranges require only skill in subtraction). With group-based interpretations out of the way, let's turn now to interpreting individual students' scores from the kinds of standardized tests commonly used in education.

INDIVIDUAL STUDENT TEST INTERPRETATION

Two overriding frameworks are generally used to interpret students' test scores. Test scores are interpreted in *absolute* or *relative* terms. When we interpret a student's test score *absolutely,* we infer from the score what it is that the student can or cannot do. For example, based on a student's performance on test items dealing with mathematics computation skills, we make an inference about the degree to which the student has mastered such computation skills. The teacher may even boil the interpretation down to a dichotomy—namely, whether the student should be classified as having mastered or not having mastered the skill or knowledge being assessed. A mastery versus nonmastery interpretation represents an *absolute* interpretation of a student's test score. Classroom teachers often use this absolute interpretive approach when creating tests to assess a student's knowledge or skills based on a particular unit of study.

When we interpret a student's test score *relatively,* we infer from the score how the student stacks up against other students who are currently taking the test or have already taken the test. For example, when we say that Johnny's test score is "above average" or "below average," we are making a relative test interpretation because we use the average performance of other students to make sense out of Johnny's test score.

As pointed out earlier, this chapter focuses on how teachers and parents can interpret scores on standardized tests. Because almost all standardized test scores require relative interpretations, the three interpretive schemes to be considered in the chapter are all relative score-interpretation schemes. The vast majority of standardized tests, whether achievement tests or aptitude tests, provide relative interpretations. Accordingly, teachers need to be especially knowledgeable about relative score-interpretation schemes.

Percentiles

The first interpretive scheme we'll consider, and by all odds the most commonly used one, is based on *percentiles* or, as they are sometimes called, *percentile ranks.* Percentiles are used most frequently in describing standardized test scores because percentiles are readily understandable to most people.

A percentile compares a student's score with those of other students in a *norm group.* A student's percentile indicates the percent of students in the norm group that the student outperformed. A percentile of 60, for example, indicates the student performed better than 60 percent of the students in the norm group.

Let's spend a moment describing what a norm group is. As indicated, a percentile compares a student's score with scores earned by those in a norm group. This comparison with the norm group is based on the performances of a group of individuals who have already been administered a particular examination. For instance, before developers of a new standardized test publish their test, they will administer the test to a large number of students who then become the norm group

figure 13.2 ■ A Typical Norm Group

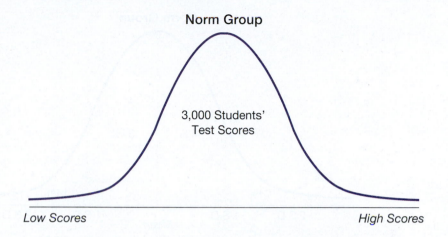

Norm Group

3,000 Students'
Test Scores

Low Scores   *High Scores*

for the test. Typically, different norm groups of students are assembled for all the grade levels for which percentile interpretations are made.

Figure 13.2 shows a graphic depiction of a set of 3,000 students' scores such as might have been gathered during the norming of a nationally standardized achievement test. Remember, we refer to such students as the norm group. The area under the curved line represents the number of students who earned scores at that point on the baseline. You'll notice, for a typical norm group's performance, most students score in the middle while only a few students earn very high or very low scores.

In fact, *if* the distribution of test scores in the norm group is *perfectly* normal, then, as you see in Figure 13.3, over two-thirds of the scores (represented by the area under the curved line) will be located relatively close to the center of the distribution—that is, plus or minus one standard deviation (S.D.) from the mean.

Not all norm groups are national norm groups. Sometimes test publishers, at the request of local school officials, develop local norms. These local norms can be either state norms or school-district norms. Comparisons of students on the basis of local norms are sometimes seen as being more meaningful than are comparisons based on national norms.

In many instances, local norms are different from national norms because the students in a particular locality are not representative of the nation's children as a whole. If there is a difference between local and national norms, then there will be a difference in a student's percentile scores. A student's raw score—that is, the number of test items answered correctly—might be equal to the 50th percentile based on *national* norms, but be equal to the 75th percentile based on *local* norms. This kind of situation would occur if the students in the local group hadn't performed as well as had students in the nation at large. National and local

figure 13.3 ■ **A Normally Distributed Set of Norm-Group Scores**

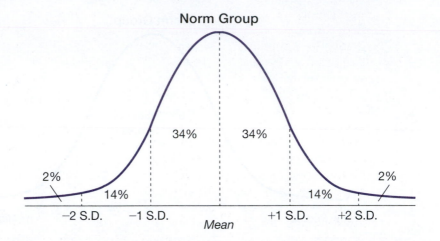

norms provide decisively different frameworks for interpreting standardized test results. When reporting test scores to parents, make sure you communicate clearly whether a child's percentiles are based on national or local norms.

It's also true that some norm groups have been more carefully constituted than others. For example, certain national norm groups are more representative of the nation's population than are other national norm groups. There are often large differences in the representativeness of norm groups based on such variables as gender, ethnicity, geographic region, and socioeconomic status of the students in the groups. In addition, many standardized tests are renormed only every 5 to 10 years. It is important to make sure the normative information on which percentiles are based is both representative and current.

Grade-Equivalent Scores

Let's turn from percentiles to look at a *grade equivalent* or, as they're often called, *grade-equivalent scores*. Grade-equivalent scores constitute another effort to provide a relative interpretation of standardized test scores. A *grade equivalent* is an indicator of student test performance based on grade level and months of the school year. The purpose of grade equivalents is to transform scores on standardized tests into an index reflecting a student's grade-level progress in school. A grade-equivalent score is a *developmental* score in the sense that it represents a continuous range of grade levels.

Let's look at a grade-equivalent score of 4.5:

A Grade-Equivalent Score:

Grade → 4.5 ← Month of School Year

The score consists of the grade, a decimal, and a number representing months. The number to the left of the decimal point represents the grade level, in this example, the fourth grade. The number to the right of the decimal point represents the month of the school year, in this example, the fifth month of the school year.

Some test publishers, using statistical schemes, convert raw scores on standardized tests to grade-equivalent scores. These grade-equivalent scores often appear on students' score reports. Grade-equivalent scores are most appropriate for basic skills areas such as reading and mathematics where it can be assumed the degree of instructional emphasis given to the subject is fairly uniform from grade to grade.

The appeal of grade-equivalent scores is they appear to be readily interpretable to both teachers and parents. However, many teachers and parents actually have an incorrect understanding of what grade-equivalent scores signify. To see why these scores are misunderstood, it's necessary to understand a bit about where they come from in the first place.

To determine the grade-equivalent scores that will be hooked up with particular raw scores, test developers typically administer the same test to students in several grade levels, then establish a trend line reflecting the raw score increases at each grade level. Typically, the test developers then *estimate* at other points along this trend line what the grade equivalent for any raw score would be.

Let's illustrate this important point. In Figure 13.4, you will see the respective performance of students at three grade levels. The same 80-item test has been given to students at all three grade levels: grades 4, 5, and 6. A trend line is then established from the three grades where the test was actually administered. The result of that estimation procedure is seen in Figure 13.5.

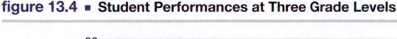

figure 13.4 ■ Student Performances at Three Grade Levels

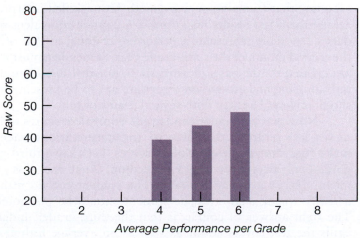

figure 13.5 ▪ A Trend Line Used to Estimate Average Performance of Students at Nontested Grades

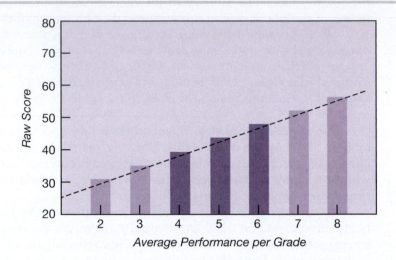

In order for these estimated grade-equivalent scores to be accurate, several assumptions must be made. First, it must be assumed the subject area tested is emphasized equally at each grade level. It must also be assumed students' mastery of the tested content increases at a reasonably constant rate at each grade level over an extended period of time. The assumption that the mastery of the test's content increases consistently over time is particularly difficult to support in subject areas other than reading and mathematics. And even in those two bread-and-butter subjects, students' consistent increases in mastery of content are definitely debatable.

The implied precision associated with a grade-equivalent score of 6.2, therefore, is difficult to defend. A 6.2 grade-equivalent score suggests a degree of accuracy that's simply not warranted. An unskilled interpreter of a standardized achievement test results may think a 6.2 grade-equivalent score indicates the student's raw score represents a performance equal to that of a sixth-grade pupil in the second month of the sixth-grade year. Remember, most grade-equivalent scores are created on the basis of estimation, not real test-score data. Because substantial sampling and estimation errors are apt to be present, grade-equivalent scores should always be taken with several grains of salt.

Now that you understand grade-equivalent scores to be, at best, rough estimates, let's return to the potential misinterpretations teachers and parents often make regarding grade-equivalent scores. Let's say a third-grade student makes a grade-equivalent score of 5.5 in reading. What does this grade-equivalent score mean? Here's a wrong answer: "The student can do fifth-grade work." Here's a *really* wrong answer: "The student should be promoted to the fifth grade." The right answer, of course, is that the third-grader understands those reading skills the test covers about as well as an average fifth-grader does at midyear.

A grade-equivalent score should be viewed as the point where a student is along a developmental continuum, not as the grade level in which the student should be placed.

If standardized tests are used in your school district, and if those tests yield grade-equivalent scores, it is important to provide parents with an accurate picture of what a grade-equivalent score means. Parents who have not been given an accurate description of such scores frequently think a high grade-equivalent score means their child is capable of doing work at the grade level specified. Some parents even use high grade-equivalent scores as a basis for arguing their child should be advanced to a higher grade. Because many parents have a misconception of what a grade-equivalent score means, some parents may have an inflated estimate of their child's level of achievement. The high frequency of parental (and teacher) misinterpretations is the reason some districts have, as a matter of policy, eliminated grade-equivalent scores when reporting standardized test results.

Remember, if a fourth-grade student gets a grade equivalent of 7.5 in mathematics, it is *not* accurate to say the fourth-grader is doing well in seventh-grade mathematics. It is more appropriate to say a grade-equivalent score of 7.5 is an estimate of how an average seventh-grader might have performed *on the fourth-grader's mathematics test*. Obtaining a 7.5 grade-equivalent score doesn't mean the fourth-grader has any of the mathematics skills taught in the fifth, sixth, or seventh grade because those mathematics skills were probably not even measured on the fourth-grade test.

But what happens when grade-equivalent scores are *below* the actual grade level tested? Let's say a fifth-grader earns a mathematics grade-equivalent score of 2.5. It doesn't make much sense to say the fifth-grader is doing fifth-grade mathematics work as well as a second-grader, because second-graders obviously aren't given fifth-grade mathematics work. About the best you can say is that, in mathematics achievement, the fifth-grader appears to be lagging several years behind grade level.

Given the shortcomings of grade-equivalent scores, most measurement specialists are delighted that the use of these scores is diminishing.

Scale Scores

Let's move, now, to the last of our three score-interpretation schemes: *scale scores*. A scale score constitutes yet another way to give relative meaning to a student's standardized test performances. Scale scores are being employed with increasing frequency these days to report results of national and state-level standardized programs.

Although scale scores are sometimes not used in reporting standardized test results to parents, scale-score reporting systems are often employed in describing group test performances at the state, district, and school levels. Because of the statistical properties of scale scores, they can be used to permit longitudinal tracking of students' progress. Scale scores can also be used to make direct comparisons among classes, schools, or school districts. The statistical advantages of scale scores are considerable. Thus, we see scale-score reporting systems used with more frequency in recent years. As a consequence, you need to become familiar with the main features of scale scores because such scores are likely to be used when you receive reports of your students' performances on standardized tests.

A *scale* used for reporting test scores typically refers to numbers assigned to students on the basis of their test performances. Higher numbers (higher scores) reflect increasing levels of achievement or ability. Thus, such a scale might be composed of a set of raw scores where each additional test item correctly answered yields one more point on the raw-score scale. Raw scores, all by themselves, however, are difficult to interpret. A student's score on a raw-score scale provides no idea of the student's *relative* performance. Therefore, measurement specialists have devised different sorts of scales for test interpretation purposes.

Scale scores are *converted raw scores* that use a new, arbitrarily chosen scale to represent levels of achievement or ability. Shortly, you'll be given some examples to help you understand what is meant by converting scores from one scale to another. In essence, a scale-score system is created by devising a brand-new numerical scale that's often very unlike the original raw-score scale. Students' raw scores are then converted to this brand-new scale so, when score interpretations are to be made, those interpretations rely on the converted scores based on the new scale. Such converted scores are called *scale scores*.

figure 13.6 ■ **A Raw-Score Scale and a Converted-Score Scale**

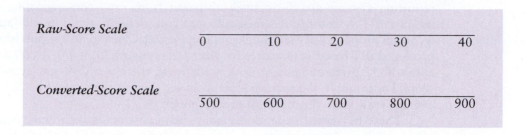

Raw-Score Scale

| 0 | 10 | 20 | 30 | 40 |

Converted-Score Scale

| 500 | 600 | 700 | 800 | 900 |

For example, in Figure 13.6, you see a range of raw score points from 0 to 40 for a 40-item test. Below the raw-score scale, you see a new, converted scale ranging from 500 to 900. For a number of reasons, to be described shortly, it is sometimes preferable to use a scale-score reporting scheme rather than a raw-score reporting scheme. Thus, a student who achieved a raw score of 30 items correct might be assigned a scale score of 800, as shown in Figure 13.7.

One of the reasons scale scores have become popular in recent years is the necessity to develop several equidifficult forms of the same test. For example, a basic skills test must sometimes be passed before high school diplomas are awarded to students. Those students who initially fail the test are, typically, given other opportunities to pass it. The different forms of the test used for such retake purposes should, for the sake of fairness, represent assessment challenges for students that are equivalent to those represented by the initial form of the test. However, because it is next to impossible to create test forms that are absolutely identical, scale scores can be used to help solve the problem. Scores on two test forms of differing difficulty levels can be statistically adjusted so, when placed on a converted score scale, the new scale scores represent students' performances as if the two test forms had been completely equidifficult.

figure 13.7 ■ **An Illustration of a Raw-Score Conversion to a Scale Score**

Raw-Score Scale

| 0 | 10 | 20 | ×
30 | 40 |

Converted-Score Scale

| 500 | 600 | 700 | ×
800 | 900 |

Most of the more popular types of scale-score systems are based on what statisticians refer to as *item response theory*, or IRT. These types of scale-score reporting systems are distinctively different from raw-score reporting systems because IRT scale-score schemes take into consideration the difficulty and other technical properties of every single item on the test. Thus, some test publishers have produced IRT-based scale scores for their tests ranging from 0 to 1,000 across an entire K–12 grade range. For each grade level, there is a different average scale score. For example, the average scale score for third-graders might be 585 and the average scale score for the tenth-graders might be 714.

These IRT-based scale scores can, when constructed with care, yield useful interpretations if one can reference them back to some notion of relative performance such as percentiles. If average scale scores are provided at different grade levels, this also can aid in the interpretation of scale scores. Without such interpretation crutches regarding a scale score's *relative* meaning, however, scale scores cannot be meaningfully interpreted by either educators or parents.

Item response theory scales are often employed by psychometricians in an effort to devise a *vertical scale* that will allow students' test performances to be tracked across a number of grade levels. Clearly, especially in an accountability context where educators are often eager to show students' growth from year to year, such vertical scales have a special appeal. But they also have a serious drawback. In order for a vertical scale to do its job across many grade levels, it is necessary for the test items being used to correlate well with a single trait—for instance, a unitary trait such as "students' mathematical comprehension." It is this global unitary trait that permits a vertical scale to do its job properly. However, because the test's items must be linked to the unitary trait on which the vertical scale is based, those items are unable to yield meaningful diagnostic information to teachers about students' differing mathematics skills and knowledge. Legitimate diagnosticity must be jettisoned when a test's developers are preoccupied with making all their items hook into the unitary trait chosen for their vertical scale. It is impossible, for example, for a test to contain a cluster of items distinctively focused on a student's geometric skills or algebra insights if all the test's items are first required to link up with the unitary mathematical trait being assessed.

So, if officials in your school or district are considering adoption of a standardized test whose chief virtue is that it supplies a meaningful vertical scale for cross-grade comparisons of students' scores, even if the test is accompanied by marketing assertions about the test's diagnostic dividends, don't be fooled. The cost of a vertical scale is the sort of diagnostic evidence that teachers need for sensible instructional decision-making.

Errors are often made in interpreting scale scores because teachers assume all scale scores are somehow similar. For example, when initially administered over 80 years ago, the mean scale score on the verbal section of the Scholastic Assessment Test was 500. This does not signify the mean score on that test today is 500 or that other tests using scale scores will always have mean scores of 500.

Scale-score systems can be constructed so the mean score is 50, 75, 600, 700, 1,000, or any number the scale's constructor has in mind.

One kind of scale score you may encounter when you work with your students' scores on standardized tests is the ***normal curve equivalent.*** A normal curve equivalent, usually referred to as an NCE, represents an attempt to use a student's raw score to arrive at a percentile for a raw score as if the distribution of scores on the test had been a perfectly symmetrical, bell-shaped normal curve. So, one of your students might get an NCE score indicating the student was performing at or near the top of a norm group's performance. Sometimes, unfortunately, neither the norm group's performance nor that of subsequent test takers is distributed in a normal fashion, so the meaningfulness of the student's NCE evaporates. Normal curve equivalents were originally created in an attempt to amalgamate students' performances from *different* standardized tests, perhaps none of which yielded normal distributions. As might be suspected, NCEs failed to solve this problem satisfactorily.

A final kind of scale score you should know about is called a ***stanine.*** Stanines are somewhat like normal curve equivalents in the sense that they assume a normal distribution for a set of scores. And this assumption, as you just read, runs counter to reality. But, as you'll soon see, a stanine score is a more gross score, so it can more easily tolerate a score distribution's departure from a normal shape.

A stanine scale divides a score distribution into nine segments that, although equal along the baseline of a set of scores (actually one-half standard deviation in distance), contain differing proportions of the distribution's scores. As you can see in Figure 13.8, the fifth stanine is at the center of a score distribution and contains about 20 percent of the scores. A ninth stanine score, however, contains only about 4 percent of the scores.

figure 13.8 ▪ Stanine Units Represented in Approximate Percentages of the Normal Curve

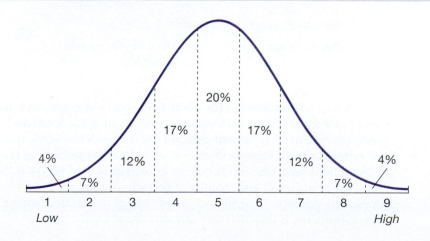

One advantage of stanines is they are *approximate* scale scores, and their very inexact nature conveys more clearly to everyone that educational measurement is not a superprecise assessment enterprise. As with most hierarchical classification systems, of course, a student may be *almost* at the next higher (or lower) stanine, yet may miss out by only a point or two. Such is the imprecision of measurement, even if you're using a deliberately approximation-engendering scoring system.

Contrasting Common Interpretive Options

We've now considered several types of score-interpretation schemes, the most frequently used of these being percentiles, grade-equivalent scores, and scale scores. (Stanines and NCEs tend to be used less frequently.) It's time to review and summarize what's really important about the three most popular ways of making sense out of standardized test scores.

We first considered percentiles. A *percentile* indicates a student's standing in relationship to that of a norm group. If a student's test score is equal to the 25th percentile, the student's performance exceeds the performances of 25 percent of the individuals in the norm group. One advantage of percentiles is they're easy to interpret. And, for the most part, people's interpretations of percentiles are accurate. A disadvantage of percentiles is the defensibility of the interpretation is totally dependent on the nature of the normative data on which the percentiles are based. Unrepresentative or out-of-date norm data yield inaccurate percentile interpretations. As pointed out earlier, because percentile interpretations are so widely used, it's imperative for teachers to be knowledgeable about such interpretations.

Percentiles
Advantage: readily interpretable
Disadvantage: dependent on quality of norm group

Next, we considered grade-equivalent scores. A *grade equivalent* indicates the nature of a student's test performance in terms of grade levels and months. Thus, a grade equivalent of 3.7 would indicate the student's test score was estimated to be the same as the average performance of a third-grader during the seventh month of the school year. One advantage of grade-equivalent scores is, because they are based on grade levels and months of the school year, they can be readily communicated to parents. A significant disadvantage associated with grade-equivalent scores, however, is they're frequently misinterpreted.

Grade Equivalents

Advantage: readily communicable

Disadvantage: often misinterpreted

Finally, scale scores were described. *Scale scores* are interpreted according to a converted numerical scale that allows us to transform raw scores into more statistically useful scale-score units. A student who gets a raw score of 35 correct out of 50 items, for example, might end up with a converted scale score of 620. An advantage of scale scores is they can be used to create statistically adjusted equidifficult test forms. Scale-score schemes based on *item response theory (IRT)* do this by weighting individual test items differently based on an item's difficulty and other technical properties in relation to those same properties for all of a test's items. A disadvantage of scale-score reporting schemes is, with the possible exception of stanines, they're almost impossible to interpret all by themselves. Unless we mentally reference scale scores back to percentiles or average grade-level scale scores, such scores are essentially uninterpretable.

Scale Scores

Advantage: useful in equalizing difficulties of different test forms

Disadvantage: not easily interpretable

It should be clear to you that each of these three score-interpretation schemes has some potential virtues as well as some potential vices. You probably realize, even if you understand the general nature of each of these three interpretation schemes, it may be necessary to secure additional technical information to interpret each reporting scheme with confidence. Such information is usually found in the technical manuals that accompany standardized tests. For example, what was the nature of the norm group on which a test's percentiles were based? What sort of mathematical operations were used in generating a scale-score reporting scheme? Is a score distribution sufficiently normal to warrant the use of NCEs? To interpret a particular standardized test's results sensibly, teachers sometimes need to do a bit of homework themselves regarding the innards of the reporting scheme being used.

The Instructional Yield from Standardized Achievement Tests

Nationally standardized achievement tests, as noted previously, are developed and sold by commercial testing companies. The more tests those companies sell, the more money those companies make. Accordingly, the representatives of commercial testing companies usually suggest that their standardized achievement tests will not only yield valid norm-referenced interpretations about the students who take the tests but will also provide classroom teachers with a galaxy of useful information for instructional decision-making. In my experiences, the *instructional* payoffs of standardized achievement tests are more illusory than real. More often than not, claims for the instructional dividends of such achievement tests reflect the zeal of a testing firm's sales force, not the reality of how teachers can actually use the results of standardized tests for instructional purposes.

INSTRUCTIONALLY DIAGNOSTIC TESTS

"Diagnostic test" is a label more often uttered than understood. Yes, although the phrase "diagnostic testing" pops up in educators' conversations every few days, it is a safe bet that most of those who use this phrase have only a murky understanding of what constitutes a genuine diagnostic test. Yet, because today's teachers are increasingly buffeted by commercial vendors trying to peddle their "instructionally powerful" diagnostic tests, you ought to understand whether vendors' claims are legitimate.

Generally, of course, diagnostic tests are thought to be good things. Most people regard such tests as useful measurement tools—often associated with medical applications, for example, when physicians employ diagnostic tests to pinpoint a patient's illness. A diagnostic test, according to my dictionary, is "concerned with identification of the nature of illness or other problems" (*The New Oxford American Dictionary,* 2001). When diagnostic testing occurs in the field of education, we see such tests used either for purposes of *classification* or *instruction.*

Classification-focused diagnostic tests are often employed by educators who are working with atypical students, that is, with students who are particularly gifted or students who have pronounced disabilities. Such tests allow educators to identify with greater accuracy the exact nature of a student's exceptionality—so that the student can then be classified in a specific category.

Instruction-oriented diagnostic tests are used when teachers attempt to provide particularized instruction for individual students so the teacher's upcoming instructional activities will better mesh with the precise learning needs of different students. The following analysis will be devoted exclusively to *instructionally diagnostic tests.*

Getting my own bias on the table immediately, I am an all-in fan of instructionally diagnostic tests—but only if they are well constructed and, then, if they are used appropriately. That is, I endorse such tests when they are built properly and, thereupon, employed by teachers to do a better instructional job with their students. Those two requirements, of course, are easier to assert than to satisfy.

What Is an Instructionally Diagnostic Test?

Because the mission of an instructionally diagnostic test is to help teachers do an effective instructional job with their students, we need to identify how using such a test would enlighten a teacher's instructional decisions—for example, such decisions as deciding *when* to give or withhold additional or different instruction from *which* students. Appropriately matching instruction, both its quantity and its type, with students' current needs constitutes a particularly important element of effective teaching. An instructionally diagnostic test, if properly fashioned, permits teachers to identify those students who need more or less instruction and, if the diagnostic test is shrewdly constructed, such a test might even help teachers determine what kinds of instruction will be likely to succeed with those students.

Here, then, is a definition of an instructionally diagnostic test:

> *An instructionally diagnostic test is an assessment instrument whose use permits teachers to draw accurate inferences about individual test-takers' strengths and/or weaknesses with respect to two or more skills or bodies of knowledge—thereby permitting teachers to take more effective next-step instructional actions.*

Several components of this definition can have an influence on the development of instructionally diagnostic tests and, thus, warrant elaboration.

Solo-Student Inferences

Let's begin with the idea that, based on students' performances on an instructionally diagnostic test, a teacher will be able to draw more valid (or, if you prefer, more accurate) inferences about an *individual* student's status. Putting it differently, a good instructionally diagnostic test will help a teacher get a more exact fix on what each of the teacher's students currently knows or is able to do. Clearly, if a teacher chooses to aggregate the individual test results of multiple students in order to make subgroup focused inferences, or even whole-class focused inferences, this is altogether appropriate. However, the preceding definition specifies that an honest-to-goodness instructionally diagnostic test must be capable of yielding valid inferences about the status of *individual* test-takers.

Strengths and/or Weaknesses

Some words (e.g., *however*) or phrases (e.g., *of course*) and some abbreviations (e.g., *e.g.*) are seen so often in our routine reading that we tend to pay little attention to them. One important example of this sort familiarity occurs with the oft-encountered, paired conjunctions *and/or*. In the given definition, however, the *and/or* has an important role to play. It signifies that a student's performance on an instructionally diagnostic test can provide results permitting a teacher to draw inferences *exclusively* about the student's strengths, *exclusively* about the student's weaknesses, or about *both* the strengths and weaknesses of the student.

Although, in most settings, teachers are likely to be more interested in either students' strengths or in their weaknesses, the proposed definition of instructionally diagnostic tests makes clear that this *and/or* should be taken seriously.

Two or More Skills or Bodies of Knowledge

The strengths and/or weaknesses addressed in an instructionally diagnostic test must be *at least two*. This is where the diagnosticity of such tests gallops onstage. If a test only helps teachers establish a student's status with respect to *one* cognitive skill, or identifies the student's mastery level regarding *one* body of knowledge, such information might obviously be useful to a teacher. For example, if a fifth-grade teacher uses a teacher-made or commercial test to measure students' status regarding a single high-level skill in mathematics, results from the test could reveal which students have or have not mastered the specific math skill being assessed. This is definitely useful information. The teacher can rely on it to make better current or future instructional decisions. But a single-focus test is not instructionally diagnostic. It's not a *bad* test; it's just not instructionally diagnostic.

Next-Step Instructional Actions

The final requisite feature of the much-discussed definition stems from the fundamental orientation of an instructionally diagnostic test—namely, *instruction*. The definition indicates that, based on the results of such tests, teachers can make next-step instructional decisions, such as what to teach tomorrow or how to teach something next week. Moreover, those next-steps instructional decisions are apt to be more effective than would have been the case had a teacher's decisions not been abetted by information about students' current status.

What this definitional requirement calls for, in plain language, are test results that can be readily translated into sound next-step pedagogical moves by a teacher. To supply such data, an instructionally diagnostic test must provide its results in an *actionable* grain-size—that is, at a level of generality addressable by routine teacher-chosen instructional actions. Accordingly, if the reports from a supposedly diagnostic test are provided at such a broad grain-size that the only reasonable action implication is for the teacher to "make students smarter," this test would be a diagnostic flop.

How Good Is an Instructionally Diagnostic Test?

Once tests have been identified as instructionally diagnostic, they are still apt to differ in their quality, sometimes substantially. The following evaluative criteria can be employed to help determine an instructionally diagnostic test's merits. A brief description will now be presented of each of the following attributes of an instructionally diagnostic test's quality: (1) curricular alignment, (2) sufficiency of items, (3) item quality, and (4) ease of usage.

Curricular Alignment

The overriding purpose of educational tests is to collect students' responses in such a way that we can use students' *overt* responses to test questions to arrive at valid inferences about students' *covert* status with respect to such variables as students' knowledge or their cognitive skills. Ideally, we would like instructionally diagnostic tests to measure lofty curricular aims such as students' attainment of truly high-level cognitive skills or their possession of genuinely significant bodies of knowledge. But the grandeur of the curricular aims that a test sets out to measure is often determined not by the test-makers but, rather, by higher-level educational authorities.

Thus, if the developers of an instructionally diagnostic test have been directed by their superiors to create a test assessing students' mastery of trivial outcomes, and the resultant test performs this measurement job quite successfully, it seems unfair to downgrade the test itself because of the paltry curricular dictates over which the test's developers had no control.

The most important judgment to be made when evaluating a test on the basis of this first evaluative criterion (curricular alignment) hinges on the answer to a question such as: "Will students' responses to items in this test provide evidence permitting valid inferences to be drawn about a test-taker's status with respect to each body of knowledge and/or skill being assessed?"

Sufficiency of Items

This second evaluative criterion for appraising an instructionally diagnostic test is easy to understand, but difficult to formally operationalize. Put simply, a decent instructionally diagnostic test needs to contain enough items dealing with each of the skills and/or bodies of knowledge being measured so that, when we see a student's responses to those items, we can identify—with reasonable confidence—how well a student has achieved each of the assessment's targets.

This is an easily understood feature of diagnostic testing because most of us realize intuitively that we will usually get a more accurate fix on students' mastery levels if we ask those students to respond to more items rather than fewer items. And here, of course, is where sensible, experienced educators can differ. Depending on the nature of the curricular targets being measured by an instructionally diagnostic test, seasoned educators might understandably have different opinions about the number of items needed. For larger grain-size curricular targets, more items would typically be needed than for smaller grain-size curricular targets. What's being sought from students is not *certainty* about mastery of what's being measured in a test. No, to reach *absolute* certainty, then we might well be required to measure students' mastery of the complete universe of items that could conceivably be generated to measure students' mastery. Such exhaustive testing would constitute an inefficient use of both students' and teachers' time.

Item Quality

With few exceptions, educational tests are made up of individual items. Occasionally, of course, we encounter one-item tests such a when we ask students to provide a writing sample by composing a single, original essay. But most tests, and especially those tests intended to supply instructionally diagnostic information, contain multiple items. If a test's items are good ones, the test is obviously apt to be better than a test composed of shoddy items. This is true whether the test is supposed to serve a classification function, an instructional function, or some other function completely. Better items make better tests. You have already seen in earlier chapters a flock of guidelines regarding how to generate high-quality items for educational tests. Those guidelines surely apply to the items used in instructionally diagnostic tests.

Ease of Usage

Testing takes time. Teaching takes time. Most teachers, therefore, have very little discretionary time to spend on anything—including diagnostic testing. Accordingly, an effective instructionally diagnostic test, if it is going to be employed by many teachers, must be really easy to use. If an instructionally diagnostic test is difficult to use—or time consuming to use—it won't be easy.

If, for example, scoring of students' responses must be carried out by the teacher personally, then such scoring should require minimal time and very little effort. These days, of course, because of advances in technology, much scoring is done electronically. But if hassles arise when using a test, and most certainly when scoring a test, these hassles will diminish the test's use.

Then there are the *results* of the test—that is, the numbers or words that help teachers (and, if the teacher wishes, can help students as well) determine what a student's strengths and weaknesses actually are. About a decade ago, one of our nation's leading test-development agencies published a test that it argued was instructionally helpful to teachers. The test's results, however, were reported on an item-by-item basis, thus requiring the teacher to consider the test's results only one item at a time. Absurd!

What the ease-of-usage evaluative criterion addresses, of course, is the inherent *practicality* of the test, meaning its administration, its scoring, its interpretation, and the *instructional actionability* of its results. Instructionally diagnostic tests that are easy to used will tend to be used. Those that aren't, won't.

By employing these four evaluative criteria to judge tests that have been identified as instructionally diagnostic assessments, it is possible to make at least rudimentary qualitative distinctions among such tests.

Looking back, then, at instructionally diagnostic tests, today's teachers will be urged by commercial testing firms to "buy our nifty diagnostic tests." Well, as you have seen, some of those allegedly diagnostic tests really aren't so nifty. Because *bona fide* diagnostic tests can be remarkably useful to teachers, if you ever have the opportunity to influence a decision regarding the potential purchase

But What Does This Have to Do with Teaching?

Depending on the grade levels at which elementary teachers teach, or the subjects secondary teachers teach, many teachers these days find their attention focused on their students' scores on standardized achievement tests. That's because students' scores on such tests are increasingly used as an indicator of educators' instructional success. So, if you're a teacher whose state (or school district) requires that standardized achievement tests be administered at the end of school for a grade level you teach, you can be assured there will be plenty of attention given to your students' standardized test performances. In Chapter 15 you'll learn why this practice is inappropriate when certain types of standardized tests are employed.

But even if you're a teacher whose students are at grade levels or in classes where standardized tests don't play a major role, you need to become familiar with the way teachers and parents should interpret such test performances. And that's because, as a professional, a teacher is supposed to know such things. Parents will sometimes ask you what is meant by a percentile or an NCE. You don't want to blubber forth, "Beats me!"

And, of course, if your students *are* assessed with a standardized achievement test, such as statewide accountability exams, you'll want to be able to interpret what students' scores signify, because this information will help you instructionally. Suppose, for example, it is the first week of school and you're reviewing your new fifth-grade students' end-of-year *fourth*-grade test performances. You discover that Martha Childs earned a 94th percentile in mathematics, but only a 43rd percentile in reading. This information should give you some insights about how you'll approach Martha instructionally.

And if Billy Jenkins's fourth-grade test scores gave him a seventh stanine in language arts, but a first stanine in math, I suggest you don't ask Billy to keep track of your students' lunch money.

The better fix you get on your students' relative achievement levels, the more appropriately you can teach them. Proper interpretations of standardized test scores will often help you do so.

of commercially created diagnostic tests, be sure you review the potential acquisitions with considerable care. Not all so-called diagnostic tests really are.

Are standardized achievement tests better than no tests at all? Of course they are. But will standardized tests provide the instructionally sensible, fine-grained diagnostic data teachers need for accurate decisions? My answer, based on many years of using these tests, is decisively negative.

If you wish to get a quick fix on the instructional virtues of a standardized achievement test, here's the most direct way to do it: Simply *find out how the test's results are reported*. This lets you know immediately whether the test's reported results are being doled out at a grain-size that can realistically help teachers know what next-steps instructional actions to take. If the results are reported at a too large grain-size, such as the test-taker "can read" or "can't read," then what's a teacher to do with such an undifferentiated lump of truth? At the other extreme, if the grain-size is so small that the teacher becomes overwhelmed with a plethora of tiny status reports about a student, then this too constitutes a dysfunctional reporting structure. To spot a standardized test's instructional utility, simply scurry to see how its results are reported.

THE SAT AND THE ACT: THREE-LETTER, HIGH-IMPORT EXAMS

Each year, millions of students put their futures on the line when they sit down to take the SAT and ACT exams, the nation's college entrance tests. Because not only students, but also students' parents, are understandably apprehensive about one or both of these college admission tests, teachers at all grade levels are apt to be questioned about the SAT or the ACT. Therefore, in the next few paragraphs I'll be describing the general nature of both exams, how they came into existence, and what their scale scores look like. I'll close out this treatment of the two tests with a candid look at the accuracy with which those tests predict a high school student's academic success in college.

The SAT

First administered in 1926, the SAT was initially called the *Scholastic Aptitude Test,* and its function was to assist admissions officials in a group of elite North-eastern universities to determine which applicants should be admitted. The original name of the test really reveals what the test's developers were up to—namely, they wanted their tests to measure the largely inborn academic *aptitudes* of high school students. Because, much later, the idea of a test's measuring innate, genetically determined aptitudes became unappetizing to many educators, the Scholastic Aptitude Test became known only as the SAT. (One wonders if the developers of the SAT took their cues from the purveyors of Kentucky Fried Chicken who, recognizing the public's concern about the health risks of fried foods, morphed their famous label into KFC. It is, of course, difficult to become genuinely negative toward any three-letter label—with the possible exception of the IRS.)

The SAT was originally conceived of as a group-administrable intelligence test designed to compare test-takers according to their inherited verbal, quantitative, and spatial aptitudes. For many years, the SAT functioned in precisely that way, although during the last few decades we have seen less attention given to the *inherited* nature of what's being assessed.

PARENT TALK

Suppose that one of your students' parents, Mr. Lopez, visits your classroom during a back-to-school evening and raises a series of questions about his daughter, Concepción. Most prominently, Mr. Lopez is concerned with Concepción's scores on the nationally standardized achievement tests administered each spring in your district. Mr. Lopez is troubled by spring-to-spring changes in Concepción's percentiles. As he says, "For the last three springs, her percentile scores in language arts have been the 74th, the 83rd, and the 71st. What's going on here? Is she learning, then unlearning? What accounts for the differences?"

 If I were you, here's how I'd respond to Mr. Lopez:

"You are certainly wise to look into what appears to be inconsistent measurement on Concepción's standardized achievement tests. But what you need to understand, Mr. Lopez, is that these sorts of tests, even though they are nationally standardized, developed by reputable testing firms, and widely used, are not all that precise in how they measure students. Many parents, of course, recognize that their children's test scores are often reported numerically in the form of national percentiles. But this does *not* signify a given child's national percentile is unerringly accurate.

"The kinds of year-to-year shifting you've seen in Concepción's language arts percentiles is quite normal because a given year's test result is not unerringly accurate. Assessment specialists even admit the *anticipated* amount of flip-flop in students' scores when they talk about each test's 'standard error of measurement.' It's something like the sampling errors we hear about for national surveys—you know, 'plus or minus so many percentage points.' Well, measurement error is similar to sampling error. And let me assure you that Concepción's scores will, quite predictably, vary from spring to spring.

"What we do see in her language arts performances over the last three years is a consistently high, well above average achievement level. When her performance is compared to that of a representative, nationally normed sample, Concepción is doing very well, indeed."

Now, how would you respond to Mr. Lopez?

Currently, the SAT is divided into 10 separately timed sections. Three sections test critical reading (70 minutes total); three sections test mathematics (70 minutes total); three sections test writing (60 minutes total); and one unscored section tests critical reading, mathematics, or writing (25 minutes total). Over the years, the specific makeup of the SAT has been periodically altered, so if teachers and students wish to remain abreast of the latest configurations of this exam, it would be wise to consult the SAT website.

Three kinds of items are included in the SAT: multiple-choice questions, student-produced responses (in mathematics only), and an essay question. Designers of the SAT believe that it assesses students' knowledge of subject matter learned in high school as well as problem-solving skills in the three measured areas—namely, critical reading, mathematics, and writing. SAT scores are reported on a scale from 200 to 800, with additional subscores reported for the essay and the multiple-choice writing items. Because the mean score on both the critical reading and the mathematics sections is roughly 500, it is possible to obtain a quick impression of the extent to which a given student's score is at, above, or below the average score of other test-takers.

Although the 2005 addition of an essay-writing task to the SAT attracted substantial media attention, students' essay scores do not contribute heavily to their overall SAT scores—or even to their scores on the Writing section.

The test is still owned by the College Board, the group that originally created the test, but since 1947 the SAT has been developed and administered for the College Board by the Educational Testing Service (ETS). Both organizations are not-for-profit entities. A less demanding version of the test, referred to most often as the PSAT, is administered once each year in October—typically to high school students in their sophomore or junior years. The College Board also offers *Readi Step*, a standardized test for middle school students. This 2-hour test, consisting exclusively of multiple-choice items, assesses students' achievement in reading, writing, and mathematics during fall and spring testing windows. The SAT itself is administered throughout the nation on several preannounced occasions during the year.

In 2014, the College Board announced its intentions to release in the spring of 2016 a meaningfully modified version of the SAT intended to be more focused and useful. The redesigned SAT will incorporate eight substantive changes that its designers believe will accomplish these hopes. Those eight features are:

- *Relevant Words in Context*. The redesigned incarnation of the SAT will focus on relevant words, the meanings of which depend on the ways they are used.
- *Command of Evidence*. Several sections of the redesigned SAT call on the test-taker to interpret, synthesize, and use evidence found in a wide range of sources.
- *Essay Analyzing a Source*. The redesigned test will call for students to read a passage, then explain how the author builds an argument to persuade an audience.
- *Focus on Math that Matters Most*. The redesigned exam will focus on "matters-most" mathematics, including (1) problem solving and data analysis, (2) the "heart" of algebra, and (3) "passport" to advanced math.
- *Problems Grounded in Real-World Contexts*. Throughout the redesigned SAT, students will be given questions drawn from the real world—that is, questions related directly to work required in college and careers.

- *Analysis in Science and in History/Social Studies.* Students taking the redesigned SAT will be asked to apply their skills to answer questions in science, history, and social studies contexts.
- *Founding Documents and Great Global Conversation.* Students completing the exam will encounter passages from U.S. founding documents and from the rich, meaningful, and often profound view of great thinkers around the world.
- *No Penalty for Wrong Answers.* The redesigned SAT will move to a rights-only scoring system.

Because, despite a major test developer's original aspirations, sometimes the early tryouts of new types of items and scoring procedures require alterations in such aspirations. If you or your students are concerned about the precise nature of the redesigned SAT, you are encouraged to look into its latest formulation of the exam's current composition by consulting the SAT website.

The ACT

Although both the SAT and the ACT are typically characterized as *aptitude* exams because they are employed in an effort to predict a high-schooler's subsequent academic performance in college, the ACT's lineage makes it a decisively different kind of "aptitude" test than the SAT. Following World War II, and the subsequent enactment of the G.I. Bill of Rights (a federal law providing college tuition for returning military personnel), many more American men and women wanted to secure a college education. There was, therefore, a substantially increased need for college entrance exams.

At the University of Iowa, a gifted professor named E. F. Lindquist believed the SAT, given its ancestry as an aptitude test designed for students attending elite colleges, was not a suitable exam for many of these post-WWII college applicants. Thus, in 1959, Lindquist and his colleagues established the American College Testing Program as a not-for-profit testing company which, in 1996, changed its official name to ACT.

From the very outset, the ACT was intended to be an unabashed *achievement* test. Architects of the ACT certainly wanted their new test to be predictive of a high school student's academic success in college, but they conceived of their new test chiefly as a measure of a student's "educational development."

The ACT is made up of separate tests in essentially the same four content areas it initially assessed: English, mathematics, reading, and science. An optional writing test is now available in which the student has 30 minutes to write an essay supporting one of two positions presented in a writing "prompt," or a task. As is true with the SAT, the ACT takes about four hours to complete.

Developers of the ACT routinely solicit content suggestions, in each of the content areas tested, from large samples of secondary teachers and curriculum coordinators as well as from college professors in the four core subject areas.

Secondary-school educators are asked to identify the skills and content that students in their school or district have an option to learn by the end of their junior year in high school. College professors are asked what skills or knowledge acquired at the secondary-school level are essential for students to be academically successful during their first year of college. Based on a combination of what's taught in secondary schools and what's considered requisite for first-year success in college, items are then developed for the ACT.

Every ACT item is multiple-choice in nature, and a student gets one point for every correct answer with no subtraction of points (or partial points) for a wrong answer—as is the case in the SAT. Number-correct scores are then converted to a new 1- to 36-point scale for each of the separate tests from which an overall (composite) score is derived that represents the *average* of the four separate-tests' 1 to 36 points (unlike the SAT, where scores from its three sections are added together). The optional writing test, equivalent to the SAT's essay test, is scored on the basis of a 2- to 12-point scale using the judgments of two scorers who can each award from 1 to 6 points to a student's essay. Additional information about many aspects of the SAT can be secured from the ETS website.

As with the SAT, there are variations of the ACT available to be used with younger students. EXPLORE is aimed at eighth- and ninth-grade students, and PLAN is available for tenth-graders. More information about these three tests is available on the ACT website.

Predictive Accuracy—And Its Implications

Because of the important decisions linked to secondary students' scores on the SAT and the ACT, test-preparations options abound for each test. These test-prep possibilities range from low-cost printed and online Internet materials all the way up to very pricy in-person preparation classes and tutorials. Although there are exceptions, the more money that's spent on a preparation activity for either of these two tests, the more effective such preparation is apt to be. This is a troubling reality, of course, because children from more affluent families have greater access to the most costly preparation options, hence tend to score better than do their less affluent classmates who can't afford high-cost preparation alternatives.

But, as important as it is, let's put test-prep bias aside for a moment. There is one, overridingly important realization all teachers must arrive at regarding the predictive accuracy of the SAT and the ACT. Here it is, all gussied up in italics:

> *Only about 25% of academic success in college is associated with a high school student's performance on the SAT or ACT.*

To calculate how well a high school student's scores on a college entrance test accurately predict his or her academic success in college, a correlation is computed between high school students' scores on the SAT (or the ACT) and their subsequent college grades—for instance, their first-year college grade-point averages.

With few exceptions, the resulting correlation coefficients turn out to be approximately .50. A predictive coefficient of .50 is statistically significant, hence certainly reflects a *bona fide* relationship between students' scores on college entrance tests and their subsequent college grades.

However, to determine the practical meaningfulness of that relationship, what we must do is *square* the .50 coefficient so it becomes .25 (.50 × .50 = .25). This tells us that 25 percent of students' college grades can be linked to their performances on college admission tests. In other words, fully 75 percent of a student's college grades are due to factors *other* than students' scores on the SAT or the ACT. Such factors would include a student's motivation, study habits, and other variables over which a student has substantial control.

Now, if you are not a numerical ninny, you'll realize a student's college grades are three times more dependent on nontest factors than they are on test factors—that is, 75 percent (test-unrelated) versus 25 percent (test-related). And yet we find hoards of students who earn only "so-so scores" on the SAT or the ACT simply writing themselves off as "not smart enough" to succeed in college. College success, and success in life, is unarguably dependent on much more than a test score. Unfortunately, because the nation's educators are often unfamiliar with the predictive *imprecision* of college entrance tests, they don't do enough to dissuade students from prematurely foreclosing their college aspirations.

Over the years, a student's SAT or ACT scores have become, to many educators, and to students themselves, an unalterable definition of one's ability. That's simply not true. And teachers need not only to know it, but to make sure their students (and students' parents) know it too.

The SAT and the ACT help college officials distinguish among applicants in the common fixed-quota setting where there are more applicants for admission to a college than there are openings to that college. But the *general* predictive power of the SAT and the ACT doesn't transform those exams into definitively accurate assessment tools for *any particular* student. Teachers at all levels need to help students recognize what the SAT and the ACT exams can do—and what they can't.

WHAT DO CLASSROOM TEACHERS REALLY NEED TO KNOW ABOUT INTERPRETING STANDARDIZED TEST SCORES?

Because results of standardized tests are almost certain to come into your professional life, at least in some manner, you need to have an intuitive understanding of how to interpret those results. The most common ways of describing a set of scores is to provide an index of the score distribution's central tendency (usually the mean or median) and an index of the score distribution's variability (usually the standard deviation or the range). There will probably be instances in which you either must describe the performances of your students or understand descriptions of the performances of other groups of students (such as all students in your school or your district).

To make accurate interpretations of standardized test scores for your own students, and to help parents understand how to make sense of their child's standardized test scores, you need to comprehend the basic meaning of percentiles, grade-equivalent scores, and scale scores. You also ought to understand the major advantage and disadvantage of each of those three score-interpretation schemes. You'll then be in a position to help parents make sense out of their children's performances on standardized tests.

Two of the more influential tests many students will ever take are the SAT and the ACT, the most widely used college entrance tests. Classroom teachers need to know that, because of their differing lineages, the SAT and the ACT represent somewhat overlapping but fundamentally different assessment strategies. Whereas the SAT's focus is more heavily on assessing students' academic aptitudes, the ACT's focus is on measuring the kinds of skills and knowledge that, having been previously learned, are necessary in college. Although both tests are predictive of a student's college grades, only about 25 percent of students' college grades are associated with students' SAT or ACT scores.

CHAPTER SUMMARY

Standardized tests were defined as assessment instruments administered, scored, and interpreted in a standard, predetermined manner. Standardized tests are used to assess students' achievement and aptitude. Tests of student achievement are developed by large testing companies as well as by state departments of education (usually to satisfy a legislatively imposed educational accountability requirement). Although most standardized tests feature the use of selected-response items, many developers of such tests attempt to incorporate modest numbers of constructed-response items in their assessment devices.

For describing a distribution of test scores, two indices of central tendency—the mean and the median—were described as well as two indices of variability—the range and the standard deviation.

Several ways of interpreting results of standardized tests were discussed: percentiles, grade-equivalent scores, scale scores, stanines, and normal curve equivalents (NCEs). The nature of each of these interpretation procedures, as well as the strengths and weaknesses of the three most popular interpretation procedures, were described.

The contribution of instructionally diagnostic tests was described. Factors to consider were presented to help teachers determine whether an instructionally diagnostic test was, indeed, present and, if so, how to gauge its quality.

The SAT and the ACT are, by far, America's most widely used college entrance tests. Because of its history, the SAT (originally known as the Scholastic Aptitude

Test) aims to assess students' academic aptitudes—for example, a student's innate verbal, quantitative, and spatial aptitudes. The ACT attempts to function as an achievement test that, albeit predictive of students' college success, measures high school students' mastery of the skills and knowledge needed in college. Although predictive criterion-related validity coefficients of approximately .50 indicate students' SAT and ACT scores are certainly correlated with students' college grades, fully 75 percent of a student's academic success in college is linked to factors *other* than scores on either of these two tests.

Determining Your Outcome Mastery

Teachers are supposed to know a great deal about instruction. Given teachers' preparation and experience, they are really supposed to be instructional specialists. Teachers are not supposed to know a great deal about educational testing. That is, teachers are not really supposed to be testing specialists. But because teachers' instructional decisions will often be directly influenced by what's going on with respect to educational testing, teachers who know little about educational testing can never be *bona fide* instructional specialists. This is particularly true when it comes to standardized testing.

Standardized testing, whether it involves state-specific accountability tests or nationally standardized achievement tests, can often have an impact—sometimes visibly direct and sometimes subtly indirect—on the instructional decisions a teacher must make. And for this reason, every teacher needs to know at least enough about the basics of standardized testing so that, when a teacher's assessment-influenced instructional decisions must be made, such decisions can be made in light of a teacher's knowledge about the basics of standardized educational testing.

In this chapter, the focus was on your acquisition of basic knowledge about how standardized testing takes place and how students' performances are reported. Although attention was given to the prominent college entrance tests and the kinds of ostensibly diagnostic tests often marketed by commercial testing firms, the chief intended learning outcome for this chapter was that you acquired

> *a sufficient knowledge of standardized educational testing's fundamentals so that, when encountering an issue related to such testing or when asked a basic question about standardized testing, appropriate responses can be supplied*

As a result, the Mastery Checks focus on assessing your knowledge of the wide-ranging content regarding standardized tests and how to report and interpret the scores. Complete both the Selected-Response and the Constructed-Response quizzes and think about the feedback you receive for each quiz.

MyEdLab *Selected-Response Check of Outcome Mastery*

MyEdLab *Constructed-Response Check of Outcome Mastery*

After completing both quizzes, go to the Learning Outcome Mastery Determination, where you will decide whether you've mastered the chapter's learning outcome or whether you need further study.

MyEdLab *Learning Outcome Mastery Determination*

References

Miller, M. D., and Linn, R. (2012). *Measurement and assessment in teaching* (11th ed.). Columbus, OH: Pearson.

Nitko, A. J., and Brookhart, S. M. (2014). *Educational assessment of students* (7th ed.). Boston: Pearson.

Phelps, R. P. (Ed.). (2005). *Defending standardized testing*. Mahwah, NJ: Erlbaum.

Tankersley, K. (2007). *Tests that teach: Using standardized tests to improve instruction*. Alexandria, VA: Association for Supervision and Curriculum Development.

Waugh, C. K., and Gronlund, N. (2012). *Assessment of student achievement* (11th ed.). Columbus, OH: Pearson.

14

Appropriate and Inappropriate Test-Preparation Practices

CHIEF CHAPTER OUTCOME

An understanding of two test-preparation guidelines intended to help teachers distinguish between test-preparation practices that are appropriate and those that are inappropriate

This chapter deals with an important assessment-related issue that never really troubled teachers a few decades ago. Unfortunately, it is a problem today's classroom teachers have to confront seriously. Faced with growing pressures to increase students' scores on achievement tests, pressures that have been ratcheted up dramatically because of today's accountability and teacher-evaluation requirements, some teachers have responded by engaging in test-preparation practices that are highly questionable. In recent years, for example, a number of reports have been made of teachers and administrators who deliberately coached students with actual copies of a supposedly "secure" examination. There are even reports of educators' erasing students' incorrect answers and substituting correct answers in their place. Teachers caught cheating on high-stakes tests have lost both their teaching licenses and their jobs. Rather than a few isolated instances, such violations of test security have become, sadly, quite common.

HIGH-STAKES ASSESSMENT ARRIVES

The preoccupation with student test scores as the definitive indicator of educational effectiveness first surfaced in the 1980s. Although attention had been given to the quality of student test performances prior to that decade, it was in the 1980s that attentiveness to student test performance became pervasive. In large measure, the focus on pupils' test scores stemmed from increasing incredulity on the part of citizens about whether public education was performing properly. Taxpayers, and their elected representatives, registered serious doubts that educational tax dollars were being well spent. Spawned by such doubts, the era of educational accountability became a reality in the 1980s when state after state enacted laws requiring students to be assessed by annually administered achievement tests.

Students' performances on such tests were used not only to determine the quality of statewide schooling but also (because of the widespread practice of publishing such test scores in local newspapers) to mirror the effectiveness of individual school districts and schools.

In every sense of the expression, these legislatively mandated achievement tests were *high-stakes tests* because there were significant contingencies associated with the test results. The contingencies were experienced either by the students who took the tests or by the educators who administered the tests. To students, the tests were significant because test scores were often linked to high school graduation or to grade-level promotion. To educators, because of the manner in which test results were publicized by the local media, high test scores were viewed as indicating an effective instructional program and, of course, low test scores were seen to indicate the opposite. Because of these contingencies, teachers and administrators found themselves frequently called on to raise test scores. Candid educators will agree that pressures to boost students' test scores are still widespread.

When NCLB was enacted in 2002, high-stakes testing in America became the law of the land. Not surprisingly, a good many educators regarded federal accountability with both fear and loathing. Some protesters came up with a variety of arguments and slogans against such testing. My favorite was "High stakes are for tomatoes!" But protesters notwithstanding, the enactment of NCLB elevated our test-related stakes to previously unforeseen heights.

Discussions with classroom teachers regarding what sorts of test-preparation practices they view as appropriate and inappropriate have led to one inescapable conclusion: Most teachers have not devoted serious thought to the appropriateness of their test-preparation practices. Given the relatively recent arrival of high-stakes testing in education, it is not surprising that scant attention has been given to the appropriateness of various test-preparation practices. Yet, because no decrease in the pressures on educators to promote higher test scores seems likely, it is apparent that teachers need to consider seriously what sorts of test-preparation practices are, indeed, appropriate.

ASSESSMENT RESULTS AS INFERENCE ILLUMINATORS

Before addressing topics related to test preparation, it is important to remember the function of educational achievement tests. An educational achievement test is employed in order for us to make a reasonable inference about a student's status with respect to the knowledge and/or skills in the curricular aim the test represents. Ideally, of course, an achievement test will sample the curricular aim representatively so the level of a student's performance on the achievement test will serve as a reasonably accurate reflection of the student's status with respect

DECISION TIME

Was It Really Wrong?

Judy Jameson is a tenth-grade history teacher in Grant High School. All tenth-graders are given statewide language arts and mathematics tests that must be passed if the students are to receive a state-sanctioned diploma from the district.

The test administration takes place during a two-day period in the school cafetorium and is supervised by Grant High teachers. During those two days, on three occasions Judy overheard Mr. Pelkins respond to students who raised their hands for clarification. Mr. Pelkins did not merely clarify; he told the student what the correct answer was to the test item. After some subtle inquiries, Judy learned that each of the students that Mr. Pelkins had helped was currently in his tenth-grade general mathematics class.

Judy is now trying to decide whether she should do anything about Mr. Pelkins's conduct and, if so, what?

If you were Judy, what would your decision be?

to the curricular aim. The nature of this relationship is illustrated in Figure 14.1 where it is indicated that a student who answered correctly 80 percent of the items in an achievement test would be expected to have mastered about 80 percent of the content in the curricular aim (and its knowledge and/or skills) the test was measuring. The relationship between a student's test performance and the student's mastery of the curricular aim represented by the achievement test, as will be seen later, is a key factor in establishing the appropriateness of test-preparation practices.

figure 14.1 ■ The Inference-Illuminating Relationship between a Test and the Curricular Aim It Represents

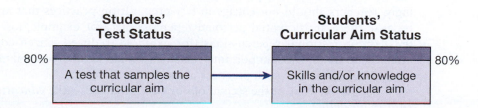

TWO EVALUATIVE GUIDELINES

Two guidelines can be employed by teachers who wish to ascertain the appropriateness of given test-preparation practices. Taken together, the two guidelines provide teachers with advice regarding the suitability of particular test-preparation activities. Here, then, is the first guideline—the *professional ethics guideline*.

Professional Ethics

No test-preparation practice should violate the ethical norms of the education profession.

This first guideline obliges teachers to avoid any unethical test-preparation practice. Ethical behaviors, of course, are rooted not only in fundamental morality but also in the nature of a particular profession. For example, physicians should be governed by general ethical principles dealing with honesty and respect for other people's property as well as by ethical principles that have evolved specifically for the medical profession. Similarly, teachers should not engage in test-preparation practices that involve violations of general ethical canons dealing with theft, cheating, lying, and so on. In addition, however, teachers must take seriously the ethical obligations arising because teachers have agreed to serve *in loco parentis*. Teachers who serve "in place of the parent" take on an ethical responsibility to serve as models of appropriate behavior for children.

When teachers engage in test-preparation practices that, if brought to the public's attention, would discredit the education profession, such practices should be considered professionally unethical. This is because, in the long term, such practices erode public confidence in our schools and, as a result, diminish taxpayers' financial support for the schools. Consequently, this erosion of public support renders the education profession less effective and, as a result, leaves children less properly educated.

Thus, according to the professional ethics guideline, teachers should not engage in test-preparation practices that involve such behaviors as violating state-imposed security procedures regarding high-stakes tests. A growing number of states have enacted serious and widely promulgated regulations so teachers who breach state test-security procedures will have their credentials revoked. Accordingly, teachers should not engage in test-preparation practices that are unethical because there are potential personal repercussions (for example, loss of credentials) or professional repercussions (for example, reduced citizen confidence in public schooling). Most importantly, teachers should avoid unethical test-preparation practices because such practices are *wrong*.

Let's look, then, at the second of our two guidelines—the *educational defensibility guideline*.

Educational Defensibility

No test-preparation practice should increase students' test scores without simultaneously increasing students' mastery of the curricular aim tested.

This second standard emphasizes the importance of engaging in instructional practices that are in the educational best interests of students. Teachers should not, for example, artificially increase students' scores on a test while neglecting to increase students' mastery of the knowledge and/or skills that the test is supposed to reflect.

An appropriate (ethical) test-preparation practice raises not only students' prepreparation-to-postpreparation performance on a test, but it also raises students' prepreparation-to-postpreparation mastery of the curricular aim being tested. This situation is illustrated in Figure 14.2 where you can see that a 20-percent prepreparation-to-postpreparation jump in students' mastery was seen both on the test and on the curricular aim it represents.

Conversely, an inappropriate test-preparation practice raises students' prepreparation-to-postpreparation performance on the test, but not students' mastery of the curricular aim itself. This situation is illustrated in Figure 14.3 where students' test performances increase, but their mastery of the curricular aim doesn't.

figure 14.2 ■ **Appropriate Test Preparation Based on the Guideline of Educational Defensibility**

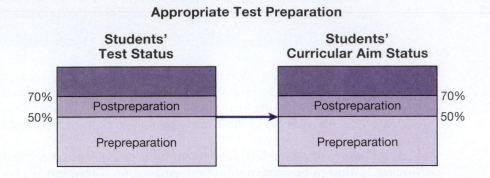

figure 14.3 ■ **Inappropriate Test Preparation Based on the Guideline of Educational Defensibility**

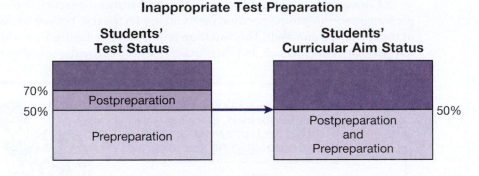

The result of such inappropriate test-preparation practices is that a deceptive picture of students' achievement is created. The test results no longer serve as an accurate indicator of students' status with respect to a curricular aim. As a consequence, students who in reality have not mastered a curricular aim's content may fail to receive appropriate instruction regarding such content. The students will have been instructionally short-changed because inappropriate test-preparation practices led to an inflated estimate of their content mastery. Such test-preparation practices, because they rob students of needed instruction, are educationally indefensible.

FIVE TEST-PREPARATION PRACTICES

We can now turn to a consideration of five common test-preparation practices. These five practices are not exhaustive in the sense that there are no other conceivable test-preparation procedures. The five practices do, however, capture most of the important test-preparation options available to teachers. Some of these involve special instruction rather than regular classroom instruction. *Special instruction* consists of extra preparation sessions, during or outside class, devoted exclusively to the readying of students for tests. In contrast, *regular classroom instruction*, although its focus may be relevant to the content of a test, occurs as part of the teacher's ongoing instructional program. The five test-preparation practices are the following:

1. *Previous-form preparation* provides special instruction and practice based directly on students' use of a previous form of the actual test. For example, if the currently published form of a nationally standardized achievement test is being used on a statewide basis as part of a state's accountability system, the teacher gives students guided or independent practice with earlier, no longer published, versions of the same test.

2. *Current-form preparation* provides special instruction and practice based directly on students' use of the form of the test currently being employed. For example, the teacher gives students guided or independent practice with actual items copied from a currently used state-developed high school graduation test.

3. *Generalized test-taking preparation* provides special instruction covering test-taking skills for dealing with a variety of achievement-test formats. For example, the teacher shows students how to make calculated guesses for certain types of items or how to allocate test-taking time judiciously.

4. *Same-format preparation* provides regular classroom instruction dealing directly with the content covered on the test, but employs only practice items that embody the same format as items actually used on the test. For example, if a mathematics achievement test includes addition problems formatted only in vertical columns, the teacher provides practice with addition problems formatted solely in this manner. Some teachers create "clone" items for same-format preparation activities—such items being almost mirror images of a test's actual items. For many of these "clone" items, the practice items are essentially indistinguishable from the actual items.

5. *Varied-format preparation* provides regular classroom instruction dealing directly with the content covered on the test, but employs practice items representing a variety of test-item formats. For example, if the achievement test uses subtraction problems formatted only in vertical columns, the teacher provides practice with problems formatted in vertical columns, horizontal rows, and in story form.

APPLYING THE TWO GUIDELINES

When these five test-preparation practices are scrutinized according to the guidelines of professional ethics and educational defensibility, only two turn out to be appropriate.

Previous-form preparation violates the educational defensibility guideline because students' test scores are apt to be boosted via such special preparation sessions without concomitant rises in students' mastery of the curricular aim being tested. In addition, because in the public's view this kind of test-preparation practice may be seen as an improper instance of coaching students *merely* for test-score gains, it may be viewed by some as professionally unethical. Previous-form preparation, therefore, is inappropriate. (This same judgment would apply to the use of commercial test-preparation materials based chiefly on specially created "parallel" forms of a currently used test.)

Current-form preparation clearly loses out on both guidelines. Not only is it educationally indefensible, but such preparation also constitutes an outright example of cheating. Current forms of the test must be stolen or surreptitiously copied in order to be used in such potentially improper score-boosting special sessions. Teachers who are caught readying their students via current-form preparation should, in fact, be caught.

Generalized test-taking preparation turns out to be an appropriate form of test preparation because such special instruction on how to take tests is, characteristically, rather brief and not seriously deflective of a student's ongoing education. More importantly, because such test-taking preparation readies students to cope with a number of different sorts of tests, students will be less apt to be intimidated by a previously unencountered type of test item. In a very real sense, therefore, generalized test-taking preparation sessions allow students' test performances to be more accurately reflective of their true state of knowledge and/or skill. Such preparation, *if not excessively lengthy,* is clearly appropriate.

Same-format preparation, although it may be ethical, is not educationally defensible. If students in their regular classroom instruction are allowed to deal *only* with the explicit item format used on a test, then those students will be far less likely to generalize what they have learned. Test scores may rise, but comparable content mastery is not apt to rise. Although many administrators may, because of powerful pressures to boost scores, endorse this form of test-preparation practice, it should be resisted because it is educationally unsound. The more "clone" items there are in a set of practice items, the more inappropriate such test-preparation activities are.

Varied-format preparation, in contrast, satisfies both of our two evaluative guidelines. Students during their regular classroom instruction are given practice not only with content as it is conceptualized on the test but also with content conceptualized in other ways. Rises in test scores will, in general, be accompanied by rises in mastery of the curricular aim being tested because students' generalized mastery of the content is being fostered.

Of the five test-preparation variants, then, only varied-format preparation and generalized test-taking preparation satisfy both evaluative guidelines. This can be seen in Table 14.1.

PARENT TALK

Mrs. Stern is the mother of Sara, one of your most talented students. Mrs. Stern, it is rumored, will be running for election to your district's school board in the fall. Accordingly, whenever Mrs. Stern raises questions about Sara's education, you always try to be especially responsive. You are no dummy.

When Sara arrived at school this morning, she gave you a brief note from her mother. The note said, "Why is so much time spent in our school, and in your class, 'teaching to the test' this year? Shouldn't our children be learning more than what's on a test?"

 If I were you, here's how I'd respond to Mrs. Stern in person or with a note (if in person, I might reply on bended knee):

"You're right on target to be raising this issue, Mrs. Stern, but I want you to understand an important difference between teaching to the test, in the sense you teach students to do well on particular test items, versus teaching to the test, in the sense you teach the students to master the skills and/or knowledge represented by the test.

"What I do in my class is the latter, and that's also what most of my colleagues do. In other words, we teach directly toward the important skills and knowledge that our tests measure. Those are the key kinds of skills and the significant bodies of knowledge that you and I both want Sara to acquire. But the classroom assessments that we use will only sample a student's mastery of such knowledge or skills.

"So it would be instructionally unwise for us to teach toward particular test items. We want Sara and her classmates to master skills and knowledge so our students can apply what they've learned in many settings, not merely on a specific test.

"Putting it simply, we do not teach toward a set of test items, but we do teach toward the skills and knowledge our tests represent."

 Now, how would you respond to Mrs. Stern?

table 14.1 ▪ **Per-Guideline Indicator of the Appropriateness of Five Test-Preparation Practices**

	Guideline Satisfied?	
Test-Preparation Practice	Professional Ethics	Educational Defensibility
Previous Form	No	No
Current Form	No	No
Generalized Test-Taking	Yes	Yes
Same Format	Yes	No
Varied Format	Yes	Yes

WHAT ABOUT "TEACHING TO THE TEST"?

If you get into any sort of meaningful discussion of test preparation, it's almost certain that someone will soon use the expression "teaching to the test." This someone should not be you! Here's why.

There are two decisively different meanings people employ when they use the phrase **_teaching to the test_**. First, they can mean a teacher is directing instruction toward the knowledge, skills, or affective variables represented by the test. Another way to put this same meaning of "teaching to the test" is that teachers are aiming their instruction so students accomplish the curricular aim sampled by the actual test. This is good instruction. A second meaning of "teaching to the test," however, is that it describes teachers who are directing their instruction specifically toward the actual items on the test itself. This is bad instruction.

So, when someone uses the expression "teaching to the test," we can't tell whether they're talking about something swell or something sordid. Conversations that take place about test preparation in which this double-meaning expression is tossed around mindlessly will, almost certainly, end up being mindless conversations.

As a consequence, I implore you _never to use this ambiguous expression_ yourself. Rather, say either "teaching to the test's items" or "teaching to the curricular aim represented by the test." To emphasize the importance of this advice, I have summarized it in this box:

> NEVER, NEVER SAY: "Teaching to the test"
>
> **SAY:**
> "Teaching to the test's items"
>
> (or)
>
> **SAY:**
> "Teaching to the curricular aim represented by the test"

If you should momentarily forget my fine advice and find yourself blurting out the foul phrase I've just been castigating, or if you are forced with pepper-spray to say it aloud, be sure to quickly follow up by saying which meaning of the expression you intended. By and large, however, you'll be better off if you expunge the phrase completely from your potential utterances.

If a _friend_ uses the phrase, you might gently and supportively seek clarification about which meaning is intended. If an _enemy_ uses the phrase, however, I recommend a crisp facial slap on the left or right cheek—depending on either cheek's proximity to you.

One way of thinking about how teachers ought to prepare their students for important assessments is presented in Figure 14.4. As you can see, a teacher's instruction should be directed toward the body of knowledge and/or skills (it

figure 14.4 ■ **Appropriate and Inappropriate Directions for a Teacher's Instruction**

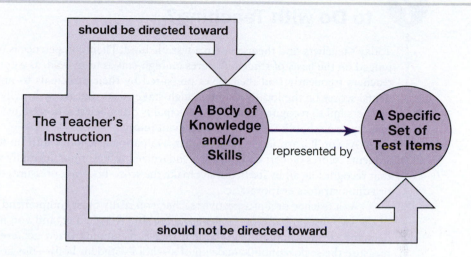

could also be affect) represented by the test, but not toward the specific set of items doing the representing.

And this way of thinking about test preparation brings us to an important point for teachers to understand. You can only direct your instruction toward the knowledge and/or skills represented by a high-stakes test if there is a suitable description of the assessed curricular aim available. You can't expect a teacher to teach toward a curricular aim if there's no clear description of that aim provided.

Unfortunately, many of the nation's teachers are now experiencing immense pressure to raise their students' scores on high-stakes test that are unaccompanied by instructionally actionable descriptions of what those tests measure. And without such descriptions, it is far from surprising that many pressured teachers have succumbed to the lure of item-focused teaching.

I've spent a good deal of time reviewing the descriptions of assessed behavior provided by publishers of all the nation's standardized achievement tests, and I can tell you, from a teacher's perspective, the descriptions of these tests' curricular targets fall way short of what teachers need. Oh, of course there are some loose descriptions of objectives or content assessed, but those descriptions just aren't sufficient if a teacher is planning day-to-day instruction.

My point is this: If the high-stakes test on which you're asked to boost students' scores is not accompanied by descriptions of what the test's items *represent*, then you should let the world know you're being put in an untenable instructional position. Teachers should not be forced to play the score-boosting game if obliged to use rules making it certain the teacher will lose. And there's no way to satisfy this chapter's two test-preparation guidelines if a curricular aim's description (suitable for instructional action) has not been supplied.

But What Does This Have to Do with Teaching?

Today's teachers find themselves in a terrible bind. Their competence is often being judged on the basis of students' scores on high-stakes tests. And, as a consequence, teachers frequently find themselves pressured by their principals to improve students' scores on the locally anointed high-stakes tests. But many heavily pressured teachers fail to recognize that their principal is often being squeezed just as hard to make sure a school's test scores take a giant jump.

As you'll learn in the next chapter, evaluating a school's staff on the basis of students' scores on certain kinds of standardized tests is fundamentally wrong. Yet that recognition, all by itself, doesn't make the score-boosting pressures on teachers or administrators evaporate.

As a teacher, or a prospective teacher, you really must comprehend the nature of the two test-preparation guidelines offered in the chapter, and you need to understand (from Chapter 15) why it is that some standardized achievement tests measure the socioeconomic makeup of a school's student body—not how well the school's teachers are teaching.

At that point, instead of assuming a school's principal is the "heavy" in this score-boosting frenzy, you need to recognize school principals are, themselves, under substantial pressure to elevate their school's test scores. Accordingly, by the time you wrap up this book, you'll know (1) how to and how not to prepare students for high-stakes tests and (2) what kinds of high-stakes tests give educators—that is, teachers *and* principals—a chance to succeed.

Therefore, why not collaborate *with* your school's principal to explain ways of responding to extant test pressures with test-preparation practices that help, not harm, children. What you need to do, frankly, is put the stuff you've already learned in Chapter 12 (about formative assessment) and this chapter (about test preparation) together with what you will learn in Chapter 15. Then, working collaboratively with your school's principal, figure out a strategy to make accurate evaluative judgments while, at the same time, benefitting kids.

WHAT DO CLASSROOM TEACHERS REALLY NEED TO KNOW ABOUT TEST-PREPARATION PRACTICES?

As a classroom teacher, you may find your own test-preparation practices may not coincide perfectly with one of the five practices described in this chapter. You'll probably discover, if you are preparing your students specifically for some sort of high-stakes test, however, your approach will be reasonably close to one of the five practices. More important than the five preparation practices, of course, are the two evaluative guidelines. You should review with care your own preparation activities linked to high-stakes tests. The two evaluative guidelines provided here—professional ethics and educational defensibility—will prove useful in such a review.

CHAPTER SUMMARY

This chapter dealt with an important assessment-related issue: how teachers should prepare their students for significant tests. After a recounting of why it is that classroom teachers are under substantial pressure to boost their students' test scores, two evaluative guidelines were supplied by which test-preparation practices can be judged. The two guidelines were (1) *professional ethics,* which indicates that no test-preparation practice should violate the ethical norms of the education profession, and (2) *educational defensibility,* which indicates that no test-preparation practice should increase students' test scores without simultaneously increasing students' mastery of the curricular aim tested. Five test-preparation variants were then described: (1) previous-form preparation, (2) current-form preparation, (3) generalized test-taking preparation, (4) same-format preparation, and (5) varied-format preparation. Having applied the two evaluative guidelines to the five test-preparation practices, it was concluded that the only two practices satisfying both guidelines were generalized test-taking preparation (if brief) and varied-format preparation. Readers were urged to eschew the phrase *teaching to the test.* Readers should also have been urged to eschew the word *eschew.* The chapter was concluded with a discussion of the necessity for the creators of high-stakes tests to supply curricular aim descriptions from which sound instructional decisions can be made.

Determining Your Outcome Mastery

As the consequences of educational testing become higher and higher, the pressures on teachers to boost their students' test scores become greater and greater. Regrettably, in response to those pressures, some teachers have engaged in reprehensible test-preparation activities that range all the way from "somewhat questionable" to "downright deplorable." Most teachers have not devoted any sort of systematic attention to the acceptability of how they ready their students to take educational tests, especially high-stakes educational tests, and some teachers unthinkingly stumble into the use of test-preparation activities that are definitely improper.

The intent of this chapter was to help you focus your attention on these issues so that you achieve the chief chapter outcome:

> *an understanding of two test-preparation guidelines intended to help teachers distinguish between test-preparation practices that are appropriate and those that are inappropriate.*

To assess your mastery of this outcome, complete both the Selected-Response and the Constructed-Response quizzes and think about the feedback you receive for each quiz.

MyEdLab *Selected-Response Check of Outcome Mastery*

MyEdLab *Constructed-Response Check of Outcome Mastery*

After completing both quizzes, go to the Learning Outcome Mastery Determination, where you will decide whether you've mastered the chapter's learning outcome or whether you need further study.

MyEdLab *Learning Outcome Mastery Determination*

References

Cannell, J. J. (1989). *How public educators cheat on standardized achievement tests.* Albuquerque, NM: Friends for Education.

Hardison, C. M., and Sackett, P. R. (2008). "Use of writing samples on standardized tests: Susceptibility to rule-based coaching and the resulting effects on score improvement," *Applied Measurement in Education, 21,* no. 3 (July–September): 227–252.

Harris, P., Smith, B. M., and Harris, J. (2011). *The myths of standardized tests: Why they don't tell you what you think they do.* Lanham, MD: Rowman & Littlefield.

Lai, E. R., and Waltman, K. (2008). "Test preparation: Examining teacher perceptions and practices," *Educational Measurement: Issues and Practice, 27,* no. 2 (Summer): 28–45.

Mehrens, W. A., and Kaminski, J. (1989). "Methods for improving standardized tests scores: Fruitful, fruitless, or fraudulent." *Educational Measurement: Issues and Practice, 8,* no. 1: 14–22.

Sacks, P. (1999). *Standardized minds: The high price of America's testing culture and what we can do to change it.* Cambridge, MA: Perseus Books.

15

The Evaluation of Instruction

An understanding of the potential contributions and limitations of test-elicited evidence of instructional quality sufficient for the identification of likely shortcomings in such evidence or in its use for the evaluation of schools or teachers

Most teachers, at the conclusion of a set of instructional activities—whether those activities consume an hour, a week, or an entire school year—do not systematically try to determine how successful their instruction actually was. But they should. In this chapter, then, we'll consider ways that teachers can tell whether their just-completed instruction was great or grimy. It's really a rather straightforward task, yet not without some significant sand traps to avoid.

Because the chapter after this one deals with the appraisal of students, I want to make sure we are using two sometimes confused labels accurately. In casual conversation, you'll sometimes find educators using the terms *evaluation* and *grading* interchangeably, but these two words really stand for distinctively different education-related activities.

There was a time when educators really didn't distinguish between *evaluation* of students and *grading* of students, but those days have passed. Because program evaluation has now become such a prominent part of educational practice, when most educators encounter the term *evaluation* these days, they think about the evaluation of an educational program such as a school district's newly installed cooperative learning scheme.

When classroom teachers engage in **evaluation,** those teachers are typically arriving at conclusions about the quality of their own instructional efforts. In this sense, therefore, you should think about evaluation as "program evaluation." Because the "program" under consideration in most classrooms is the instructional program provided to students by the teacher, then *evaluation* will be used in this chapter to signify the attempt on the part of teachers to determine how well they're doing instructionally. The evaluation of instruction, then, can be roughly equated with "teacher evaluation" because when teachers evaluate their instructional endeavors, they're really evaluating the quality of the instructional program they put together as well as the way they delivered that program. The focus of *evaluation* in this chapter, therefore, is on teachers' evaluation of their instruction.

In contrast, the focus of **grading** is on *students*. When a teacher grades a student, the teacher is assigning some kind of symbol (we'll discuss several options in the next chapter), such as letter grades of A, B, C, D, or F, that signify "how well the student has done." Although in most classrooms there's surely a relationship between the quality of the teacher's instructional program and the grades students receive, those two notions are really independent. For example, Mrs. Bevins, a third-grade teacher, could evaluate her own language arts program very negatively because her instruction seemed to confuse many students. Nevertheless, Mrs. Bevins would still award grades of A to numerous students who, despite the confusing language arts instruction, effortlessly seemed to grasp the language arts concepts being considered.

Although I've tried to draw a nice, crisp distinction between *evaluation* as the appraisal of an instructional activity and *grading* as the appraisal of a student's performance, don't be surprised if you encounter colleagues who don't slice their appraisal cake in the same way. Some educators (I think mistakenly) refer to the grading of students as the "evaluation" of students. Other educators (also, in my view, mistakenly) talk about "grading" the quality of instruction. So, prepare yourself for some semantic stumbling when you discuss these concepts with others.

There are two types of evaluation bearing on teachers' appraisals of their instructional efforts. *Teachers'* self-evaluation refers to the personal appraisal of the teacher's instructional program for purposes of improving the program. For example, suppose you're teaching a three-week social studies unit on International Cooperation to a class of fifth-graders for the first time. You want to improve the unit so that the next time you offer it, your teaching will be more effective. That's a task for self-evaluation, and students' assessment results will surely help you. *External teacher evaluation*, in contrast, is often not improvement focused. This kind of evaluation frequently refers to appraisals of teachers' competencies in order to make significant decisions about those teachers such as (1) continuation of employment or (2) awarding of tenure. When teachers are evaluated externally, they're almost always evaluated by an administrator or supervisor.

External evaluations of teachers are typically divided into two categories: summative teacher evaluations and formative teacher evaluations. **Summative teacher evaluations** focus on the sorts of high-stakes personnel decisions mentioned in the previous paragraph. **Formative teacher evaluations,** often made by teachers in collaboration with a supervisor or school-site administrator, are intended to help teachers improve their instructional effectiveness.

Classroom teachers usually do their own self-evaluation because they wish to spruce up their instruction. For external teacher evaluation, classroom teachers may be called on to supply evidence (such as students' test results) to supervisors who will then use such evidence evaluatively.

The evaluation of a teacher's instructional effectiveness will also be influenced by the presence of relevant state or federal laws that, for many teachers, may require students' scores on standardized tests to be used for evaluating schools and, by implication, for evaluating the teachers who teach in those schools. If you find yourself teaching a grade level or in a subject field where federal or state accountability tests are given annually, you can bet that your students' scores on those tests will figure into any evaluation of your effectiveness.

A FOCUS ON CONSEQUENCES

You can't tell how well teachers teach by watching them do it. Instead, to determine the effectiveness of a teacher's instruction, we need to focus on the *effects* a teacher's instruction has on students. There are precious few exceptions to this "focus on consequences" strategy for the evaluation of instruction. To illustrate one such exception, on the ineffective end of the quality scale, this would occur if we were to observe a teacher engaging in a series of badly explained, mind-numbing, and off-target activities—all of which were taking place in the midst of loud-talking, misbehaving, and clearly out-of-control students. Anyone walking into such a cacophonous classroom would instantly be able to conclude, with good reason, that some seriously shabby instruction was taking place. At the other end of the quality yardstick—the good end—we might observe a teacher who is carrying out a galaxy of diverse, research-supported instructional practices in a classroom where well-behaved students are clearly engaged in what is taking place and, when asked by the teacher, actively participate in a series of cleverly devised learning activities. This second "does it all perfectly" teacher is likely to be regarded as successful based on just about any evaluative factors we might choose when judging instructional quality. But, with the possible exception of such spectacularly wonderful or spectacularly woeful teachers, we really can't tell by *watching* how successful a teacher is. The vast majority of teachers are neither phenomenally fabulous nor flat-out flops; they're somewhere in the middle. Accordingly, in the vast majority of instances we really need to evaluate a teacher's instruction according to its *consequences*—that is, by determining its effect on students' learning.

To properly evaluate a teacher's instruction, we should employ a rather traditional ends-means model. Using such a time-honored paradigm, the curricular aims sought by a teacher represent the teacher's intended *ends,* whereas what the teacher does in an effort to achieve those ends constitutes the teacher's instructional *means.* When we assess students at the close of an instructional sequence, therefore, we are attempting to determine whether the teacher's instructional means have, indeed, promoted students' attainment of the curricular ends being sought by the teacher.

For years, empirical evidence has shown conclusively that there is no "one best way" to teach something. The instructional procedures used marvelously by a particular teacher in a particular setting with a particular set of students might turn out to be thoroughly ineffectual in the hands of another teacher in a different setting with a dissimilar set of students. Put simply, for almost all teachers, the only way to evaluate instruction accurately is to determine what happens to students as a consequence of the teacher's instruction. And this is where assessment evidence comes bounding onto the scene, *for it is only by using assessment evidence that we can tell what was taught has actually been learned.* Assessment evidence, therefore, helps us arrive at accurate evaluations of a teacher's success, whether this evidence is used as part of a teacher's own self-evaluation or in connection with an externally imposed evaluation of teachers.

If a teacher's instructional success is going to be evaluated on the basis of students' learning, then what evidence of students' learning ought to be employed to arrive at such an evaluation? Well, there are two prominent kinds of assessment evidence that should, if at all possible, be included in any sort of instructional-evaluation sweepstakes. First off, evidence of students' learning that is collected via *classroom assessments* is clearly one source of assessment data to be considered. Second, if a teacher's students are required to complete one or more *external accountability tests,* then students' performances on such tests should definitely be used in the evaluation of instruction.

In a moment, we'll look at ways of collecting both of these kinds of evidence, but please realize that not all results of classroom assessments *or* accountability tests should be treated equally. In earlier chapters you tussled with a number of test-development and test-refinement ideas that, clearly, bear on the quality of the data collected by the use of teacher-made classroom assessments. Obviously, there is a profound difference in the persuasiveness of students' test results depending on the caliber of the tests themselves. For instance, let's assume that a teacher's classroom tests assess students' mastery of a set of several genuinely high-level cognitive skills, and those tests do so by using a collection of items that assiduously follow all of the item-guidelines given earlier in this book. Students' performances on such a well-built test ought to play a prominent role in evaluation of instructional activities. On the other hand, let's assume that a teacher's classroom test not only measures a collection of trifling curricular aims, but does so with items that reek of wretchedness. In short, this second fictional test measures unimportant stuff and measures it badly. Clearly, students' performances on this second test should be given little if any importance when evaluating a teacher's instruction.

A second source of assessment evidence we should employ to evaluate instructional quality occurs when external achievement tests are used as part of a governmentally required accountability program. Obviously, a teacher has far less influence over the makeup of such tests—in contrast to the teacher's own classroom assessments. But external accountability tests, such as the annual exams administered in accord with a statutorily required accountability program, also vary dramatically in quality. As you will see later in the chapter, many of the accountability tests now being used in the United States are seriously flawed from an evaluative perspective, and thus should really not be employed to evaluate instructional quality. So, just as we saw with the evidence collected by teacher-made tests, the appropriateness of evidence provided by external accountability tests also can vary considerably. It is a mistake to automatically regard external accountability tests as trustworthy merely because they take more time to create and are more expensive to develop than teacher-made tests.

Okay, so when we set out to evaluate instructional quality, two potentially useful kinds of evidence to be considered are students' performances on (1) classroom assessments and (2) external accountability tests. As already noted, because both of these two categories of tests can vary in their quality, caution is clearly warranted when using students' performances on either type of test.

But there's one additional factor to consider when teachers evaluate their instruction, and it's an important one that should be considered every time an instructional evaluation takes place. That additional factor consists of the *unintended side effects of instruction.* With test results, whether from classroom assessments or external accountability exams, teachers have at least a general idea of what's to be assessed, hence they can usually engage in instructional activities aimed at improving students' test performances. But what happens if, although the teacher has not planned on it, some significant side effects on the teacher's students are seen as a consequence of instruction? Shouldn't these side effects be taken into consideration in the evaluation of instruction? Of course they should.

To illustrate, let's say a middle school mathematics teacher has done a simply spectacular job in getting her students to perform well on a series of exams she personally constructed, and she's even seen dramatic increases in her students' performances on the state's annual mathematics assessments. So, clearly, students' scores have soared on both kinds of assessments we have been considering as potential evidence for the evaluation of instruction. Unfortunately, what also happened in this teacher's math classes is that almost all of the students acquired seriously negative attitudes toward math, some of the students claiming privately that they "would never take another math class voluntarily." So, despite the teacher's test-based evidence of success—seen on both classroom tests and statewide accountability tests—a serious side effect seems to have soured this teacher's instructional soufflé. If a math teacher's instruction makes students abhor mathematics, then this constitutes a significant side effect to be taken into consideration when evaluating the teacher. Unanticipated side effects, both negative and positive, should *always* be considered when evaluating instructional quality.

But how, you might be asking, does a teacher identify the side effects of a completed instructional sequence? Well, that task is a truly tough one. As a teacher, what you most need to do is *be on the lookout for any consequences of instruction that you had not foreseen.* You might, as you near the close of an instructional sequence, ask a colleague to help you think about such a question. You might also try to poll your students with anonymous self-report inventories similar to those you learned about in Chapter 10. But the chief thing is for you to be *looking for* such unanticipated side effects, and never regard a set of instructional activities as having been properly evaluated without raising the possibility that some unforeseen positive or negative effects might have taken place because of the instruction.

The evidence a teacher uses regarding unforeseen side effects might be collected by fairly traditional data-gathering approaches, or more innovative assessment ploys could be used. And in some cases, side effects will be found without any reliance at all on assessment devices. For example, let's think of a sixth-grade teacher whose hyperdemanding and stressful style, when used with recently arrived immigrant children, apparently leads to massive dropouts on the part of those children. (Fully half of those children have already left school during the current school year.) The evidence of such an adverse side effect might not be collected by using any sort of typical or even innovative assessment tactics. Instead, the school's attendance office might be the source of such information. For identifying side effects, all legitimate sources of information are fair game.

Summarizing, then, to evaluate the quality of your instruction, I encourage you to structure your evaluative strategy around the following three factors:

1. Assessment evidence collected via classroom assessments
2. Assessment evidence collected via accountability tests
3. Evidence pertaining to any positive or negative side effects

As noted before, the quality of the assessment devices used is critical when we set out to appraise instructional quality. Good assessments—ones that measure worthwhile things—typically provide good evaluative evidence. The opposite is also true. In earlier chapters, we've already taken a look at how teachers can devise appropriate classroom assessments. In the remainder of this chapter, we will be giving serious consideration to external accountability tests because those kinds of tests are currently being used to supply the dominant evidence regarding most teachers' instructional success. But before leaving the evidence available from classroom assessments, let's take a brief look at *how* a teacher can use classroom assessments to collect evaluative evidence regarding the teacher's instructional success.

CLASSROOM ASSESSMENT EVIDENCE

Most teachers realize that if they collect assessment evidence from their students only *after* instruction is over, they won't be able to determine the effectiveness of the instruction they're trying to evaluate. After all, students might have known already—before any instruction took place—what the teacher was setting out to teach. Thus, whether evidence is being collected for teachers' self-evaluation or for external teacher evaluation, some sort of *pretest versus posttest* data-gathering model is usually employed. Let's consider two such models, both of which can make a contribution to teachers' efforts to evaluate the quality of their instruction.

Pretests versus Posttests

Whether for self-evaluation or external evaluation, the classic pretest–posttest model presented in Figure 15.1 will prove serviceable for gauging instructional impact. If you assess your students prior to teaching them, then assess your students after you've taught them, any difference between their pretest and posttest performances ought to be chiefly attributable to what went on in between—your teaching.

figure 15.1 ■ A Classic Pretest versus Posttest Model for Determining Instructional Impact

Certain problems are associated with the classic pretest-posttest scheme for discerning instructional impact, of course, but as a general paradigm for figuring out whether your instruction is making any dents in your students, the approach represented in Figure 15.1 isn't all that bad. One of the difficulties with the pretest–posttest model you need to watch out for is the possibility the pretest will be *reactive;* that is, it will sensitize your students to "what's important" so they behave atypically when being taught about what was on the pretest. In other words, the effects measured by the posttest will really be a function of your instruction *plus* the pretest. However, if the posttest results for Topic X truly turn out to be what you want when you use a reactive pretest, then you might decide to toss in a pretest every time you teach Topic X.

For purposes of external evaluation, such as when you are being evaluated by school district officials for purposes of continued employment, there's a really difficult problem to consider, and this is the extent to which pretest-to-posttest assessment results for students will be influenced by the caliber of the students you happen to be teaching. If you're teaching a ninth-grade geography class and have been blessed with a group of bright, motivated, and well-informed students, it is certain the pretest-to-posttest gains you obtain will be quite different from the gains you might see if you were teaching a collection of dull, unmotivated students whose conception of geography stops at the boundaries of the schoolyard.

It is imperative, however, that those who use student-assessment data for purposes of external teacher evaluation do so in the context of the situation in which the teacher teaches—the most important feature of which is the specific students being taught. For your own self-evaluation purposes, there's somewhat less need to get caught up with the "dissimilar students" problem. After all, you'll know your own students and will be able to judge whether you have a group of fast-thinking wizards whose pretest-to-posttest gains will be astounding or a group of slow-thinking students whose progress will be substantially less electrifying.

To the extent you're using gain scores (that is, posttest-minus-pretest scores), you should be aware of another technical problem likely to get in your way. If your students do *very* well on the pretest, it's more difficult for them to show gains than if they'd scored lower prior to instruction. When students score very high on tests, they tend to "top out" because of what is called a *ceiling effect.* Sometimes, in fact, if your students score really poorly on a pretest, they'll be likely to score higher on the posttest *by chance alone.* (If you want to intimidate your colleagues during faculty meetings, this is called a *regression effect,* wherein extremely low-scoring (or high-scoring) students tend to regress toward the mean when retested. By casually asserting your "students' progress, of course, might be attributable to a regression effect," you'll surely awe a few of your fellow teachers.)

There's another potential way of dealing with the difficulties of a simple pretest-versus-posttest evaluation design, and that's to use different but *equidifficult* tests. The only problem with this solution is it's almost impossible for busy classroom teachers to create two truly equidifficult forms of a test. So, if the form used as a posttest is easier than its pretest counterpart, the teacher's instruction might look terrific, but students' high posttest performances could be caused chiefly by the softer posttest. Or, worse, if the posttest form is tons tougher than the pretest form, then a pretest-to-posttest comparison might suggest that the impact of the teacher's instruction has been to make students "unlearn" what they knew when they took the pretest. No, two test forms, even if they are intended to be equidifficult, won't save the day.

The Split-and-Switch Design

There is a simple modification of the classic pretest–posttest design that will work for you if you have a reasonably large class of, say, 25 or more students. It's called the *split-and-switch design,* and here's how it works.

First, you need two forms of the test you're going to use as a pretest and as a posttest. The two forms ought to be *somewhat similar* in degree of difficulty, but need not be equidifficult or all that close to it. Let's call the two forms Test 1 and Test 2.

Second, you *split* your class into two roughly equal *half-class* groups, perhaps by counting half-way down your class roster so all students whose last names start with the letters A through L are in Half-Class A, and all students whose last names start with the letters M through Z are in Half-Class B.

Next, you administer one of the two forms to each half-class, but ask students *not* to date their test forms. Ideally, in fact, students should write their names only on the *back* of their completed tests. You should then *code* the two sets of pretests (Test 1 and Test 2) so you can tell they are pretests. You can even use the pretest to help you plan your instruction. But you should not score, or write on, the pretests (on the actual test forms) at this time.

Then you should instruct all your students for as long as you have allowed for the instruction. Suppose, for example, you were trying to teach your students how to write an effective narrative essay. This might take several months or even a full school year. Let's say, however, you devote one full semester to the teaching of this skill.

At the end of instruction, you then *switch* your two half-classes so if Half-Class A took Test 1 as a pretest, it now takes Test 2 as a posttest. Similarly, if Half-Class B received Test 2 as a pretest, at the end of instruction it will receive Test 1 as a posttest.

You then *code* the posttests so *you* can distinguish them, after consulting the codes, from the pretests. You next *mix* together all the copies of Test 1 (both pretests and posttests). You do the same with Test 2.

Next, you, colleagues, or even parents judge the quality of the mixed-together Test 1s. That is, the tests are subjected to **blind-scoring.** The same is then done for the mixed-together Test 2s. *After* all scoring has been done, the codes are consulted so the blind-scored papers are separated into pretests and posttests.

This data-gathering model, one I've called the *split-and-switch design,* provides you with *two* indications of whether your instruction promoted posttest improvement—that is, the pretest-to-posttest changes for Test 1 as well as those for Test 2.

Because the pretest and posttest comparisons are made using the *very same test,* there is clearly no problem caused by differential test difficulty. Moreover, because your students will not have previously seen the posttest they receive, the reactive impact of the pretesting is minimized.

In essence, you have taken two 50-percent samples of your class, at both pretest time and posttest time, to help you determine whether students have made the progress you wish. The split-and-switch design, of course, becomes less accurate as class sizes get smaller, but it does help you dodge some of the more troublesome aspects of the simple pretest-versus-posttest data-gathering model. The evidence this atypical data-gathering design provides can be particularly compelling if you secure *nonpartisans* (such as parents) to supply the blind-scoring.

The split-and-switch design is depicted graphically in Figure 15.2. If you are not sure yet in how it is supposed to function, please consider the Figure 15.2 diagram until you see what happens when. Note that the appropriate comparisons, and there will be *two,* are signified by the arrows.

Teachers can use pretest results to guide their instructional decision-making. And they can use posttest results to assign grades (remembering to make allowances for test forms of differing difficulties). But, of course, no permanent marks should be made on any tests until after they've been mixed together and blind-scored.

figure 15.2 ■ A Split-and-Switch Data-Gathering Design

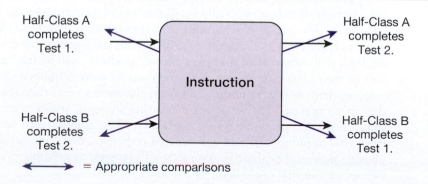

Half-Class A completes Test 1.

Half-Class A completes Test 2.

Instruction

Half-Class B completes Test 2.

Half-Class B completes Test 1.

= Appropriate comparisons

DECISION TIME

To Buttress or Not to Buttress?

Madeline teaches fifth-graders in an inner-city school. In recent years, her school's students have performed poorly on the state's annual accountability tests. Madeline's principal, Mr. Jenkins, is convinced that the state accountability test is little more than a measure of students' socioeconomic status, and that students' scores on the test definitely do not accurately reflect the instructional success of his school's teachers.

Accordingly, Mr. Jenkins recently issued an invitation to all the school's teachers to evaluate their ability to promote their students' mastery of a high-level cognitive skill in any subject area by collecting pretest-to-posttest evidence regarding whether their instruction was, in fact, successful. The purpose of this activity is to supply evidence to buttress students' scores on the annual accountability test—and to "show the community that our teachers are doing a good job." Mr. Jenkins asks all volunteers to pursue a cognitive skill requiring students to generate their own responses on the pretests and posttests. The instruction should take at least two months to complete, and the collected pretests and posttests would be coded, then mixed together so scorers could not tell whether a student's response was written prior to or following instruction. The test responses would be blind-scored by parent volunteers, then separated into pretest and posttest groups after the blind-scoring had been completed. Mr. Jenkins plans to summarize the results from all participating teachers, prepare a brief report, then send that report to all of the school's parents.

Madeline realizes that if the pretest-to-posttest results are positive, this would surely have a positive impact on parents' perceptions of the faculty's effectiveness. However, if the results are not positive, then this evidence would confirm the view, based on the annual state tests, that the school's staff is not very effective. She must let Mr. Jenkins know by the end of the week whether she will be a volunteer in this proposed activity.

▶ *If you were Madeline, what would your decision be?*

The split-and-switch design should be used for determining students' achievement of only a relatively small number of particularly significant cognitive outcomes—for instance, a handful of curricular aims calling for students' attainment of truly high-level cognitive skills. If this data-gathering design is overused, students will soon realize that their future "posttest" will be the "pretest" taken by half of their classmates prior to instruction. As a consequence of this realization, some students will start finding out from classmates what they remembered about the "other pretest." However, for measuring students' mastery of a few genuinely significant curricular outcomes, especially when nonpartisan scorers have been employed to judge students' constructed responses, this data-gathering design can provide powerful evaluative data that will be seen as credible even when used as part of an external evaluation of a teacher's effectiveness.

What to Assess

Whether you use your students' assessment results yourself for the self-evaluation of your teaching or, in contrast, supply those results to others who will use such evidence for an external evaluation, you still have to decide what to assess. Think back, if you can remember that long ago, to Chapter 2's discussion of what to assess. Remember the key factor governing what you should assess in your classroom is always the educational decision(s) you need to make. For purposes of your self-evaluation, you'll have to think through for yourself what kinds of evidence you'll need in order to tinker with or to fundamentally overhaul your instructional activities. Surely you'll want to know how well your students have learned the most important things they were supposed to learn.

You should also seriously consider the assessment of students' *affect*. Affective assessment is of little utility for decisions about individual students because, as seen in Chapter 10, such measurement is too imprecise for defensible inferences about particular students. However, for judging the effectiveness of your instructional efforts, group-based inferences about students' pretest-to-posttest shifts in affect are useful. The split-and-switch design, incidentally, works wonderfully when affective data are being gathered because it minimizes pretest reactivity.

If a classroom teacher is stuck with a small class (tough luck!), so small that a split-and-switch design wouldn't work, then I recommend the straight-out pretest-posttest model with all its problems. You can still use blind-scoring of coded pretests and posttests after having mixed them together. And you can also round up one or more nonpartisan scorers. Such pretest-to-posttest evidence is surely way better than none.

In sum, students' performances on classroom assessments are clearly important when teachers evaluate themselves or when others evaluate teachers. Although there are several important sources of evidence to be used in appraising a teacher's instructional efforts, what happens to students as a consequence of instruction is, unarguably, the most significant source of evidence.

EVIDENCE FROM EXTERNAL ACCOUNTABILITY TESTS

"If we're going to evaluate teachers, why don't we simply do so by seeing what their students have learned—as shown by those students' scores on significant achievement tests?" This statement, or statements similar to it, can often be heard these days as part of an ever-rising chorus demanding that teachers be evaluated chiefly on the basis of their students' test scores. And the test scores referred to in these entreaties for test-determined teacher evaluation are, almost always, the scores earned by students on externally imposed, standardized accountability tests—not scores on teachers' home-grown classroom tests. This is because most proponents of such an approach to teacher evaluation fear that *teacher-made* classroom tests, if employed to evaluate teachers, will often be softened in a self-slanted manner so that many teachers will appear to be more effective than, in fact, they truly are.

Thus, in the last few years we have seen an enormous increase in the clamor for *test-based teacher evaluation* —that is, teacher appraisals in which the dominant (but not the only) determiner of a teacher's quality is the performance of a particular teacher's students on an externally imposed standardized achievement test. Typically, the tests selected for this purpose are the annual accountability tests that have been administered each year for well over a decade in all of our 50 states. Those state-level accountability tests were required by federal law, especially by recent reauthorizations of the Elementary and Secondary Education Act of 1965. To appraise the teachers in a particular state's schools, these annual accountability tests were often the only available standardized test that appeared to be up to this sort of evaluative task.

In the near future, as mentioned earlier, the anticipated availability of accountability exams generated by two multistate, federally funded consortia is likely to present an attractive alternative for advocates of test-based teacher evaluation. As those two sets of consortium-built assessments have become widely available, then the advocates of test-based teacher evaluation can point to another collection of carefully constructed educational assessments that can be used to measure students' achievement status.

It should be noted, however, that the assessments built by the Partnership for the Assessment of Readiness for College and Careers (PARCC) and Smarter Balanced Assessment Consortium (SBAC) will be focused on measuring students' mastery of the Common Core State Standards chiefly in mathematics and English/language arts (ELA). Many teachers, of course, are responsible for instruction not addressed by the consortium-built tests (for example, K–2 teachers as well as teachers of the arts, physical education, and various other subjects). Clearly, then, if test-based teacher evaluation is to become widespread in the United States, provisions must be made for supplying suitable measures of students taught by *all* teachers, not only teachers of math and ELA.

The demand for increasingly rigorous teacher evaluation has surely been spurred in part by dissatisfaction on the part of some observers with what they regard as a less than lustrous performance by our nation's public schools. More and more taxpayers are registering dismay with what they regard as the inadequate quality of America's tax-supported schools. This dissatisfaction has often morphed into a straightforward call for teachers to be more stringently appraised, and for the bulk of that appraisal to be determined by the performances of teachers' students on external accountability tests.

Two federal initiatives in 2009 (the Race to the Top Program) and 2011 (the ESEA Flexibility Program) functioned as powerful catalysts for states to overhaul their often dated teacher-evaluation systems. One of those programs, Race to the Top, provided substantial fiscal incentives for those states awarded federal grants from a program funded at $4.35 billion. The other program, the one focused on ESEA flexibility, permitted states to secure a waiver that exempted a state from satisfying certain conditions of the No Child Left Behind

Act (NCLB). The Race to the Top Program, therefore, employed a "carrot" while the ESEA Flexibility Program relied on a "stick." To qualify for *either* of these programs, a state's educational officials were required to install a teacher-evaluation system in which teachers must be evaluated using multiple sources of evidence. In that array of evidence, federal officials insisted that student growth must be "a significant factor." These federal initiatives—both of which emphasized summative teacher evaluation more heavily than formative teacher evaluation—have sparked what most observers regard as an unprecedented re-look at how the nation evaluates its teachers. Clearly, test-based teacher evaluation satisfies the requirement that student growth will be a significant consideration in the appraisal of teachers. Other evidence of a teacher's instructional quality can be appropriately included in a sensible teacher-appraisal program. For example, systematic classroom observations of a teacher in action, as well as students' anonymous ratings of teachers, can both make contributions to the accurate evaluation of a teacher's skill. I have treated this issue more extensively elsewhere (Popham, 2013).

Following is a four-point logic chain underlying the argument in favor of test-based teacher evaluation featuring external achievement tests:

- *Point 1.* Teachers should be evaluated carefully so that (a) effective teachers can be rewarded and (b) ineffective teachers can either be helped to improve or, if improvement does not transpire, fired.
- *Point 2.* In evaluating a teacher's success, the most important factor must be the depth, breadth, and quality of students' learning that takes place because of instruction provided by the teacher.
- *Point 3.* The depth, breadth, and quality of student learning will best be represented by students' performances on carefully created, externally determined, and properly administered achievement tests.
- *Point 4.* Therefore, the scores of a teacher's students on externally administered exams, such as a state's annual accountability tests, should be the dominant determiner of a particular teacher's evaluated success.

If the foregoing logic chain is to be implemented properly, however, a pivotal requirement is that the tests on which such a teacher-evaluation system is based must be unarguably suitable for this significant evaluative task. In other words, in order for Point 3 to be satisfied, the "carefully created, externally determined, and properly administered" tests must be capable of accurately differentiating between well-taught and badly taught students. When such exams are "carefully created," those who are developing the exams must do their best to make sure the exams can correctly detect the depth, breadth, and quality of student learning. This is easier to say than it is to do. What is imperative, if test-based teacher evaluation is going to work properly, is that the tests being used are sensitive to the *quality of instruction* provided by the particular teacher who is being evaluated.

Comparative Estimates of Progress: Student Growth Percentiles

In 2002, when the No Child Left Behind Act first frolicked into American educators' lives, we learned that our schools would soon be seen as unsuccessful unless ever-increasing proportions of students' annual test scores represented "adequate yearly progress" (AYP). The term *AYP* was defined as the percent of students—overall as well as for students in NCLB-designated subgroups—who were test-classified as "proficient" or "advanced."

But, because NCLB's minimum proportions of AYP proficient-and-above students were federally influenced, and those proportions became more and more stringent as time went by, many school leaders began to chaff under these required AYP minima. Such educators were dismayed because, although their students may have been displaying substantial improvements in how well they were learning, those increases might not be sufficient to push a school's students over the AYP-required proportions of students who needed to score at proficient or advanced levels on a state's annual accountability tests.

Accordingly, a widespread clamor from the field was heard for schools to be evaluated, at least in part, according to *how much growth* a school's students had displayed—even though this growth might not be enough to reach a given year's AYP targets. For the past several years, therefore, various approaches to the determination of a school's test-based growth have been introduced. Of these, the most widely accepted model has been the system devised by Betebenner (2007). Often referred to as the "Colorado Growth Model" for it was first used on a statewide basis in Colorado, Betebenner's approach has also been adopted by several other states. Because today's teachers are apt to encounter colleagues who approve or disapprove of such growth-focused approaches, a brief description of this increasingly popular model seems in order.

The Colorado Growth Model is predicated on a particular numerical quantity representing an individual student's comparative progress in one school year. This quantity, the heart of Betebenner's approach, is called a ***student growth percentile.***

Student growth percentiles are really straightforward to understand, and here's how they work. First off, students who scored at a given point on the *previous* end-of-school-year accountability test (Year 1) are identified. Let's say we're looking at students who earned a scale score of 214 when 300 scale-score points are available. Then, in the next year (Year 2), using those same students (Year 1's 214-scorers), we employ their Year 2 scores to compute how much gain (that is, growth) each student made from the first year to the second year. The amount of gain students make from Year 1 to Year 2, however, is *not* reported according to how many scale-score points those students advanced (or retreated) but, instead, is reported as a *student growth percentile.* On such a percentile scale, students at the 95th percentile have made as much growth as 95 percent of students in the state whose Year 1 scores were 214. Similarly, students at the 40th growth percentile have made as much growth as 40 percent of the state's students who had a Year 1 score of 214.

Student growth percentiles, however, are calculated for students with Year 1 scores at *all* points on the score scale. Thus, there is a set of student growth percentiles computed for students with a Year 1 score of 212, another set of student growth percentiles for students with Year 1 scores of 213, and so on—across all Year 1 scores at which students have scored in sufficient numbers to calculate student growth percentiles.

We can calculate a particular teacher's *average* student growth percentile (Betebenner recommends that we use the median, rather than the mean, as this average) based on the performances of that teacher's students on the Year 2 accountability test. But because a given teacher's students will have earned Year 1 scores all over the lot, we base a particular teacher's median student growth percentile on the complete collection of student growth percentiles earned by all the teacher's students. Similarly, such an amalgam median growth percentile could be calculated for all students in an entire school or for the students at a particular grade in that school. The interpretation most often made when a school's (or a teacher's) average student growth percentile is above the 50th percentile is that the school (or the teacher) promoted better than average growth among students. Conversely, an average student growth percentile below the 50th percentile would indicate that whatever growth had been promoted among students, it was below average.

Statistical adjustments can be made in this approach to compensate for the real-world problem that some teachers (and some schools) end up serving very high-achieving students who actually have little room to grow on tests. This is because they are already bumping up against a ceiling effect due to a test's limited difficulty. At the other end of the achievement spectrum, teachers (and schools) dealing with very low-achieving students are working with students who have much more room to grow—because they have scored so dismally on the previous year's tests. Thus, in a sense it may sometimes be "statistically easier" for teachers who instruct particularly low-achieving students to demonstrate that their students have grown during a school year.

If you've never encountered the concept of student growth percentiles, it may take you a bit of time to grasp how they work. Fortunately, these quantities are fairly easy to explain to parents and policymakers. As a way of representing how well a teacher's students perform in a given school year—relative to other students who entered the school year with comparable achievement levels—student growth percentiles, when abetted by an example or two, are intuitively comprehensible to most people.

To the degree that the architects of an accountability program wish to incorporate a legitimate representation of the degree to which students have grown in their mastery of what was to be learned, Betebenner's approach incorporating student growth percentiles is definitely worth considering.

Instructional Sensitivity

Children learn, thank goodness. But this learning takes place both inside a school and outside of it. Students learn at home from interactions with family members. Students learn at the park or at a shopping mall. Students learn from watching television programs, even reality shows. Students learn darn near everywhere. And aren't we happy that they do! But when we tie the evaluation of a teacher to students' performances on tests supposedly measuring what students *have learned in school,* we must be reasonably certain that the tests being employed do, in fact, measure what a particular teacher has taught those students. In other words, we need to make certain that any test used to evaluate a teacher's competence can accurately gauge students' mastery of what has been taught. We need, in fact, to ascertain the ***instructional sensitivity*** of a test. Here's what this concept, a remarkably important one when we set out to evaluate teachers or schools, involves:

> *Instructional sensitivity is the degree to which students' performances on a test accurately reflect the quality of instruction specifically provided to promote students' mastery of what is being assessed.*

Notice in the definition of instructional sensitivity that the focus is on *instructional quality*—that is, the caliber of instruction that's directed toward students' achievement of whatever is being measured by a test. An instructionally sensitive test, therefore, would be one that can accurately distinguish between effectively taught and ineffectively taught students. Instructional sensitivity of a test, however, is not an either/or variable. A test need not be *completely* insensitive or *completely* sensitive to instruction. Tests can vary in the degree to which, based on students' performances, they can properly distinguish between students who have been taught splendidly and those who have been taught shabbily.

The push for test-based teacher evaluation comes from a variety of quarters, but sometimes even the most ardent advocates of this evaluative strategy fail to recognize a potential problem with this approach—namely, that if the tests being used for such evaluations do *not* do a good job in distinguishing between successfully and unsuccessfully taught students, then test-based teacher evaluation simply can't work. To illustrate, suppose that a state's education officials have created brand new accountability tests for the specific purpose of evaluating teachers' skills. More specifically, the new tests are to be used so see how well individual teachers have done in promoting their students' mathematics and reading achievements. Further, suppose that the new tests were built by following fairly traditional test-construction practices, and that students' performances on the newly developed accountability tests turn out to be closely linked to the socioeconomic status (SES) of students' families. In other words, when the tests are administered, students from more affluent families almost invariably outperform students from less affluent families—*no matter how effectively those students have been taught.* In other words, SES-status invariably trumps teachers' skills because of the

SES-linked nature of the test. Given those circumstances, genuinely skilled teachers in schools serving low-SES kids would often be seen as ineffective (because of their students' weak performances on the new SES-linked accountability tests) while genuinely weak teachers in schools serving high-SES kids would be seen as effective (because of their students' strong performances on the new SES-linked accountability tests).

In such a fictitious scenario, inaccurate decisions would often be made about many teachers' skills, and the ultimate losers in such a situation would be the students themselves. Truly strong teachers might be bounced out of the profession, and truly weak teachers might be retained or even applauded. It is to prevent these sorts of errors, and their subsequent impact on students' educations, that any tests used in test-based teacher evaluation should be accompanied by compelling evidence they are, in truth, instructionally sensitive. (And, by the way, in many states during recent years this "fictitious scenario" is not fictitious at all.)

Determining Students' Progress: With Value-Added Models

As part of attempts to isolate the instructional success of particular teachers, or particular schools, considerable attention has been given to an approach known as a *value-added model (VAM)*. This approach represents a statistical strategy aimed at isolating the cause of students' progress—or lack of such progress. The VAM procedures employ students' prior achievement and/or background characteristics as statistical controls to help isolate the effects on student achievement of specific teachers, schools, or school districts. Relying on often exotic statistical gyrations, VAMs try to contrast the effects on students' test scores of (1) *school-unrelated variables* such as family or friends and (2) the *instructional impact* of a given school or teacher.

The very name given to this statistical strategy usually evokes a positive response from people who are interested in getting a fix on the effectiveness of teachers or schools. After all, when we refer to a "value-added" contribution to students' achievement, we typically think of increases in students' learning attributable to educators *above and beyond what might have taken place simply because students grew older*. Accordingly, the "value-added" label generates a fair amount of support—sometimes unthinking support—from educational policymakers and the public in general. Anything that is "value-added" sounds so darn good. But is this widespread support warranted?

The most widely known VAM is the Tennessee Value-Added Assessment System (TVAAS) devised by William Sanders. However, because the statistical machinery of TVAAS is proprietary, and unavailable to public scrutiny, many proponents of VAMs have sought to employ other VAM approaches. Basically, all of these procedures require data tracking students' academic growth across several years, usually in different subjects, to estimate the contributions that teachers have made to this growth.

Increasing numbers of technical reviewers of value-added procedures, however, have identified several serious methodological problems when such strategies are employed to identify teachers' contributions to students' achievement. To illustrate, a significant shortcoming with these approaches is that VAMs produce a statistically massaged *estimate* of a teacher's relative contribution to a particular student's learning. Making causal attributions for these estimates are most defensible when teachers are randomly assigned to classes and when students are randomly assigned to teachers. As we know, however, randomized assignment of teachers and students is rarely encountered in most school districts. Parents frequently influence the schools their children attend and, beyond that, parents often have a serious say in the teachers to which their children are assigned. The less random is the undergirding of VAM procedures, the less credible will be the causal inferences about teachers' impact that we can base on these approaches.

Moreover, students' academic progress is influenced by a substantial array of variables beyond a teacher's control—for instance, the physical condition of a school, the instructional resources at hand, the quality of a school's administrators, a district's instructional policies, and the degree of parental encouragement of their children's learning. Because these variables often vary systematically across a district's schools, they can substantially erode the accuracy of VAM conclusions.

Another serious shortcoming of most VAMs is that their use is frequently advocated *irrespective* of the suitability of the achievement tests to be used in the analysis. Earlier in this chapter, instructionally *insensitive* achievement tests were described. Such tests often contain numerous items linked closely to students' socioeconomic status (SES). These items tend to be answered correctly more often by students from affluent families than by students from impoverished families. Well, if the results of achievement tests being employed in a VAM are highly correlated with test-takers' SES, all the statistical high-jinks in the world will be unable to transform SES-governed test results into data that accurately gauge teachers' instructional effectiveness. Such tests may permit students' scores to be compared—as is the measurement mission of traditional achievement tests. But such tests—even when all their causality implications have been statistically squeezed out of them—can't tell us which teachers are effective.

A final shortcoming of value-added models is that it is nearly impossible to explain to normal human beings how VAMs work. The statistical operations associated with these value-added strategies are often so esoteric that their opacity defies description.

In a highly readable introduction to the topic of VAMs, Braun (2005, p. 4) concludes that "VAM results should *not* be used as the sole or principal basis for making consequential decisions about teachers." He argues that too many mistakes will be made when VAM approaches use the kinds of data typically available from school districts.

Value-added models, although enticingly labeled and enthusiastically touted by their devoteés, are regarded by most nonpartisans as inappropriate for evaluating the quality of educators' endeavors.

The Genesis of Instructional Insensitivity

How do educational achievement tests, especially those that are carefully developed by reputable test-development organizations, become instructionally insensitive? Is this some sort of plot, perpetrated by assessment agencies, to subvert the test-based evaluation of the nation's schools and teachers? No, there's no discernible malevolence on the part of those who crank out the standardized achievement tests we have historically used in our schools. Rather, the cause underlying today's instructionally insensitive tests flows from a traditional, long-standing manner in which U.S. psychometricians have viewed the tests they have built and polished.

The traditional mission of U.S. educational achievement tests, you see, has been to produce results leading to accurate score-based *comparisons* among test-takers. Indeed, almost a century of large-scale educational testing in the United States has revolved around the creation of comparative score-interpretations. And, giving credit where it is due, educational psychometricians have become darn good at providing such comparative score-interpretations. We can usually do a pretty decent job of determining that Millie's reading scores put her at the 84th percentile whereas Althea's reading scores are only at the 63rd percentile. Conceding that educational tests scores are not as precisely accurate as most people think, it is frequently useful to educators to find out how students compare to one another.

Much of the impetus for the generation of comparative score-interpretations can be traced back to World War I (not World War II) when the United States, having become involved in an unprecedented world conflict, found itself in need of a way to identify young men who would be successful in the Army's officer-training programs. Army officials approached the American Psychological Association (APA) for assistance in developing a suitable screening tool, and soon a committee of APA appointees met at Vineland Training School in Vineland, New Jersey, to develop the *Army Alpha,* a group-administrable intelligence test that presented verbal and quantitative problems to examinees in an effort to get a fix on new Army recruits' intellectual aptitudes. The *Alpha* was administered to about 1,750,000 Army recruits during World War I, and it was regarded as a major success because it allowed test-takers' to be *compared.* The highest-scoring recruits were placed in officer-training programs, and their success in those programs substantially exceeded the success rates of pre-*Alpha* placement efforts. The *Army Alpha* was most certainly an *aptitude test,* for its intent was to locate those Army recruits who had the most cognitive aptitude to succeed in the Army's officer-training programs. Interestingly, however, the comparative assessment strategy employed in the *Alpha's* aptitude test soon became the prototype for a range of educational assessments—not all of which were focused on the measurement of test-takers' aptitudes.

For example, as soon as World War I was over, several assessment firms in the United States began to create educational *achievement* tests using the psychometric approach embodied in the *Alpha.* To illustrate, the *Stanford Achievement Tests,* a widely used set of nationally standardized achievement tests that have been revised almost a dozen times, were first published in 1923, shortly after the close of World War I. And, although the Stanford Achievement Tests were *achievement* rather than *aptitude* tests, they nevertheless cleaved closely to the comparison-oriented mission of the *Army Alpha*. Indeed, for almost 100 years, the psychometric community in the United States has been committed to the creation of tests intended to yield comparative score-interpretations for test-takers.

One key tenet of assessments intended to yield comparative score-interpretations is that they produce sufficient *score-spread*—that is, differences among test-takers' total scores so that those scores can be meaningfully contrasted with scores earned by other test-takers. For example, other things being equal, for tests intended to provide comparative score-interpretations, it would be better to have a test's items answered correctly by roughly half of the test-takers than for items to be answered correctly by 100 percent of the test-takers or answered incorrectly by 100 percent of the test-takers. Items answered by all or none of those taking a test make no contribution whatsoever to creating the kind of score-spread that contributes to accurate, fine-grained comparisons of test-takers' scores.

Over the years, traditional psychometricians have frequently enhanced an educational test's score-spread by linking its items to socioeconomic status or to students' inherited academic aptitudes. Both SES and inherited academic aptitudes tend to be nicely spread out variables, and they're also variables that are not readily altered. Thus, if an item on an educational test can be linked to either SES or inherited academic aptitude, then this item is likely to produce the kind of score-spread that brings joy to a traditional psychometrician's heart. Let' look briefly at both of these kinds of items.

SES-Linked Items

A particularly troubling kind of item on standardized achievement tests chiefly assesses what students have learned outside of school. Unfortunately, you'll find more of these items on standardized achievement tests than you'd expect. If children come from affluent families, then those children are more apt to succeed on certain items contained in standardized achievement tests than will other children whose environments don't mesh as well with what the items measure. Hopefully, the item in Figure 15.3 will illustrate what's actually being assessed by a number of the items on standardized achievement tests.

This fourth-grade reading item asks students to tell from context what the meaning of a multiple-meaning word is. I have no problem with this as a skill children should acquire. But I have a big problem with the item itself.

Notice the fourth-grader's task is to figure out how the word *field* is being used in the item's item. And, of course, answer Option C is correct. But please recognize that parents who are physicians, attorneys, or journalists do, indeed, have a *field*. If a child's parents, however, work in a car wash or as a cashier in a convenience store, the child's parents will rarely, if ever, refer to their *field* of employment.

figure 15.3 ■ A Fourth-Grade Reading Item

> My uncle's *field* is computer programming.

■ Look at the sentences below. In which sentence does the word *field* mean the same as it does in the boxed sentence above?

   A. The softball pitcher knew how to *field* her position.

   B. They prepared the *field* by spraying and plowing it.

   C. I know the *field* I plan to enter when I finish college.

   D. The doctor used a wall chart to examine my *field* of vision.

Those parents have *jobs*. Clearly, kids from affluent families in which one or more parents are professionals will be more likely to do well on Figure 15.3's reading item than will kids whose parents are employed in menial jobs. This item is clearly linked to children's socioeconomic status.

Suppose you're a teacher at a school in which most students come from a genuinely low socioeconomic environment. How are your students likely to perform on a standardized achievement test if a substantial number of the test's items are linked to the affluence of your students' backgrounds? In other words, how will your students do if many of the test's items are SES-influenced? That's right, your students are not apt to earn very high scores. Does this mean your school's teachers are doing a poor instructional job? Of course not.

Conversely, let's imagine you're a teacher in an affluent school whose students tend to be the offspring of upper-class, well-educated parents. Each spring, your students' scores on standardized achievement tests are dazzlingly high. Does this mean your school's teachers are doing a superb instructional job? Of course not.

One of the chief reasons children's SES is so highly correlated with standardized test scores is that there are a number of items on standardized achievement tests really focused on assessing knowledge and skills learned outside of school. Most of such knowledge and skills are more likely to be learned in higher-level SES settings than in lower-level SES settings.

Again, you might ask, Why would developers of nationally standardized achievement tests place such items on their tests? As usual, the answer is consistent with the dominant measurement mission of those tests—namely, to spread out students' test scores so that accurate and fine-grained comparative (norm-referenced) interpretations can be made. Because there is substantial variation in children's socioeconomic strata, and this variation doesn't evaporate overnight, items reflecting such variation are efficient in producing the traditional psychometrician's much-cherished spread in test scores.

Items Linked to Inherited Academic Aptitudes

We turn now to another kind of item favored by traditional psychometricians in their quest for sufficient score-spread in their tests—that is, items linked to the *inherited* academic aptitudes of students. That's right, items hooked up to how lucky a student happened to be from birth.

I wish I believed all children were born with identical intellectual abilities, but I don't. Some kids were luckier at gene-pool time. Some children, from birth, will find it easier to mess around with mathematics than will others. If children came into the world having inherited identical academic aptitudes, teachers' pedagogical problems would be far more simple.

Current thinking among many leading educators suggests there are various forms of intelligence, not just one (Gardner, 1994). A child who is born with less aptitude for dealing with quantitative or verbal tasks, therefore, might possess greater "interpersonal" or "intrapersonal" intelligence, but these two abilities are not tested by conventional achievement tests. For the kinds of items most commonly found on nationally standardized achievement tests, children differ in their innate aptitudes, especially their verbal, quantitative, and spatial aptitudes. And some items on nationally standardized achievement tests are linked directly to such *inherited* academic aptitudes.

Consider, for example, the social studies item in Figure 15.4. This item attempts to measure a sixth-grader's ability to "figure out" what the right answer is. I don't think the item measures what's taught in school. The item—at least in part—measures what students come to school with, not what they learn there.

In Figure 15.4's item, look carefully at the four answer options. Read each option and see if it might be correct. A verbally advantaged student, I contend, can figure out that Choices A, B, and D really would not "conserve natural resources" particularly well; hence, Choice C turns out to be the winning option. Verbally adept kids will have a better time with this item than will their less verbal classmates.

figure15.4 ■ **Sixth-Grade Standardized Achievement Test Item in Social Studies**

■ If a person truly wants to conserve natural resources, one good way to do so is to:

A. leave the radio turned on even if no one is listening to it.

B. wash tiny loads instead of large loads in an automatic dishwashing machine.

C. write on both sides of a piece of paper.

D. discard used magazines in the trash.

You'll find many such "native smarts" items in any of today's nationally standardized achievement tests. The items I find particularly galling are the ones that measure a child's inborn spatial aptitude. To illustrate, one math item in a current fourth-grade standardized achievement test presents four letters to students (such as "F, L, R, and B"), then asks, Which letter, "when bent in half," will have two equal parts? The answer, in case you weren't born with adequate spatial aptitude, is the B. But what kind of a silly skill is involved in mental letter-bending? Yet, many standardized achievement tests contain items that tap the spatial-visualization aptitudes children have obviously inherited because of the gene-pool lottery.

But why, you might be thinking, do developers of nationally standardized tests include such items on their tests? The answer is really quite simple. Remember, these sorts of items, because they are based on nicely spread out innate academic aptitudes not readily modifiable in school, do a wonderful job in spreading out test takers' scores. The quest for score-spread, coupled with the limitation of having only a few items to use in assessing students, makes such items particularly appealing to those who construct traditional standardized achievement tests.

Yet, items that primarily measure differences in students' inborn academic verbal, quantitative, and spatial aptitudes obviously do not contribute to valid inferences about "how well children have been taught." Would we like all children to do well on such "inherited aptitudes" items? Of course we would. But to use such items to arrive at a judgment about a teacher's instructional effectiveness or a school's educational success is absurd.

PARENT TALK

Suppose you're a teacher in a large suburban high school whose students score consistently high on almost any kind of statewide or national test they're obliged to take. Indeed, anyone who knows much about your state's schools would be surprised if your school did not score among the top schools on any standardized achievement test. Nonetheless, at a recent Back-to-School Night, one of your students' parents, Mr. Carney, corners you with a barrage of questions about the meaning of these test results. He prefaces his questions with an indication he is pleased with his daughter's test scores, but then says, "Okay, I know our school serves super-affluent families, and I know students' test scores are always high, but I also know that there is some seriously shabby teaching going on here. When my daughter Wendy has her girlfriends come to our place for sleepovers, they level with Wendy's mom and me. They often tell us about really boring classes they have had to sit through. How can the school's test scores be so darn high, and yet have this sort of poor teaching take place?"

 If I were you, here's how I'd respond to Mr. Collins:

"Well, for openers, Mr. Carney, I'd have to say that I've definitely not heard reports of the sort of weak teaching Wendy's friends have described to you. I'm sure that in a school as large as ours, not all teachers are wonderful, but let's assume—just for the sake of discussion—that some less-than-lustrous teaching is going on in the school. What you want to know is how our school's high test scores can be produced by weak teaching.

"Here's how that sort of thing can happen. First off, you need to know that almost all standardized achievement tests are developed in a very traditional way. That is, those tests are intended to provide *comparative* interpretations of different test-takers' scores—so that the students can be compared with one another. To produce the range of different scores needed for such comparisons, many of the items on these tests are closely linked to students' socioeconomic status—in other words, their SES. As you probably know, SES is a variable that's well spread out, and really doesn't change very rapidly. Kids who come from more affluent families will tend to answer SES-linked items correctly, while kids from less affluent families will tend to miss those same items. This gives a school such as ours a tremendous edge when it comes to such tests. Our school's students are likely to score well on SES-linked items no matter how well or how badly they have been taught. That's just what happens.

"If there are many SES-linked items on a standardized achievement test, you can bet that our school's students will always shine. Personally, what I find myself worrying about is how the teachers who teach low-SES kids feel about this. I might have as easily been teaching students from disadvantaged backgrounds. Remember, Wendy attends a school where, to the outside world, teaching seems to be wonderful. But in a low-SES school, students' scores on SES-linked items are, with few exceptions, destined to be low. It's really not fair."

 Now, how would you respond to Wendy's father?

Avoidance of Instructionally Insensitive Items

It is easy to forget that most educational tests are nothing more than a collectivity of items to which students must respond. If the items are good, the test will be good; but if the items are bad, then the test itself will be similarly bad. So, when we are trying to create an instructionally sensitive accountability test, we must be inordinately attentive to the items themselves. If teachers have effectively taught students to master a curricular aim that's being measured by a collection of, say, 6 to 12 items, will the bulk of those items be answered correctly by the teacher's students? And what about a teacher whose instruction is focused on the same curricular aim, but produced a less-than-effective instructional effort? For those same 6 to 12 items, what we need to see is that most of the teachers' students come up with incorrect answers.

One way to discern how many instructionally insensitive items there are on an accountability test is to have a group of properly oriented reviewers—usually experienced teachers—consider each item on the test, one at a time, then respond to a review question such as the following:

> Attention reviewers: Please note the specific curricular aim which, according to the test's developers, this item is assessing, and only then answer this question: *If a teacher has provided reasonably effective instruction to promote students' mastery of the specific curricular aim being assessed, is it likely that the bulk of the teacher's students will answer this item correctly?* (Choose one: YES, NO, NOT SURE). ___

The nature of the orientation provided for any instructional-sensitivity reviewers should focus on the kinds of factors that might render an item instructionally insensitive. Reviewers must be completely conversant with such factors. For example, consider the following six qualities of an item that might cause the item to be instructionally insensitive:

1. *Alignment leniency.* If an item has been too leniently judged to be in alignment with the curricular aim it ostensibly assesses, that alignment is questionable. Teachers will be trying to get their students to master a specified curricular aim, but the test's items will be measuring something else.
2. *Excessive easiness.* If an item is so very easy that completely untaught students would answer it correctly, then the item is apt to be measuring students' achievement of something other than what the teacher was trying to teach.
3. *Excessive difficulty.* If an item is so very difficult that even marvelously taught students might not answer it correctly, then the item can't distinguish between well-taught and poorly taught students.
4. *Item flaws.* If an item has serious deficits such as ambiguities or garbled syntax, these flaws will prevent well-taught students from answering it correctly, thereby making it impossible for the item to accurately distinguish between well-taught and poorly taught students.

5. *Socioeconomic status links.* If an item gives a meaningful advantage to students from higher SES families, then the item will tend to measure what students bring to school rather than how well they are taught once they get there.

6. *Academic aptitude links.* If an item gives a meaningful advantage to students who possess greater inherited quantitative, verbal, or spatial aptitudes, then the item will tend to measure what students arrive with at school instead of how well they are taught.

By establishing item-review committees to scrutinize all under-development items, much as is currently done by bias-review committees, it would be possible to identify items that might be instructionally insensitive on the basis of one or more of the factors just listed. If, after further analysis, there is a reasonable chance that an item might be insensitive to the accurate detection of instructional quality, then it can be modified or jettisoned from the test before being used. Will we ever completely excise all instructionally insensitive items from our accountability tests? Probably not. However, we need to make sure that the proportion of instructionally insensitive items on any accountability tests—tests presumed to accurately measure the quality of educators' instructional efforts—will be small indeed.

In addition to the use of judgmentally based procedures for identifying instructionally insensitive items, empirically based procedures are also available for this purpose. By identifying two groups of "outlier" teachers who have, based on several years' worth of previous instruction, been identified as both extraordinarily successful and also extraordinarily unsuccessful in promoting students' growth, any unpredictable per-item performances by students taught by those two outlier groups can help spot items likely to be instructionally insensitive. Such empirical approaches to the detection of instructionally insensitive items, however, require very large samples of students as well as accessible test-score records for several years—and a heap of statistical hijinks. Those sorts of empirical studies of instructionally insensitive items, therefore, would need to be undertaken at the state level or by very large school districts.

WHAT'S A TEACHER TO DO?

Those who evaluate teachers need to make up their own minds about the degree to which students' test performances should figure in the appraisal of a teacher. In my opinion it is foolish for teachers to be evaluated without at least some consideration of the assessed display of students' learning. However, the *degree of emphasis* to be placed on students' test performances should be linked directly to the caliber of the tests being employed to provide such evidence. If an external accountability test, for instance, measures students' mastery of important skills and knowledge that have been approved by relevant policymakers (such as a state board of education), and the test is demonstrably sensitive to instruction, then I'd argue that the results of such a test should play a prominent role in the evaluation of teachers. If no evidence exists that the tests being employed to evaluate teachers are instructionally sensitive, then we should assume the tests are instructionally *insensitive,* and should therefore play a minimal, if any, role in the evaluation of teachers' effectiveness.

This assumption applies not only to the major, externally administered assessments that are used to appraise teachers and schools but also to teacher-made tests that, for teachers whose students are not tested by large-scale assessments, might be created by individual teachers or by groups of teachers. Putting it simply, if policymakers have mandated that students' test performances are to play a key role in the evaluation of teachers, then it may be necessary for teachers to rely on teacher-made tests to supply the needed assessment evidence. Yet, for test-based teacher evaluation to function properly, so evaluation errors are minimized, even teacher-made tests should be fashioned in such a way that they are as instructionally sensitive as possible.

Remember, although the assessments being touted for use in test-based teacher evaluation are almost invariably some form of "achievement test," do not succumb to the widespread misconception that what's measured by such achievement tests represents what's been taught in schools. It is certainly possible that achievement tests do, in fact, assess what students have been taught by their teachers. But it is also possible, especially if the tests have been built by measurement traditionalists, that the tests being employed actually measure what students have brought to school, not what they've learned once they arrive.

Even the staunchest advocates of test-based teacher evaluation typically recommend that factors other than students' test scores play a role in the appraisal of a teacher. For example, evidence based on observations of teachers' classroom activities, students' anonymous appraisals of their teachers, or administrative ratings frequently are mentioned as additional reasons to consider when appraising a teacher. But you're reading a textbook about classroom assessment, and whether the assessments administered in a classroom are teacher-generated instruments or externally created assessments, how much weight to give students' test performances should be heavily dependent on the energy expended in rendering the tests involved as instructionally sensitive as possible.

I recommend that you attempt to assess students' mastery of genuinely significant cognitive skills, such as their ability to write effective compositions, their ability to use lessons from history to make cogent analyses of current problems, and their ability to solve high-level mathematical problems. If the skills you choose (1) measure really important cognitive outcomes, (2) are seen by parents and policymakers to be genuinely significant, and (3) can be promoted instructionally by competent teachers, then the assembly of a set of pretest-to-posttest evidence showing substantial student growth in such skills can be truly persuasive. Earlier in this chapter you saw how a split-and-switch design (with blind-scoring of students' responses by nonpartisan raters) can be employed to collect compelling evidence of a teacher's instructional effectiveness. Use of pretest-to-posttest designs to gauge your own instructional success makes much more sense than succumbing to the senselessness of measuring your teaching prowess with the wrong kinds of tests.

Right Task, Wrong Tools

Teachers should definitely be held accountable. The teaching of a nation's children is too important to be left unmonitored. But to evaluate educational quality by using unsound assessment instruments is a subversion of good sense. Although teachers need to produce accurate evidence regarding their effectiveness, you've seen that instructionally insensitive accountability tests are the wrong tools for this important task.

When students' test performances are being used to evaluate schools or teachers, what's needed is *evidence* supporting the appropriateness of such an evaluative measurement mission. And this is why the 2014 AERA-APA-NCME standards presents—as the *overarching* standard for validity—a call for the clear explication of each of a test's intended uses as well as "appropriate validity evidence in support of each intended interpretation" (AERA *Standards*, 2014, p. 23). Evidence regarding the suitability of a test to perform an educational evaluation function must, of necessity, attest to the instructional sensitivity of that test.

If inappropriate standardized tests are chosen by a state's officials to satisfy the provisions of federal accountability laws, you can bet that a good many public schools are going to be labeled as failing when, in fact, they are doing a good instructional job. Equally disturbing, many schools will appear to be doing a stellar job based on their students' test scores, but those high scores are chiefly attributable to the composition of the advantaged students who make up such schools' student bodies. In contrast, instructionally *sensitive* accountability tests are the right kinds of assessments to use when evaluating schools. Teachers should, solo or in collaboration, use whatever influence they can so the proper kinds of accountability tests are used with their students.

WHAT DO CLASSROOM TEACHERS REALLY NEED TO KNOW ABOUT ASSESSMENT-BASED EVALUATION OF TEACHING?

You must realize that when you use students' test results as indicators of your own instructional prowess, a major determiner of how well your students perform will be the particular students with whom you're working. Even using a straightforward pretest-posttest evaluation approach doesn't circumvent the problem created because of the dissimilarity of different teachers' students. For purposes of teacher's self-evaluation, disparities in students' entry behaviors don't pose all that

But What Does This Have to Do with Teaching?

It is inconceivable that an entire profession would allow its members to be judged using the wrong measuring tools. Yet, in education, this is precisely what is going on. And some teachers, largely because they do not understand specifically why certain kinds of accountability tests ought not be used to evaluate schooling, compliantly accept this profound misuse of educational tests. Such teachers may have an intuitive idea that students' scores on some accountability tests don't provide a clear picture of instructional quality, but they can't tell you why.

If, as a teacher, you don't help people understand why it is that particular sorts of accountability tests should not be used to judge instructional effectiveness, then you probably deserve what you'll get—thoroughly inaccurate judgments about your skill. But you're not the only one who gets hurt because of this glaring miscarriage of measurement-based justice. Your students will get hurt too. And *that's* why you need to first understand the ins and outs of this important issue, then you need to let others know about the misuse of certain kinds of tests to judge educational quality.

Who are those "others" you need to acquaint with this issue? Well, start off with your colleagues. Few teachers or administrators really understand, at a meaningful level, why some accountability tests aren't the answer for judging schools. Then there are parents who need to understand. And, of course, there are educational policymakers. They definitely need to learn what constitutes solid evidence of instructional quality and what evidence ought never to be used.

In short, if you don't want your own teaching to be appraised using the wrong microscope, then outfit yourself in evangelical garb and start doing a bit of educative gospel-spreading!

much of a problem. However, for purposes of external teacher evaluation, particularly *summative* teacher evaluation, disparities in the abilities and motivation levels of different teachers' students should induce caution in the evaluative use of students' test results. Judgments about the caliber of growth attained by a given teacher must be made in the context of the instructional situation in which the teacher is functioning. A useful way of collecting evidence regarding a teacher's instructional effectiveness is the split-and-switch design.

Perhaps one of the most important understandings you should carry from this chapter is the recognition that certain kinds of accountability tests—instructionally insensitive ones—should not be employed to evaluate a teacher's instructional effectiveness. You need to understand *why* such tests are inappropriate for this purpose. And once you recognize why the evidence derived from the wrong kinds of accountability tests is unsuitable for the evaluation of a school staff's quality, then you should see that other evidence, more defensible and more credible, needs to be collected by educators. The public has a right to see how well their tax-supported schools are doing. The public doesn't have the right to do so by using the wrong evidence. It was suggested that *instructionally sensitive accountability tests in concert with teacher-made assessments* could provide accurate evidence of teachers' success.

CHAPTER SUMMARY

This chapter argued that the most defensible way to evaluate instruction, whether such evaluations are to be used for a teacher's self-evaluation or for external teacher evaluations, is to focus on the consequence of instruction—that is, the impact of instruction on students. Three sources of evaluative evidence were considered: (1) students' performances on classroom assessments, (2) students' performances on accountability tests, and (3) evidence regarding unanticipated effects of instruction. For the two test-elicited forms of evidence, it was stressed that the caliber of the tests themselves must be considered when deciding how much weight to give certain kinds of assessment evidence.

For the collection of classroom assessment evidence, two forms of a pretest-to-posttest data-gathering design were described: (1) a pretest–posttest design and (2) the split-and-switch design. Instructional sensitivity was described as the degree to which students' performances on a test accurately reflect the quality of instruction specifically provided to promote students' mastery of what is being assessed. When evaluating the quality of instruction, educators were urged to rely exclusively on instructionally sensitive tests. For the identification of unanticipated side effects of instruction, teachers were encouraged to be constantly attentive to the possibility of such unforeseen effects.

Educators were urged to learn more about both the appropriateness and the inappropriateness of certain kinds of evidence regarding instructional quality, then relay their conclusions to concerned constituencies.

Determining Your Outcome Mastery

This chapter took a hard look at how instruction ought to be evaluated and how instruction ought not to be evaluated. Two things to keep in mind were, first, an evaluation of instructional quality can be focused directly on the evaluation of a teacher *as an individual*. Such evaluations of specific teachers are seen increasingly in state-sanctioned or district-devised annual teacher evaluations. Second, teachers can be evaluated *as a collectivity* whenever the success of their school's instruction is evaluated. Annual schoolwide evaluations, for example, are often seen these days in response to federal regulations calling for the annual evaluation of a state's public schools. In both teacher evaluations and school evaluations, evidence of students' learning can make a major contribution to the evaluations that are ultimately made.

The breadth of the discussion of instructional evaluation in Chapter 15 is reflected in its chief intended learning outcome:

an understanding of the potential contributions and limitations of test-elicited evidence of instructional quality sufficient for the identification of likely shortcomings in such evidence or in its use for the evaluation of schools or teachers

To assess your mastery of the outcome, complete both the Selected-Response and the Constructed-Response quizzes and think about the feedback you receive for each quiz.

MyEdLab *Selected-Response Check of Outcome Mastery*

MyEdLab *Constructed-Response Check of Outcome Mastery*

After completing both quizzes, go to the Learning Outcome Mastery Determination, where you will decide whether you've mastered the chapter's learning outcome or whether you need further study.

MyEdLab *Learning Outcome Mastery Determination*

References

American Educational Research Association. (2014). *Standards for educational and psychological testing.* Washington, DC: Author.

Betebenner, D. W. (2007). *A primer on student growth percentiles.* Dover, NH: National Center for the Improvement of Educational Assessment.

Braun, H. I. (2005). *Using student progress to evaluate teachers: A primer on value-added models.* Princeton, NJ: Educational Testing Service.

D'Agostino, J. V., Welsh, M. E., and Corson, N. M. (2007). "Instructional sensitivity of a state's standards-based assessment." *Educational Assessment, 12,* no. 1: 1–22.

Gardner, H. (1994). "Multiple intelligences: The theory in practice." *Teacher's College Record, 95,* no. 4: 576–583.

Grossman, P., Cohen, J., Ronfeldt, M., and Brown, L. (2014). "The test matters: The relationship between classroom observation scores and teacher value added on multiple types of assessment," *Educational Researcher, 43,* no. 6 (August/September): 293–303.

Jennings, J. L., and Bearak, J. M. (2014). "'Teaching to the test' in the NCLB era: How test predictability affects our understanding of student performance," *Educational Researcher, 43,* no. 8 (November): 381–389.

Jones, N. D., Buzick, H. M., and Turkan, S. (2013). "Including students with disabilities and English learners in measures of educator effectiveness," *Educational Researcher, 42,* no. 4 (May): 234–241.

Marzano, R. J. (2013). "How to show student learning," *Educational Leadership, 71,* no. 2 (October): 82–83.

Master, B. (2014). "Staffing for success: Linking teacher evaluation and school personnel management in practice," *Educational Evaluation and Policy Analysis, 36,* no. 2 (June): 207–227.

Nichols, S. L., and Berliner, D. C. (2008). "Why has high-stakes testing so easily slipped into contemporary American life?" Phi Delta Kappan, 89, no. 9 (May): 672–676.

Popham, W. J. (2009). *Unlearned lessons: Six stumbling blocks to our schools' success.* Cambridge, MA: Harvard Education Press.

Popham, W. J. (2010). *Everything school leaders need to know about assessment.* Thousand Oaks, CA: Corwin.

Popham, W. J. (2013). *Evaluating America's teachers: Mission possible?* Thousand Oaks, CA: Corwin.

Popham, W. J. (2013). "Tough teacher evaluation and formative assessment: Oil and water?" *Voices from the Middle, 21,* no. 2 (December): 10–14.

Popham, W. J., and DeSander, M. (2014). "Will the courts save teachers?" *Educational Leadership, 71,* no. 5 (February): 55–59.

Popham, W. J. (2014). "The right test for the wrong reason," *Phi Delta Kappan, 96,* no. 1 (September): 46–52.

16

Assessment-Based Grading

CHIEF CHAPTER OUTCOME

A sufficient familiarity with goal-attainment grading to be able not only to describe its key steps, but also to identify when teachers are or are not employing goal-attainment practices in their grading determinations

Teachers give grades. One supposes when the original blueprints for "teacher" were drawn, there must have been a mandatory grade-giving component included somewhere. Other than tradition, however, why is it that teachers dispense grades to students so regularly?

The answer's fairly simple. A teacher needs to let students know (1) how well they're doing, as when a teacher assigns interim grades on various assignments during the course of the school year; and (2) how well they've done, as when a teacher dishes out end-of-year grades. For teachers to find out how well they've *taught*, as we saw in the previous chapter, the level of students' achievement must be determined. For students to find out how well they've *learned*, the extent of their achievement must also be determined.

Although, as you'll soon see, there are a number of factors teachers sometimes consider when grading students—other than simply how well those students performed on classroom assessments—there's little argument that a *major* consideration in the grade a student receives should be the quality of the student's assessment performances. In this final chapter, we'll be looking at different ways those assessment results can be incorporated into students' grades.

THE PURPOSE OF GRADING

How teachers grade their students stems chiefly from what those teachers believe the purpose (or purposes) of grading should be. I know, as a beginning high school teacher, my understanding of the potential purposes of grading was almost nonexistent. Oh, sure, I knew that good grades should be given to students who performed well on my tests, and that students who performed poorly on those tests should end up with low grades. After all, teachers who—as students themselves—have gone through years of schooling surely recognize that students' test performances and students' grades are closely linked. But is that all there is to it? In truth, when I began teaching, I simply had not devoted any thought, *any at all,* to how I was going to grade my students. In retrospect, I'm certain I made a number of bone-headed grading mistakes as a tyro teacher.

The mission of this final chapter in *Classroom Assessment* is to encourage you to give some serious think-time to the topic of grading. In almost every school setting, teachers will need to grade their students. And although teachers will probably never acquire a precise, zero-errors grading strategy, teachers can at least come up with a defensible way of thinking about this important task. Such defensibility begins by a teacher's understanding the purpose of grading.

Susan Brookhart (2009), who writes often and well about grading, contends that the primary purpose for grading, whether for individual assignments or report cards, should be to communicate with students and parents about students' achievement of curricular aims. At first glance, this sensible statement might appear to be little more than the sort of educational platitude teachers routinely encounter. It isn't. Indeed, if you agree with what Brookhart thinks the purpose of grading should be—namely, *communicating information to both students and their parents about students' goal attainment*—then this stance will profoundly influence how you grade your own students.

Brookhart's conception of grading identifies not only *who* are the targets of the information that's being communicated (in this instance, students and parents) but also *what* is being communicated (in this instance, students' goal-attainment status). You'll find most educators agree that the target audiences of grading should be students and their parents. Where more disagreement bubbles up, however, is with what's being communicated to those audiences. Brookhart's exclusive focus is on *goal attainment.* But some educators want grades to communicate not only students' goal attainment but also to incorporate evaluations of students' effort, attendance, attitudes, classroom behavior, and so on. Clearly, if teachers are grading students only on the basis of students' goal attainment, those teachers will arrive at substantially different grades than will teachers who try to incorporate such factors in their grading as students' attitudes and effort.

As Brookhart (2009, p. 4) points out, "In a perfect world, there would be no need for the kinds of grades we use in school today." She would prefer replacing grades on individual assignments with discussions about strengths and weaknesses—based on a student's progress toward goal attainment—and these discussions would take place among students themselves as well as between the student and the teacher. The focus would be on how to improve. There would be no "failures" because students would continue with additional tasks and assignments until a curricular aim had been achieved. All performances would be seen as capable of being improved. As she points out, however, "The demands of schooling as we know it have kept us from reaching that utopia" (p. 4). Yet, even in such a utopian educational world, the focus of all these improvement-oriented evaluative discussions among teachers and students would revolve around the level of students' goal attainment. Thus, whether you are a seasoned teacher or a teacher-in-training, an early decision you must make is precisely *what it is* that you want to be communicating to your students and to their parents.

Okay, what about teachers giving grades—at least in part—on the basis of their students' effort, attitudes, levels of class participation, behavior, attendance, tardiness, and punctuality in assignment submission? Should factors such as these have *any* role in the awarding of grades? Well, Ken O'Connor thinks not.

O'Connor is another colleague who has devoted much of his career to helping teachers decide how best to award grades to their students. "For grades to have real meaning," wrote O'Connor, "they must be relatively pure measures of each student's achievement of the learning goals" (O'Connor, 2009, p. 90). He, too, advocates that teachers relate their grading procedures to learning goals. In fact, he recommends that when officially sanctioned content standards exist, as is true now in almost all jurisdictions, students' achievement of those standards should be the *only* determiner of students' grades. O'Connor would definitely supply students and their parents with information about such factors as class participation or punctuality in assignment submission, but this would be done separately. (We'll look at techniques for doing so later in the chapter.)

I must confess that the laser-like focus on using students' attainment of curricular aims as an exclusive grading criterion, the stance taken by both O'Connor and Brookhart, was surely not the way I approached grading when I was a neophyte teacher. I sometimes gave higher than deserved grades to certain underachieving students as a way I thought might jolt them into an "I can do it" mood. I also graded some students according to what I believed were the levels of effort they were giving to their studies. I graded hard-working, albeit low-performing, students generously, while also grading lazy, yet high-performing, students harshly. I also used the lure of high grades as a motivation ploy—that is, as a way of getting students to study harder. In hindsight, my grading practices would have earned condemnation from my friends Sue Brookhart and Ken O'Connor. They would have been right. My grading practices were an ill-conceived mess.

When I became a college professor, merely because students' achievement seemed to be the only thing my fellow professors deemed worth grading, I nestled into a comfortable, achievement-dominated approach to grading. But this professorial grading stance was not dictated by careful thought on my part. Rather, it was a knee-jerk acceptance of my peers' expectations.

So, with the hope that my now-confessed grading sins will ultimately be forgiven, I want to go on record as saying the central grading position taken by O'Connor, Brookhart, and those who share their views, is one I recommend to you with enthusiasm. I now believe that truly defensible grading requires the teacher to make students' achievement of clearly understood curricular aims the solitary consideration in determining the grades to be communicated to students and parents. For report-card grading, this typically means the teacher will be relying on assessment-based evidence concerning students' status regarding the curricular aims themselves. For assignment grading, or for grading en route assessments, the teacher must decide on the contribution those assignments and en route assessments will make to students' mastery of the target curricular aims. Certain en route tests, for example, may deal with knowledge or subskills deemed more significant to students' mastering the target curricular aims than will other en route tests. The more significant tests (or assignments) would obviously carry more grading weight than would the less significant ones.

I realize that all curricular aims are not created equal. Many teachers simultaneously promote their students' attainment of several curricular aims, and some curricular aims are more important than others. It is perfectly acceptable, therefore, for a teacher to assign more significance to some curricular aims than to others. If teachers try to make their grading decisions transparent rather than cloud-cloaked, a teacher can announce in advance which curricular aims, if any, are regarded as more significant than others. The same sort of thinking would apply to the assignment of grades for en route tests or for grades given to students' assignments. Those aimed at more important curricular aims would be assigned more grade-determining import than would those aimed at less significant curricular aims.

To review, then, when arriving at a sensible stance regarding grading, teachers must first make up their minds about what the fundamental purpose of grading is. I have suggested teachers adopt a position that grading should be regarded as a communication activity aimed at students and their parents, and that this activity should be based exclusively on a student's status with respect to the mastery of curricular aims. I understand that, in many settings, a teacher has little choice about which curricular aims should be regarded as important—because governmental agencies will have already made those curricular decisions. Thus, in those settings, teachers will characteristically endorse students' attainment of officially sanctioned curricular aims. Accordingly, what's communicated to students and parents will be a student's status regarding each of these official curricular aims. In sum, I recommend without reservation that you adopt a grading strategy based only on students' goal attainment.

How Does Goal-Attainment Grading Take Place?

Let's assume that you see a mite of merit in the idea of linking students' grades to their progress in mastering curricular aims. How, precisely, would a teacher go about using this approach? Let's take a look at a few nuts-and-bolts of such a goal-attainment grading strategy.

I am presuming that teachers will want their grading approaches to be as transparent as is practical. I know that some teachers might prefer to keep grading a mysterious enterprise. Most such teachers, of course, are reluctant to bring their grading practices into the sunlight chiefly out of fears that those practices would be found wanting. This is all too understandable. My early grading practices were so deplorable that the only way I could have defended them was by hiring well-armed mercenaries. But if teachers accept the view that the grading of students is a less than completely scientific enterprise, and mistakes will inevitably be made, then letting the world know what went into the teacher's grading decisions seems so much more responsible than trying to camouflage what transpired while grades were being determined.

Step 1: Clarifying curricular aims. The first step in any grade-giving approach that's wedded to students' attainment of curricular aims is to make certain all participants in the grading game understand the nature of the curricular aims involved. What this means, in practice, is that teachers must provide *understandable* renditions of all curricular aims to those involved—specifically, to students and parents. Sometimes those understandable versions of curricular aims will employ identical language for both students and parents. In most instances, after students have entered middle school, any statements of curricular aims thought suitable for students will probably also be suitable for their parents. But for younger children, especially those in primary grades, separate "kid-friendly" versions of curricular aims are usually needed in addition to the descriptions of curricular aims provided for parents.

These statements of curricular aims are often more readily understood when accompanied by illustrative test items. It helps both students and parents to see sample items that might be used to assess a student's mastery of a particular curricular aim. Care must be taken, however, to indicate that these sample items do not exhaust the assessment techniques that might be employed to measure students' mastery. The accompanying items should be identified as "illustrative, but not exhaustive" examples of how students might be asked to display mastery of a particular curricular aim. We want our students to master a curricular aim so they possess a truly generalizable mastery of this aim, not merely one way of displaying such mastery. Genuine mastery of a curricular aim signifies that a student can display this mastery in a variety of ways, not only one or two.

To truly understand the nature of a curricular aim, it is often necessary for us to know the nature of the criteria by which a student's mastery of the aim will be determined. Such criteria are the factors to be used in determining the student's level of aim mastery. For instance, when judging the quality of a student's ability to write expository essays, the scoring guide/rubric that's employed for this purpose might isolate judgmental criteria such as the quality of an essay's (1) organization, (2) content, and (3) avoidance of mistakes involving the mechanics of writing. When the absence of such criteria would appreciably reduce someone's understanding of what mastery of a curricular aim really means, then the teacher must identify and, if necessary, explain what those criteria are.

For both the improvement of instruction as well as for the clarification of a grading process, it is almost always helpful to supply students with examples of acceptable and unacceptable responses to assessments or to assignments. When students are just starting to learn about something, for example, when they're just beginning to acquire mastery of a sophisticated new skill, it typically makes sense to provide exemplars at the extreme ends of the quality continuum. For example, once more using our expository-essay example, a teacher could pass out a truly terrific expository essay as well as one that was sublimely shabby. Ideally, both examples would be actual responses made by previous students. Later, when students become more conversant with the nature of the curricular aim being sought, exemplars exhibiting more fine-grained differences in quality could be distributed. The idea here, of course, is to help students understand what is being sought and how students' mastery of it will be appraised.

Step 2: Choosing goal-attainment evidence.   After identifying and describing the curricular aims (goals) on which grades are to be based, the teacher then decides on the *evidence* that will be used to help arrive at a determination of the student's progress toward mastery of each curricular aim being sought. It is altogether appropriate to let parents, as well as students, know what's coming in the way of evidence-eliciting assessment approaches. Well-described goals communicate effectively to students and parents. Well-described goals along with well-described assessments communicate *really* effectively to students and parents.

Most of today's teachers, when they were students themselves, saw their teachers typically rely on important exams to assign grades. To illustrate, a final-exam grade counted more toward an end-of-course grade than did a midterm exam or weekly quizzes. The final exam was, in other words, the test that made the most difference in the grade a student received. It is the assumption in such instances, and this is often a warranted assumption, that the more significant the exam, the more influential should be its contribution to a teacher's judgment about a student's mastery of curricular aims. In many instances, this may be true. But sometimes it isn't.

Step 3: Weighting goal-attainment evidence.   The third step in goal-attainment grading calls for the teacher to judge whatever assessment evidence is available regarding students' goal-attainment status. Here's what's typically going on when a teacher arrives at a judgment about a student's mastery of a specific curricular aim. First off, the teacher decides what evidence might be germane to a "goal-mastery" decision. Perhaps there are two homework assignments the teacher's students were obliged to complete, as well as one classroom quiz, and also about 40 percent of the items on the midterm exam. Well, when the teacher looks at those four chunks of evidence, it is up to the teacher to decide which evidence will best support an interpretation about a student's mastery of this particular aim. It may well be that the two homework assignments actually give the teacher a better idea about the student's mastery-status than the evidence provided by either the classroom quiz or the items on the midterm exam. What the teacher must do, then, is decide how much weight to give each source of evidence, and be prepared to let any concerned individuals know about the nature of those weighting decisions. Again, transparency is the motive here. If grades are to be awarded on the basis of the degree to which a student has mastered a curricular aim, then a teacher should make clear (1) the evidence being relied on when the teacher makes those mastery-inferences and (2) the teacher's judged importance of this evidence.

In earlier editions of this book, I advocated assigning more grading weight on the basis of the type of assessment involved, with final exams and midterm exams trumping en route quizzes and homework assignments. I hope I was assuming that those exams would supply the most useful evidence in helping teachers arrive at inferences about students' goal attainment. But, for the record, if you have adopted the grading posture recommended so far in this chapter, it may well be that your most significant evidence in support of an inference about students' goal attainment might come from "lesser" exams. All you need to do is decide how much significance to assign to different sources of evidence, and then let the world know—preferably in advance—what your weighting decisions were.

Step 4: Arriving at a final goal-attainment grade.   Let's assume there are several curricular aims being pursued, and there are several sources of assessment-evidence at hand related to each of those aims. This is when the teacher focuses on the overall status of a student with regard to the attainment of the complete array of goals. More-important goals will count more than less-important goals. More-significant assessment evidence of goal attainment will be counted more heavily than will less-significant assessment evidence of goal attainment. Clearly, arriving at a reasonably coalesced conclusion with so many things to keep track of is not a task for the dull-witted. But, in the final analysis, that's what grading boils down to. And, at least with the overriding grading consideration being a student's attainment of goals, a teacher is at least playing an understandable grade-giving game.

Elementary school teachers, of course, often are concerned about grading considerations of less interest to teachers in middle schools or high schools. For instance, first-grade teachers may think a significant *educational* aim in their classrooms is to have children develop self-control in a social setting. For example, a 7-year-old boy who pounds on male or female classmates during recess would not be behaving in an appropriate manner, nor would a 7-year-old girl who pounds on male or female classmates during recess. (A teacher afflicted with many such students might consider establishing a "cooperative pounding group.")

As students become older, a teacher's grading scheme might be based on typical academic criteria. Teachers who work with younger children will often need to describe—and weigh—a much more developmentally appropriate set of factors. The essentials of such teachers' grading practices are identical to the approach used in later grades. But elementary teachers need to think through what they regard as relevant curricular aims, describe them, then weigh their contribution to a child's grade.

GRADE-GIVING SPECIFICS

When teachers award grades, there are several options available to them. For final, end-of-term or end-of-year grades, it is necessary to adhere to whatever grade-descriptor system has been adopted by the district. Thus, if the district's policy is to use grades of A, B, C, D, or F, then the district's teachers must use those grades even if, during the course of the year, the teachers employed a different grade-descriptor scheme in class. Although many school districts, or schools within those districts, have grading policies that are quite general, some grading policies are particularly restrictive—setting forth specific limits on the percentages of particular grades that can be awarded by teachers.

Generally speaking, there are three major options available to teachers when they describe how well a student has performed. Teachers can use (1) letter grades, (2) numerical grades, or (3) verbal descriptors. Most of us are familiar with *letter grades* because such grades have been widely used for a long, long time. A grade of A is yummy and a grade of F is crummy. In some districts, teachers are also allowed to add pluses or minuses to letter grades, thus transforming a grading scale that has 5 points (A, B, C, D, or F) to one with 15 points. We can assume that a grade of F– reflects genuinely abysmal rock-bottom performance. A *numerical grading system* is usually organized around some chosen number of points such as 100, 50, or 10. Students are then given a number of points on each classroom assessment so that when students see their grade for the assessment, they realize they have earned, for example, "7 points out of a possible 10." *Verbal descriptors* are used instead of numerical or letter grades when teachers rely exclusively on phrases such as "excellent," "satisfactory," and "needs improvement." The number of such phrases used—that is, the number of possible verbal-descriptor grades that might be employed—is up to the teacher. If verbal-descriptor grades are used throughout an entire district, the choice of verbal descriptors is typically determined by district officials.

One increasingly common form of a verbal-descriptor grade is the *achievement-level* classification system used to describe performance on the National Assessment of Educational Progress (NAEP). When NAEP tests are administered, students' performances are classified as Advanced, Proficient, Basic, or Below Basic. (Although "Below Basic" is not an official NAEP-designated reporting category, it is typically employed so that students' totals add up to 100 percent!) This four-category achievement-level classification model has become widely used across the United States. Because the NCLB Act called for states to use at least three of these descriptive labels (that is, *Basic, Proficient,* and *Advanced*), many states simply adopted the NAEP four-category model. Thus, the use of the NAEP achievement-level labels is clearly a prominent variation of verbal-descriptor grades used in the United States. A number of districts have tried to devise *standards-based report cards* wherein the quality of each student's mastery of each content standard (curricular aim) is described. In many instances, the level of detail being used in such reporting systems has proven overwhelming to students, their parents, and more than a few teachers.

These standards-based report cards, a fundamentally sensible approach—especially given the increasingly widespread advocacy of basing grades dominantly on the basis of students' attainment of curricular aims (content standards)—is dependent on the *artistry* of those who crafted the content standards in the first place. If the grain-size (breadth) of the content standards is too small, then teachers end up being obliged to evaluate students' status with respect to an often overwhelming litany of such standards. The teachers might know what each content standard means, but there are simply too darn many of them! As a result, teachers tend to give less than careful attention to the whole array of standards, and both students and their parents become overwhelmed. In contrast, if the grain-size of the standards is too large, then what the content standards truly mean sometimes vanishes into too-general verbiage. That's why it truly takes verbal artistry for those who craft standards-based report cards to arrive at versions that make those report cards educationally useful. I have seen many examples of standards-based report cards, all of them well-intentioned. I have seen few examples of standards-based report cards I regarded as educationally useful.

The only sensible way to wrestle with the grain-size dilemma when relying on standards-based report cards is to *prioritize, prioritize,* and, for good measure, *prioritize*. If standards-based report cards can be structured around a manageable number of understandable curricular aims, then the standards set forth in such report cards can be crafted at a suitable grain-size so this grading strategy pays off for both teachers and students. If grading is seen as a way of communicating about a student's level of goal attainment, then it is difficult to conceive of an approach to report-card grading that is not chiefly dependent on the quality of the content standards involved.

In contrast to more traditional letter grades, or even some of the alternative grading descriptors considered earlier, teachers should recall the dividends of *descriptive feedback* presented in Chapter 12's treatment of formative assessment. Descriptive feedback is rooted in a three-step operation in which the teacher lets the student know (1) what the curricular aim is—or what the building blocks are leading to master of the aim, (2) where the student is in relation to that aim's attainment, and (3) what the student should do to reduce the gap between the student's current status and desired status. Insofar as possible, teachers should try not to dispense grades that have few implications for students' learning. Instead, teachers should replace those grades with descriptive feedback whose function is to guide students toward the achievement of the curricular aims which, if the teacher adopts a goal-attainment approach to grading, will ultimately determine the student's grade.

Evaluative Options

Let's look at three common grade-giving approaches. Each of these approaches can be used not only for end-of-term or end-of-year grades but also for grading the classroom assessment performances and assignments of students during the school year. In other words, these grading approaches can be applied whether you are assigning Johnny an end-of-term grade in your science class or grading his two-week experiment dealing with "Psychological Depression in Earthworms."

You're probably already familiar with the three grading approaches to be described because, when you were a student, you most likely encountered them all:

- *Absolute grading.* When grading *absolutely,* a grade is given based on a teacher's idea of what level of student performances is truly necessary to earn—for instance, an A. Thus, if an English teacher has established an

"Mr. Rath really does dispense his final grades with a flourish."

absolute level of proficiency needed for an A grade, and in a given class no student performs at the A-level of proficiency, then no student will get an A. Conversely, if the teacher's absolute grading standards were such that all students had performed beyond the A-level requirements, then the teacher would shower these students with A grades. An absolute system of grading has much in common with a criterion-referenced approach to assessment. If the teacher has adopted a goals-attainment approach to grading, then an absolute implementation of this strategy would revolve around a teacher's judgment about the levels of goal attainment needed for all to-be-awarded grades.

The major argument in favor of an absolute approach to grading is that there are, indeed, legitimate levels of expectation for students that, although judgmentally devised by teachers, must be satisfied in order for specific grades to be awarded. And, of course, it is always the case that people form their absolute expectations based on seeing how folks usually perform. Thus, there's a sense in which *absolutes flow from relatives.*

■ *Relative grading.* When teachers grade *relatively,* a grade is given based on how students perform in relation to one another. Thus, for any group of students, there will always be the *best* and the *worst* performances. Those students who outperform their classmates will get high grades irrespective of the absolute caliber of the students' performances. Conversely, because some students will always score relatively worse than their classmates, such low scorers will receive low grades no matter what. This system of grading is somewhat analogous to a norm-referenced approach to assessment.

As noted earlier, there is a sense in which even a teacher's *absolute* expectations regarding the level of performance needed to achieve an A, B, C, D, or F are derived from years of working with students and discerning how well similar students are usually capable of performing. But a relative grading system uses the students *in a given class* as the normative group, and does not take into consideration all the students whom the teacher has taught in the past.

The chief argument in favor of a relative system of grading is that because the quality of the teacher's instructional efforts may vary, and the composition of a given group of students may vary, some type of class-specific grading is warranted. Teachers who use a relative-grading approach tend to appreciate its flexibility because their grading expectations change from class to class.

■ *Aptitude-based grading.* When grading on *aptitude,* a grade is given to each student based on how well the student performs in relation to that student's academic potential. To illustrate, if a particularly bright student outperformed all other students in the class, but still performed well below what the teacher believed the student was capable of, the student might be given a B, not an A. In order to grade on aptitude, of course, the teacher needs to have an idea of what students' academic potentials really are. To estimate each student's academic aptitude, teachers either need to rely on the student's prior performance on some sort of academic aptitude test or, instead, must form their own judgments about the student's academic potential. Because academic aptitude tests are being administered less frequently these days, in order to use an aptitude-based grading approach, teachers will generally need to arrive at their own estimate of a student's potential.

The main argument in favor of aptitude-based grading is it tends to "level the playing field" by grading students according to their innate gifts and, thereby, encourages students to fulfill their potential. A problem with this grading approach, as you might guess, is the difficulty of deciding on just what each student's academic potential really is.

As indicated earlier, any of these three grading approaches can be used to assign grades for individual efforts of students, such as their performances on a short essay examination, or for arriving at a student's total-year grade. For instance, thinking back to Chapter 9's treatment of portfolio assessment, it would be possible to use any of the three grading approaches in order to arrive at students' portfolio grades—grades dispensed in letter, numerical, or verbal form.

What about Effort?

Students' effort is, educationally, so profoundly important. If a teacher can engender in students the inclination to expend effort in their school and nonschool endeavors, those students will be well served in the future. Students who believe the level of their effort will make the most difference in their success will be students who are more likely to succeed than will their classmates who rely on luck or on inherited smarts to carry them through life.

Okay, if students' effort is so significant, why shouldn't we take it into consideration when we grade students? In other words, why shouldn't we give higher grades to kids who put out the effort—regardless of their assessed levels of achievement? Regrettably, as Wormeli (2006) points out, "We don't have a commonly accepted, legally justifiable, non-subjective method for measuring how hard or sincerely someone is working" (p. 108). This single sentence, sadly, torpedoes any hope of a worthwhile "effort-grading" approach. Even if, as a teacher, you would desperately like to incorporate effort into your grading approach, *you can't get an accurate fix on your students' effort levels*. Although you might identify anecdotal evidence that seemingly tells you how hard a student is trying, such evidence can be misinterpreted. And such evidence *is* misinterpreted—way too often. We simply don't have an effort-determining measuring stick on which we can rely.

DECISION TIME

Should Level-of-Effort Be Rewarded?

Karl Kramer teaches second-graders at Twelfth Street Elementary School. He's been doing so for 6 years. During the past year, however, Karl has seriously been reconsidering his whole approach to grading. This reconsideration was stimulated by three students who in the past would have been placed in some form of special needs program, but now have been included in Karl's second-grade class.

Although the three students, Marie, Floyd, and James, are having difficulty with much of the content treated in class, all three are obviously trying hard to succeed. In fact, if Karl were to grade on effort alone, the three students would probably get the highest grades in class.

In the past, Karl has given no credit for student effort when grades were awarded. Now, however, he finds that he's rethinking that decision.

 If you were Karl, what would you do?

Let's suppose a teacher (we'll call him Elmer) cares so much about incorporating effort into students' grades, he goes totally overboard to try to accurately identify a student's level of effort. Indeed, in this fictional fantasy, Elmer even rents a set of pricey lie-detection equipment, and also hires an expensive lie-detector technician to operate it. Okay, there is Elmer and the technician (in the teachers' lounge), interviewing students one at a time to reach a conclusion about each student's level of effort. What scale will Elmer employ to represent students' effort levels? Will the scale range from 10 for "Loads of Effort" to a 1 for "Little Effort"? And what about the personal judgments of our truth-telling students when they try to identify their own levels of effort? Is a self-identified effort level of 9 by Sally Lou the same as a self-identified effort level of 9 by Billy Bob? When we are dealing with such a covert, person-specific variable, even completely honest respondents can't help us arrive at an unerring fix on students' levels of effort. Effort levels are decidedly squishy. Effort is almost as elusive as it is important.

Accordingly, teachers who try to incorporate effort into their students' grades are usually fooling themselves. They simply can't arrive at an accurate identification regarding a student's effort associated with a given assignment or a particular assessment.

What about Those Important Intangibles?

Suppose that a teacher accepts the central grading guideline that's been endorsed in this chapter—namely, that students' grades should be based only on the degree to which a student has achieved the curricular aims set forth for the student. What about the many variables other than goal attainment that most teachers regard as important? If those are significant education-related variables, shouldn't teachers find a way to let students and their parents know how a student is doing with respect to, for instance, *social skills* (such as showing respect for classmates and adults) and *study skills* (such as working independently)? The answer is definitely *yes*. But the way to communicate such information is not by trying to piggy-back it onto a goal-attainment grade. Rather, the solution is to employ report cards embodying what O'Connor (2009, p. 238) calls "expanded format reporting" in which teachers render judgments about what I'll call *evaluative factors*.

These evaluative factors are the educationally relevant variables that educators believe students and those students' parents should know about. For instance, we know that "effort" is a potent consideration in the way a student prospers—not only in school but also after schooling is over. Yet, there's no way of accurately measuring an individual student's effort level. Nonetheless, if a report card clearly indicates that a teacher's estimate of a student's level of effort is just that, *a judgment-based estimate*, then both students and parents may benefit from those estimates.

As a practical matter, of course, individual teachers cannot craft their own report cards, so what's on a report card is typically decided at a district, state, or provincial level. Typically, an expanded format report card lists a series of evaluative factors, then provides an interpretation key so that a teacher can indicate whether—for each listed evaluative factor—a student is, for example, "Excellent, Good, Satisfactory, or Needs Improvement."

Ideally, the report card itself, or an accompanying letter, will provide an explanation regarding the judgmental nature of the teacher's estimates regarding each evaluative factor that's included in an expanded format report card. Such "disclaimer" explanations can play a powerful role in educating both parents and students about the difference between "teacher's *evidence-based* grades about a student's goal attainment" and "teacher's *judgmental estimates* regarding a student's status on key evaluative factors."

In Figure 16.1 you will find an example of an expanded format report card in which, at the right, you see a listing of the five curricular aims (called goals in this instance) and a place where at the close of every quarter, a student's status with respect to each goal is to be given a "mastery-status grade" by the teacher—namely, *Complete Goal Mastery (CGM)*, *Developing Goal Mastery (DGM)*, and *Inadequate Goal Mastery (IGM)*. A total-course grade is supplied at the bottom of each quarter. (In this example, the total-course grade would be based on a teacher's judgment about the student's composite goal mastery.) On the right of Figure 16.1's report card, you will see two sets of evaluative factors (Social Skills and Study Skills), each of which is given a mark by the teacher on the basis of the

figure 16.1 ■ An Illustrative Expanded Format Report Card

Student's Name: _____

Goal Mastery

Interpretation Key: The letters below indicate a student's assessment-based mastery of each goal. Goal descriptions were distributed at the beginning of school. The *overall grade* (A, B, C, D, F) represents a student's overall goal mastery.

Mastery Status Grade:

CGM = *Complete Goal Mastery*

DGM = *Developing Goal Mastery*

IGM = *Inadequate Goal Mastery*

Evaluative Factors

Interpretation Key: For the factors listed to the right, you will find a teacher's *judgmental estimate* of the student's effort to improve.

3 = *Consistent*

2 = *Inconsistent*

1 = *Minimal*

Curriculum Goals

	Q1	Q2	Q3	Q4
Goal 1				
Goal 2				
Goal 3				
Goal 4				
Goal 5				
Overall Grade				

Social Skills Factors

	Q1	Q2	Q3	Q4
Respects classmates				
Follows rules				
Is self-disciplined				

Study Skills Factors

	Q1	Q2	Q3	Q4
Stays on task				
Organizes work				
Uses time well				
Employs technology				

teacher's judgmental estimate of whether the student's effort to improve has been *Consistent* (3 points), *Inconsistent* (2 points), or *Minimal* (1 point).

As you consider the report card presented in Figure 16.1, I'm sure you will realize that the mastery-status grades or, indeed, the overall course grade itself, is going to make no sense if the persons on the receiving end of such a report card do not understand the nature of the five goals on which the course grades will depend. This information (distributed at the beginning of the school year in this illustration) needs to be written in language readily understandable both to students and parents. Providing an additional description of those goals whenever report cards are issued is usually a smart move.

Again, recognizing that not all of a district's teachers are apt to have a hand in carving out the specifics of how a district's report cards are constructed, there may be some occasions when you might actually have an opportunity to register your personal preferences regarding the structure of district report cards. If you do have a chance to toss your ideas into such mix, please remember that in the reporting of students' grades, a profound truth is that "less is more." Too many grading dimensions incline both students and parents to become so swamped with information that they end up paying only superficial attention to any of those dimensions. And, of course, if there are too many grading tasks for teachers to undertake, they will typically end up racing through the "grading agony" as quickly as they can—often thoughtlessly. Really influential report cards will be crafted so that the number of judgments a teacher must make are intellectually manageable. This will lead to a modest, understandable interpretation task for both students and their parents. This will also lead to teachers' more thoughtful decisions regarding students' grades.

Electronic Record Keeping

Although many seasoned teachers have traditionally kept records of their students' accomplishments by making handwritten entries in a gradebook, the dramatic increase in the use of teacher-friendly computers promises to alter that practice. As more and more youthful, computer-canny teachers enter the field of education, we will surely see marked expansions in the use of computer-based records regarding students' performances.

A number of readily usable programs to help teachers keep track of their students' performances now exist, and more will surely be available in years to come. The mission of these electronic grading programs is to simplify the teacher's tasks, so even a rudimentary notion of how to use a computer will allow teachers to save tons of record-keeping time. Some observers of America's classrooms predict, within a decade or so, teachers' entering grades by hand in a traditional gradebook will be quite rare.

Student-Involved Grading Conferences

One useful supplementation to the exclusive reliance on traditional report cards is the use of grading conferences. Grading conferences, when first introduced,

PARENT TALK

Imagine that one of your students' parents, Mrs. Aquino, wants to discuss her daughter's grade in your class. Specifically, she wants to know, "What goes into Mary's grade?"

 If I were you, here's how I'd respond to Mrs. Aquino:

"I'm delighted you want to look into how Mary is graded in my class. What I'd like you to do is look over my classroom information system I've been able to get up and running this year on my lap-top computer. Why don't you come to my class before or after school and I'll show you how I arrive at each of the components contributing to Mary's grade. I'll also show you how I've tried to weight the grade-determination importance of certain tests and other assignments Mary and her classmates complete. I am especially concerned about the progress Mary is making toward the nine state-set curricular aims that are to be achieved by students this year.

"What you need to understand, Mrs. Aquino, is that any grade given to any student is almost always a teacher judgment based on an amalgam of different sorts of evidence. And, to be honest, because teachers' judgments are involved, and teachers are altogether human, there will invariably be some teachers' errors in grading.

"But I assure you, the other teachers in our school and I are trying to do the fairest and most accurate job we can when we grade our students. Why don't you visit and we can review what goes into Mary's grade?"

 Now, how would you respond to Mrs. Aquino's concerns?

usually involved only teachers and students' parents. Increasingly, however, these conferences are taking place in which students themselves play a role. There is, of course, a considerable range of involvements for students in such grading conferences. This range starts off with the student being present but not taking any part—other than being a listener—in the conference. At a greater level of involvement, the student participates actively in the conference. At the most substantial level of involvement, the student actually *leads* the grading conference. Clearly, for most variations of student-involved grading conferences, students will need to be carefully prepared by their teachers so that the resulting conferences will be maximally productive. (The vast majority of students possess no experience in grading themselves, and definitely no experience in supplying *goal-attainment* grades for themselves.) Remember, if the grading conference is based on a goal-attainment conception of grading, then all three parties in the conference (student, teacher, and one or both parents) will need to consider the *evidence* regarding a student's level of goal mastery. And that, of course, is where assessment provides the key information around which the grading conference is structured.

Let's recall that the basic purpose of grading is for teachers to communicate to students and parents the degree to which a student is making progress toward the goals this student is supposed to master. To the degree a teacher accepts this conception of grading, then when students understand the chief thrust of the grading process—by being actively involved in that process—this provides those students with information they need not only to evaluate their own achievements but, just as importantly, to monitor their ongoing progress toward goal attainment. Student-involved grading conferences can be a powerful *instructionally* relevant way of grading students so that they and their parents comprehend, if they are the recipients of descriptive feedback, where students currently are and what students need to do in order to achieve complete goal mastery.

Grading's Inherent Imprecision

Wouldn't it be nice if teachers never made mistakes when they grade students? But, as you probably know all too well from having been the recipient of too-low or too-high grades during your own years as a student, teachers do make grading errors. Certainly, teachers don't want to make mistakes in the grades they give to their students. However, grading is a judgment-based enterprise in which flawed decisions will surely be made.

Fortunately, in the long haul, such errors tend to balance one another out. Do you recall from Chapter 8 that there are three kinds of rater bias—namely, generosity bias, severity bias, and central-tendency bias. It is true that many teachers are biased in one of these three ways when they grade their students. Thus, over the years, a given student will probably be on the receiving end of some undeserved high grades and some unwarranted low grades. What you need to remember is that if you do the best job you can in dispensing grades to your students—that is, if you assign grades carefully and with the kind of deliberateness suggested in this chapter—you'll have done your grading as well as you can. Human judgment, as potent as it is, is not flawless. And it certainly isn't flawless when it comes to grading students.

WHAT DO CLASSROOM TEACHERS REALLY NEED TO KNOW ABOUT ASSESSMENT-BASED GRADING OF STUDENTS?

It is now apparent to me that adoption of a goal-attainment approach to grading makes solid educational sense, and that separating grading from a teacher's judgments about other evaluative factors is the way to proceed. First off, there will be greater clarity about grades on the part of teachers who base their grades on students' goal attainment of well-described goals. Students and parents will better understand the resultant grades than they would understand such traditional grading approaches as simply comparing the relative achievement levels of the students in a particular classroom.

But equally important as the communication dividends derived from goal-attainment grading is the manner in which such an approach will mesh with the way teachers should approach their *instructional* tasks. Let's face it, the chief reason teachers teach kids is to help those kids acquire skills and knowledge. The skills and knowledge to be promoted by teachers are called *goals, curricular aims,* or some synonymous label. Those are the *ends* of a teacher's instruction, and *teaching* is what the teacher does to promote students' mastery of those curricular ends. Indeed, as you saw in the previous chapter, the quality of a teacher's instructional efforts should be dominantly evaluated on the basis of whether the teacher has promoted students' attainment of curricular goals. So, from an instructional perspective focused on students' goal attainment, why not devise a student appraisal system that meshes perfectly with the fundamental reason teachers teach?

But What Does This Have to Do with Teaching?

The purpose of teaching is to bring about worthwhile changes in boys and girls. Most of these changes focus on students' acquisition of knowledge and skills. In truth, the very act of teaching can be seen as the use of the instructional means a teacher used in order to promote students' attainment of worthwhile ends—that is, curricular goals. If this is to be the teacher's chief aspiration—to have students master the curricular aims set forth for those students—why not evaluate students according to precisely the same framework? To the degree that both the teacher and the teacher's students are using the same targets to orient their activities, and to judge the success of those activities, then the resulting synergy from having both teacher and students pursuing identical aspirations will surely prove educationally beneficial. Goal-attainment grading pushes students to attain the very same goals the teacher wants those students to attain. Instruction will follow aspiration. Learning, too, will follow aspiration. Evaluative structures alter conduct. Why not alter students' conduct in a manner that leads to a greater likelihood of goal attainment?

Grading based on students' goal attainment, therefore, is an approach that makes sense from both an evaluative perspective and an instructional perspective. Regarding those other important factors that teachers would like to communicate, adoption of an expanded reporting format seems to be the way to go, as long as the evaluative factors don't overwhelm. Remember, the converse of "less is more" embodies every bit as much truth—namely, "more is less." An expanded format report card whose grade emphasis is students' goal attainment, yet that deals with a modest number of evaluative factors other than goal attainment, seems to represent the most sensible way to proceed.

CHAPTER SUMMARY

Conceding that the grading of students is a process fraught with imprecision, this chapter argued that the most defensible system of grading should be rooted in teachers' judgments about the degree to which students have mastered the curricular aims a teacher is promoting for those students. The guiding premise of the chapter was that the purpose of grading is for teachers to communicate with students and their parents about the degree to which students have attained the goals they are supposed to achieve. Thus, a goal-attainment approach to grading was advocated.

Four steps for teachers when implementing a goal-attainment approach to grading were presented: (1) clarifying curricular aims, (2) choosing goal-attainment evidence, (3) weighting goal-attainment evidence, and (4) arriving at a final goal-attainment grade.

Regarding the incorporation of factors other than assessment-based evidence of a student's goal attainment, it was suggested that an expanded format type of report card be employed to allow the teacher to provide judgmental estimates regarding the student's status with respect to these educationally relevant variables. However, it was stressed that the *grades* awarded by teachers should be based exclusively on assessment-obtained evidence of goal attainment rather than attempt to incorporate any of these other factors.

Determining Your Outcome Mastery

In this chapter, an attempt was made to defend a particular approach that teachers could use in awarding grades to their students. Conceding that other approaches to the grading of students are possible, and might be preferred by someone reading this book, I argued that the most defensible strategy for grading students is *goal-attainment grading*. This approach to grade-giving is rooted in the determination of how well a student had mastered the curricular aims being pursued by the teacher.

As a reminder, here is the chapter's chief outcome:

> *A sufficient familiarity with goal-attainment grading to be able not only to describe its key steps, but also to identify when teachers are or are not employing goal-attainment practices in their grading determinations*

The Mastery Checks are therefore preoccupied with goal-attainment grading. Complete both the Selected-Response and the Constructed-Response quizzes and think about the feedback you receive for each quiz.

MyEdLab *Selected-Response Check of Outcome Mastery*

MyEdLab *Constructed-Response Check of Outcome Mastery*

After completing both quizzes, go to the Learning Outcome Mastery Determination, where you will decide whether you've mastered the chapter's learning outcome or whether you need further study.

MyEdLab *Learning Outcome Mastery Determination*

References

Brookhart, S. M. (2009). *Grading* (2nd ed.). New York: Merrill.

Brookhart, S. M. (2011). *Grading and learning: Practices that support student achievement*. Bloomington, IN: Solution Tree.

Guskey, T. R. (Ed.). (2008). *Practical solutions for serious problems in standards-based grading*. Thousand Oaks, CA: Corwin.

Guskey, T. R. (2015). *Challenging the conventions of grading and reporting*. Bloomington, IN: Solution Tree.

O'Connor, K. (2009). *How to grade for learning: Linking grades to standards* (3rd ed.). Thousand Oaks, CA: Corwin.

O'Connor, K. (2011). *A repair kit for grading: 15 fixes for broken grades* (2nd ed.). Boston: Pearson.

Pattison, E., Grodsky, E., and Muller, C. (2013). "Is the sky falling? Grade inflation and the signaling power of grades," *Educational Researcher, 42,* no. 5 (June/July): 259–265.

Sadler, P. M., and Good, E. (2006). "The impact of self- and peer-grading on student learning," *Educational Assessment, 11,* no. 1: 1–32.

Townsley, M. (2013/2014). "Redesigning grading, districtwide," *Educational Leadership, 71,* no. 4 (December/January): 56–61.

Welsh, M. E., D'Agostino, J. V., and Kaniskan, B. (2013). "Grading as a reform effort: Do standards-based grades converge with test scores?" *Educational Measurement: Issues and Practice, 32,* no. 2 (Summer): 26–36.

Wormeli, R. (2006). *Fair isn't always equal: Assessment and grading in the differentiated classroom*. Portland, ME: Stenhouse.

Wormeli, R. (2011). "Effective grading in standards-based schools," *Educational Leadership, 69,* no. 3 (November): 40–44.

glossary

absence-of-bias   The degree to which an assessment instrument is free of qualities that offend or unfairly penalize test takers because of those test takers' personal characteristics such as race, gender, socioeconomic status, or religion.

accessibility   The extent to which students are readily able to display their abilities with respect to what is being assessed such as a student's mastery of a cognitive skill or a body of knowledge.

achievement tests   A measurement of the knowledge and/or skills a student possesses. Although often thought to assess what a student has *achieved* in school, some commercially published achievement tests contain many items measuring a student's out-of-school learning or the students' inherited academic aptitudes.

affective assessment   A measurement of a student's attitudes, interests, and/or values.

alignment   The substantive agreement between two or more of the following: curriculum, instruction, and assessment.

alternate assessments   Meaningfully different tests intended for students with disabilities so that more valid inferences can be made about the students than if the original test were used (even with assessment accommodations).

alternate-form reliability   The consistency of measured results yielded by different forms of the same test.

analytic scoring   A method of scoring a student's constructed responses involving the application of multiple evaluative criteria, one criterion at a time. After having employed the evaluative criteria separately, there may be an aggregation of these separate judgments into a final, overall evaluation.

anonymity-enhancement procedures   The steps a teacher takes so that a student accurately perceives his or her responses to self-report affective assessment inventories are truly untraceable.

aptitude tests   A measurement device intended to predict a student's likelihood of success in some future setting, often an academic one. Although formerly referred to as *intelligence tests,* and thought to assess a person's innate potential, aptitude tests often contain a number of the same sorts of items one finds in achievement tests.

assessment   A formal attempt to determine a student's status with respect to an educational variable of interest. Synonyms: *measurement, test.*

assessment accommodations   The techniques used when assessing a student with disabilities or a language-minority student in order to secure more valid inferences about such students' knowledge and skills. Typical accommodations include allowing increased time to complete a test or, perhaps, presenting a test's items in a manner more suitable for the student's limitations.

assessment bias   If an assessment instrument offends or unfairly penalizes a student because of personal characteristics—such as race, gender, ethnicity, or socioeconomic status—the instrument is biased against that student.

assessment literacy   An individual's understandings of the fundamental assessment concepts and procedures deemed likely to influence educational decisions.

assessment task   The part of an essay item or performance test that describes what it is the student should do to complete the assessment.

authentic assessment   Performance assessment in which the student's tasks resemble real-life tasks.

binary-choice item   A test item requiring a student to select one of two presented options.

blind scoring   When a student's tests are judged without the judges' knowing whether a test was completed as a pretest or as a posttest.

classification consistency   A representation of the proportion of students who are placed in the same classification category on two testing occasions or by using two forms of the same test.

cognitive assessment   Measurement of a student's knowledge and/or intellectual skills.

cognitive demand   The essence of the intellectual operation(s) a student must carry out in order to respond successfully to a test's items or tasks.

Common Core State Standards (CCSS)   These are curricular goals developed as targets for the nation's instructional programs. The reading and mathematics curricular aims created for the *Common Core State Standards* have been accepted as official curricular aspirations by many of the 50 U.S. states.

computer-adaptive assessment   Computer-adjusted presentation of test items to students so that, depending on students' responses to previous items on the test, new items can be chosen that mesh most appropriately with a student's demonstrated level of achievement.

computer-based assessment   When computers are employed not only to present assessment tasks to students but also when those students provide their responses to such items by computers.

construct-irrelevant variance   Factors unrelated to the construct being measured which diminish the accuracy of what is being assessed.

construct-related evidence of validity   Empirical evidence that (1) supports the posited existence of a hypothetical construct and (2) indicates an assessment device does, in fact, measure that construct.

constructed responses   A student's answers to assessment tasks, such as essay items, that require a response to be generated by the student "from scratch."

content-related evidence of validity   Evidence indicating that an assessment instrument suitably reflects the content domain it is supposed to represent.

content standards   The knowledge and skills that a student is supposed to learn.

content underrepresentation   An instance when the content being assessed, for instance, a collection of curricular aims, has not been satisfactorily addressed by the items constituting a test.

convergent evidence of validity   When students' performances on a test are positively related to their performances on other tests intended to measure the same variable or, perhaps, similar variables.

correlation coefficient   A numerical index reflecting the nature and strength of the relationship between two variables—for example, between students' scores on two different kinds of tests. The strongest positive relationship is signified by a correlation coefficient (r) of +1.00; the strongest negative relationship is signified when r equals −1.00. An r of 0.0 indicates no relationship between the two variables under analysis.

criterion   A variable deemed to be of such significance that it is regarded as the most prominent variable involved, for example, when a predictor test measures students' aptitude levels to predict a criterion such as students' college grades.

criterion-referenced measurement   An approach to assessment in which a student's test performance is interpreted according to how much of a defined assessment domain has been mastered by the student.

criterion-related evidence of validity   Evidence demonstrating the systematic relationship of test scores on a predictor test to a predicted criterion variable.

criterion variable   An external variable that serves as the to-be-predicted target for a predictor exam, such as an aptitude test.

curricular aim   A skill, body of knowledge, or affective outcome that teachers intend their students to acquire.

curriculum   The set of educational aims—for instance, goals or objectives—teachers wish their students to achieve.

Depth of Knowledge   The level of cognitive demand needed by students to master a given curricular aim or to respond successfully to a test item. A lower Depth of Knowledge (DOK) might call for mere memorization, but a higher DOK could require students to employ evaluation of synthesis.

descriptive feedback   Information communicated to students about their performances intended to help students determine how to narrow the gap between their current achievement and the achievement embodied in the curricular aim(s) they are pursuing. Descriptive feedback moves beyond mere comparative reporting so that the specific quality of the student's test performance is delineated.

disparate impact   If test scores of different groups (for example, different ethnic or religious groups) are decidedly different, this is described as an assessment procedure having a disparate impact on test takers.

distractor analysis   Scrutiny of a student's empirical performances on the different answer options contained in multiple-choice and matching items.

distribution   A term used to describe a set of test scores, such as when one says, "The final exam score distribution from the students in Ms. Hill's class was very homogeneous."

educational accountability   The imposition of required evidence, usually a student's test scores, as a way of holding educators responsible for the quality of schooling.

educational defensibility guideline   A guideline for test preparation stipulating that no test-preparation practice should increase a student's test scores without simultaneously increasing his or her mastery of the assessment domain represented by the test.

empirical item-improvement   Improving an item's quality based on a student's performance on the item.

English language learners (ELLs)   A diverse group of students whose first language is not English. Such students are often referred to as limited English proficient (LEP) students and, sometimes, simply as language learners.

essay item   A test item eliciting a response of one or more paragraphs from a student.

evaluation   An appraisal of the worth of an educational program or, in the case of classroom teachers, either the effectiveness of an instructional activity or the competence of the teacher.

evaluative criterion   A factor with which, along with other such factors, we judge the quality of a student's performance.

evidence based on response processes   Validity evidence that generally comes from analyses of individual test takers' responses such as when students are, after having been tested, questioned about their thought processes during an examination.

evidence of validity based on test content   Formerly referred to as *content validity* or *content-related validity,* this validity evidence stems from a formal scrutiny or the content assessed by a test's items or the procedures employed to choose that content.

extended-response item   An essay item that gives a student few constraints about how he or she is to respond, especially with respect to the length of his or her responses.

fairness   The validity of test-score interpretations and uses for students from all relevant subgroups. Fairness is present when assessments are developed, administered, scored, and reported in ways that are evenhanded for all students.

formative assessment   A planned process in which assessment-elicited evidence of students' status is used by teachers to adjust their ongoing instructional procedures or by students to adjust their current learning tactics.

formative teacher evaluation   The appraisal of a teacher's instructional performance with the exclusive purpose of improving the teacher's performance rather than supporting such summative decisions as tenure denial, reward recognition, or job termination.

grade-equivalent scores   An often misinterpreted estimated score based on the grade level and months of the school year represented by a student's test performance.

grading   An assignment of a quality-designating label (numerical or verbal) to describe the caliber of a student's work.

grain-size   The breadth of a curricular aim, ranging from small grain-size to large grain-size aims. Typically, the breadth of a curricular aim—that is,

its grain-size—is directly linked to the amount of instructional time it is thought will be required for students to master the curricular aim.

halo effect   The error of allowing a test-scorer's overall impression of a student to influence any criterion-by-criterion evaluations of the student's response to a test.

high-stakes test   An assessment whose consequences have important implications either for students (such as grade-to-grade promotion) and/or for educators (such as when schools are qualitatively ranked on the basis of students' test scores).

holistic scoring   The method of scoring a student's constructed responses that calls for the synthesized application of multiple evaluative criteria—that is, simultaneously using several distinguishable factors to arrive at an overall judgment about the quality of a student's response.

hypergeneral rubrics   Scoring guides whose evaluative criteria are described in excessively general—hence, dysfunctional—terms.

individualized education program (IEP)   A federally required document describing the specifics of how a child with disabilities is to be educated.

instruction   The activities carried out by teachers with their students intended to help students achieve teachers' curricular aims.

instructional sensitivity   The degree to which students' performances on a test accurately reflect the quality of instruction specifically provided to promote students' mastery of what is being assessed.

internal consistency reliability   The degree to which a test's items are functioning in a similar (that is, homogeneous) fashion.

item alternatives   The answer options used in a multiple-choice test item.

item-discrimination index   A numerical indicator contrasting, on a particular test item, the proportion of high total-test performers and the proportion of low total-test performers.

item distractors   The wrong-answer options in multiple-choice items.

item response theory (IRT)   This scale-score approach to reporting a student's test performances takes into consideration not only a student's raw score but also other factors such as item difficulty, the guessability of items, and so on. The computation of IRT scale scores requires considerable computer-based statistical analysis.

learning progression   A sequenced set of building blocks—that is, subskills or bodies of enabling knowledge—it is thought students must master en route to mastering a more remote target curricular aim.

Likert inventories   Affective assessment devices organized around a respondent's self-reported degree of agreement with a series of presented statements.

limited English proficient (LEP) students   A label, often used in governmental publications, referring to students whose first language is not English. These students are frequently described as English language learners, ELL students, or language learners.

matching item   A test-item format that requires students to associate items, as directed, from two different lists.

mean   The arithmetic average of a set of scores.

measurement   A formal attempt to determine a student's status with respect to an educational variable of interest. Synonyms: *assessment, test.*

measurement-driven instruction   An approach to educational reform in which the installation of high-stakes assessments is intended to influence teachers to teach toward the knowledge and skills those assessments purport to measure.

median   The midpoint in a set of scores when the scores are ranked from lowest to highest.

multiple binary-choice item   A binary-choice item that, along with other binary-choice items, is based on a single, usually somewhat lengthy set of stimulus material.

multiple-choice test item   A test item requiring a student to choose a response from three or more presented options.

normal curve equivalent   Often referred to as an NCE, a normal curve equivalent is a scale score representing a raw score's relative position in a distribution of scores that is assumed to be normally distributed. The meaningfulness of this scale-score approach, of course, depends on the degree to which the score distribution involved is, in fact, normal.

norm-referenced measurement   An approach to assessment in which a student's test performance is interpreted relatively—that is, according to how the student's performance compares with that of other test takers.

offensiveness   A test is offensive when it contains elements that would insult any group of test takers on the basis of their personal characteristics, such as religion or race.

opportunity to learn   Because several important court cases indicate that if a test's consequences are significant for the test taker, then that test taker must have been given an instructional program constituting a reasonable opportunity for the student to learn what is being tested. This test-relevant instruction is often described as opportunity to learn.

p value   An indicator of an item's difficulty based on the percent of students who answer the item correctly. Thus, an item answered correctly by 67 percent of students would have a *p* value of .67.

Partnership for the Assessment of Readiness for College and Careers (PARCC)   One of the two state assessment consortia established with substantial federal funding to create "next generation" tests to assess students' mastery of the *Common Core State Standards.*

percentiles   An interpretive score based on the percent of students in the norm group outperformed by a given student. For example, a student whose raw score exceeded the performance of 84 percent of norm group students would have earned an 84th percentile score.

performance assessment   A form of testing in which a student is given a task, typically a demanding one, then asked to respond to the task orally, in writing, or by constructing a product.

performance standard   The level of proficiency at which content standards should be mastered.

portfolio assessment   An assessment approach centered on the systematic appraisal of a student's collected work samples.

preassessment   A pretest given prior to instruction, typically to (1) determine a student's entry skills and knowledge or (2) employ as part of a pretest-posttest collection of evidence regarding instructional quality.

premises   A matching item's listed elements (on the left) for which a match is sought from a list of responses (on the right).

professional ethics guideline   A guideline for test preparation stipulating that no test-preparation practice should violate the ethical norms of the education profession.

professional learning community   A group of educators who meet periodically, over an extended period of time, to enhance their competencies related to one or more particular topics.

prompt   The assessment task, typically for a writing sample, that indicates what the focus of a student's composition should be.

psychomotor assessment   Measurement of a student's small-muscle or large-muscle skills.

quartile   One of three points in a distribution of test scores dividing those test scores into 25 percent of the scores. Those three points are the 25th percentile, the 50th percentile, and the 75th percentile. Often mistakenly referred to as representing a quarter of a set of test scores (e.g., "He scored in the top quartile" *(sic)*, quartiles refer to points, not proportions of a test-score distribution.

range   An infrequently used measure of a score distribution's variability that is calculated simply by subtracting the value of the lowest test score from the value of the highest test score.

raw score   The number of items, without any sort of numerical transformation, answered correctly by a student.

reactive   The often confounding effect of early assessment on a student's subsequent learning, most vividly seen in the impact caused by preassessment of an affective variable, wherein the student is unduly sensitized to the affective variable with which a teacher is concerned.

regression effect   A well-known statistical phenomenon in which extremely high scorers or extremely low scorers will, when retested, tend to earn scores closer to the mean of the score distribution.

reliability   The consistency of results produced by measurement devices.

reliability coefficient   The numerical indicator of whatever type of reliability evidence has been assembled to represent the consistency with which a test measures—most commonly presented as a correlation coefficient in which higher, positive coefficients represent greater measurement consistency.

reliability/precision   The degree to which scores of a particular group of test-takers are consistent over repeated administrations of a test, thereby leading to the inference that scores for an individual test taker are similarly dependable and consistent.

responses   In general, a student's answer to an assessment task (or test item). For matching items, responses are the listed elements (on the right) from which matching selections to premises (on the left) are made.

restricted-response item   An essay item that markedly limits the form and content of a student's response to the item.

rubric   A scoring guide employed to evaluate the quality of a student's responses to performance tests, a student's portfolios, or any kind of student-generated response.

scale scores   Converted raw scores that employ a new, arbitrarily chosen scale to represent a student's performance. A considerable number of scale scores are used in education. (See *normal curve equivalent, stanine*.)

score-spread   The degree to which a set of test scores is dispersed (that is, spread out).

selected responses   A student's answer to test items that present options from which the student must choose—for instance, multiple-choice or binary-choice items.

self-report inventories   An assessment tool, often completed anonymously, wherein a student's responses reveal his or her values, behaviors, attitudes, and so on.

short-answer item   A test item eliciting a brief response, usually a word or phrase, from a student.

showcase portfolios   Collections of a student's "best work"—that is, the work samples deemed to be of the highest quality. Such portfolios are typically used for celebrating students' accomplishments with parents, policymakers, and so on.

skill-focused rubrics   Scoring guides whose evaluative criteria are applicable for judging a student's responses to any suitable skill-measuring task.

Smarter Balanced Assessment Consortium (SBAC)   One of the two state assessment consortia formed to generate assessments suitable for measuring students' mastery of the *Common Core State Standards*.

socially desirable responses   Responses of a student that do not represent the student's actual sentiments but, instead, reflect how the student believes he or she *should* respond.

split-and-switch design   A data-gathering design in which a class is split into two halves, each half taking a different pretest. Then, after instruction, the tests are switched so that students take the other test form. Two comparisons are then made between students' pretest-versus-posttest performances on the same test form.

stability reliability   The consistency of assessment results over time. Synonym: *test-retest reliability*.

standard deviation   A statistical index revealing the degree to which the scores in a group of scores are spread out from the group's mean score, larger standard deviations reflecting more score-spread than smaller standard deviations.

standard error of measurement   An estimate of the consistency of an individual's test performance(s) represented by an index of how likely it is that another test performance (on an equidifficult test) would yield a comparable score.

standardized test   Any test that is administered, scored, and interpreted in a standard, predetermined manner.

stanine   A scale score based on the division of test scores into nine units of one-half standard deviation distances (on the score distribution's baseline). The highest stanine, number 9, contains about 4 percent of the scores—as does the lowest stanine, number 1. The middle stanine, number 5, contains about 20 percent of the scores if the distribution is fairly normal in shape.

stem   The initial part of a multiple-choice item—that is, the stimulus to which one of the multiple-choice options serves as the best response.

student growth percentile   A norm-referenced representation of students' relative changes in test performances during a single school year—such changes being represented on the current test by percentile comparisons of all students who had scored identically on the prior year's test. The growth of a given teacher's students would therefore be determined by an average of those growth percentiles based on different starting points.

summative assessment   When tests used to make final judgments about students or the quality of a teacher's instruction.

summative teacher evaluations   When the quality of a teacher's instruction is appraised not to improve it but, rather, to support more high-stakes decisions such as the teacher's job status or recompense.

task-specific rubrics   Scoring guides whose evaluative criteria deal only with scoring a student's responses to a particular task, not the full range of tasks that might represent the skill being measured.

teaching to the test   When a teacher directs instruction toward the assessment domain represented by the test *or* toward the specific items that make up the actual test. Because of this dual meaning, and the confusion apt to result from its use, the expression should be avoided or immediately defined.

test   A formal attempt to determine a student's status with respect to an educational variable of interest. Synonyms: *assessment, measurement.*

test-based teacher evaluation   Teacher appraisals in which the dominant determiner of a teacher's quality is the performance of a particular teacher's students on an externally imposed standardized achievement test.

test-criterion relationship   When validity evidence regarding a predictor test, such as an aptitude exam, is collected with respect to the empirical relationship between scores on the predictor test and the student's status on a criterion variable such as the student's subsequent grades.

test-retest reliability   Often referred to as *stability reliability,* evidence of a test's consistency of measurement is collected by testing a group of students, and then re-administering that test to the same group of students at a later point in time.

true–false item   A common binary-choice item in which a student's two options regarding the accuracy of a presented statement are *true* or *false.*

unfair penalization   A test item unfairly penalizes test takers when there are elements in the item that would disadvantage a group because of its members' personal characteristics, such as gender or ethnicity.

universal design   A "from-the-get-go" approach to assessment development that strives to maximize the accessibility of a test for all those who are intended to take the test.

validity   The degree to which evidence supports the accuracy of test-based inferences (interpretations) about students for a test's specific purpose.

validity argument   A justification of the degree to which accumulated evidence and theory support the proposed inferences (interpretations) about a student's test performances.

value-added model (VAM)   A statistical procedure intended to employ students' prior achievement and/ or background characteristics as statistical controls to estimate the effects on student achievement of specific teachers, schools, or school districts.

working portfolios   Ongoing collections of a student's work samples focused chiefly on the improvement, over time, in a student's self-evaluated skills.

writing sample   A student-generated composition intended to allow inferences about a student's writing abilities.

index